Organizing & Organizations

Organizing  Organizations

An Introduction

Second edition

Yiannis Gabriel • Stephen Fineman • David Sims

SAGE Publications
London • Thousand Oaks • New Delhi

First published 1992

Reprinted 1994, 1995, 1996, 1997, 1998

This second edition first published 2000, Reprinted 2000

 SAGE Publications Ltd
6 Bonhill Street
London EC2A 4PU

SAGE Publications Inc.
2455 Teller Road
Thousand Oaks, California 91320

SAGE Publications India Pvt Ltd
32, M-Block Market
Greater Kailash - I
New Delhi 110 048

British Library Cataloguing in Publication data

A catalogue record for this book is available from the British Library

ISBN 0 7619 6279 4
ISBN 0 7619 6280 8 (pbk)

Library of Congress catalog card number available

Typeset by SIVA Math Setters, Chennai, India.
Printed in Great Britain by The Cromwell Press Ltd, Trowbridge, Wiltshire

Contents

Preface to the second edition

Published in 1993, *Organizing and Organizations* broke new ground. Instead of the usual litany of conventional academic topics and theories (e.g. motivation, leadership, groups, communication), it invited students to use their own experience as part of the learning process. It challenged teachers to trust and build on this. The lived experiences of organization members provided the conceptual glue for the book.

The book was something of an experiment, academics being rather conservative about the texts they recommend to students. We have been delighted that this did not prevent it being well used. Indeed, its widespread adoption on degree and professional courses far exceeded our expectations, signalling to us that we had hit the right note. We therefore approached the present updating and revision with enthusiasm; we were no longer in uncharted territory.

The first edition pioneered a number of areas in the presentation of organizations to new students, including morality, emotions, sexuality and humour. Some of these issues are now more widely discussed in organizational studies. The students who engage in the study of organizations have changed, with an influx of more mature and more experienced people taking up or resuming academic studies. Meanwhile, work organizations are transforming – into smaller, leaner and more loosely organized units. The challenges of globalization, intense competition, environmental damage, and ever greater uncertainty are becoming more pressing.

In producing this second edition, we have reflected on our own experiences in using the book and have listened to the views of colleagues, reviewers and students. We have kept the main features of the book intact – the informal tone, the absence of excessive theoretical material in the text of the book, the loose sequencing of chapters, the Thesaurus. We have updated many of the ideas and examples, drawing upon more recent research. We have also included a 'reading on' section at the end of each chapter. Some of the chapters have undergone deep transformations, reflecting our changing ideas and the developing nature of the subject matter.

Others have evolved organically from their form in the earlier edition.

We have added three new chapters: on organizing and the environment, the management of differences, and the relation between production and consumption. We are confident that this new edition will continue to provide a stimulating introduction to the fascinating world of organizing and organizations.

We would like to acknowledge the help of colleagues and students who have used our book and given us feedback. We would also like to acknowledge the help of Rosemary Nixon and all the people at Sage who have helped produce this second edition.

Yiannis Gabriel, Stephen Fineman, David Sims
Bath and London, 1999

Preface to the first edition

Over the years we have tried to convey to our students something of the excitement and mystery of life in organizations – with the aid of one or more textbooks. But often the neat (and usually similar) topic headings have left us feeling dissatisfied. Typical of our students' comments are:

- 'Yes, but when I worked in my uncle's shop it was nothing like that.'
- 'These books don't tell you what working really *feels* like.'
- 'It all reads so rationally – can it really be like that?'
- 'They don't say much about the life you bring with you into the organization – like that row, or busting up with your boyfriend.'

There is a gulf between the lived experience of organizing and being organized by others, with its uncertainty and confusion, and the tidy, rather sanitized, texts on organizational behaviour. In this book we attempt to bridge this gulf.

We have done this in three ways. Firstly, we have written chapters which reflect live issues and activities of organizational life. We could have added many more if we had the space. After the introductory chapter, you can start reading any chapter that catches your interest; they are not sequenced or divided according to conventional textbook topics.

Secondly, our narrative is often based on stories told by, or about, organizational members. This includes the work experiences of our students and ourselves, our research in organizations, and what managers and working people of all sorts have related to us. These are knitted together with plain-speaking accounts of some of the key concepts in the study of organizations.

Finally, to enhance the accessibility of the book, we have avoided the usual reference formats and extensive citations of research studies. However, research underpins all of our endeavours, and references to many studies may be found, in user-friendly form, in the Thesaurus at the end of the book.

This book is the product of a truly co-operative effort – so much so that we had to toss a coin to decide the order of authors on the front cover. Initially, we divided the chapters equally between us, but thereafter it was a group activity. We discussed and argued each chapter, and shared re-writes. A valuable part of this process was a consumer test on our own undergraduate students – who spotted things we missed and relished 'marking' the work of their lecturers. We are grateful to our colleague Ian Colville, nearly a fourth author. Ian played a key role in the inception of this work, but unfortunately had to withdraw because of other commitments. We also want to thank Sue Jones of Sage Publications, whose exceptional drive, encouragement and critical feedback were a valuable source of support. And, finally, the fine-tuning of the book was enhanced by the very helpful comments of Craig Lundberg, Barbara Czarniawska-Joerges and Barry Turner.

Any book reflects the backgrounds and partialities of its authors, and this one is no exception. We have taught courses on organizations and organizational behaviour for many years, and share the joys and tribulations of teaching both undergraduates and postgraduates at several universities. Together, we bring teaching, research and consultancy backgrounds in psychology, sociology and management to our courses – and to this book.

How to use this book

Unlike most books on organizations which are structured in a sequence (the individual, the group, the organization), you may think of this book as a wheel. The introduction and conclusion are the centre, Chapters 2–20 are the spokes, and the Thesaurus is the rim. We invite you to move from section to section as your fancy takes you – but please read the introduction, Chapter 1, first. We also offer a tabulation of common organizational topics and our chapter headings (on p. xii). With this you can locate directly which chapters to turn to if you want information on a more conventional organizational behaviour topic (e.g. 'change', 'motivation', 'personality').

Theories provide and clarify many of the concepts used in discussing the experiences of organizing. Such concepts are flagged in the text through the use of **bold** print and can be studied in the Thesaurus, which covers much of the material you will find in other textbooks. Thesaurus entries are listed at the end of each chapter, and are cross-referenced in the Thesaurus itself to enable you to study whole clusters of interrelated concepts. The match between a bold word in a chapter and an entry in the Thesaurus is not always perfect. For example, 'bureaucratic' and 'unemployed' are not in the Thesaurus, but 'bureaucracy' and 'unemployment' are.

We would regard our effort as successful if, as you read this book, you begin to see organizations in a different light; things which might have escaped your attention in the past may suddenly become full of meaning; things which you may have taken for granted in the past may begin to look rather less solid. In doing so, you can share some of the pleasure and excitement which we experienced in planning and writing this book.

Chapter headings in this book ⇨

Traditional topics ⇨

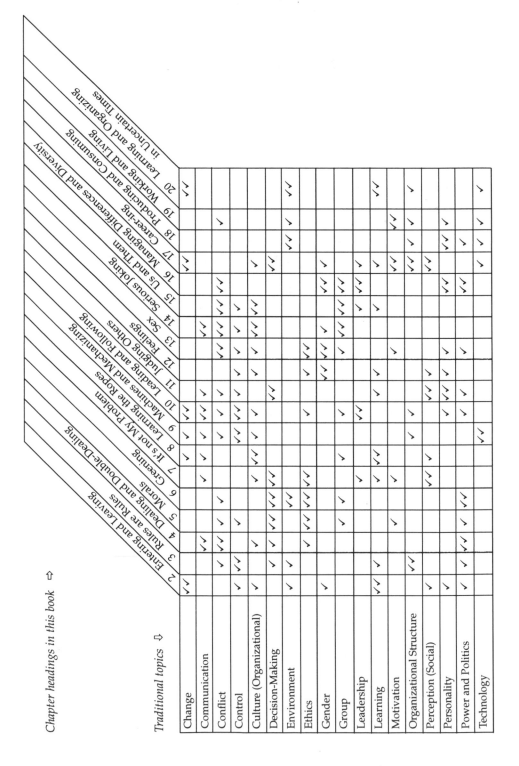

Traditional topics	2 Entering and Leaving	3 Rules are Rules	4 Dealing and Double-Dealing	5 Morals	6 Greening	7 It's not My Problem	8 Learning the Ropes	9 Machines and Mechanizing	10 Leading and Following	11 Judging Others	12 Feelings	13 Sex	14 Serious Joking	15 Us and Them	16 Managing Differences and Diversity	17 Career-ing	18 Producing and Consuming	19 Working and Living	20 Learning and Organizing in Uncertain Times
Change	✓✓					✓	✓✓	✓✓							✓✓				✓✓
Communication		✓✓			✓	✓	✓✓	✓✓								✓			
Conflict	✓✓	✓✓	✓				✓	✓	✓										
Control	✓	✓✓	✓				✓✓	✓	✓	✓		✓							✓✓
Culture (Organizational)	✓		✓	✓✓	✓✓		✓	✓	✓	✓	✓✓	✓✓	✓✓		✓				
Decision-Making		✓	✓✓	✓✓	✓✓			✓✓							✓✓				✓✓
Environment	✓	✓	✓✓	✓✓	✓✓										✓✓				
Ethics		✓					✓		✓✓	✓✓					✓				
Gender	✓						✓			✓✓	✓✓	✓✓	✓				✓		
Group						✓	✓			✓✓	✓✓	✓✓	✓✓						
Leadership				✓	✓	✓✓	✓✓		✓	✓✓	✓✓	✓	✓✓	✓				✓✓	
Learning	✓✓	✓		✓	✓		✓	✓	✓	✓		✓	✓			✓✓			✓
Motivation			✓	✓												✓			
Organizational Structure		✓✓				✓	✓		✓✓	✓✓	✓				✓✓	✓			
Perception (Social)	✓			✓✓	✓				✓✓	✓✓	✓				✓✓	✓	✓		✓
Personality	✓								✓	✓					✓✓	✓			
Power and Politics	✓	✓✓	✓	✓✓		✓✓	✓		✓	✓	✓				✓	✓			✓
Technology															✓	✓			✓

1

Introduction
Organization and organizing

What is an organization? Everyone knows: universities, airlines, chemical plants, supermarkets, government departments. These are all organizations. Some have been around for a long time, employing numerous people across many continents – Shell, IBM, McDonald's, Toyota. Others are smaller, locally based – a school, a family-owned restaurant, a small law firm, a pottery.

Organizations enter our lives in different ways: we **work** for them, we consume their products, we see buildings which house their offices, we read about them in the newspapers and absorb their advertisements. When we look at organizations, especially the larger, older, famous ones, they seem solid, they seem permanent, they seem orderly. This is, after all, why we call them organizations. Images of organizations as solid, permanent, orderly entities run through many textbooks. But, in our view, these books tell only half the story. They obscure the other half: the life and activity that buzzes behind the apparent order. Sometimes this bursts into view, revealing chaos even – such as when computer systems break down, when there is delay or an accident on an airline, when products are sent to the wrong destinations or when bookings are made for the wrong dates. They also obscure the immense human efforts and energies that go into keeping organizations more or less orderly.

In this book, our focus is not on 'organization' but on 'organizing' – the activities and processes of doing things in organizations. We do not take organization for granted; after all, many large and well-known organizations have faded or died for one reason or another. Instead we focus on the *processes* of organizing and being organized. We highlight the *activities* which go on in organizations. We look at our emotions, the stories and gossip which we trade, the deals we strike, the games we play and the moral dilemmas we face when in organizations.

Organizations get likened to many things – machines, armies, garbage cans, theatrical plays, the human body, and so on. We find the analogy of a river helpful. Like a river, an organization may appear static and calm if viewed on a map or from a helicopter. But this says little about those who are actually on or in the moving river, whether swimming, drowning or safely ensconced in boats. Our aim in this book is to highlight the experiences of those people who actually know and understand the river well, to present their stories and learn from their adventures. We are hoping that the images of organization which we generate have more in common with the moving, changing, living river than the tidy lines of a map.

WHAT DO YOU KNOW ALREADY ABOUT ORGANIZING?

Probably far more than you think. If you have been formally employed you have already peeped behind the organizational screen; felt what it is like to be told what to do; to do boring or exciting work; to interact with a wide range of people; to day-dream; to see inefficiency around you; to try and meet deadlines; to feel stress; to experience elation and excitement; to see how differ-ently different managers do their work; to give and receive help from others.... If you have not had a job, you have been part of organizing in project groups at school, sports meetings, family holidays, Christmas dinners, pub crawls, cinema outings with friends, trips to clubs and so forth. You do not have to have had a leadership **role** in these to be part of organizing, and already to know, through experience, what seems to operate successfully and what seems to fail. Trust these experiences; they are very impor-tant. Use them actively as you read this book; build on them with the concepts, stories and studies that we relate.

ORGANIZING – KEEPING THINGS IN ORDER

In this book organizing is treated as a continuous set of activities. We all have different perceptions of, and tolerances for, disorder – revealed classically in the contrast between a teenager's view of a 'tidy' bedroom and that of his/her parents. In work settings 'get-ting organized' means different things to different people. Some people seem to operate effectively for years in offices with papers and files strewn all over the place, using their memory as a diary. When challenged about the apparent chaos they will usually retort that it is fine for them, as long as no one else moves things around.

But not all of us find organizing easy or agreeable. This is how one manager described his 'typical day':

Getting organized is something that I don't find easy. I have in front of me a book called *Get Yourself Organized* offered by a friend, who was perhaps trying to give me a hint. It looks appealing; it looks sensible. It is written in clear type, with a bold 'key message' printed on every other page:

- DECIDE ON YOUR MAJOR PRIORITIES.
- PUT A TIME-SCALE AND DEADLINE ON EACH PRIORITY.
- IF YOU CAN DO IT TODAY, DO IT!
- WHO DO YOU NEED TO CONTACT TO MAKE THINGS HAPPEN?
- INTERRUPTIONS – AVOID THEM!
- AT THE END OF THE DAY LEAVE YOUR DESK CLEAR.

Well, I kept a diary of some of the things that happened to me the other day. Here are some snippets:

It's 7.30 in the morning and I'm driving to work, the loose ends of yesterday still in my head. I've got a 9.30 meeting with the strategy committee and I'm not looking forward to it. I need to get my ideas straight on how we market the new truck, or I know John will screw me and get the cash for his new project.... Mobile rings. It's my secretary, Alice – have I remembered the lunch meeting with Dr Hosikkii from our Japanese subsidiary? I'd clean forgotten about it.

At my desk and a screen full of e-mails. I'll answer the important-looking ones first. Bill phones; he urgently wants to see me before the 9.30 meeting.... He comes in, looks awful. He tells me he needs a few days off because his son's very ill. Of course he must go home, but how am I going to manage with him away?

I'm ten minutes late for the meeting; I feel embarrassed and the Chief Executive looks disapproving.... It's a tense meeting but I seem to have at least one ally – Jean from Sales. I can trust her, but it's Alan from Production who I can't figure out. Sometimes he's with me, sometimes he's really obstructive. I must take him out for a drink and have a bit of a chat....

The meeting breaks up and I take the opportunity to walk back with the Chief Executive. I explain my lateness and manage to get him to hear my plans for shifting the staff around in my section and the problem of overload. At least he didn't say a new appointment was out of the question....

Back to my office and Alice looks tense. The main computer is down and we need the financial forecasts for the annual report. I phone Helen in Accounts – she's helped me in the past. Meanwhile a call-waiting from Germany on the spec for the new truck. They need to go to press on it this week. I'm really angry with the agency who were supposed to co-ordinate this. I phone them and lay it on the line. They cost us a small fortune; I'm going to have to look around for a new agency....

A good lunch with Hosikkii; I realize now that I'm going to have to visit him in Tokyo much sooner than I thought. It's an exhausting journey and I can't stay away more than three days. I'm away from my kids yet again....

2.15 p.m. The Chief Executive calls me – I've won! Great! Not only will I get what I wanted for marketing the truck, but I can also hire a new assistant. Sometimes I love this job.... I tell Alice to pass the news around. I dash over to Mark's office and congratulate him. He persuaded me in the first place to increase our bid.

I stop at Brenda's desk in the big, open-plan office: 'I know you want something from me', she says; 'that's the only reason you ever visit me.' 'How can you say that!' I reply, sounding offended. She's right, of course. I ask her if she has any advance news on the customer survey we conducted last month. She feigns ignorance, and then slips a computer printout from her drawer. 'I need this back today please; it's red hot.'

I find a quiet corner to hide and read the report. Wow! Two of our products have done disastrously. We are going to need a completely revised PR plan. Is that why the Chief Executive's been so accommodating? More work for me?

Alice bleeps me. Says I need to call Eric. I call right away. Never keep your Director waiting. He wants me to stand in for him at an executive meeting tomorrow because 'something's come up'. I dutifully agree; I bet it's the customer survey stuff. But it also means cancelling the appraisal interview I'm doing on Marcus. He'll get even more stressed now. I'll get Alice to make my excuses.

Two more meetings. The first is terminally tedious: a presentation from a consultant on a computer information system. He couldn't sell me a washing machine. Fortunately I'm interrupted; a query over the copy on our new trade brochures; are we being sexist?! The second was an hour with a research student from a university who was looking at marketing in the automotives sector. She actually had some thought-provoking questions; it's a shame I couldn't give her more time. And it was hardly quality time – my phone rang four times, each time with someone wanting an instant decision or opinion.

4 p.m. already. Grab a coffee. Meet Jane at the machine. Had I heard that Martin was leaving? No I hadn't. It's rumoured that he's got a plum job in Wales with one of our competitors. 'More re-organization for us', I quipped. The rest of the afternoon I found I couldn't get Martin's leaving out of my head. Maybe that's just what I should do....

It's 6.15 p.m. and things, at last, have quietened down. I'll see what's left of the e-mails and what new messages there are. Oh yes, I must get the agenda for tomorrow's executive otherwise I'll look a prat. 'Alice, are you still there...'.

AT THE END OF THE DAY LEAVE YOUR DESK CLEAR, says the book.

They must be joking!

Organizing, in this account, involves tensions, preferences, interruptions, politics, power and personalities. Maybe the manager could have been a better organizer, but his account chimes with what we know about the experienced realities of managing. It is often a whirl of activity; quick switches from one issue to another; gossip and speculation; people dependent on each other; bargaining and compromise; developing contacts and friends; reconciling work pressures with domestic demands. Time is always precious. The picture of the cool, rational thinker, quietly planning the day, is a myth.

FRONT STAGE, BACK STAGE

The process of organizing defies tidy, universal, categories. As consumers (customers, students, passengers, etc.) we take for granted that things will get done. Lectures, meetings, examinations, happen. Individual and group effort come together to create the hard product – the car, hi fi, vacuum cleaner, pen, paper; or the service – delivering a meal, cutting hair, preaching a sermon, policing a city, running a train. We hardly bother with the organizing processes behind these events. The struggles, politics, negotiations, anguish and joys of actual organizing remain, for the most part, invisible to the consumer: they are backstage. When they are inadvertently revealed, showing how precarious organization can be, it can come as something of a shock – as the following tale from one of us reveals;

> Once I was booking tickets for a European rail holiday at a local, family-run, travel agent. They were busy, and I queued for a long time. Eventually I was served by an elderly gentleman who fumbled with a weighty European Rail Timetable. He got very confused. The queues behind me were growing ever longer. The staff were getting hopelessly overloaded and stressed. The tension was growing, but, like good British customers, no one in the queue complained. The breaking point came with a loud, sharp, whisper from a younger, female, member of staff to the man who was serving me:
> 'For Christ's sake, give it up, Dad! He only wants a rail reservation; it's not worth our trouble.'
> The man turned on her immediately and retorted, through clenched teeth: 'How dare you! A customer is a customer; that's what we're here for!' He then proceeded to tell me that 'they only tolerated him in the shop at weekends now' and they had their 'differences of opinion'.
> Some of the entrails of the organization had suddenly been revealed. I had seen something I should not have seen, and I was uncomfortable. I did not want to witness a row or receive a confession – I wanted a ticket! I now mistrusted the service. I could not play my customer role properly if they did not play out their role as 'travel agents'.
> I decided to go elsewhere.

ORGANIZING AS A MEANING-CREATING PROCESS

When we get close to the experience of people organizing, there is the impression of a lot of personal and interpersonal work going on. In the above exchange, the protagonists were not just observing or responding to each other's actions; they were also making judgements and creating **meanings** for themselves.

Seen through the eyes of different individuals, what happened may have seemed very different. Each may have told a different story about what 'really' happened. For example:

- the elderly gentleman's story: 'Customers were happy to queue for personal, caring service.'
- his daughter's: 'Customers were in a hurry, dear old Dad all at sea.'
- the story-teller's: 'Customer pressure reveals cracks in the organization.'
- other customers': 'Incompetent travel agents', 'rude young people'.

The meaning of the incident is not obvious. Even the meaning of particular words or sentences may be ambiguous. 'It's not worth our trouble' could be interpreted as a personal insult, or as an expression of frustration with Dad – or with customers in general. 'A customer is a customer' could be taken as a brave assertion of good old-fashioned service. But, in this case, what about all the customers waiting? Does their inconvenience count for nothing? Alternatively, it may have been a dig at the way young people conducted business, just for the money. We are continuously creating meanings for ourselves; a better understanding of organizing can help improve our understanding of others' meanings.

While most of us in organizations seem to be 'doing a job', listening to someone talking, tapping keyboards, talking into telephones or soldering electronic components, we are also making and exchanging meanings – a fundamental human/social process. Organizing, as we are presenting it in this book, is intimately concerned with the way that people create meaning for themselves, with others, during their working lives. As we interact with others at work, we bring our personal histories and our past experiences with us – finding common ground, compromising, disagreeing, negotiating, coercing. This is a vibrant, mobile process, often full of tensions, frustrations and possibilities.

Some portraits of organizations present a bleak picture – the isolation of the individual, lost in an impersonal **bureaucracy**. Some employment is indeed experienced in this way. But this is only part of the picture. People at work also create their own **realities**, an ever-rich **symbolic** life providing a sense of who we are and where we belong. Amongst other things, this involves swapping rumours, stories, gossip, **jokes** and laughter. We pick up and contribute to the chat about the organization's heroes, villains and fools. In this way 'the organization' takes on a special, personal meaning.

ORGANIZING AS A SOCIAL PROCESS

For much of the time organizing is a social as well as a personal process, involving groups working together – part of the raw material of meaning-making. This is well illustrated when organizing something from scratch. We invite you to imagine doing this with some colleagues – such as organizing a welcoming event for new students on your course.

A host of initial questions can spring to mind. What exactly are you meant to organize? What is the real purpose of the function? What kind of function is it going to be? 'Serious'? 'Light-hearted'? A mixture of both? What is your budget? What are the possible dates and venues for the event? What events may compete or clash with yours? How are you going to publicize it? It is beginning to look rather complicated – so it is comforting to know that there are others there to help out.

Yet sharing with colleagues seems to make things worse – more disorganized. Different people have different ideas, opinions and interests. Some sound downright **prejudiced**. The stress level rises and sometimes people seem to be speaking different languages – and getting quite angry with each other. And this is just about organizing a welcoming event for students! It is impossible to move forward without making some compromises – and you feel you have made lots.

But things are starting to shift. People are now listening more to each other – maybe they are getting tired or just fed up. New meetings are scheduled but in the meantime people chat about the event in corridors, at the Union bar and over the telephone. There's some whispering about 'awkward' and 'ignorant' people in the **group**. But, more constructively, one person has set up an e-mail discussion list called 'Welcoming Ideas' which has attracted some good thoughts – as well as some outrageous ones! Some people in the group come over more powerfully than others, which makes you feel uncomfortable. But they sometimes have interesting ideas and are able to push things on.

Finally a plan of action is agreed; things are beginning to fall into place at last. Different individuals now have different tasks to do (some more willingly than others). A **leader** has emerged from the group to co-ordinate things (you like her and are secretly pleased it is not you).

As the key day approaches, up pop the snags. The grand plan is far from perfect and it has to be re-negotiated several times – usually when someone fails to deliver on what they promised or the group has neglected an important item. The leader proves to be excellent – gently nagging and persuading. Some (not you) find her too bossy, too controlling; they get sulky or irritated. But they hang in nevertheless, as the time pressures are enormous and the whole group now wants the event to succeed. **Communication** and co-ordination are essential – often easier said than done.

ORGANIZING AND IMPROVISING

Things, it seems, rarely go entirely according to plan; even the best laid plans occasionally come to grief. On the day of the event you face near calamity: the food and wine for the reception are delivered late; there is a bus strike in the city. Your group has no contingency plans – how were you to know this would happen?

What have you learned? Successful organizing may depend on a sound plan but planning alone is no guarantee of success. Planning ahead provides a needed sense of security and direction, but a rigidly planned event can fail because it does not allow people sufficient opportunity to improvise when things are not working out. When crisis strikes, your group may fall apart. Those who had expressed reservations about the plan may say 'We told you so. You insisted on doing things your way, now you sort out this mess.' Being able to work effectively as a team, thinking on your feet, maintaining your cool and the goodwill of those involved under pressure, are all important in ensuring the success of your project.

There are, of course, individual differences here. Some people are quite happy improvising and managing crises. They can live with uncertainty and chaos, placing their faith in 'muddling through'. They believe that 'it will be all right on the night', and they are frequently proven right – to the intense annoyance of others. These others seek to **control** uncertainty. They are serious, methodical people; they like order, plan, routine and do not generally like 'fooling around'. They mistrust improvisation, chance and spontaneity; but what they really abhor is unpredictability.

SUCCESS OR FAILURE?

Some of the causes of success and failure in organizing are common, no matter what the specific organizing at hand seeks to achieve. Placing excessive reliance on a machine, an animal, a person or the weather, on anything over which you have limited control, may undermine your plan. Poor communication, inadequate budgets, irreconcilable differences, personality clashes, unanticipated events, low motivation can frustrate any organizing.

However, even if things run smoothly, it does not make an event a success. In fact, success and failure are themselves meanings which we attribute to events, meanings which we usually develop as we **talk**, joke and gossip with others. Imagine if, a few days after the function which you organized and which everyone enjoyed, your group comes under criticism from the head of your department for 'misspending the college's money on irrelevant activities, like that farce of a drunken party organized recently'.

You may be surprised at such an **attitude**. Instead of thanks for organizing what seemed, eventually, a much-enjoyed event, you come in for criticism. This may be one of the best lessons that the example teaches us: just when we think that we are free to organize others, we may ourselves be part of someone else's organizing activities. Your event may have been a success in terms of your objectives and values, but a resounding failure in terms of theirs – and they have the power to make their judgement stick.

Under such circumstances, it may be helpful to present to the departmental head some arguments and evidence, showing that most of those participating in the function found the event not just enjoyable but also extremely useful. This type of evaluating and assessing is itself an important aspect of organizing. Would you do things differently if you were organizing the same function all over again? Are there any shortcuts that you have learned? Might you have opted for a different event? Would you like to work with the same people again?

Some major events are organized on a one-off basis, as in the example above. A military campaign, the staging of the Olympic Games, a business takeover, a wedding: such events seem to call for their own unique organization. Most events, however, are not organized like this. They are part of on-going processes of organizing. Admitting a new class of undergraduates to a degree, preparing a company's accounts, taking in new stock, recruiting new staff, purchasing new equipment and many other activities are like painting the Golden Gate Bridge in San Francisco: by the time you have finished, it is time to start all over again.

IN SUM...

We have argued for a shift from the notion of organization to organizing. Organizing is to be seen as a social, meaning-making process where order and disorder are in constant tension with one another, and where unpredictability is shaped and 'managed'. The raw materials of organizing – people, their beliefs, **actions** and shared meanings – are in constant motion, like the waters of a river. And, like a river, they look quite different depending on how close you are. In the chapters that follow we attempt to communicate the feel of this flow; to portray something of the richness, variety and surprise of life in organizations.

THESAURUS ENTRIES

action	meaning
attitude	organization
bureaucracy	prejudice
communication	reality
control	role
group	symbolism
jokes	talk
leadership	work

2

Entering and leaving

Joining a new organization is usually a memorable experience because of its mix of emotions – apprehension, excitement, tension, confusion. Each new encounter, each new person introduced, adds to the impression of what the place is like. It is the first of many steps through which we become part of something called 'the organization'. But while we gradually fuse with the organization, we also help make it what it is – we reproduce it and, perhaps, change it.

Our initial experiences set some of the psychological and physical boundaries to the space that we call **work**. We cautiously experiment with what we say or do. What is the reaction? Is it acceptable? We are **learning** the ropes; finding where we fit in. In social science terminology, we are seeking clues to the culture, norms and values of the community we are entering. None of this appears in the organization's recruitment literature. No one told us about it. There may be a hint of things to come in unofficial prospectuses, as can be found in some colleges and universities where existing students tell something of what things are really like. But mostly we have to find out as we go along.

Leaving the organization is a different matter altogether. It may occur smoothly and comfortably at the statutory end of a working lifetime, celebrated by the presentation of the proverbial gold watch – for 'long, loyal service'. We witness similar rituals when people leave for another job, for marriage, to have a baby, or simply to retire early. The usual warmth of such occasions contrasts strikingly with the 'letting go', 're-structuring', 'retrenchment', 'laying off' or 'redundancy' which are now commonplace in our times of boom or bust. These actions can mark a pragmatic approach by companies: when times are tough, people will lose their jobs. Or they may be a part of new management fashion to create a 'leaner, fitter' organization. But dismissal, for whatever reason, is a harsh way of separating a person from an organization. Like most separations or drastic changes, it quickly exposes the raw elements of the relationship.

GETTING IN – FIRST IMPRESSIONS

Each year many companies undertake a tour of higher educational institutions. They set up their stalls and hand students glossy brochures containing colourful descriptions and photographs of corporate life. The exercise is designed to extol the benefits, and delights, of joining the organizations. Collectors of recruitment brochures will detect common images – which are not difficult to exemplify:

–   On the inside cover: a head-and-shoulders colour picture of a smartly dressed, serious-looking man (usually). The Managing Director gives a message of welcome and reassurance:
    Implicit message: *'Do not think that this is a fly-by-night company. We mean business; we know what we are doing, and someone important is in charge.'*
–   Pictures of people working at computer terminals, talking and smiling:
    Implicit message: *'There is nothing old fashioned or fussy about us. We are an up-to-date, high technology company.'*
–   Pictures of men and women, black and white, looking earnest, discussing things, making important decisions:
    Implicit message: *'There is equal opportunity here. Anyone can get on if they work hard. It's ability and performance that count.'*
–   Pictures of people in a classroom; a tutor heads the group:
    Implicit message: *'You will not vegetate here. We believe in training. We will give you opportunities to improve your skills and qualifications; we will look after you.'*
–   Pictures of people playing sport:
    Implicit message: *'It is not just work, work, work. We have places for you to relax.'*
–   Picture of someone getting off a plane in an obviously foreign land:
    Implicit message: *'We are not just a local firm. We have international interests and there are opportunities for you to travel.'*

In this way the **organization** parades its best costume, tailored carefully by its public relations department. The business of self-presentation has begun. The *formal* apparatus of organization has swung into action – and there is more to come. Wooing new, desirable-looking employees means presenting an attractive organizational image. Blemishes are heavily camouflaged, or simply omitted from the picture. It is assumed, not unreasonably, that when people have to make a difficult decision on what job to choose, relatively unambiguous information is helpful. Given that the organization wants your skills, they gain little by revealing that, actually, very few black people or women get to the top, that international travel is reserved for senior managers, that the computer system is in desperate need of renewal, or that the training budget has just been substantially cut. Moreover, it is likely that many potential applicants will *want* to believe the organization is glamorous, international, aggressive, or whatever, because that represents some ideal image they hold of themselves. They are therefore content to collude in the myth of the exemplary organization – especially if jobs are in short supply. The business of selection has begun – both parties, candidate and organization, are exchanging the impressions they want to present to one another.

Typically, interested job candidates will groom themselves for the part. 'Respectable' suits and shirts replace the usual jeans and T-shirts – for males and females alike. To deviate too far from conservative dress risks being labelled as 'unreliable', 'radical', or 'will not fit in'. First appearances are notoriously poor guides to character, nevertheless we use them all the time in our interpersonal judgements. Street-wise job applicants know this, and learn to adjust their CVs or résumés to the apparent requirements of the job – accentuating some features, playing down others. They also research the company in advance to demonstrate the seriousness of their intent to an interviewer. Some will have topped off their armoury of **skills** with special training on being an effective interviewee to create the right **impression** or **perception** (countered, ironically, by interviewers trained to see beneath a feigned presentation).

RITUALS – TO REDUCE UNCERTAINTY

The initial coming together of company and candidate involves careful make-up and posturing. At first sight this may appear irritatingly trivial – 'What's it got to do with the real me, and the actual job?' But the way we *present* ourselves to others, through a rich array of social protocols – **language**, dress, gestures, **rhetoric** – constitutes an essential part of social reality. These protocols are

embedded in customs and rituals. From an early age we learn
certain social conventions through which we can interact – with a
fair amount of shared **meaning**. 'Reading' the rituals correctly and
getting our **performance**, appearance or act right – doing what is
socially correct within extant conventions – is vitally important.
That is the social currency, whether we like it or not. If we fail in
our judgement or act, we risk rejection. This sometimes means a
strange 'double take', of the sort: 'I need to give that person interviewing me a strong impression of my strengths and enthusiasm
for the job. But I'm sure he knows I'm doing that, so will he believe
what I say?' Customs do decay and transform over time as they get
challenged by their users and other observers. For example, as we
write there is debate as to whether English barristers and judges
should still be required to wear wigs in court.

THE SELECTION

The time and effort a company wishes to devote to selecting its personnel can vary enormously. A selection decision could be made on
the basis of a letter of application and a short **interview**. On the
other hand, it is not uncommon for large companies to expose candidates for managerial and professional jobs to a sequence of interviews, **psychological** tests, group discussions and exercises.
Assessors will record their observations, and candidates will be
judged against a set of previously agreed criteria of competence.
This is the questionable science of selection. Questionable, because
there are many studies which reveal that devices such as selection
interviews and **personality** tests have modest to poor reliability
and validity, or predictive value. Judging people's competence in
areas such as leadership, interpersonal relationships, working
under pressure and so forth, is notoriously difficult, not least
because, as hinted above, a candidate's performance in a selection
procedure can reveal more about that procedure than about the
candidate's actual work behaviour. But an elaborate selection
process offers the *apparent* reassurance that a poor decision is
unlikely, and that it is possible to **control** entry to the organization.
It is also a **ritual** through which impossibly difficult decisions can
be made to appear possible. With tools that promise 'objectivity',
selector and candidate alike can feel that a thorough and fair job is
being done (see Chapter 11, 'Judging Others').

The ritual of selection can border on the absurd when some of the
common methods are omitted – such as face-to-face interviews. For

example, United Kingdom applicants for some jobs in Australia can expect to be accepted or rejected after a telephone interview (considerably cheaper than a flight plus expenses). This normally means that they receive a pre-arranged conference telephone call at their home in the early hours of the morning. They then have to respond intelligibly to serious questions from a group of dis-embodied voices, many miles away. People on the receiving end of this process report a sense of surrealism, only slightly reduced by changing from their pyjamas to a smart suit.

...AND POLITICS

It is likely that who gets selected for a job results more from **poli-tics** than from the elegance of the entry structure. Politics focuses attention on the personal interests and idiosyncrasies of the selec-tors, and their power to make their own particular judgements pre-vail. It also demonstrates that we often need to turn our attention to *informal* mechanisms in the organization for a more complete understanding of what is happening.

An associate of ours recently failed to win a top appointment with a London-based publishing company. She was one of two shortlisted candidates, and she had attended four separate inter-views, the last one being with a panel of directors in the company. To all outward intents and purpose the job should have been hers. She had a fine reputation in her field – she outshone the other can-didate. Furthermore, the night before the final interview she heard, from an 'inside source', that the job was hers. So what went wrong?

It was hard to find out – details of the proceedings were secret, as they often are. But the insider, now much embarrassed, was determined to uncover the reason. It transpired that, in the final interview, our colleague had mentioned that if she were offered the job, she would have to commute to work for a time. Her family were well settled in their home town outside London where her children went to school. She would consider setting up a second home if necessary, but first she would like to take the commuting route. The point was well taken, with apparent sympathy, during the interview. Her honesty, however, proved to be a tactical error. After the interview the Managing Director, who was chairing the selection panel, declared firmly that this was not his idea of com-mitment or loyalty to the job; it was not what he would do if he were in the applicant's position. He would not permit the appoint-ment of someone who did not move to the job right away.

This is a clear example of 'homosocial reproduction', a rather inelegant shorthand for the phenomenon of hiring people who are similar to those already in place. Put another way, people feel less anxious about working with others who are similar to them, so they will consciously, or unconsciously, veer towards people who seem, on first impressions, like them in social **values, gender, attitudes**, educational background and age. This is the psychological explanation of the 'old school tie' phenomenon. It also accounts for why certain organizational cultures perpetuate themselves – that 'Shell', 'Procter and Gamble', 'IBM' or 'Marks and Spencer' feeling. And it is a reason why fairly drastic changes in key personnel have to take place if strong organizational values are to shift significantly – a frequent tactic of new chief executives who wish to make their mark.

Job applicants who dutifully respond to advertised vacancies can unwittingly fall foul of invisible political structures. Personal contacts and friendship networks bring some people, and not others, to the special attention of employers. In close communities, informal channels (rumour, casual chat) can keep many available jobs filled – especially in times when work is scarce. Sometimes, when various people are involved in an appointment, unknown to most of the selectors and applicants taking part in the event, there is already a favoured candidate. Indeed, it is not unknown for an applicant to be processed right through a selection procedure, ignorant of the fact that the job has already been offered to someone else – secretly.

SETTLING IN

The period of settling in can be a confusing time. Taken-for-granted ways no longer fit; the familiar customs and practices of the previous job or role are inappropriate. Things begin to happen which remind newcomers that they are indeed part of a new **environment**, but which also point the way to what they have to do, or be, to become part of the social group. For example:

• John, straight from secondary school at 19, joined a prestigious retailing chain as a management trainee. After a couple of days feeling lost, a departmental manager approached him: 'I suppose you are used to getting long holidays, eh? Well, you can forget that here. It's 8 till 6.30 six days a week. That's what it takes to get on here.' John was stunned at what sounded like a prison sentence. A week later he was called to see the Store

Manager, who asked him to recite the names of the staff in the store. John stumbled through most of their first names. The manager was furious: 'How can you ever expect to be taken seriously as a manager if you call people by their first names!?'

- 'OK then, young upstart lady, get a hold of this and put it in the car', said an assembly line worker, handing Helen, a young management trainee, a windscreen. Eventually he helped her fit it. All the men gathered around to witness the incident. After some tense moments: 'She's all right lads, nearly one of us now.'

- Hassan discovered he had made a mistake and mentioned it to his boss. 'Listen', retorted the boss, '*you* haven't made a mistake. The *system* has. Whenever something is wrong you must come and tell me the accounts system has screwed up. Then we can look at the problem and try to improve the system. The system will lose prestige, whereas you have gained recognition because you spotted the error. You see, this company likes winners.'

Anthropologists refer to events such as these as **rites of passage**; ways by which established organizational members induct new people into the actual working customs of the organization. Some inductions are gentle; others are harsh, even humiliating. Groups as diverse as military personnel, prisoners and public school children will use degradation as a way of initiating the newcomer.

Rites of passage are part of the unwritten procedures of organizational life; they are not to be found neatly listed in a job description. They are akin to a second selection system, but every bit as important as the first one. Rites of passage reveal themselves most clearly and consistently in 'strong' **culture** companies – those that have the same clear beliefs and values throughout all aspects of their business. For example, the IBMs and Procter and Gambles of the world present new recruits with a series of specific hurdles to jump – surviving punishing working hours; performing very basic work to remind them of their humble status in the face of all they will have to learn; complete immersion in one part of the company's core business, until they have full mastery of it; sacrificing domestic and leisure time for the company.

McDonald's, the pervasive hamburger chain, is meticulous in ceremonially rewarding its staff with badges and certificates as they move from one hurdle to the next. In this way one's progress is visibly delayed until one conforms to the company's expectations. Such is the potency of this form of conditioning that it can take a remarkably short time for people to fall into line. They soon speak the corporate language and perform according to the rules. Those who do not will be delayed in their progress, or dismissed. Some will leave voluntarily because they cannot stand it any more.

... AND LEAVING

The farewell party is perhaps the most common organizational ritual, or final rite of passage, for the leaver (who has not been dismissed, or resigned in anger or disaffection). There are the complimentary farewell speeches tinged with nostalgia and humour, and the presentation of a gift. A mix of alcohol and bonhomie helps transcend political frictions which may have existed, and the leaver should feel able to quit gracefully, with a sense of completion to his or her endeavours. A brief period of mourning may follow, with people talking about how things used to be when the leaver was around. If the person strongly influenced the direction of the organization (for good or ill) his or her memory may be enshrined in stories which are passed on to future employees.

As well as marking an end to someone's organizational efforts, the farewell celebration legitimizes vacating the job, for someone else. It is problematic if this point is misread or misunderstood. To illustrate. Many a leaver will exit to the sentiment, 'It will be great to see you around here any time'. Those who respond literally to such an invitation may be disappointed, as the following tale from a personnel manager reveals:

> Brian was a production executive. He loved his work with us; I guess he was a workaholic. He's been retired about a year now. We gave him a lavish send-off, a huge party. He was a popular man, you see. About a month after he left he popped in to see us. Of course it was great to see him and to exchange stories. I got the feeling then that he wasn't adjusting too well to retirement. He said he'd keep in touch with us, and that he did! It seemed like every week he'd be in – trying, really, to be where he thought he belonged. Eventually one of his old colleagues came to see me, in despair. 'He's driving us mad', he said. 'He's a nice guy, but we don't want him any more. He wants to do our job for us; he can't let go.'

The emotional bonds of organizing are very real, but often temporary, and heavily entwined with daily work routines. The leaving ritual effectively marks an end to a person's organizational membership, and disenfranchisement can be rapid. Only special friendships survive. Without the everyday sharing of work, old inter-personal feelings are left without roots, or a proper context for expression. This can come as quite a shock to people who quickly find their old school, college or workmates relative strangers once they have left the organization. More cynically, one can regard many organizational relationships as a means to an end. We try to get on with people because we have to – to get the job done, to get through the day.

There is another image of leaving, which is far removed from the canapés and congratulations. This is the world of redundancy and restructuring. People have to leave because their jobs are no more. The vagaries of the market economy can, sometimes overnight, turn a 'caring, family' organization into a beast which consumes its own children – in order to survive. 'Our most important asset, people' rarely survives a severe downturn in trade, or new mechanization; other interests take precedence. When people invest fair parts of themselves and their security in their employing organizations, job loss comes as a very worrying event. For the first-time **unemployed**, the loss of income, **status** and routine activity can feel like a collapse of meaning at the centre of their lives. Those who have been made redundant more than once tread warily through the world of work, cautious about their commitment to any one company. While we now live in times where a job for life is becoming a thing of the past, moving in and out of many jobs can still be very disturbing, like a series of losses or redundancies. To cope with this, some people develop a sense of detachment, or **alienation**, so that when the job ends they can retain their sense of self-worth.

The anxiety and threat which surround job loss are also reflected in the ways organizations manage the process. The closest one finds to a supportive ritual are attempts to soften the blow through generous redundancy payments and 'out placement' support – to help people find new jobs or other activity. Otherwise, there is a mish-mash of responses. Some senior managers cannot face the task of announcing redundancies themselves, so they delegate it to an internal, or external, 'hatchet person', some of whom are well practised at that kind of work. Then there are people who find out about their own redundancy from what they read in their local newspaper. Others hear by letter, or return from a break to find that their job, and office, has disappeared – perhaps the ultimate symbol of redundancy and rejection. Deceit and camouflage flourish in the emotional confusion of redundancy.

We cannot but wonder at the apparent courtesy and charm which can bring a person into an organization, and the acrimony and disarray which can, sometimes, mark the leaving. Perhaps, most of all, it reminds us of the curious fragility of social orders and of organizing.

- Entering and leaving organizations are critical transitions in our work lives.
- Entering and leaving are marked by both formal and informal social rituals.
- The rational procedures of recruitment and selection are often overlaid with political interests – which may not give the candidate a 'fair' hearing or decision.
- Most organizations wish to present a glossy image to the outside world; but once inside an organization you get a different picture.
- There is a gradual process of getting to know one's place in an organization – learning its customs and practices. This is crucial to survival, and can sometimes be very testing.
- An organization can soon become part of our self-image and identity.
- Rapid job changes, sudden unemployment or retirement can leave people confused; they are often unprepared for a life without paid employment.

THESAURUS ENTRIES

alienation	performance
attitude	personality
control	politics
culture	psychological testing
environment	rhetoric
gender	rite of passage
impression formation	ritual
interview	skill
language	status
learning	unemployment
meaning	values
organization	work
perception	

READING ON

The way we present ourselves to others in social settings is described as 'dramatic performance' in the extensive work of sociologist

Erving Goffman. He speaks of *The Presentation of Self in Everyday Life* – how we don particular 'masks' and use role 'scripts' to give the right social impressions to others. An overview of this work can be found in Fontana (1980). Following such ideas, some writers have looked at the nature of impression-formation in key organizational events or settings – see Giacalone and Rosenfeld (1991).

The social rituals of organizations are captured at a broader level by organizational anthropologists seeking to interpret the meanings of such events – see Kuper (1977) and Czarniawska-Joerges (1992). Such events are also explained by Bate (1994) and Brown (1995) as features of organizational culture. The socialization of new employees has been discussed by Schein (1988), who argues that individuals may accept socialization and conform, or rebel, or even adapt the organizational norms to their own needs. The extent to which rational selection procedures (e.g. job descriptions, person specifications, psychological tests) determine how people are actually selected and socialized into a new job, is much debated. However, there is no doubt that many firms put much energy into such procedures; a good overview can be found in Bowen et al. (1991).

The way employment can become incorporated into our self-image is most graphically represented in studies on the effects of unemployment – see Fineman (1983) and Fryer and Ullah (1987). Some individuals can find it extremely difficult to survive outside the familiar routines of paid work, yet such conditions are becoming more the norm as long-term, unbroken employment is becoming less available.

3

Rules are rules

'PASSWORD!' – MIKE'S STORY

I applied to Securecops on the off-chance. I attended an interview in their fortress-like headquarters on the Thames Embankment. It lasted all of five minutes. I would get my first job the following week. What I had to remember, at all times, was SECURITY, they said. I would be given a secret password, which would be changed each night. All communications with HQ, and with any caller to the place I was guarding, had to use the password.

I left HQ with my free kit under my arm: an ill-fitting blue uniform, a cap with a peak, a whistle, a torch and a truncheon.

A week later I turned up to my first job. It was a US Navy stores depot in an isolated spot in North London. As far as I could tell it contained things like Coca-Cola, soap and paper towels. I could not figure out why the US Navy should have such a place in London. I felt self-conscious – a bit of a nerd in my new uniform. A Securecops supervisor met me to show me around. The rules the supervisor told me were these:

- Keep everything locked.
- Patrol the building and the perimeter wire once an hour.
- Ring in and report to HQ after each patrol. They'll chase you if you don't call.
- Get the password from HQ at the start of each shift, and use it in all calls.
- *Don't* smoke on patrol.
- *Don't* let anyone in unless they give the password.
- *Don't* fall asleep on the job, or you will be sacked.

The supervisor left. The guard I was replacing packed up his stuff. As he was leaving he winked at me and said: 'Listen. Skip a patrol or two and get all the sleep you can.' I was puzzled.

I got through the first night, exhausted. It was really scary going around the dark buildings. The very thought of *using* my truncheon on a human being filled me with horror. I decided the best thing to do was to run it against the wire fence and along doors as I patrolled. It made a hell of a racket but that should deter an intruder – I hoped.

Night two. I realised that I could easily skip a few patrols – as long as I rang HQ on time. Also, I found myself plotting other ways of bucking the system. Surely, you could do a deal with another guard, elsewhere, to ring HQ on your behalf? You'd then get more sleep some nights, and he could sleep while you were doing it for him. I later learned that such a dodge was well known, but no one had prevented it.

I found myself falling asleep between patrols, so I kept an alarm clock to wake me on time to report to HQ. In the middle of such a slumber, at about four in the morning, I was jolted awake by the loud, persistent hooting of a car horn. I scrambled for my uniform jacket, and grabbed my truncheon. I dashed outside, my heart racing.

I was facing the headlights of a van, shining through the wire mesh of the locked main gate. In front of the lights was the silhouette of a tall man. 'Christ, where the hell have you been? Let me in!'

I got a bit closer and saw the guy was wearing a Securecops uniform. I plucked up courage and shone my torch in his face. I recognized the supervisor. What a relief! I fumbled for my keys – and then hesitated. Hell, this could be a trick, I thought. To test me out. I'd better watch it. 'Oh hi', I said. 'Could you tell me the password please?'

The man looked confused. Then he shouted at me: 'Like hell I can! Open these bloody doors and let me in. Just stop fooling around!'

I fingered the keys nervously. What on earth should I do? I was sure he was OK, but I was breaking a cardinal rule if I let him in. And he still might be tricking me. I tried very hard to sound authoritative: 'I can't let you in unless you tell me the password. *Rules are rules.*'

'I don't know the bloody password for tonight', he retorted, getting more and more wound up.

Fearing for my physical safety, I eventually phoned HQ, who were not in the slightest bit interested in the man's identification. I should let him in. He marched past me, saying not a word. He left the same way – after a very cursory check.

RULES IN ORGANIZATIONS

Mike did not last long in this job. But the incident raises important issues. Entering the organization is entering a world of formal **rules** and procedures. They govern every aspect of work, and seem to leave little room for discussion. 'No smoking' means precisely 'No smoking', no matter who you are, how badly you wish to smoke or what it is that you would choose to smoke. Yet, after a few days at Securecops, Mike **learned** that rules were sometimes disregarded, broken or bent, occasionally with the consent of **management.**

Train drivers found out long ago that if every rule and every procedure of starting their locomotives were followed, the trains would never leave the stations or reach their destinations on time. 'Work to rule', sticking to every small rule and regulation in the book, was recognized as a very effective way of paralysing organizational performance. Sometimes it takes a major accident before it is realized that official procedures have been flouted for so long.

Organizational rules can be usefully distinguished from social **norms**. Norms are the 'unwritten rules'. Employees of many companies, for example, go to work wearing casual clothes on Fridays, even though this is not enshrined in any formal rule. Nor is it a rule of the road that truck drivers should flash their headlights to indicate to an overtaking truck that it is safe to pull back, or for the overtaking truck to flash their indicator as a sign of appreciation. Social norms guide many of our **actions**, both inside and outside organizations. Some of the other chapters highlight their importance and implications. This chapter focuses instead on the formal, written rules and regulations which seem to set modern organizations apart from other types of human **group**, like families or truck drivers on highways.

Rules and Factory Despotism

Formal rules and regulations are not a new phenomenon. Medieval monasteries had rules banning different types of behaviour and specified detailed penalties for different offences. For instance, a monk guilty of sexual intercourse with an unmarried person was required to fast for one year on bread and water; a nun guilty of the same offence between three and seven years (depending on the circumstances), a bishop for twelve years (see Morgan, 1986: 208). However, the proliferation of rules at the workplace coincides with the rise of the factory system and especially of large **bureaucratic organizations**. Consider the following extracts from the rules of a 19th-century mill in Lancashire.

RULES
TO BE OBSERVED AND KEPT BY THE PEOPLE
EMPLOYED IN THIS FACTORY

1   Each person employed in this factory engages to serve THOMAS AINSWORTH AND SONS, and to give one month's notice, in writing, previous to leaving his or her employment, such notice to be given in on a Saturday, and on no other day. But the Masters have full power to discharge any person employed therein without any previous notice whatsoever.

2   The hours of attendance are from Six o'clock in the morning until half-past Seven at Night, excepting Saturday when work shall cease at half-past Four....

---

5   Each spinner shall keep his or her wheels and wheelhouse clean swept and fluked, or in default thereof, shall forfeit One Shilling....

10   Any person smoking tobacco, or having a pipe for that purpose, in any part of the Factory, shall forfeit Five Shillings.

12   Any person introducing a Stranger into the Factory without leave of one of the Proprietors, shall forfeit Two Shillings and Sixpence....

17   Any Workman coming into the Factory, or any other part of these Premises, drunk, shall pay Five Shillings.

18   Any Person employed in this Factory, engages not to be a member of, or directly or indirectly a subscriber to, or a supporter of, any Trades Union, or other Association whatsoever.

19   Any Person destroying or damaging this Paper, shall pay Five Shillings.

Such rules may shock us as unfair and one-sided. Imposed unilaterally by the employer, they make no secret of whose interest they seek to protect. Their aim was **control**. Like political dictators, Messrs Ainsworth and Sons and other early capitalists sought to bolster their **power**. They made little pretence that the rules served anyone's welfare other than their own.

Rules and Modern Organizations

There are still organizations in some countries with rules not unlike those above. Most Western organizations today, however, shy away from such brutal rules, especially when they emphasize the potential for **conflict** between employers and employees. Nevertheless, when we join an organization, we usually undertake, through a written contract, to obey its rules and procedures. These are *impersonal*, they apply to all, and are laid down in company manuals and ordinances, dictating, sometimes in minuscule detail, what we can and what we cannot do, our rights and our obligations. Not all organizational rules are written down; each organization has many tacit rules, rules which are part of a psychological contract between itself and its members. Such tacit rules may include working after hours or refraining from talking to reporters about matters that may embarrass the organization. In exchange, organizations are perceived by individuals to offer reciprocal favours and rewards to their members, such as promotion and training opportunities.

What has changed since the days of Messrs Ainsworth and Sons is not the nature of the rules but our perception of their rationale. Instead of 'Do A, B and C because I say so', rules in modern organizations proclaim 'Do A, B and C because it is sensible to do so'. Unlike the exploitative rules of the illustration, the rules of modern organizations appear **rational**. In this sense, they resemble the rules of the road. Most of us will stop at a red traffic light, not because we are afraid of the policeman or because of our sense of moral duty, but because we recognize that stopping at red lights is a rational means of regulating traffic. At times a red light will cause us great frustration, especially if we are in a great hurry, it is late at night and there is no other traffic on the road. Nevertheless, this does not make us argue that stopping at red lights is silly, senseless or unfair.

In a similar way, we recognize most of the organizational rules we obey as rational. To appreciate the exact sense of 'rational' consider a rational rule next to a patently irrational one. Most colleges and universities have formal rules requesting students to write essays when asked by lecturers. They have no rules requiring students to wash their lecturers' motorcars, much as some lecturers might appreciate it. Is this accidental? Hardly. What formal *educational* or *organizational* purpose could possibly be served by rules authorizing superiors to order their subordinates to carry out personal favours? Such rules would not merely be immoral, but also irrational. Of course, the fact that there is no car-washing rule does not imply that no personal favours are ever requested. Favours, bribes, backhanders can all be part and parcel of doing business, embedded in the norms of some organizations. But they are not in any of the rulebooks (see Chapter 4, 'Dealing and Double-Dealing' and Chapter 5, 'Morals').

Organizational rules are rational inasmuch as they are seen to be means of enhancing the achievement of organizational ends. This type of rationality is often referred to as instrumental or means–end rationality. Information regarding alternatives and technical **knowledge** are indispensable ingredients of this type of rationality. Ideally, rational rules would be the result of a methodical comparison and analysis of alternatives and the choice of those alternatives which are best suited to the organization's **goals**. In practice, this is not always the case. While most members of an organization may agree that the organization has goals, there is often disagreement about the nature of these goals or the order of priority in which they are placed. For instance, a doctor, a hospital porter, a secretary, a personnel manager, a nurse and a patient may have very different notions of what a hospital's goals are. Is the hospital's goal to cure patients, to relieve pain, to improve the health standards of people, to carry out large numbers of operations, to offer a very high quality of medical care, to carry out world-class research, to make patients feel happy, or to make profit?

Formal technical rules, therefore, underpin the single-minded pursuit of efficiency that characterizes many organizations. The frying and serving of potatoes becomes the object of extensive 'scientific' study for a fast food organization. This determines specific types of potatoes, fats and fryers, the design of a new wide-mouthed scoop and other hardware and the drafting of 26 different rules on 'how to fry chips'. All this is aimed to ensure that even a person who has never cooked at home can produce, after a minimum of training, a standardized 'market-winning product', without accidents or waste.

BUREAUCRACY

Formal rules affect not only employees of an organization. Next time that you visit a park, have a look at the 'by-laws' stating what you are and what you are not allowed to do. Or consider the regulations governing behaviour in a swimming pool:

No eating	No drinking	No running	No smoking
No bombing	No kissing	No shouting	No spitting
No swearing	No singing	No ducking	No jewellery
No verrucas	No pushing	No diving	No petting

During a conference in Copenhagen, someone brought to the attention of the delegates a set of regulations issued by the Fire Brigade:

In the event of a fire:

1 Stay calm.
2 Locate the fire.
3 Call the Fire Brigade.
4 Close windows and doors.
5 When the Fire Brigade arrives, introduce yourself.
6 If possible, put out the fire.

We all had a good laugh at these regulations. Fortunately no fire disrupted the proceedings. Had there been one, however, it is unlikely that anyone would have remembered the regulations or acted according to them, as people would hurry to the nearest fire escapes.

Seen through the eyes of delegates, rules like those above are the products of bureaucrats, who have little sense of the chaos and confusion that a fire would cause (see Chapter 1, 'Introduction: Organization and Organizing'). They treat an event like a fire as something which can be controlled, or at least contained, through neat and orderly procedures. Their concern for organizing, order and plan blinds them to the forces of disorder that a fire would unleash. Seen through the eyes of those who devised them, both the fire regulations and the swimming pool regulations are not daft at all. They are quite rational, seeking to minimize damage, injuries, insurance liabilities and to contain the disorder. They also help satisfy certain political requirements – such as reassuring Head Office and the safety committee that 'there is a policy in place'.

Managers and administrators spend a lot of time fine-tuning rules and procedures; they are always on the lookout for new rules which will do what old rules did, only better. They believe that this is very important. What they sometimes fail to do is to question the objectives served by these rules and procedures. Are the objectives themselves appropriate? Have they become outdated? Are all the different objectives in harmony? Are there any other objectives which should be served? Whose interests do these objectives serve? Is it realistic to expect people to follow rules like those above?

Organizations vary in their emphasis on rules. Some offer a considerable margin of freedom to their members, allowing them to use their judgement and discretion in making **decisions**. Here is 'the rulebook' of Nordstrom, a North American retailing company.

WELCOME TO
NORDSTROM

We are glad to have you with our company.

Our number one goal is to provide *outstanding customer service*.

Set both personal and professional goals high. We have great confidence in your ability to achieve them.

Nordstrom Rules:

Rule 1: *Use your good judgement in all situations*.

There will be no additional rules.

Please feel free to ask your department manager any question at any time.

Other organizations, like Securecops in our opening example, appear to be strict and regimented, but insiders soon realize that their bark is worse than their bite. Most of their rules are routinely side-stepped. Yet other organizations seek to control everything through precise prescriptions and procedures. Employees are expected to 'do everything by the book', without asking questions. In such organizations, the rules become ends in themselves, rather than means of achieving organizational objectives. In a French hospital, a rule stipulated that receptionists in the Accident and Emergency Unit were to admit only patients arriving by ambulance. The aim of the rule was to ensure that only genuine emergencies were given priority. Once, a seriously ill patient brought to the Unit by taxi was refused admission and sent to the Outpatients' Department; he died while waiting to be admitted.

Organizations in which rules are inflexibly applied, with no regard for the particulars of each individual case, are frequently referred to as bureaucracies. Such organizations remind us of machines. Order, predictability, reliability are the qualities towards which they strive. Judgement, improvisation and fun are dismissed as the enemies of order. Standardization, **hierarchy** and **structure** are of the essence. By contrast, the term 'adhocracy' is sometimes applied to organizations which treat each case on its individual merits, and have few general rules and procedures to guide behaviour. Such organizations must rely on training, trust and strong shared **values** to ensure co-ordination and control. Adhocracies are never particularly orderly or predictable. But they appeal to individuals with artistic or anarchic temperaments.

How Rational are Bureaucratic Rules?

What is important is that you should *understand* why your work has to be done in a certain way and that you do it properly, to the best of your ability. *Not because you have to, but because you want to. In the end this is the BEST WAY.* (Handbook of fast food company)

But is 'the book's way' always the best way? Most of the time, we assume that if a rule is there, it is there for a reason. The rules governing behaviour in the swimming pool may displease us, but most of us would not really question whether they are rational or not. We take on trust that 'experts', who have studied the situation, have developed these rules for everybody's benefit. We assume, for example, 'no running' is there to stop people from slipping and injuring themselves, 'no bombing' to stop people intimidating or injuring others, etc. We take the rationality of many organizational rules and procedures for granted and do not question their legitimacy. We rarely complain about them and tend to disregard the inconvenience in which they result. Some of these rules eventually are observed mechanically, they become part of ourselves. Life without them becomes inconceivable.

Yet, no rule can anticipate all contingencies. If *every* situation involved an appropriate set of rules, the odds are that paralysis would follow; there would be so many rules that few employees would be able to remember them all or be able to apply them appropriately. The risk of rule overload is one that administrators often overlook. Adding ever-increasing numbers of rules can be as counter-productive as failing to have a suitable rule when an unusual situation arises. The ambulance rule at the hospital was rational *until* the arrival of the fated patient; until then it had served what most would regard as a useful purpose. However, one would have to suffer from bureaucratic blindness to argue that when it led to loss of life, it was still rational. Whether a rule is rational or not depends largely on circumstances. No rule can be rational at all times. There comes a time, usually under exceptional or unforeseen circumstances, when it is rational *not* to apply a particular rule. Some organizations recognize the constitutional inability of rules to be rational at all times. They also trust their employees. They allow them to use their discretion.

This, however, may lead to different kinds of difficulties. Imagine if the hospital allowed receptionists to exercise 'discretion' as to whom to admit directly and whom to refer to the Outpatients' Department. This is likely to put great pressure on the receptionists; how can they judge after all who is an 'emergency' and who is not? Besides, patients may complain that they are not treated fairly; why should a drunkard with a broken jawbone be admitted and the child with a fever referred?

Dependence on Rules and Impersonality

Officials become dependent on rules to guide and justify their actions. They sometimes feel that any rule, *even a non-rational one*, is better than no rule. Rules save one the trouble of having to make awkward decisions and then having to explain and defend them. **Impersonality** means that each decision is unaffected by the specific circumstances of individuals. No amount of begging, pleading or arguing will alter the decision. Some of the decisions people make in organizations are very unpleasant. Sacking an employee, putting a patient on a long waiting list, failing a student, are not easy or agreeable decisions. Impersonality cushions us from the suffering and misery of others. 'It was nothing personal, Mrs Jameson, but rules are rules!' But impersonality can also have advantages for those affected by decisions. If everyone is treated according to the rule, if everyone is treated the same, there is no cause for complaints.

Rules can become the opium of bureaucratic officials. Without the rules, they are lost, paralysed. With the support of the rules, they are persons with **authority**. Without rules, chaos. With rules, order and organization. Unlike the authority of the father or the mother in a family or of the founder of a movement, the officials' authority is legal: it rests on the rules which define their rights and responsibilities. Their authority lies not in who they are but in the hats they wear, that is, in the positions they occupy.

Impersonality underwritten by rules seeks to ensure that a task will be performed in a uniform way, no matter who is performing it. Officials will discharge their duties unaffected by erratic factors like their mood, their passions and their idiosyncrasies. Finally, it means that staff in organizations are replaceable, since they are appointed not for who they are but for what they can do.

Impersonality, its Costs and 'Personal Service'

As the size and power of organizations has increased, impersonality has become a dominant feature of Western societies. Constrained by countless rules, stripped of initiative and discretion, increasingly the players of **roles**, we frequently relate to others not as full human beings but as names on forms, numbers on computer terminals, voices at the end of telephone lines or distorted faces behind counters. Many of us feel that we know the characters of television soap operas better than we do our co-workers. Our decisions frequently affect people we scarcely know: a mastectomy may be a life-shattering ordeal for a woman and her family, but for the hospital administrator it is an extra demand on hospital beds; for the medical secretary a mere tick in box 6B.

We are all aware of the frustrations that impersonality causes. Generally we do not like being treated as numbers and many organizations will try hard to create the impression of a personal service. The air stewardess will address business-class passengers with their names and the waiter in certain restaurants may introduce himself saying, 'Hello, I am Pierre, your host for the evening'. Some of us feel uncomfortable or embarrassed about such personal touches, which smack of premeditation and artifice. We may also suspect that they will increase the figure at the end of our bill. A fast food employee said:

> It's all artificial. Pretending to offer personal service with a smile when in reality no one means it. We know this, management know this, even the customers know this, but we keep pretending. All they want to do is take the customer's money as soon as possible. This is what it's all designed to achieve.

The irony, of course, lies in the fact that the 'personal service' is itself often the result of carefully planned rules. As if offering an efficient service were not enough, the rulebooks of some organizations seek to control our **emotions** and our thoughts. Thus, in addition to the physical and intellectual work that they do, many employees find themselves performing *emotional labour* – having to display a caring and friendly attitude, always ready to smile or to exchange some personal words with the customer (see Chapter 12, 'Feelings').

Faced with mock personal service, many prefer the no-nonsense anonymity of the machine. When cash dispensing machines were first introduced by banks, it was thought that people would prefer the personal touch of the bank teller over the fully impersonal transaction with the machine. It did not take long to find that most people given a choice prefer the latter. Anonymity and impersonality have advantages not only for the organization but also for the customer. For one thing, they remove the need to reciprocate false smiles and other unfelt pleasantries.

BENDING THE RULES

We have seen that the rigidity with which organizations enforce their rules varies. The more bureaucratic organizations are fastidious in the application of rules while others take a more relaxed attitude and allow their members a measure of discretion. We sometimes laugh at bureaucracies and their ridiculous regulations, like those of the Danish Fire Brigade. Rules which seem to serve no useful purpose are derided as 'red tape'. Bending such rules appears more rational than enforcing them.

But bending rules has its own difficulties. For one, it undermines one of the most important functions of rules: their guarantee of equal and consistent treatment. Some may fear that once a rule has been bent or violated once, a *precedent* is created for future bigger violations. The rule may then lose all credibility. In most British universities, students must get 40 per cent in order to pass a particular course. Student A has obtained 39.5 per cent. Should he/she pass or not? Common sense and tolerant judgement may argue for lenience. What should then happen to Student B on 39 per cent? Or Student C on 38.5 per cent? Bureaucratic rationality would suggest that a line has already been drawn at 40 per cent and should be observed.

Bureaucratic rationality often rules in organizations. The student on 39.5 per cent may be failed. But then, he/she may not. If every organizational rule was rigidly applied, life could grind to a halt. The fear of creating a precedent, frequently referred to in emotive terms like 'opening the floodgates' or 'the thin end of the wedge', is often based on imaginary dangers; most precedents are quickly forgotten or brushed aside with suitable excuses. Other 'precedents' may be entirely fictitious – having no foundation in an organization's history, yet being regularly invoked to stop change. What seems to happen in the majority of organizations is the establishment of a range of permissible deviations from rules. To new recruits all rules and procedures may seem unbreakable. Nevertheless, as our opening example illustrated, individuals quickly realize that not all rules and regulations are equally sacrosanct. Some of them (like stopping at red lights) are fairly inflexible, but most of them contain loopholes or can be dodged in different ways. Many rules are highly circumstantial, applying only in specific situations, for instance during visits by inspectors. Others have fallen into total neglect. Yet others are the topic of constant conflict and negotiation, a continuous give and take between different organizational members.

Even in fast food restaurants, rules are routinely bent. At peak times, more than four pieces of fish may be fried simultaneously, or chips may be kept for more than seven minutes. Such practices are against the regulations but essential in meeting the demand. What is more, managers themselves are seen bending the rules or turning a blind eye when others violate them. Side-stepping a rule is often essential to meet the demands of a job, but equally individual workers may earn exemptions in the form of privileges. A particularly hard-working employee who turns up to work on a busy day wearing an ear-ring ('not allowed') or having forgotten to wear his deodorant (an 'essential' requirement) is unlikely to be disciplined or turned away.

It is important, then, to emphasize that rules are not things, blindly controlling our behaviour in organizations. They permit different interpretations and their enforcement becomes tied in with the **culture** as well as the power relations of organizations. The same rule may have very different **meanings** in different organizations or even to different individuals within the same organization. Contesting the meaning, the interpretations and the implications of rules is one of the central activities contributing to the instability, unpredictability and richness of organizational life.

CONCLUSION: CHANGING FASHIONS IN THINKING ABOUT RULES

In general, where there are rules, people will look for ways of getting more elbow room. Even in the strictest organizations they are likely to get some, with or without the collusion of their superiors. A study of the behaviour of people in organizations, therefore, must examine both the rules that guide behaviour and the ways in which the rules are interpreted and challenged. It would be shortsighted then to reduce all behaviour in organizations to a passive following of rules; yet it would also be short-sighted to disregard the profound and far-reaching implications of rules in our lives.

Management thinking about rules and procedures is changing. At one time the fine-tuning of rules and procedures was regarded as the secret of organizational success. Flexibility and initiative, embodied in the Nordstrom rules illustrated earlier, are the current fashion. In the past, the frictionless machine represented the managerial ideal of an organization. The lean, highly responsive organism lies more close to current thinking. It is increasingly argued that rules and procedures, however carefully designed, cannot cope with a highly complex and changing organizational **environment** or with massive **technological changes** (see Chapter 9, 'Machines and Mechanizing').

In the past, some bureaucratic organizations prospered because of their predictability and order. Inflexibility and sluggishness were no problem in a stable, friendly environment. After all, dinosaurs ruled the earth for over 200 million years, inflexible and sluggish though many of them were. No one knows for sure why dinosaurs died away, but we all assume that it had something to do with their inability to adapt to new environmental conditions, whether these were brought about by a colliding asteroid or some other cause. The same, argue modern management theorists, is the fate of rigid bureaucratic structures. They stifle innovation, discourage new ideas, fail to capitalize on advantages conferred by modern technologies and are generally too slow and cumbersome to meet **competition**. It is for these reasons that they are already giving way to quicker, smaller, more adaptable, more enterprising organizations.

Such organizations seek to unleash human potential and creativity rather than constrain it through rules and regulations. **'Empowerment'** has replaced control as a management buzz word. This does not mean that control has faded away or that organizational rules and discipline have been replaced by trust and autonomy. It does mean, however, that many organizations seek to complement bureaucratic regulations with subtler forms of organizational control. Selection procedures aimed at ensuring highly committed staff, organizational values, reward structures and corporate culture are currently much-favoured mechanisms of control; their importance will become clearer in some of the other chapters in this book.

- Most organizations have formal, impersonal and highly specific rules.
- Rules can be seen as 'rational' if they are carefully chosen to serve generally agreed organizational goals.
- Rules are an important means of achieving control over individuals' behaviour in organizations.
- Organizations differ in their reliance on rules and on the rigidity with which they apply them.
- At times it becomes more rational to bend or disregard a rule than to enforce it.
- Bending rules may lead to ever-increasing violations and eventual anarchy; but in most organizations, a degree of rule-bending is accepted as normal and necessary.
- Officials often become dependent on rules to justify their actions and decisions and to bolster their authority.
- Rules give organizations an impersonal quality; they reduce the influence of emotions on the way people do their job, and control the way emotions are displayed.
- People in organizations frequently contest the meaning of rules and try to interpret them or change them to their advantage.

READING ON

Bureaucracy is one of the most popular subjects in the study of organizations. Many theorists have engaged with Weber's theory of bureaucracy (1958) which envisaged an ideal type of bureaucracy as the most efficient form of administration. Gouldner (1954), for example, sought to distinguish between rational rules, punitive rules and mock rules, whereas theorists like Jaques (1976) and Drucker (1989) have elaborated and refined arguments of how organizational efficiency can be enhanced through planning, procedures, rules and control.

Peters and Waterman (1982) and numerous other writers, on the other hand, have attacked bureaucracy as the cause of virtually every organizational ill and have advocated more loosely structured organizations, coupled with strong organizational values and a heavy reliance on individual initiative as the recipe for success. Numerous writings by successful business people have attacked bureaucracy along similar lines, notably Carlzon (1989), Morita (1987) and Roddick (1991). Charles Handy (1976) has argued that bureaucracy is itself a feature of the culture of certain organizations, which he terms 'role cultures', whereas other cultures (including power cultures, task cultures and support cultures) lay far less emphasis on standardized procedures and regulations.

The material presented in this chapter also addresses issues of power and control in organizations. Rules in organizations, like the laws of wider society, are not merely means for the achievement of agreed-upon goals, but are also mechanisms of control, safeguarding the interests of those in positions of power. Robert Michels (1949), arguing against Weber's view of rational bureaucracy, envisaged bureaucracy as a smokescreen behind which a ruthless power game goes on, a game through which the few rule the many. This is what he described as the 'Iron Law of Oligarchy'. Two chapters in Morgan's *Images of Organization* (1986) discuss organizations as political systems and as instruments of domination; both are of considerable use to the reader who wishes to explore further the political dimension of the stories introduced in this chapter.

In a series of pioneering studies focusing on the mental asylum, the prison, the clinic, the army and the school, Michel Foucault (1965, 1971, 1977) has argued that these institutions signal the arrival of a new type of control over the masses, a form of control pervasive enough to be absorbed into each and every individual's subjectivity. Rules and bureaucratic procedures of observation, classification and punishment are, according to this view, powerful instruments of control not because of their tangible, visible effects, but because they create a pliant, self-controlled, disciplined population who are unable to envisage themselves outside of these procedures. Our society becomes patrolled by ever-vigilant watchdogs.

A number of neo-Marxist theorists have developed theories of resistance, sometimes drawing on Foucault's work: according to these, organizational subordinates can find more or less indirect ways of contesting, undermining or evading control mechanisms, such as those embodied in rules and regulations (see Jermier et al., 1994; Knights and Willmott, 1990). According to these arguments, there are instances when organizational red tape (such as that encountered in this chapter) is neither a dysfunction of bureaucracy nor a smokescreen for management control but rather an attempt by subordinates to reclaim some control by excessive or ritualistic adherence to rules and procedures.

4

Dealing and double-dealing

While interviewing staff at an historic hospital in the centre of London, I was surprised to find that Mick, a porter, came to work by car. Now everyone knows that there is no parking in this part of London, so I asked him where he left his car. He became quite defensive and indicated vaguely that he found a place within the hospital perimeter. I interviewed numerous other catering workers, none of whom drove to work. I was sufficiently intrigued to ask one of his colleagues about Mick's parking. 'Mick's got his own private parking space, with his name on it, right next to the consultants', I was told. 'How come?' I asked, quite perplexed. 'Politics', came the answer.

Later I learned that Mick received his parking space as a reward for strike-breaking. A few years earlier, a tough new manager had imposed a strict roster regime in the hospital's kitchen and had clamped down on pilfering and over-time. This infuriated the catering staff and they went on strike. Eventually, though, they were forced back to work on management's terms.

During the strike, the managers had provided service with the help of a few workers, including Mick, who were smuggled into the hospital in taxis. All of these workers had been rewarded with promotions, benefits or simply by being assigned the most desirable jobs in the kitchen, the 'gravy jobs'. Those who had joined the strike were denied overtime work and were systematically landed with the 'stinkers', those jobs no one wants to do.

It is hard to think of organizing without **politics**. Differences of opinion, value and interest, clashes of personality, limited resources and personal ambition add to the tension, as well as the buzz and excitement, of organizing. People sometimes describe their organization as 'all politics', to suggest a devious, conflictual atmosphere where intrigue, gossip and whispering are endemic. They appear to be 'looking over their shoulders' much of the time and the language of politics – what secret deals are happening; who is abusing the system; who is the boss's favourite – permeates the corridors and coffee rooms. At its extreme politics can be harsh, vindictive and conflictual, where power is used and abused. It can also bring about strange alliances. In a **conflict** situation, such as above, it is clear that **power** is not always simply a matter of the boss's prerogative. It is the 'lowly' porter on whom the boss ultimately depends in a crisis – a collaboration that he needs for his own ends, and one that also rewards the porter.

Secret deals and plotting behind closed doors are fascinating. But just as fascinating are those organizations where such events seem rare, or non-existent. These may be happier (or duller, depending on your perspective) organizations to work in, but does that mean there is no politics? We think not. Politics is both the expression and the resolution of inevitable differences between people and their preferences. But these do not have to be expressed and tackled using devious means: some organizations handle their differences in a more open manner, without rancour or distrust. Let us examine this a little further.

DIFFERENT GAMES?

One way of looking at the dealings that people have with each other is as **games**. Referring to dealings as games does not mean that they do not have serious intentions, nor that they may not have serious consequences. The game is a metaphor for the way that people attempt to influence, or score 'points' off, one another. Indeed, one psychologist, Eric Berne (1964), has suggested that many of our conflicts can be unravelled by seeing them in terms of the games we play, with rules that are sometimes so taken for granted that we do not see how they operate or what they do. The games can be complex and intertwined; multiple games each with rather different rules and different outcomes. Games can be played coolly and calculatively, or aggressively and passionately.

In organizations we often have a sense of some of the **rules** of play, the turns, the refereeing and so on. We learn about their intricacies, such as that it is OK to criticize John when you are talking to your friend Sue, but not when you are talking to Mary (who is John's boss). If such niceties are misunderstood or ignored, there can be a cost (e.g. personal embarrassment, a lost friendship or working relationship, even your job). Another 'rule' might be that new product ideas must always be taken to the development committee before the production department is asked to comment on them.

Organizations abound in such tacit rules of the game – rules that do not appear in writing or a rulebook (see Chapter 3, 'Rules are Rules'). Many organizational games are of the someone-wins-someone-loses sort. For example, in the 'game' of appointments and promotions, if there is only one vacancy, and one person gets it, another does not – he/she loses. However, there are organizational games where one person's gain is not necessarily another person's loss. These are rather like the informal games at a children's party: if one person or **group** wins too convincingly or too often, the others will not want to play with them any more. So the art is to learn just where to co-operate sufficiently to make sure that your opponents are doing well enough not to quit: a win–win situation. Skilled negotiators in industrial relations conflicts on pay, productivity or working conditions know this only too well. A complete loser is likely to feel demotivated and refuse to bargain on another occasion. They may find other ways of scoring off an opponent – such as wrecking the efforts of others through poor workmanship, blocking initiatives, spreading rumours, **sabotage** or sheer bloody-mindedness. This reminds us that winning and losing can have different meanings for different actors – to the extent that one person's 'obvious' win may not feel that way to him, and another person's 'clear' loss is regarded by him/her as a personal victory. Such apparent inversions attest to a range of social and psychological processes – such as perceptions of fairness, defensiveness and the kind of audience to whom the success or failure is presented. We see such behaviours in, for example, the way football supporters handle their team's losses and how heads of state, who have lost a war, claim a 'moral victory'. The careful use of **language** and **rhetoric** is crucial to this process.

Some organizational activities resemble a constellation of games such that winning at one level allows you to proceed to the next level. For example, competing successfully for a budget is used as entry to bidding for a larger contract, and then for entry to compete for promotion. It may also be that succeeding in one game, against a particular set of rules, excludes you from another game. A typical example here is 'rate busting'. Exceeding the work rate – how much and how long to work – that immediate colleagues informally agree is appropriate may win praise from senior management (for more production, more profit), but at the cost of being snubbed or excluded by colleagues.

Some games go on invisibly, behind one's back. This is amply illustrated by a student's account of her experiences on her work placement:

> On 1 October I [Mirella] arrived in Paris to join a headquarters team of six people in the department specializing in hairdressing products. I became assistant to Carol, a charming Irish lady, and shared an office with Peter. Three

months before my arrival Peter had been transferred with his family from Australia to work in our office.

The atmosphere at work was so informal and friendly that I soon became really close to Peter and Carol, my mentor. In less than a week I was considered part of their team, and had access to all sorts of informal discussions that were going on in the organization. Through Carol I learnt that Peter had found his move from Australia very difficult; what was supposed to be a promotion had turned out to be a major upheaval. Life in Paris was far more expensive than in Australia; his wife and daughters, born and brought up in Australia, were struggling to learn French, his wife unable to get a work permit in Europe. They were therefore stuck at home without many opportunities for integrating into French society.

Still, Peter claimed that he was very happy to be in Paris, a city he loved. He was happy to have made it to the headquarters, and happy for his family to get to know France. He felt it would take some time for them to settle down, but that things would get better

Then, during one of our increasingly frequent chats, Carol revealed to me that Peter would not stay at the headquarters in Paris permanently, but would go and occupy a vacant position in Germany. Paris was merely a stopover for him – but he and his family did not know that yet.

For the organization, it did not really matter that he and his family were struggling to settle down in France. What really mattered to them was that Peter was the perfect man for the German job: his German was excellent and he would be able to carry out a job in Germany in the French way – which he was learning.

The organization is willing to provide its employees with considerable privileges and good working conditions, but their identity is taken away from them in return. These are the rules, and once you are in the mechanism it is very difficult to get out; almost impossible. The situation reminds me of those games where a child is supposed to fit an object of a particular shape into a hole of corresponding shape: the employees are just like the objects; there is a suitable hole for each one of them. The invisible hand, or rather, the decision makers that nobody ever sees or hears, are only concerned with finding the right holes for the right objects, because that is the solution of the game.

Such shadowy games highlight the way that different rules can apply at different levels of an organization: one group's interests are pursued by devaluing the 'interests' of others – who are less powerful. The games also sow the seeds of mistrust.

There are occasions when the principle at stake for both parties is so high that nothing but an all-out win will do; yet that win seems unattainable. It is not uncommon to observe the sad and destructive spectre of two-loser games in organizations: a strike which leaves the workers none the richer and a company in ruins; an interdepartmental rivalry in which each department effectively blocks the other's efforts; a price war between two firms driving both of them to bankruptcy. But, interestingly, even such losses can be described by the warring parties as victories of a sort, given that

they have safeguarded their principles. Organizational history is
littered with examples of Pyrrhic victories.

If some organizational games disintegrate into apparently no-
win situations, others generate multiple winners. Situations that
appear stubbornly win–lose can suddenly be unlocked through the
arts of politics and diplomacy. There is the delightful tale of two
pharmaceutical companies after the same resource – ugli oranges –
which contained the essential raw ingredients for their products.
The oranges were in very short supply so both companies were
prepared to pay 'any price' to obtain them. Two senior executives
from each of the two companies had a meeting to see if they could
reach a compromise. But they soon discovered that they were both
in an all-or-nothing situation: they were both after the full supply
of oranges.

Just as they were preparing to part and declare war on each
other, it occurred to one of them to ask the other *how* they were
going to use the oranges.

'Exactly which part of the orange do you need?'

'Why, the juice, of course!'

'Good grief, let's celebrate…we only need the rind!' (Adapted
from Hall et al., 1978.)

ABOVE AND BELOW THE TABLE

Some conflict or **competition** in organizations is built into the
structure. So the board of directors will have members with **roles**
which invite them to fight for different interests within the company. The Marketing Director, the Production Director and the
Finance Director are appointed to represent different interests.
Although they need to collaborate for the good of the company,
they are also expected to do the best deals they can for their department and to see their own department's point of view. This is a
way of formalizing conflict, containing it by establishing rules and
formulae within which it takes place. In many commercial organizations certain conflict is legitimized as competition, a force for
profit, growth and constructive contest. Competition has its rules,
such as there being a 'level playing field', undistorted by monopoly power or special privileges. Organizations which engage in
international trade can often be seen to be in dispute or conflict
because the tax, legal or employment conditions in one country
give organizations there a competitive edge: a little like a runner in
a race starting from a point ahead of all the rest of the field.

Once certain rules and formulae are recognized as the sensible way of doing business, they acquire special significance: they become institutions. Institutions shape our expectations and generate a sense of fairness. Consider the democratic institution of general elections through which much political conflict is channelled. Your party loses the elections; you may not be happy about this, but you accept it. You do not like some of the laws which the government passes, but you observe them. The party in opposition is not pleased, but they do not try to mobilize the army to gain power by force. In this way institutions, rarely perfect, can work.

The same goes on in organizations. You fail to gain promotion. You are not happy about this. But you are able to live with it if (a) it is the result of a clearly stated procedure, and (b) your colleague who got promoted instead of you was noticeably better on the stated criteria. In other words, the decision appears fair and by the rules. This does not mean that people always accept the rules as they find them. In organizations the referees are often themselves players. Trying to change the rules, twist them, re-interpret them, is itself a major part of organizational politics. Nevertheless, having some rules which give all sides a 'winning chance' is necessary if people are going to accept the outcomes as fair. This may be seen more clearly in the dealings between management and trade unions. The declining power of trade unions in the UK in the 1980s was widely admired by many. But it was regretted by some managers who found that the **institutionalization** of conflict through collective bargaining made their lives easier. They could deal with a clear negotiating partner, but were much less comfortable when it was less obvious who the negotiating partner was, or what rules governed any agreements that were made.

Is it better for conflict to come out into the open? There are no hard and fast answers. Sometimes we feel better if a conflict that has been bubbling away for some time becomes open and acknowledged. A middle manager in a high-volume factory producing biscuits told of his own experiences:

> It's funny. You can be supervising a bloke who has been cheerful for weeks on end, and then suddenly he turns on you – for no apparent reason. This has happened to me a number of times. I'm always caught unprepared, and I'm always baffled by it. It has worried me a lot. I've now started to talk about it more with the people involved. I've noticed that their anger is nearly always about something that happened weeks ago – maybe at work, maybe outside. The blokes have been sitting on it until it becomes just too much to hold.

A big storm can sometimes clear the air. At other times small quarrels can escalate into major disputes. Sometimes the very act of declaring a conflict creates one. As soon as there are two sides in a dispute it becomes difficult for people not to join up with one side or the other. The theatre of conflict is enlarged, making a resolution tougher to achieve. So unleashing conflict may or may not be a wise thing to do. This creates some dilemmas. For example, the advantages of cohesive, strife-free, work groups are extolled by many managers. The groups instil a positive team spirit in their members, they are pleasant to work in, and they are not split by differences of opinion. The down-side is that, in their desire to remain cohesive, the group members suppress internal conflicts and disagreement which could lead to more creative actions or solutions; and worse, they become blind and deaf to disturbing information. This phenomenon has been called **groupthink**, and it has been used to explain events as calamitous as the failed invasion of Cuba at the Bay of Pigs in 1961, and, less dramatically, the failure of an organization to see critical changes in the demand for its product. The moral, it seems, is to be suspicious of conflict-free zones in organizations.

WHO WILL GET THE RESOURCES...?

An oft-cited source of conflict in organizations – where politics, haggling, dealing and double-dealing, flourish – is in the getting and giving of resources. Resources are the people, buildings and equipment that a manager requires to run and develop his or her part of the business. They are funded from a budget allocated from the total monies available to the organization. Given that the cake is rarely large enough to meet the appetites of all managers, its division is almost bound to disappoint someone.

The fact that the vast majority of organizations have to function with less resources than they would ideally like (and considerably less in times of recession), means that there is potential for serious conflict at least once a year, perhaps every quarter, when budgets are decided. Also the legacy of such allocations, with its winners and losers, can rumble on for a long time, setting the tone of working relationships both within and between working groups.

The players in the conflict are already in place. As mentioned, the various directors – marketing, production, finance, sales, personnel, training, quality control, research and development – each have their own interests to fight for and protect, and they are in continuous **communication** with one another. Their interests will include their personal careers as well as the size, prestige and effectiveness of their particular department or function. Given the centrality of budget-setting in an organization's functioning, one would expect it to be well institutionalized, with clear, rational and fair rules to play by. In practice it is institutionalized, but the rules are not all that apparent or clear. They are much contested and negotiated. We gain a glimpse of just how from a production director of a medium-sized clothing manufacturer:

> We were about three months off the new financial year, and things had been tough for the company. I knew I could do much better with a special new cutting machine – made only in Germany. The Chief Executive knew of the problem, but said that the £175,000 was just too much; it was cheaper to keep repairing the old one. I disagreed, but I couldn't shift him. I knew that Bob from Sales was after a new fleet of trucks, and Alan was determined to increase his marketing staff, and get them all into a decent office. They each had a strong case, so I had to do something. Firstly, I found an excuse to get the Chief Executive down on the shop floor on the next breakdown, to see the waste and chaos. It happened three times; some people think I actually fixed the breakdowns! Next, I had a long chat on the phone with the German supplier. I got them to knock 15 per cent off the price and give us one-year interest-free credit, and install the machine. A brilliant deal, I thought. Finally, I got their rep to call by with a sample of the cutter's work at a time when I knew I'd be with the Chief Executive. The Chief Executive was noncommittal – but that was better than a refusal. Then, on 3 April, I received my new budget – with an allowance for a new machine! Bob and Al didn't get half of what they wanted, and they aren't too happy. Bob says he's now looking for a new job, and Al seems to avoid me and the Chief Executive.

We see here the reality of lobbying, politicking and creating alliances. The Chief Executive, for his part, was faced with a number of competing, but plausible, claims for extra resources. He also had to try and make a wise budget distribution for the overall survival, and ultimate success, of the organization. In such difficult and ambiguous conditions he is likely to find it hard to ignore special pleading – especially if it is handled skilfully and seems to link with his own aims and plans. In this particular case, however, his decision was costly in certain non-financial ways – the disaffection of two of his senior managers. In the longer term that could translate into financial costs as a result of the poorer effectiveness of the managers, and their possible replacement. There are no simple recipes for **decision making** in these sorts of circumstances. Skilled managers will need to acknowledge the political and **emotional** features that underlie such resource allocations, and, as shrewdly as possible, steer a path between the various interests involved.

There are a number of variations on the theme of this case. In some organizations groups will fight hard, and bitterly, over available resources. Others will do secret deals with colleagues to their mutual advantage. Less furtively, senior managers may sit around a table in a private room and not emerge until they have thrashed out a budget allocation with which they can all live, accepting that not everyone can get all they want. Many would argue that this is the best way of making the most of a seemingly impossible situation. On the other hand, some executive teams are so divided from the outset that nothing short of a directive from 'above' will sort it out.

AND CRITERIA ...

Inextricably entwined with resource allocation are the goals and criteria by which individuals and groups are judged (see Chapter 11, 'Judging Others'). The likelihood of conflict is high when one group regards **organizational goals** as less realistic, or less attainable, than another group. Each group wishes to have organizational criteria adopted that will make them look the best. Universities, for example, are known for such behaviour. As well as for teaching, universities are mandated to produce original research; they are judged, and rewarded, according to their publication record. But how do you compare the impressive number of publications which come out of a department of physics, reporting many small experimental variations on a number of themes, with a modern languages department which produces far fewer publications – but some weighty tomes on linguistics? And when is a publication a publication? Which journals count? What is the worth of a long article in a quality newspaper compared with a research note in an obscure academic journal, compared with a chapter in a book?

The contention that surrounds such questions leads to all sorts of anxiety, and much political behaviour – partisan negotiations, lobbying heads of department to have the criteria changed, 'creative' declarations of what one has published, and contesting the research record of a colleague, boss or other department. At worst it produces an air of divisiveness and mistrust. More whimsically, it serves as a challenge for those who wish to send up the system (see Chapter 14, 'Serious Joking'). We have a colleague who works in a department of education at a university. By choice, he does precious little research. However, he has a passion for gardening and writes a weekly column in a popular gardening magazine. He insists that these are bona fide publications, and should be treated as his contribution to his department's efforts. So each year, when his department's publications are collated, amongst the learned articles on topics such as classroom violence, syllabus design, and ethnic differences on attainment tests, there are titles such as 'Geraniums in a drought', 'Lawn care without tears', and 'Weeds to treasure'.

RESOLVING CONFLICT?

The natural flow of conflict and co-operation in organizational life, and its attendant politics, means that the removal of all conflict, were it possible, is an unrealistic ideal. Furthermore, as we have illustrated, there are ways in which conflict can contribute to the richness of organizational life.

It is tempting to extract conflict from its organizational context, and seek universal managerial 'fixes' to damaging disputes. Some typically promoted are:

- smoothing the differences between conflicting parties by providing them with new information;
- voting – the majority wins;
- seeking compromise: everyone gets a bit of what they want;
- seeking consensus: a solid best solution worked out by those in conflict;
- confrontation: encouraging straight talking between opposing parties.

Each technique has its pros and cons. For example, smoothing conflict only works if the information given is trusted; majority rule can be felt as unfair if you are often on the losing side; compromise is fine if people resist the urge to exaggerate their demands in the first place. More importantly, though, conflict management needs to be sympathetic to, or in tune with, the prevailing political **culture** of the organization. An organization that 'thrives' on deals and double-deals is unlikely to respond well to consensus-seeking. In an organization that prides itself on its strong culture people will be puzzled if asked to vote. And an open confrontational style would be hard to implement in a company predominated by power and **status** divisions.

TO SUMMARIZE ...

In this chapter we have presented organizations as a 'natural' reflection of the people who comprise them. It should come as no surprise that, in some way or another, people will bring their interests, attitudes, prejudices and allegiances into the making of organizational life. And whom they meet, whom they work with, and whom they are controlled by, will influence how people 'present' themselves, and what they choose to do. This is organizational politics. So 'dealing', tacitly or openly, nicely or nastily, with or without open conflict, is part of organizational life. How much, though, and in what form, depends on the issues faced and the political culture of the organization – and we have offered a framework to indicate the range of possibilities.

- Politics is a normal feature of organizational life.
- Politics is as much about trust and loyalty as about deception and corruption.
- Organizational politics does not have to be conducted in a destructive way.
- Conflict in organizations is often regarded as acceptable and even good if it is kept within bounds.
- Many of the deals and games within organizations are about resource allocation.
- The criteria by which departments and proposals are evaluated are a key issue in organizational politics.
- Different ways of handling conflict may be appropriate in different organizational cultures.

THESAURUS ENTRIES

communication	institutionalization
competition	language
conflict	politics
culture	power
decision making	rhetoric
emotion	role
games	rules
goals	sabotage
group	status

READING ON

Morgan (1986) explores organizations as political systems and offers an extensive account of the way power and politics operate in organizations. A deeper analysis of these issues – especially interpersonal rivalries and coalitions in multi-interest settings – is provided by Kotter (1979, 1982), Pfeffer (1992) and Lukes (1975). Lukes, as well as French and Raven (1959), offers widely used typologies of power.

Charles Handy (1976) notes different manifestations of conflict – 'argument', 'competition' and disruptive 'conflict'. More radical theorists, such as Salaman (1981), avoid the notion that conflict is disruptive, preferring to focus on how it emerges from the tensions, contradictions and ideologies of organized life. A consideration of how people respond to conflict is to be found in the work of Thomas (1977), who speaks of various classes of response – from avoidance to collaboration.

Game theory is used to analyse conflict in business (Gardner, 1995; Radford, 1986), an approach that stresses different game strategies: risk, information, competition and co-operation. Maccoby's (1976) vivid portrayal of executive games reveals some of the finer detail of what happens in practice, while Mangham's (1986) lively perspective links political games with dramaturgy – the way game players shape their public images and postures. Game theory has its critics, most notably Morgan (1986), who analyses its strengths and weaknesses and Lasch (1980) who is despairing of the game mentality that he sees permeating social life.

5

Morals

Some years ago, the Bank of England took a sudden and extraordinary step: it shut down the London base of a major international bank (the Bank of Credit and Commerce International). The bank served considerable financial interests in Arab countries and Asia, as well as in the UK and America. It was known for its philanthropic use of funds, inspired by the religious beliefs of its founder. It provided banking facilities for individuals as well as major corporations, including the accounts of a number of British charities. It also laundered drug money, supported shady arms deals, bolstered military dictatorships, underpinned a secret nuclear bomb project involving Libya, Argentina and Pakistan, was party to a CIA deal on the prosecution of General Noriega, ex-dictator of Panama, and consistently falsified its records. How could this happen? How could the principles of a respectable and cautious part of the business community become so corrupted?

Elsewhere, completely out of the news, a manager at a prestigious British firm of chartered accountants confidently adds an administration charge to a client's account, based on an invented item of 'work done'. And, in the forecasting department of a multinational cigarette company a clerk wryly alters the sales forecasts for a fourth time – because top management 'still don't like them'. The clerk has learned that she needs to produce work which will back up management's objectives for end-of-year sales.

These are actual events. How are we to understand them, both great and small? Are they all part of the **game** of business and organizing (see Chapter 4, 'Dealing and Double-Dealing')? Does it not matter what you do, as long as you are not found out? Is it **power** that determines what has to be done – who wields the biggest stick? What unite the incidents are questions of **value** and morality: the distinctions between what is right or wrong in organizational behaviour, and whether, and how, such distinctions are made and acted upon.

KNOWING RIGHT FROM WRONG

We can add further examples which, in their different ways, go to the heart of moral beliefs:

- police officers who fabricate a confession;
- the 'charity' organizer who takes our money, and then steals it for himself;
- a multinational oil company which massively pollutes the environmentally sensitive Alaskan shoreline.

When we look closely at such incidents there is a cluster of 'dubious' behaviours – lying, deceit, fraud, evasion, negligence. In most cultures, such behaviours generate strong feelings of disapproval and indignation. We may argue that no organization should be run that way. But many are, and organizational members invent terms which help them to do so – such as 'creative accounting', 'being economical with the truth', 'tidying the books', 'not rocking the boat', and 'safeguarding the interests of the shareholders', symbols of a sub-morality – to which we shall return.

But when are issues really *moral* ones? And who makes such judgements? This is problematic. At a psychological level the distinction has been drawn between actions which produce feelings of guilt in the actor, and those which produce embarrassment. The former relate directly to morality. So, if an engineer knowingly fails to properly service a valve on a gas line which then leaks and kills a colleague, the guilt he feels relates to his feeling of culpability in harming another human being. The principle of not harming somebody through one's actions, directly or indirectly, lies at the heart of moral concepts. The person who lets down colleagues by not turning up for a key meeting, which leads to the loss of a client, may feel deeply embarrassed. She has transgressed the expectation of her work **group**, but it is not felt as a moral issue. The harm is neither as devastating nor as irreversible as that which followed the engineer's actions. The roots of the harm principle go deep into society's codes of conduct, but it is expressed in different ways according to the cultural and religious history of a country.

We start to make moral judgements early on in our lives, as we learn to distinguish right from wrong, partly by noting our parents' approval and disapproval of different types of behaviour. Some of these judgements reflect the values of our culture, which become part of us as we grow older. Early on, we may resist the temptation to steal our sister's or brother's book or to break their favourite toy for fear of punishment. Gradually, however, we learn to tame our impulses not so much for fear of punishment, but because we accept that certain types of behaviour are intrinsically wrong. Stealing, lying, hurting or insulting others, deceiving, destroying, killing: these are acts that offend our moral conscience – unless they are experienced as serving a still more fundamental moral principle. For instance, lying in order to save someone from unnecessary hurt may be seen as permissible – a 'white lie'. Yet, as we grow older, we find ourselves facing moral dilemmas, situations where different moral principles are at odds, and no clear right and wrong options are readily available. Is peace more important than justice? When is it right to use violence in pursuit of moral objectives? Is our duty to our parents greater than that to our children? Is it right to lie in order to protect someone's honour and dignity? Is our loyalty to our friend more important than our right to criticize and castigate him or her when they act wrongly?

Moral dilemmas can cause us much unease and anxiety. We each discover different ways of defending ourselves against these unpleasant feelings. As we saw in Chapter 3, one way is to shield ourselves with organizational rules, denying that our actions have any moral import at all – they are merely the enactment of someone else's regulations. Another way to avoid the anxiety brought about by moral dilemmas is to deny their importance or to overlook the implications of our decisions. Alternatively, we invent plausible-sounding reasons as a way of persuading ourselves of the correctness of our actions. We did not really mean to hurt someone; we only wanted to have a laugh. We did not lie, we just forgot to present a piece of information. We did not get someone dismissed, we just let them go. These plausible-sounding excuses are referred to as **rationalizations**. They can be the product of much reflection and self-questioning or, more commonly, they are ways of deceiving ourselves, buying ourselves an amnesty for acts which would cause us feelings of guilt and remorse. If we can convince ourselves that someone has hurt many others, he/she becomes a legitimate target for aggression and violence, which would be thought of as immoral if aimed at an innocent party. In this way, as humans, we can easily deceive ourselves into believing that we are gentle creatures who would never harm anyone without being provoked.

Another way of coping with awkward dilemmas is by sustaining two or more stories about our actions. These can be at odds with each other, yet each serves to rationalize our actions in a different way. Even a trivial matter, like the appropriation of somebody else's book, can become the focus of numerous stories or half-shaped thoughts in our minds. For example, we did not really steal our friend's book; we only 'borrowed it and then forgot to return it'. Besides, our friend 'borrowed' our favourite T-shirt and kept it for several weeks. And anyhow, he had no use for the book, whereas the book was very useful for us. Besides, it was not even his book, but his sister's.

ORGANIZATIONS AND MORALITY

Institutional processes can wreak havoc with our sense of right and wrong. They can subvert, even obliterate, moral judgement, producing their own counter-morality or amorality. Police officers have knowingly falsified confessions which have sent innocent people to jail – or to their execution. Any feelings of guilt are rationalized away in terms such as 'well, that sort of person deserves what they get', or 'it was important to get a conviction at all costs, the man was a menace to society'. Many organizations so strongly inculcate their members with their own values that people become blind to individual moral issues. In effect, the organization's values come to stand for what is moral and what is not. This was most horrifically demonstrated in Nazi Germany. The defence offered by German officers who systematically brutalized and annihilated millions of human beings was, 'I was only obeying my orders'. Indeed, the response to organizational 'orders' says much for the frailty of human moral conduct. The Nazi doctrine had an additional feature to help crush conventional moral thought: Jews, gypsies, the mentally ill and others were to be considered as sub-human, or even as the diseased parts of society, who threatened to infect everyone else, thus they merited their fate.

Organizations present their members with various tests of loyalty – situations where they have to decide whose side they are on – which can seriously stretch ideas of right and wrong. In the example used in Chapter 4, 'Dealing and Double-Dealing', Mirella, a temporary employee at a cosmetics multinational, is presented with such a test. In the course of a conversation with Carol, her boss, Mirella discovers that Peter, a colleague, is due to be moved from the company's headquarters in Paris to an outpost in

Germany. Mirella knows that Peter, who has moved his family to Paris from Australia, will be devastated when he hears the news. Should she tell him, warn him or prepare him? Or should she stay quiet?

> In the space of five minutes the destiny of a man I did not know that well, had been revealed to me. I felt I had become an accomplice in this 'multinational mechanism', where an invisible hand allocates resources in the most efficient way. I knew things about him that he would probably find out about in about a year's time, by which time his family would have only just settled down. However, I could not warn him. My information came from the grapevine and was therefore not reliable. I was supposed to mind my own business and pretend I did not know. That was what everybody else was doing; this is how you were supposed to behave if you were working in that organization. The fact that Carol was meant to be a close friend of Peter implied that she should be the one to talk to him, I thought. I realized later that loyalty to the organization came first, even before friendship; nobody would ever dream of arguing against a decision made by the 'invisible hand'. Certainly, I thought, an offer to move to another country can be refused, but that is true only in theory. Once your destiny has been decided somewhere up in the hierarchy, the invisible hand will make sure you will find it too disadvantageous to refuse. In other words, the organization is willing to provide its employees with considerable privileges and good working conditions, but their identity is taken away from them in return. These are the rules, and once you are in the mechanism it is very difficult to get out; almost impossible.

In this example, Mirella's sense of right and wrong is overwhelmed by what she regards as an organizational code which requires her to be silent; while she finds numerous rationalizations for staying silent, she experiences feelings of discomfort or even guilt about the situation. She certainly does not look forward to the day when she finds herself in Peter's position:

> I still cringe at the idea of having one day a comfortable office in one of these organizations. Deep down, I will be conscious of the fact that I have become like a circle-shaped object and someone I don't even know is desperately trying to find the corresponding circle-shaped hole.

When morality is replaced by organizational **norms**, or by a professional code of practice, people can defer to those as the arbiters of the rightness or wrongness of their action. They provide a shortcut to moral **decision making**, relieving people of much of the burden of having to make up their own mind. This can, step by step, move people into self-justifying positions, rationalizations, which, by any other criteria, would be immoral. So it is 'just tough', or part of the 'realities of doing business', that Joe's job will be removed when he is away on holiday and he will not know until he gets back. And 'we'd lose the contract' if community representatives were told the true noise levels of the new factory that is going to be built near their village. 'If we don't harvest that old forest, someone else will.' Leaders in many organizations set the moral tone for their followers. In some organizations, a sense of deep social and moral responsibility is continuously reiterated, emphasizing the need for each and every member to be morally scrupulous and above reproach. Some organizations pride themselves on their respect for human rights, for the environment, for the rights of minorities, and so forth. Such organizations may attract public attention, as journalists, politicians and academics test the strength of their claims, especially when they clash with harsh financial realities. Other organizations may institutionalize the turning of a blind eye, disregarding what they view as moral niceties (such as giving employees advance notice of redundancies or offering them re-training packages) and emphasizing business objectives rather than a wider moral or social agenda.

Immorality and corruption can sometimes infect an entire organization, turning every member into a silent accomplice to shameful acts. Occasionally, cases come to light of companies which have embezzled or recklessly speculated vast amounts of shareholders' money, of children's homes where children have been systematically abused, of hospitals which run roughshod over patients' health, or of firms which ruin or jeopardize the natural environment. Questions are then asked: 'Why wasn't any action taken to prevent this? Why was it not made public earlier? Why did nobody spill the beans?' Answers to such questions are difficult to find, without recognizing the psychological vulnerability and corruptibility of individuals, when exposed to an environment where the normal precepts of morality are routinely flouted by everybody, from the top down.

Some medical, research and other organizations have '**ethics committees**' to consider the morality of adopting new programmes or procedures in their work. Ethical codes of practice, like professional ethics, are meant to guide individuals when faced with moral dilemmas. However, decisions in most organizations are rarely subjected to such scrutiny. Most just happen, a product of the personal beliefs of the actors involved, their **roles** and professional expectations, and the **politics** and **culture** of the organization. All these come into play when, for instance, a board of directors is deciding on which bit of their company to close down, whether to continue promoting a product with a poor safety record, or the extent of their own pay rises compared with those of their employees.

Moral logic is fluid when it comes to protecting vested interests. It is not uncommon for one group to challenge another in morally toned language, while the defenders offer an 'obviously reasonable and practical' explanation for their actions, disclaiming the relevance of moral considerations. Moral accusations make powerful **rhetoric**, and it is sometimes seen as wiser to disengage from such **discourse** and fight on other terms. Throughout the 1990s the directors of many large British corporations awarded themselves massive pay increases (ranging from 50 to 300 per cent) while insisting that their staff receive modest pay rises – 'in order for the company to survive'. 'It makes good economic sense,' asserted the directors, 'to pay the market rate for leadership talent.' 'It is greedy, unfair and extraordinarily insensitive,' cried the workers.

Many organizations will claim that their prime obligation is to serve their shareholders, to give them as good a return on their investment as possible. Then, they say, as long as they operate within the law (although some will fight it or bend it), issues of moral culpability are not really relevant to their actions. Such pragmatism has justified the commercial exploitation of the seas, rivers and forests, despite the devastating harm that has been wreaked upon the earth – its animals, plants and human communities. Only recently has there been a slight convergence between these patently moral concerns and the amoral logic of economics. The latter can begin to incorporate the former if the earth itself is not considered akin to income – something that can be spent and used because there will always be more of it (see Chapter 6, 'Greening').

PERSONALIZING AND DEPERSONALIZING

We are most likely to *feel* issues as moral ones when they touch us personally: the disquiet or guilt from feeling party to a possible injustice or harm. There are decisions which some people find hard not to experience as morally problematic, such as sacking, takeovers, not promoting, demoting. The anguish can be seen in the following comments from a senior computer analyst:

> There are parts of my job that I hate. Today I've written a report where I've almost suggested that there ought to be redundancies in certain areas. I've felt dreadful about it. It's the first time I've done anything like that, and I'm really not sure what I'm doing. I'm talking about people I know. It would be a new

computer system which would replace two people with one part-timer. I never thought I'd be in a position where I would be making these recommendations. But it's just a recommendation, not a decision.

Advice on how to handle these situations is usually aimed at damage limitation, not at confronting the moral dilemma. So we find instructions to the carriers of bad tidings to 'offer help and constructive criticism along with the bad news'; 'present the broader organizational and economic picture', or 'hire an external expert to do the job'. A crisp and soothing organizational language exists to help decision makers depersonalize and rationalize their anxieties and put them into the organization's 'moral' framework – where it is just part of the job; the rules of the game. For example:

- On dismissing someone:
  'Sometimes you have to be cruel to be kind; it's in their ultimate interests to work for someone more suitable.'
  'It's your job or theirs.'
  'The organization's efficiency is at stake.'
- On promising an unlikely delivery date:
  'Well, we must win the contract first. We'll worry about delivery later.'
- On selling an environmentally damaging product:
  'It's our job to make profits. It's the government's job to protect the environment.'
  'It's not illegal yet. If we don't sell them, someone else will.'
- On selling weapon-potential chemicals to an unreliable military regime:
  'As far as we are concerned they are for agricultural purposes, and the government has not opposed an export licence.'

In the world of economic rationalizations winning a contract, staying in business, satisfying shareholders, is 'what it is about'. Lies are not lies; they are 'part truths' which 'make good economic sense'. Someone has to get hurt in market-place competition and **conflict**, goes the argument; there 'must be winners and losers'. Additionally, there is the concern that **motivates** people to protect the security and income which, in our culture, are obtainable only through a job; fine altruistic values cannot survive the cut-and-thrust world of business. In these various ways, tough and potentially harmful decisions are transformed into an organizational procedure or control device – and a seemingly enduring feature of organizational functioning (see Chapter 3, 'Rules are Rules').

BETWEEN THE CRACKS

Not all morally questionable actions are easy to hide or neutralize within the organization. **Harassment** is a case in point. Verbal, sexual or physical harassment is usually felt as a moral violation. The perpetrator, however, might talk about it as 'simply a bit of fun', 'a game', or 'all part of everyday working'. Individuals are often alone with their moral conscience when they experience, or witness, harassment. Should they complain? If it is happening to them, will anyone be sympathetic? Helen, one of our students, recalls her first week in a major corporation:

> We were in this boardroom, three male managers and me. One pointed to the large table in the middle of the room, and said to me: 'Go on, lie out on that. We'll all have a go then.' I felt dizzy, sick and horrified. I wanted to run out, but I held on. They thought it was a great **joke**.

Joanne, another student, describes the constant sexual taunts, disguised as humour, from male managers in the oil company in which she worked. It went on so long that she eventually summoned up the courage to turn on the men responsible. They immediately chided her for her 'over-reaction'. She ended up feeling embarrassed and humiliated.

With Helen and Joanne we enter the realm of the sexual politics of organizations (see Chapter 13, 'Sex'). In many companies codes of sexual conduct and 'acceptable' sexual attitudes are dominantly male, and male dominated. This can be powerfully oppressive, leaving women vulnerable and unsupported. The male-centred ideology can also contribute to a devaluation of the worth of women when it comes to decisions on selection and promotion. The 'gender logic' of the organization, like the commercial logic, is influenced by the values of the dominant coalition of people who hold the power.

Other social and interpersonal matters are also affected in this manner – from AIDS, gays, blacks and the disabled, to policies on maternity leave, paternity leave, job sharing and crèches. The tension is between decisions which, at one level, may be regarded as about morally significant issues, but at another level as a matter of **conformity** to the values, or convenience, of the organization.

POWER, AND THE ORGANIZATIONAL IMPERATIVE

People will act with apparent moral integrity in one situation, but then with little moral concern elsewhere. The key to this paradox lies, as already hinted, in the power that different organizations (the 'church', the 'office', the 'business') can have over what we do. One social psychological experiment forcefully illustrates the point. Forty seminary students, who expressed particularly high standards of moral behaviour, were told to prepare a lecture on one of two topics – the parable of the Good Samaritan or job opportunities for graduates. Half the students in each group were told they had a very tight time schedule; the rest were told they had plenty of time. Then, sneakily, the experimenters made it impossible for the students not to pass an obviously 'distressed man' on their way to the lecture room. Only 16 stopped to help him, most of them being from the group that thought they had plenty of time to get to the lecture. Those who were going to do a Good Samaritan lecture were just as likely to walk past the man as those who were not.

So here we have morally aware people acting in a way quite contrary to their expressed values – in order 'to get the job done'. An even more alarming, and famous, experiment, was conducted by social psychologist Stanley Milgram in the 1960s (Milgram, 1974). Forty males, of various ages, volunteered for paid participation in an experiment on 'the effects of punishment on learning'. They were instructed to administer electric shocks to a 'learner' who was strapped to a chair in an adjoining room. Each time the learner gave a wrong answer, or no answer, the shock had to be increased. The volunteers operated their own control switch which was marked from 'slight shock' through to 'danger: severe shock', ending with an ominous 'XXX' marking. As the shocks increased the volunteers would hear cries from the learner, and pounding on the adjoining wall. Any hesitation to go on was met with a cool instruction from the experimenter to the effect that they had to continue in order to complete the experiment. Milgram found all the volunteers were prepared to administer 300 volts to the learners, and 26 of them went to the end of the shock series, despite the fact that the learner had gone silent by then. The experiment (itself criticized as morally dubious) was rigged so that the learner would deliberately give wrong answers and feign distress. There were no actual electric shocks.

There are two important messages that we can take from these studies. Firstly, that we may firmly *espouse* a moral stance to help, or not to injure others, but organizational life is a severe testing ground where the best of us can fail to support our belief with moral *action*. Secondly, obedience to commands from a superior is a strong force in our society, even if it means we will hurt another human being.

CHEATING – INSTITUTIONALIZED 'IMMORALITY'

The revelation of massive fraud and criminality in some very large organizations leaves most people with a mixed response. On the one hand there is the sense of moral indignation that such empires can cheat and exploit in the way that they have done. On the other hand there is the growing expectation that all businesses have their seamy side and some are simply more seamy, and more hypocritical, than others.

It is likely that few organizations operate without some form of hidden economy: individual profits made from **fiddling** – bending the rules, pilfering, short-changing or overcharging. Our moral appraisal of fiddling depends on where we stand. If we do the fiddling ourselves we can view it as a 'fair perk', or a 'necessary action'. If we are the victims of fiddling we become morally indignant. Also *who* we fiddle from comes into the moral equation. We might regard the wealthy, and well insured, superstore as fair game for a little pilfering. The same action towards the small corner shop could inflict unacceptable injury on its owners.

Fiddling has a long history. There are records of theft from ancient Egyptian storehouses which reveal a remarkably similar pattern to today's thefts (Mars, 1982). An insider supplied grain and fabrics from the storehouse to an outside ship's captain (the 'fence') who in turn bribed the temple scribes to alter the stock records so no one would notice the shortfall. Fiddling can take various forms – from organized theft to unauthorized phone calls, and 'borrowed' pens, paper and computer disks. The persistence of fiddling suggests it is intrinsic to the social organization of work, acting as a necessary adjunct to other financial and psychological rewards. Fiddling offers some people the opportunity to rectify, or compensate for, felt injustices in their working arrangements. It can offer an escape from stifling **bureaucracy** and arbitrary **control**. For a minority, fiddling can make the difference between a job they can financially survive on, and one they cannot. Such was the rationale presented for fiddling time sheets in a building-repairs organization where one of us once worked:

> Every Friday we had to fill in our time sheets for work done that week. Bert, the tradesman I worked with, called them 'fiddle sheets'. It was soon apparent why. At the bottom of the sheet was a space for hours' overtime worked. Every week Bert put in 15 hours, and told me to do the same. The first time this happened I was astonished. We hadn't worked 15 hours overtime; in fact we hadn't worked any overtime. We hadn't even worked our required 42 hours! Bert reassured

me: 'Listen. You do exactly what I do. Our pay is lousy and this bumps it up a
bit, helps us get by. As you work with me we both put down the same hours,
OK? It will be all right'. And it was all right. The foreman received our time
sheets and immediately signed them – without a blink. It soon became apparent that he was in the same game. I felt really torn to start with, as it was so
plainly dishonest. Soon, though, I saw their point. Their take-home pay was
amongst the lowest in the country.

Here we see a guilty conscience transformed with a rationalization
of the sort: 'Well, it's fair to lie in these particular circumstances.'
Usually, fiddles have a complex set of internal rules and checks –
small fiddlers do not automatically turn into big ones; lone fiddlers
do not necessarily progress to gang fiddlers. How much is taken,
and by whom, is usually fairly well worked out within the group.
For example, restaurant workers on the fiddle will work out a hierarchy of reward – the food, alcohol and other products – which
each person can take. There are shop assistants in clothing stores
who have bought similar clothing, on discount outside the shop, to
re-sell it – just one or two items a month – at a personal profit in the
shop. Fiddling is taken for granted in some big corporations by
fiddlers and fiddled alike. It is built into the overall running costs,
and is tacitly accepted as part of the informal organization of work.
Often preventive policing simply gives rise to more cunning fiddling, and the costs of heavy surveillance may soon outweigh the
company's losses.

BLOWING THE WHISTLE

There are, as we have shown, social processes within organizations
which create their own particular brands of morality. They permit,
and often encourage, conduct which is self-serving; conduct dislo-
cated from the values the organization might publicly profess, and
from the principles by which, privately, organizational members
try to live. Sometimes, the uneasy balance between these different
forces is dramatically upset: someone blows the whistle. The whistle blower may reside within the corporate ranks, or be an outsider.
Either way, the motive is the same: a deep disquiet about something that is going on in the organization that they regard as very
wrong. So wrong that they are prepared to take on the organization
in order to ensure that the 'malpractice' is brought to public attention, and prevented from recurring. Typically, whistle blowers will
act from an overriding sense of moral conscience, whatever the
personal consequences. Because the personal risks are high, there

are not many whistle blowers. The Mafia is an example, albeit extreme, of an organization which has a distinctive way of dealing with members who blow the whistle on them.

Some external whistle blowers have strengthened and protected themselves by becoming organized as pressure groups. They act as watchdogs, sniffing out dubious or immoral organizational practice. In the 1960s Ralph Nader started a consumer watch after he publicly exposed the American Ford Motor Company which was, it seemed, deliberately continuing production of a car they knew was liable to explode on impact. His style of work is reflected in some of the activities of consumer associations across the world. Certain whistle blowers focus on particular areas, such as Friends of the Earth and Greenpeace, who make it their business to expose companies whose actions are harming the natural environment.

The status of whistle blowers in broader society is usually high. Some are elevated to the level of hero or heroine, depending on the cause they espouse and the risks they take. Not surprisingly, they are seen rather differently by the enterprises they attack. If they are employees they can be branded as traitors, disloyal. Complaints based on moral grounds are often met by a wall of organizational defensiveness. The organization is keen to demonstrate its moral integrity.

Big pressure groups, such as trade unions and consumer organizations, may be a reasonable match for large corporations in the slog which usually follows whistle blowing. On their own, though, individual employees are far more vulnerable. Their intimate knowledge of the organization and its secrets poses an enormous threat to those who have profited from irregular practices, negligence or law breaking. Whistle blowers are to be feared, and some corporations will go to extraordinary lengths to disable them. Robert Jackall (1988), an American anthropologist, tells the tale of a major food-processing company, which amply illustrates the point. We paraphrase:

> Brady, a conscientious financial officer (trained as a chartered accountant) noticed that a peer of his in marketing had overshot his budget, and had faked $75,000 of invoices to cover the discrepancy. He submitted a report on the matter to the CEO, but was dismayed to find the report blocked before it got to him. Brady was asked, several times, to drop the matter.
>
> Gradually, he was frozen out of key decisions and his authority cut back. Nevertheless, he stumbled across further, even larger, financial irregularities – the manipulation of pension funds which guaranteed large personal bonuses for top managers. Brady was deeply troubled and, for want of some access to

the CEO, informed a friend in the company who had the CEO's ear. The information reached the CEO, without Brady's name being mentioned. Immediately following a meeting between the CEO and his top aides, Brady's friend was fired and escorted from the building by armed guards.

Brady then realized that the CEO was part of the conspiracy, and took the matter to the corporation's chief lawyer – who 'did not want to touch it with a barge pole'. Brady was advised by a senior manager to accept it as 'part of the game in business today'. He could not. He was summarily fired and was ejected from the company building by a security guard.

This story poignantly characterizes the way an organization can evolve a 'working' morality to suit parts of itself. Using power and fear, certain members can twist the professional conventions of business to serve their positions and greed. As fear and secrecy take hold, moral concerns give way to the pragmatics of 'keeping your nose clean', 'doing what you are told', and 'obeying orders'. As one manager in Jackall's study pithily asserts:

> What is right in the corporation is not what is right in a man's home or in his church. What is right in the corporation is what the guy above wants from you. That's what morality is in the corporation. (Jackall, 1988: 105–11)

It would be wrong to conclude that organizations inevitably sap the moral energy of those who work in them. However, what we do need to appreciate is that in organizations as varied as food-processing, churches, steel manufacturing and schools, the most moral of human beings can gradually find themselves doing things that they never would have imagined they could – or should.

- Caring, upright, moral citizens can change dramatically when they arrive at work, breaking their personal moral codes.
- People's personal morality can be subverted by strong organizational norms.
- Organizations can invent their own brand of morality which may be in conflict with more conventional moral behaviour.
- Self-interest, drive for profit and fear can induce individuals and corporations to harm others and the environment.
- Organizational humour can disguise acts such as harassment and abuse.
- Cheating, to some degree, is a part of most enterprises; it can be organizationally helpful as well as destructive.
- Whistle blowers act as the organization's conscience – and are often treated roughly for doing so.

THESAURUS ENTRIES

bureaucracy	institution
conflict	jokes
conformity	motivation
control	norm
culture	politics
decision making	power
discourse	rationalization
ethics	rhetoric
fiddling	role
games	sexual harassment
group	values

READING ON

The issues of business morality and the moral responsibility of business have emerged as important areas in organizational studies in recent years. The view that it is not the responsibility of business to provide a moral example (Friedman, 1970) or that managers are essentially technocrats with no moral awareness (MacIntyre, 1981) has receded in favour of approaches which view organizations as arenas of moral behaviour, sometimes flawed, sometimes tacit, but always vital. Moral behaviour in organizations often does not follow from grand moral principles of right and wrong – these tend to be redefined according to pragmatic demands for survival, finding a suitable person to blame or avoiding conflict and embarrassment. Jackall (1988) has elaborated the concept of 'moral rules in use' to describe how organizational norms subvert moral behaviour, a perspective related to Argyris and Schön's (1974) contention that 'theories in use' rather than people's declared 'theories in action' determine actual behaviour. Fineman (1996b) has further developed this thesis in terms of 'enacted moralities' to show how managers take actions which end up damaging the natural environment. Cannon (1994) offers a readable and wide-ranging discussion of the social and ethical responsibilities of business organizations.

6

Greening

There is, it seems, much for us to worry about. The last decades of the twentieth century have brought with them a bleak picture of the environmental costs of industrialization. There are holes in the ozone layer, polluted rivers and seas, air in cities that is difficult to breathe, loss of unique wildlife habitats, rain forest depletion on a massive scale, waste mountains. In return we, especially in Western nations, have a myriad of consumer goods and machines: computers, cars, aircraft; heating and cooling systems; plastics, chemicals and synthetic building materials. These represent comforts and choices that a generation or two ago would have seemed unattainable, and are ones to which industrially emerging nations aspire.

But with our craving to produce and consume (see Chapter 18), are we eroding the very basis of what sustains us as a planet? Like the *Titanic*, are we steaming blindly to our destruction on an unalterable course? Or is this all undue scaremongering, another one of history's many doom-laden, end-of-the-world prophecies that fails to come true? Somewhere in this, industrial organizations need to respond – because much of the blame, rightly or wrongly, is placed at their doorstep. It is they, goes the argument, who produce the goods and services and persuade us, through their advertising and marketing, to buy. It is they who look for quick, competitive returns as they serve themselves and their shareholders, often ignoring environmental concerns. And it is they who are very pleased to sell what they have to offer, but are often uninterested in the environmental after-effects – such as the pollution caused by the product, or its disposal.

What, then, is it like for organizations that go green or stay grey? What does greening of industry, making it less environmentally damaging, teach us about organizing and organizations – their politics, ethics and dilemmas?

WHAT ENVIRONMENTAL DAMAGE?

Many of us have been brought up to have faith in science. So when 'hard' science says that something is hazardous, polluting, toxic or destructive, that is the time to take immediate action. Furthermore, much damage we cannot see, so we have to trust science to define its existence. But it does not take the student of the environment long to discover that the scientific community is often divided over what is happening and how dangerous it is. Is the ozone hole a 'hole' and how much does it repair itself? How much global warming is due to industrial activity and what will happen if the icecaps melt and the seas rise? Will they rise – and by how much? Losing various species of flora and fauna has been intrinsic to our planet's evolution, so why should we worry about current changes? What are the risks? Biologists will argue with other environmental scientists as well as with each other, and from time to time a consensus may emerge – only to be challenged by another set of experts at a later date. We end up confused about what to believe. Sometimes it is a crisis that defines what is important – such as an explosion at a nuclear plant, a chemical fire, a massive oil spill at sea or an uncontrollable forest fire. The environmental damage is clear, palpable. The public outcry (orchestrated by the media) is then such that industry and governments have to listen and act – at least for a time.

Opinion surveys continue to record our concern about environmental pollution, especially air quality. But in Western societies few of us are prepared to significantly modify our lifestyles, or the use of the machines and products that make those lifestyles what they are. Environmental degradation is, in sociological terms, *contested terrain*. Scientific authority is challenged as various different interests – industry, green activists, governments, consumers – make their case and shape perceptions of what is or is not an 'environmental problem'. For example, it may well be in its commercial interests for a chemical company to interpret the statistics on the damage or toxicity of their new fertilizer as 'not significant' while, for Friends of the Earth, just the opposite is the case. They have different partialities, or **perceptual** sets. This is not to suggest that certain forms of environmental damage are not universally judged as appalling. The long legacy-effects of radioactive fallout from the ill-fated Chernobyl power station in the Ukraine in 1986 is a case in point. Its damage to the environment and to the health and welfare of local communities – both contemporaries of the disaster and the subsequent generation – is undisputed. Radiation-related ill-ness remains an awesome problem. Yet the remaining reactors of this dangerous power station are still in operation because the Ukrainian government has no alternative sources of power for the region.

Given the political nature of claims and responses to industrial environmental damage, another principle has been suggested – the *precautionary principle*. This 'better safe than sorry' notion means that absolute proof is unnecessary. We should err on the side of cau-tion, limiting those industrial processes that we think might cause serious ecological damage – even though we are not sure how much. The precautionary principle encourages changes, especially technological ones, along the whole spectrum of the design, manu-facture and disposal of industrial goods and services. While it does not eliminate squabbles between experts, it reflects a broader, pro-environment, form of thinking. It moves away from crisis manage-ment and who is right or wrong in environmental debates and attempts to infuse green thinking into all our industrial processes – from 'cradle to grave'.

THE ETHICAL 'SPIN'

Rather than viewing environmental protection as a scientific or technical problem, it can be seen in ethical terms. The natural envi-ronment is so precious to us all, something upon which we all depend, that it is morally wrong to damage it knowingly. We should care for the environment – for what it is, not just for what we can extract from it. This applies as much to the small company that dumps its waste in a nearby stream to avoid the costs of safe disposal, as to the transnational mining corporation that transfers its damaging mining work to a country where 'people don't ask too many questions'.

In the previous chapter we discussed how ethics in organizations can end up morally empty, devoid of conscience. Does this apply to recent trends in environmental protection? At first glance it appears not. In the 1990s, especially, many of our major inter-national corporations – oil, chemical, automotive, mining, power generation – have appeared to take the green message very seri-ously. Various **stakeholders**, groups who have a special interest or stake in the corporation's performance, helped pushed them in that direction – citizens' groups, Greenpeace, Friends of the Earth, stockholders, the media. As a consequence, their mission statements have been reassuring. For example:

> Protecting the earth and its natural resources is indeed one of the most critical issues facing mankind. As a concerned corporate citizen and a manufacturer of automotive products that have environmental impacts, we are supportive of initiatives that have a positive effect on the environment.

Or,

> Environmental protection is a primary management responsibility as well as the responsibility of every employee here. Our concern for the environment extends beyond the fence lines of our chemical producing facilities and into the communities in which we live and work.

These statements suggest a green organizational **culture** where the environment is part of all key organizational **decisions** – because this has become proper and ethical. Such companies will usually conduct environmental audits of their activities – production, waste, energy, recycling, land use – and sometimes extend this to their suppliers. Some will set up a department with special responsibility for environmental management while their Chief Executive publicly proclaims his or her commitment to the green cause. They may also put in place environmental management systems that can qualify for national or international accreditation.

Such moves offer a decidedly brighter picture of industry than that associated with belching smokestacks, arid landscapes and greedy entrepreneurs. But is this the 'fix'? Self-proclaimed ethical corporations have still been responsible for leakages of nuclear waste, oil pollution, chemical explosions and deforestation. It is notoriously difficult to find out what a company has actually done or failed to do – except when things go dramatically wrong. Some companies do offer accounts of environmental accidents and improvements, in their annual reports, but these are usually somewhat sanitized: independently audited environmental reporting is not yet a legal requirement in industry.

NEGOTIATING THE ENVIRONMENT

Imagine a smart, panelled boardroom. You are inside the headquarters of the truck division of a worldwide automotive corporation which boasts of its advanced environmental policy. Around the large table sit seven senior managers with different functions and an external environmental consultant. The meeting is chaired by the manager from Corporate Environmental Affairs:

> The mood of the meeting is cool; little sense of urgency. The agenda is a long one. The first item is about entering a national environmental award competition. The Chairman says, 'We have no choice but to enter this one.' The meeting struggles for some 30 minutes. What could they offer? The new tyres? The energy-saving in the plant? Nothing feels right, or is sufficiently outstanding to boast about. The item fizzles out.
>
> A new agenda item: the consultant delivers his specially commissioned environmental audit to the group. Everyone is now faced with what to do with the long, neat list of 'actions required'. People look glum. There is a fair amount of ducking and weaving around the table before the Chairman begins mechanically to tick off the jobs and allocate them to each manager around the table. The Production Manager suddenly springs to life, slightly panicky. He rummages in his briefcase and produces various environmental action forms and other bits of paper. He had been busy, he said. We should appreciate that.
>
> Another agenda item: plastic cups. The meeting gets excited and it turns out to be the emotional high spot of the morning. How can they prevent people taking two plastic cups from the drinks machine to stop burning their hands? There are re-usable cup-holders provided, but people keep throwing them away. And how about recycling the cups? People clearly enjoy this item and the debate is prolonged, animated, and sometimes humorous. No solution is found.
>
> Final item: beautifying the work's grounds and physical environment. The Chairman waves a brochure from the Groundwork Action Trust, a charitable organization devoted to working with industry to improve their sites. 'They have approached us before,' says the Chairman. 'Maybe the time's right to do something...'. The room is silent. After a while the Chairman fills the uncomfortable vacuum. 'Mm...planting trees and all that; not sure we're equipped to get involved with that sort of rubbish.' The item is dropped and the meeting closed.

This is a real account from our own research. Here the environment is condensed into 'items' to deal with in a **bureaucratic** fashion. Other than with the plastic cups, there is little passion or enthusiasm to the meeting. The trucks themselves hardly get a mention and protecting the planet is, seemingly, many miles from people's thinking. This is a kind of 'greenwashing', looking green on the outside but being rather greyer on the inside. Why? Do the managers simply not care? Maybe not. Can they not try a bit harder? Perhaps. But the most likely explanation lies in the way that technical responsibilities in organizations tend to displace wider moral concerns. For the corporate actor, the natural environment is both everywhere and nowhere. In a busy, stressful work life, the meaning of ozone holes or even traffic pollution seems pretty remote. The environmental damage caused by the company's overseas operations is out of sight and mostly out of mind. It is sometimes hard for a manager, or other worker, to connect his or her relatively self-contained position inside the organization with wider moral responsibilities to the environment 'outside'. The job of meeting production deadlines, sorting out sales targets and, ultimately, making profits, is all, and it is in these areas that the employee is individually judged. So environmental demands are seen, at best, as a nuisance; at worst, as a threat. The organization is something of a psychic prison, entrapping its members in a particular way of thinking and feeling. The Environmental Director of another automotive manufacturer summed it up as follows:

> It's all about 'can we afford it?' What will it give us in return? How long will we have to wait? Any competitive advantage? No fine moral sentiments in this.

The ethics of business, in this view, is primarily to compete and to make profits, and the natural environment has to take its place accordingly. Pro-environmental policies are OK as long as they deliver direct profit. Some companies are less hard nosed than this. They will run their business as 'green' enterprises and use this as a key advantage point in the market – to capture green consumers. Typically, such companies have strong environmental champions at the top of the organization, a feature of corporate environmental leaders such as the Body Shop, Ben and Jerry's and B&Q. These firms claim to make a positive environmental policy pay by carefully minimizing the environmental impact of all their operations: from ensuring the recyclability of their containers to the welfare of flora, fauna and communities that supply their raw materials. Greening is regarded as a sound business opportunity as well as a matter of ethical commitment.

SHALLOW GREEN, DEEP GREEN

Organizations such as the Body Shop are committed to economic growth on a national and international scale. They are often lauded as the acceptable, green face of capitalism, where environmental care, consumerism and profits can comfortably coexist. And this is exactly where the problem lies, according to deep-green critics of industry. It is false, they argue, to believe that making products and services greener solves our environmental problems. At best it slows down the *Titanic* rather than changing its course. The crucial challenge is to the belief that progress is an ever-increasing gross national product, and that happiness is the accumulation of ever more material goods. Eco-feminists have a distinctive view here, speaking from a less controlling, more nurturing, perspective on organizing. They stress that preserving nature is more than reducing industrial pollution. All natural entities deserve to be valued in their own right, not just in terms of what they deliver to us. This means respecting all associations with the environment; nature and humans are one, in a holistic relationship.

The alternatives proposed by critics of our current economic system vary from a radical reappraisal and transformation of our **values** and lifestyles, to a reform of the instruments by which we judge economic success. The latter approach takes issue with the economic indices such as gross national product (GNP). GNP is taken as a mark of a nation's prosperity; it is the sum of the values of all the produced goods, services and labour of a nation's economic activities, *regardless of their particular purpose or ends*. So into the GNP calculation goes the money value of the labour and materials involved in checking or repairing the effects of pollution and environmental damage (e.g. rescue services, firefighting, hospital treatment, rebuilding, policing, ecological care, pollution control). Also included is work involved in caring for those who suffer **stress** or **unemployment** in our industrial systems. But if, instead, all such activities were regarded as the costs of industrial growth, the down-side, then the curve of progress would look substantially less attractive.

Once, environmental concerns were expressed only by fringe members of society, 'awkward' critics of the establishment. Now such voices can be heard across the political and social class spectrum. In the USA, Canada and Europe there have been citizens' protests against industry and government in the creation of new roads, housing developments, nuclear power, dams, and the destruction of wildlife areas. Some of these protests have been remarkable in that they represent temporary **organizations** in their own right, of very different people, held together by a common cause – to prevent unwanted changes to the natural landscape. Their motives vary, though. Some are NIMBYs (Not In My Back Yard). They object to local environmental changes which adversely affect their own lives, but are less fussed when these happen elsewhere. Others are more deeply committed to preventing environmental despoliation (as they see it) anywhere. They might lash themselves to trees or burrow underground, confidently face TV cameras and give press interviews. **Leadership** is often *emergent*, sometimes *charismatic*, as certain people take control of events or tasks when it seems appropriate. To a casual observer such settings can appear disorganized, even chaotic, but the shared purpose and mutual enemy often create sufficient cohesion to mobilize people's efforts in a similar direction. Other protests rely on organizations that also have a very mixed membership, but have a much clearer, more formal, core structure to hold together members' shared concerns. Friends of the Earth and Greenpeace, for example, are now international organizations with paid officers, including experts in environmental matters and media relations. Also, like other large organizations, they have their splits and dissensions about who does what, and in particular the choice of target for the next campaign. These organizations are dependent on voluntary **labour** as well as donations, so their resources are always somewhat uncertain or precarious.

How have industrial organizations responded to these pressures?

KEEPING AWAY THE GREEN FOE

> Why on *earth* should we be driven by a particular group that shouts the loudest? [Thumps his desk.] Who do they think they are?! Well, they're not going to have my scalp. I'm certainly not going to make strong environmental claims for anything.

This is a corporate director of a major supermarket, and no friend of the green movement. He felt his autonomy and role profoundly compromised, and lashed out in anger. Essentially he was deaf to the green arguments and, as with other supermarket managers, liked even less the unorthodox ways they were expressed – such as 'throwing blood over frozen fish'. Another supermarket director makes a similar point:

> I'm sure the hundreds of letters I've had in here aren't written by our customers, but campaigners from these [green] organizations. If they were our customers I'd be *really* impressed. We can't be seen to buckle to that sort of pressure!

These defensive responses, if extreme, can be regarded as understandable in an industrial sector relatively new to public scrutiny and traditionally more concerned with what sells fast than with what ought to sell, by wider ethical criteria. They do, however, illuminate how the **emotionality** of responses can be extremely important in shaping organizational behaviour. Pressure from green activists has generally not been welcomed by industry, although some sectors (such as power generation and chemicals) are cautiously accepting of some of them, mainly because of the sector's high pollution profile and long experience with environmentalists. A site manager of a large chemical firm makes the point:

They've brought to us and to the public all the problems that are out there. There's no doubt that you can't just go on digging holes in the ground and throwing stuff in it and pretending it doesn't exist. From that point of view they've done a good job.

As the various green organizations – from 'eco-warriors' and local citizens' groups to national and international organizations (such as English Nature and the World Wide Fund for Nature) – have mustered their influence, they can, and do, embarrass organizations. For this reason alone they cannot be entirely ignored by industry. They are able publicly to expose environmental performance or transgressions that some organizations would prefer to hide. Bad public relations are bad for business even if, as the target industry or organization often claims, the accusations are exaggerated or simply wrong. Some companies have tried to head off the attention of green pressure groups by launching their own green publicity in advance. Others have attempted to discredit their efforts by demonstrating the inaccuracy of their accusations. Still others have managed to gain green kudos by bringing the enemy on board – recruiting high-profile environmentalists on to their own environmental campaigns.

Recently, however, there has been evidence of a systematic and concerted backlash by powerful industrial groups aiming to undermine the environmental movement. One approach to this has been to hire global public relations firms to promote anti-environmentalist images – such as environmentalists as 'religious fanatics', 'communists', 'Nazis', 'anti-American', 'destroyers of civilization'. One US PR company, John Davies Communications, has been described as follows:

John Davies helps neutralise [green protesters] on behalf of corporate clients including Mobil Oil, Hyatt Hotels, Exxon, American Express and Pacific Gas and Electric. He describes himself as 'one of America's premier grassroots consultants', and runs a full color advertisement designed to strike terror into the heart of the bravest CEO. It's a photo of the enemy – literally a 'little white-haired old lady', holding a hand-lettered sign that reads, 'Not In My Backyard!' A caption imprinted over the photo says, 'Don't leave your future in her hands. Traditional lobbying is no longer enough.... To outnumber your opponents call Davies Communications.' (Stauber and Rampton, 1995: 89)

Efforts such as these underline some of the divisions and conflicts that arise as industry faces pressures to be greener. What is construed by environmental groups as obvious good sense is seen by some industries as a threat to their business, their freedom and their independence. When the battle lines are drawn the rules of the game may not always be fair and clean.

LEGISLATING GREEN CHANGE

There are other pro-environmental forces acting on industry, in addition to green pressure groups. When industry fails to protect the environment the law can step in. Environmental protection is now a feature of national and international legislation. This obliges industry to take certain measures to ensure its processes do not pollute the atmosphere, land or water – a formal application of the precautionary principle mentioned earlier. There are directives on the storage and disposal of waste, on recycling and on packaging, as well as special provisions for very toxic chemicals and nuclear waste. Environmental law is interpreted and administered by special regulators, such as the Environment Agency in the UK and the Environmental Protection Agency in the US. These are substantial organizations themselves. For example, the UK Environment Agency employs over 9,500 environmental specialists and managers deployed in offices throughout England and Wales. Agency inspectors visit industry and grant permits to operate processes – if the company meets the required environmental standards. If they do not, the inspector has the **power** to prosecute the company.

Typically, most companies take the regulator very seriously. If environmental groups can embarrass a company, so can the regulator. But regulators also have the power to inflict financial and reputational damage; consequently most 'environmental' boardroom time will be devoted to handling regulation and its demands. This turns out to be less straightforward than it might appear. As in their dealings with other officials (e.g. tax, employment, monopolies), managers treat environmental regulation as a *negotiated* and **political** process where the regulator presses for more changes while the regulated try to avoid the costs of going beyond basic compliance. A production manager in car manufacturing describes his side of events:

> The inspector from the Agency comes in. It's obvious where she stands. She takes the view that big, multinational corporations like us have the money and she'll insist that we spend it on controlling pollution emissions from our chimneys. I say that we're probably the highest ratepayers in the County and we employ 1,000 people and they need to realize what they're playing with. It might well be that this company decides it's not worth the gamble. She doesn't believe that, but I do.

From the inspector's point of view it's a balancing act, as one explained:

> It's how can I push him to do as much as possible? You can turn the regulatory screw and make life hell for them, but that's rarely necessary. It requires sitting down and talking; chats over lunch.

Large firms, especially, employ their own experts to try and outgun the regulator. In the UK, in particular, environmental standards are contested and greatly reshaped through informal discussions, behind closed doors (the US approach is more open and litigious). On the whole, regulation increases pollution control, which some will see as good news for the environment. But the danger is that regulator and regulated get too close to one another, mutually 'captured', so diluting the regulator's power. However, regulation does little to ease the anxieties of deep-green critics of industry. If anything, it buttresses the values of the market economy; it is not designed to overthrow them.

ECO-CENTRED OR EGO-CENTRED?

The sober reality of the present state of greening is that while we, as citizens, may express our concern about environmental degradation – ours and others' – few of us are prepared to forgo the many apparent benefits of industrialized society, or contemplate alternatives. These might include leaving our cars at home; cycling more; buying less; owning less; being less slaves to fashion; using local produce; conserving energy; using aircraft less; working more from home. For many of us, though, some of these are tough, if not impossible, choices because of the way society and employment are structured and, more simply, because of what we take for granted. We, ourselves, are the products of societies where self-interest and materialism dominate as *positive* values in national and international relations. In this way we are imprisoned by what we have all helped to create. The influential economist, Milton Friedman, has stated that it is not for businesses to take on any responsibilities *other* than looking after themselves by making money and accumulating wealth, a creed that has been especially influential in the USA and Britain. In other words, making a profit *is* being socially responsible and that is all a company has to consider in order to discharge its civic duty. Supporters of this view note, paradoxically, that such greed can end up as good for the environment because it produces the wealth to fund environmental clean-ups.

There is some truth, as well as perversity, in this perspective. Technological know-how in pollution abatement, and investment in special equipment, are costly and affordable only by rich countries or industries. On the other hand, many ecologists and other experts will argue that industrialization has caused, and continues to cause, irreversible damage and losses, sometimes far away from the original point of pollution and distant from corporate headquarters. Indeed, many countries have serviced foreign powers or industries, helping them get rich while shouldering the bulk of the environmental costs. Such was the accusation made against Shell in the 1990s: that it had despoiled land in Nigeria during its oil operations there. The local communities protested loudly as Shell, in the West, made much of its green environmental image.

When the green agenda and business agenda coincide, it is money and profit that links them – not altruism. If greening pays, or can be made to pay, then it fits well with the dominant logic of business. If it provides **competitive** advantage, then that is even better for some business. Environmentalism becomes a tool to displace a competitor and to gain more power and control. For this reason some firms have welcomed regulation because they have the resources to comply, or to go beyond compliance, whilst their competitors cannot do so. It is not a scenario that comforts the deep greens; it is 'more of the same', a reinforcement of the structures of power that caused the problem in the first place. A dilemma for some environmentalists is whether to work with industry or against it. To work with industry ends up with light greening, and industry calling much of the tune. To work against industry invites a harsh backlash. Environmentalists have yet to discover how to transform us from our glimmer of ecological awareness into a society of green idealists, although they have edged some countries more than others in this direction. If industry is part of the problem, and cannot really contribute to the solution, how do we move forward? If social revolution is the only route to the necessary value change, how will this be achieved?

BUSINESS – AS USUAL?

Meanwhile, back in the boardrooms and side offices of industry, the environment is treated with more or less seriousness according to its perceived business benefit. Perhaps unsurprisingly, we find very small, cash-starved, enterprises claiming to have problems enough without worrying about the environment. For some of them, avoiding the costs of environmental protection makes a lot of business sense. There is a twilight zone where, for example, the illegal disposal of waste flourishes – truckloads of garbage and industrial residue tipped into remote country lanes, ponds, canals and rivers. Indeed, as the regulation of waste disposal has become tighter and more expensive for industry – in order to encourage recycling and waste minimization – the extent of illegal dumping has increased.

Greening has also spawned its own industry of officials and services. Apart from regulatory agents, we have many environmental consultants content to ride the 'green boom', offering services ranging from environmental audits to specialist technical advice on pollution control. As the legal penalties for environmental damage have increased, some industries have taken greening predominantly to be a legal challenge to be fought in the courts. This has created a new breed of lawyers, experts in environmental law, able to defend (or prosecute) industry. The company lawyer has now become a prominent person in shaping an organization's environmental strategy.

We are still a long way from radical moves towards greening, and many organizations are still very reluctant to take environmental damage seriously. In this category we have the type of company where yesterday's health and safety manager becomes today's environmental manager – but with poor top-level support and an insufficient budget to discharge his or her new responsibilities. Some will create elaborate green defences to shield the company – for as long as they can afford to. One supermarket manager we interviewed illustrates this response. The interviewer complimented the manager on the literature he had sent in advance: a substantial folder, printed on recycled paper, containing details of the many environmental initiatives in the company. It included descriptions of outreach activities with schools and local community groups, lectures from high-profile environmentalists, and statements on the company's 'commitment', and its 'passionate belief' in making its business environmentally friendly. The manager looked a little startled at being praised:

> Oh, …when did I send you that? Well, have you seen our trading figures for the last quarter? They're awful. All that green stuff has been stopped now.

Such responses seem cynical, but they are mostly hard-headed reactions to what many managers regard as the hard-headed realities of business. Rarely will such managers as individuals simply not care about what happens to the environment, but characteristically they feel impelled, first and foremost, by business imperatives. The economic demands of capitalism can easily ride roughshod over environmental concerns. The more optimistic news, environmentally speaking, is that much can be achieved within the current system. It might fall short of deep-green ideals, but it can make a considerable improvement to the quality of air, land and water. The recipe for success, organizationally, seems to be a combination of firm external regulation; a sincere green champion at the top of the organization; green structures and training throughout the organization; green considerations in all major functional policies; and regular auditing of progress.

As citizens and consumers, is there anything we can do? The fact that industry's values and actions are shaped, to a degree, by its stakeholders is an important social truth. So what we buy (or do not buy), what we preserve, how we travel, where we invest our money, the environmental groups we join and what we protest about, can make a difference. Living our lives according to the precautionary principle, and perhaps more holistically, makes sound environmental sense, given the uncertainties of prediction about environmental damage. Together with regulatory and economic incentives that push industry down an environmental path, it is perhaps the best chance we have currently of leaving our planet in reasonable shape for our children and our children's children.

- What constitutes environmental damage is not straightforward; it is contested terrain.
- There are different stakeholders who have an interest in, or claim on, industry's environmental performance.
- Environmental protection can be viewed as a technical or an ethical issue; more often it is the latter.
- Often corporate environmentalism amounts to relatively minor shifts in work practices rather than major green cultural transformations.
- Legislation, forcing green organizational **change**, is often the most potent force.
- Those industries most threatened by green pressures have tried to undermine the efforts of environmental groups.
- Creating a green organizational culture requires commitment from the top of the organization as well as structures at all levels to promote green beliefs and practices.

THESAURUS ENTRIES

bureaucracy	organization
change	perception
competitiveness	politics
culture	power
decision making	stakeholder
emotion	stress
labour	unemployment
leadership	values

READING ON

The complexity of appraising environmental damage is discussed by Hannigan (1995). He draws attention to *who* makes environmental claims, how they are popularized and what authority is attributed to them, particularly claims by scientists, politicians and environmental groups. Green issues have implications for all functions of business – from production to marketing. A useful set of readings on this is McDonagh and Prothero's (1997) collection. For more critical accounts refer to Eden (1996), Bansal and Howard (1997) and Smith (1993).

Studies of the multi-stakeholder perspective on organizational greening (e.g. Fineman and Clarke, 1996) reveal how important it is to take account of managerial perceptions of stakeholders in understanding what action firms will and will not take to protect the environment. This is taken to a deeper level by Fineman (1996b, 1997) who looks at the prejudices and fears of managers as they decided whether or not to become greener. The significant role of regulation in some of these is described by Smith (1997).

More general discussions on the ethical influence of green stakeholders on business can be found in Sorrell and Hendry (1994). Richard Welford, a significant writer on the mechanics of greening business strategy and culture, is also a strong critic of business conservatism. He argues strongly for a radical appraisal of our lifestyle and business values: see Welford (1995, 1997).

7

It's not my problem

One of my problems, Helen, is that whenever I have a problem to face, I always have another problem concurrent with it, which seems to take precedence. So bear with me if I seem abstracted. I cannot give my full attention to anything, because too many things require my full attention. My life has chosen to arrange itself on ramshackle lines, like a badly wrapped parcel about to burst open; I can secure one corner of it only by disturbing the others, which then must be secured in turn. (Keith Waterhouse, *Billy Liar on the Moon*, 1975)

An important part of what people are employed to do in organizations is to 'solve **problems**'. But that phrase conceals much of what happens in the handling of problems. In this chapter, we are going to suggest that people may do other much more important things with problems than solve them. For example, they may create them, or craft them in the style that they most enjoy working with. People may like having problems, and may organize their lives so as to keep themselves supplied with problems; they may go out of their way to make sure that they always have enough problems. It can be important to know who 'owns' problems; and at any particular time, there are some problems which are the fashionable ones to be associated with. We shall also be recognizing that problems sit within an institutional framework, which influences the kind of problems we are likely to have. Finally, we shall look at the activities of those who help others with problems – such as consultants.

To save confusion, we need to make a clear distinction. We are going to say that someone may view a situation as a *problem* when something is not as they would like it to be, they feel unsure about what to do about it, and have some anxiety about whether they can do anything. We will distinguish this from a *difficulty*, where something is not as someone would like it to be but they feel reasonably confident that they will be able to deal with it. For example, if someone is lost in a strange town, that could be a difficulty. They will probably have confidence that they will eventually find their way. They have procedures that they can adopt (asking a policeman, buying a map, telephoning the person they are going to see) which mean that they are sure that they will get there. If, on the other hand, they are trying to persuade a department to accept a reorganization, they may view this as a problem; they want the department to accept it, but they may not be sure how to go about persuading them or whether they will be able to exercise such **leadership**.

THE REAL PROBLEM IS...

What do we mean when we say that the *real* problem is something rather than something else? Often in organizations, it means that we think our way of looking at the situation should prevail over other people's views. We describe our view as 'real' to imply that other views are not, and therefore that everyone should accept our view.

We know that different specialists have different **perceptions** of the same situation. If a person describes a situation which they see as a problem in the same way to a friend, to a counsellor, to a doctor, to a tutor or to a priest, each of those people may well hear different problems in what that person says. In the same way, in a company, if the same data are given to the Marketing Director, the Finance Director and the Production Director, they will probably see different problems in it. They have different backgrounds, training and responsibilities, different ways of **learning** and **knowing**, and they are looking for different things. Which of these people is seeing the *real* problem? In our view, the notion of a 'real' problem is misleading. Problems are neither real nor unreal; they are a way of describing one person's view of a situation, just as a landscape painting represents one person's interpretation of a landscape; they are a way of 'constructing' a situation. Complete **objectivity** is not available. This can be extremely frustrating; there is so much going on in an organization, so much confusing material, that we would like the reassurance of at least knowing what the 'real' problem is. The answer, of course, is elusive. There are different specialists responsible for – and paid for – seeing things differently. It may be frustrating, but it is also a crucial and inevitable part of organizing.

Not only do people see different problems in the same situation, but very often some people see a certain situation as a 'problem' while others do not. For example, some people seem to take the most horrendous series of personal tragedies calmly; they do not like them, but they do not construe them as problems. Others might like to be able to do that, but find it an unattainable ideal. There are people who, given a lunch menu, become bogged down in the **decision-making** problem which this offers them. Such people may seem very amusing except to their workmates, who cannot see why anyone should see so many problems that they cannot handle, and tend to find them very irritating.

There are those who seem to have a set of personal **constructs** that make some of their problems insoluble. Consider the problem for a middle-aged man who finds that his hair is steadily becoming thinner. Not everybody will recognize this as a problem. It is 'just one of those things' – all part of ageing, which in itself is outside anyone's control, and so does not need to be taken as a problem. Other people of the same age will not accept either hair loss or ageing as inevitable, but will instead take them as problems; they then begin to look for solutions in hair transplants, hair restoring creams and so on. Sometimes in companies a particular individual gets blamed for everything that goes wrong. This may happen to a powerful person who has now left the organization, or even to a student who has finished a placement. 'You know, it is amazing how many mistakes old so-and-so made.' It may not be a very realistic description of the cause of the problem, and it is not a very useful one in that it is too late to do anything about it, but it is very popular when people leave jobs. It provides a **scapegoat**, and it offers a way of understanding the situation without having to do anything about it. This can be attractive because the potential solutions are likely to be costly, and the people concerned may well prefer to turn their attention to something else.

CONSTRUCTING ALTERNATIVE PROBLEMS FROM SITUATIONS

Suppose you pass a car showroom and see a car that you want. You do not have enough money for it. You could construct the situation as follows: 'Successive governments have run the economy so badly that I do not get enough money to buy that car.' That could be a very convenient way of constructing the issue, because you know you cannot do anything about it. This means that it cannot produce the anxiety of not knowing whether you will be able to deal with it, and thus it is not a problem in the sense that we have defined the word at the beginning of the chapter. Alternatively, you could construct the issue that you spent too much on your holiday last year, and that is why you do not have enough money for the car. Once again it is too late to do anything about it, but this way of constructing a problem out of the situation does have some implications for action – for example, when considering how much to spend on your holiday next year. Or you could construct the problem that you are not deeply enough involved in your work, and that is why you are wasting time and energy looking at car showrooms, and daydreaming about the cars afterwards. This construction of a problem leaves you looking in a completely different direction for solutions, because it implies an area over which you have more control. Or consider a student whose grades are not as good as they would like. They can start to work longer hours, to look for an improvement in their study skills, they can complain about the quality of the marking, or the quality of the teaching, they can buy an extra textbook or befriend a student in the year above who can talk to them about the subject. Each of these strategies is a solution which implies a different way of constructing the situation as a problem. Alternatively, they can become happy with how things are, including those lower grades, and not construct a problem at all.

There is a general principle about problem construction here which is shown in Figure 7.1.

In this diagram, the nearer one is to the origin, 'me, this, now', the more chance there is that one can do something with the problem that one has constructed. Problems that are constructed in terms of *me, now* and *this* may be possible to work on, while

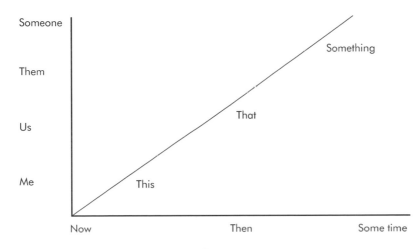

FIGURE 7.1 *Domains of Problem Definition*

problems that are constructed in terms of *them, some time* and *something* cannot. As we said above, we should not imagine that we want to construct all problems in such a way that we can do something about them. There might be other things that we would prefer to do with our resources, or we might prefer to do nothing. It is a favourite pastime in organizations to complain about company policy, but without any real intention of doing anything, and if anyone does start suggesting that something should be done, they are spoiling a popular leisure activity – 'having a good whinge'. The same is true for some conversations in pubs and cafés about governments or football managers: the problems constructed are not meant to be acted on. The conversation is being held for entertainment, and for the fun of talking about what fools the powerful people are. The fun is spoiled if you go away feeling you have to do something about it.

A PERSONAL EXAMPLE – A PROBLEM 'SOLVED'

The point is illustrated by a true story from one of the authors:

> When I was drafting this section of the book for the first time, the doorbell rang. As my wife was downstairs and I was upstairs I ignored it. A few minutes later the screen of my word processor went blank and the fan fell silent. The electrician had come to check the earthing of our mains, and he had done what electricians do – turned the power off. Several paragraphs of precious prose had been forever lost to humankind. So what was the problem? Here are some possible constructions of the situation which lead us to several different problems:
>
> 1   My wife should have remembered that I was upstairs working, and that a disruption of the power supply was likely to cause a disruption both to my work and to family life. She was 'the problem'.
> 2   I should have understood the 'autosave' facility in the software better, to ensure that not too much was lost if the power went off. My incompetence was 'the problem'.
> 3   I should have known what I was saying well enough to be able to say it all again without trouble. My memory was 'the problem'.
> 4   I should have a device for ensuring continuity of power supply to my PC. My reluctance to buy equipment was 'the problem'.
> 5   I should learn handwriting, rather than depending on fragile technology. My dependence on machines was 'the problem'.

The first of these constructions of the problem is of a common sort – blame another person. But, in terms of Figure 7.1, the 'she' and 'then' qualities of the definition show that it is likely to be frustrating. The second construction implies an equally unrealistic expectation, that a person can stop being lazy in learning software packages; of course everyone should know how the autosave works, but equally they should know that they cut corners to save time, and are likely to continue to do so. The third construction is another way of producing self-punishing but impossible solutions. The fourth is technically possible, but very expensive, and is rather like building a concrete wall behind the stable door through which the horse has just bolted. The fifth construction, to learn to write by hand, is sensible but too boring; what we find interesting or boring may be an important part of the problems that we are prepared to construct out of our situations.

The reader can see how the problem construction was eventually handled: the situation was turned into an example of how different problems can be constructed from the same circumstances. In this case, it did not have to be a problem at all.

BEYOND OUR CONTROL?

It may sound as if we are saying that all problem constructions are freely chosen, and each individual can be held responsible for the problems they experience. It is not as simple as that, and we could be at risk of blaming the victim if we say that it is up to you whether or not you choose to find a situation problematic. Consider the case of Joanna, who has just been passed over for a promotion at work in favour of John, whom she regards as less competent and less qualified than herself. Should she be framing her problem in terms of *me, now* and *this*, or should she be thinking of it as *them, then* and *that*, as in: 'The board have shown blatant sexism once again'?

This is a genuine dilemma for victims of **discrimination**. If they construct problems in terms of themselves, they will look for a construction about which they can actually do something, and they will put more stress on themselves. At the same time they are rejecting more comfortable and possibly more realistic alternatives, such as acknowledging that they have been treated very badly. In cases such as Joanna's, she can look for what she was failing to do to gain the promotion – and can almost certainly find answers to that question. Or she can say that she has hit the glass ceiling, in which case she may feel that there is nothing she can do, or she may complain within her organization about the discrimination she feels. One of the painful and damaging aspects of discrimination is that we can never know the 'truth' of these situations. Are we being badly treated or are we not as good as we thought we were?

All this is made even more difficult because of the **emotions** involved. Handling problems is not a cool, **cognitive** activity, but is immensely involving. In the grip of anger or anxiety, it may not be easy to see that one is making choices among alternative problem constructions. Choice-making is difficult once you have engaged with the problem. There are organizational pressures, discriminatory factors, and emotional commitments which considerably reduce the extent to which everybody has a free choice of problem construction. But there may well be premature closure on the construction of problems by which people in organizations allow their freedom to be restricted, or the effectiveness of their action to be curtailed, more than is necessary.

AS IF I DIDN'T HAVE ENOUGH PROBLEMS

Problems do not always get solved, nor do we always want them to be. There can be situations that are problematic according to the definition at the beginning of this chapter; the person with the problem is not sure what to do, and feels anxious as to whether they will be able to deal with the situation. But at the same time they may not really want to lose the problem. A problem can be a way of making **meaning** for ourselves in our situation.

For example, one of us had a boss whose holidays were a miracle of complexity. On the way to his holiday, he would swap cars with friends, often twice in different countries; he would pick up materials from several different suppliers on the way to the port, make sure that he had persuaded the shipping company to load a case of his favourite holiday wine for him to buy duty-free on the ferry, fix a range of meetings to tie in with parts of the holiday, and so on. Then one year everything was going wrong in his job. He was being threatened with losing most of his responsibility, and was working hard to save a department that he had built up. That year he and his family simply went on holiday. It seemed that, in contrast to his past way of life, where he knew what he was doing and how to control most situations to his advantage, he was now fully extended in handling all the problematic situations he could. When it came to the holiday he did not need any more problems, so he broke the habit of many years, and did not construct any more problems.

To say he did not 'need' any more problems is not meant ironically. We need problems. Some of us need more than others. But if we did not have problems, we would probably have to invent them. If we have no problems we can get bored, or feel that we are under-performing. And if we do not have any problems in one part of our life, we may look for some in another area of our life. So if your relationships outside work are nicely settled, you may find your-self stirring things up at work. We may seek adventure as a means of causing extra problems, whether at the career, holiday, hobby or personal relationship level. Problems provide challenge, goals, purpose and excitement for some people.

This sounds very neat. If that were the whole story, we could all be content generating just the number of problems that we need and can cope with, and then working on them. Most of us do not experience as high a degree of control over the supply of problems as this would imply, for two reasons.

Firstly, each person's world consists of more than just them-selves, and different people will have different problems that they like to deal with, and different sources of problems. At the time when someone is experiencing all the problems they need at work, their partner may be bored and needing a family problem to work on. That is when one gets the Billy Liar feeling, from the beginning of the chapter, of a badly wrapped parcel about to burst open.

Secondly, everybody has vulnerable points where they do not feel in control. The death of someone they love; being in a new and frightening organization; having a cold; feelings of despair and meaninglessness; all of these leave a person in a state where they may have no sense of control over their problem supply.

FASHIONABLE PROBLEMS

Problems can be an important part of how we see ourselves. One writer said that if you solve someone else's problem for them, that is robbery (Cook, 1982). They had something which they had taken some time making, and you go charging in and solve it for them. A participant on a course was talking about a problem he wanted to work on:

> *Participant*: The trouble is, I am not sure that I am any good at my job.
> *Tutor*: I see, the trouble is that you are not sure that you are any good at your job?
> *Participant*: No, you have not heard me right. The trouble is that I went straight into this job after university, and I think maybe I should have stayed on and done a master's degree first.

Tutor: I see, you think you should have stayed on and done a master's degree first?

Participant: No, that's not it. The thing is, really, that I got married last year, and in some ways it is very rewarding, but in other ways I find it restricts my freedom a lot.

Tutor: I see, your marriage restricts your freedom?*

Participant: Well no, it's not really that. It's more that I am not sure if I am any good at my job....

The conversation continued along these lines for an hour and a half. The two parties resumed discussion the following day, and concluded that in the middle of that circle of reasoning was a favourite problem, though they were not sure at that stage which of the different problem constructions was the favourite. If you have a problem that you do not want to lose, you make it slip around like the soap in the bath, so that every time someone thinks they have got hold of it, it slips away somewhere else. This is because it can be an important part of how you see yourself, your **identity**. 'I am the sort of person who has this sort of problem.'

Some favourite problems go in fashions. In many large companies, **stress** is currently the problem to be seen with. People know that stress is bad for them, and stress is a problem because they do not like taking health risks, feeling tired, being bad tempered, and its various other symptoms. But do they want to lose this problem? If they are *not* stressed, what is wrong with them? Are they not important? Don't they care about the organization? Are they not committed? Thus stress can easily become a favourite problem, something that is worth parading in front of admiring onlookers.

When problems are **communicated** to others, you may use those problems as part of a statement to them and to yourself about who you are, and you will try and make sure that your problems are big ones. 'Mine is bigger than yours' is as important a boast (and as awkward to prove) with problems as with other 'achievements'.

OFFICIAL AND UNOFFICIAL PROBLEMS

There is often an 'official', or 'organizational', problem that you are supposed to be concerned about, which may have little to do with what you are personally concerned about.

People at work spend a lot of time on 'illegitimate' activities – that is, things that play no part in their formal contract of employment. For example, it is not unknown for people to think about sex. But the boss who asks someone what they are doing rarely gets the answer, 'I was just thinking about sex, and about how I could either get more of it or stop thinking about it so much'. Instead, a more 'appropriate' answer will be given. If a person has an official problem to work on, and also one that they are interested in for themselves, it will be the latter which will get most energy. **Motivation** issues may often be traced to just such a conflict of problems.

In organizational life, people do actually work on problems of how to get promoted, how to avoid having to work late on Tuesday, how to avoid working with someone they dislike, how to build their **informal network**, or how to have more dealings with someone to whom they are attracted. A clue to the difference between official problems and the ones the person is interested in can be found in the **language** which is used. If it is full of Business-speak, with lots of macho words like 'strategy', 'business plan', 'mission statement', 'the bottom line', 'focus', 'quality', then it is at least possible that we may be hearing about a problem that they feel they ought to be working on rather than one with which they are actually engaged.

Job titles quite often imply that the occupant of the job should be focusing on a particular problem. In a university department, two people were appointed as 'placement officers'. Their appointments happened at a time when the department was having trouble finding enough good-quality industrial placements for its students, and the placement officers' titles associated them clearly with an attempt to solve this problem. The staff who were appointed were well organized and effective, and produced an ever-increasing supply of placements, without compromising quality. This in itself led to a problem for the two members of staff. Others started to suggest that there was no problem with placements (which was true because those two were continuously preventing it from coming back into existence as a problem), and that the placement officers therefore had an easy job, and that too many resources were being put into that activity. People are often employed to solve an official problem, and being too successful in preventing that problem from arising may make other people think that there is nothing there to be dealt with.

A PROBLEM SHARED IS A PROBLEM HALVED

When we tell someone about a problem, we know that it is often impossible to tell them everything, so we make more or less conscious choices about the communication. Sometimes we forget some details. When we are in the middle of a problem, it is often hard to see any one detail as more salient than all the others. We can never tell the other person the *whole* of a problem; problems are only problems because of their context, the total situation of the person who construes them as a problem. We may believe that we have told somebody 'all about' a problem, but what we usually mean by that is that we have told them as much as we could put together; we know there is more that we decided to define as irrelevant, but which we might have recounted on a different occasion.

The aspects of our problems that we choose to share with others, and the way we present them, depends on the **impression formation** that we are engaged in with the other person. We may not wish to come over as incompetent, or soft, or hard, or whatever. We sometimes do not have a set of words ready as a description of our problem; more often, we make the description up as we go along, and quite often we are surprised by what we hear ourselves saying. People sometimes say, 'It helps just to talk it over', or 'Thank you – what I needed was a sounding board'. We may be influenced by wanting the other person to be interested in our problem, so we give them an account of the kind of problem we think they want to hear about. You may not trust the other person; for example, you may think that they will tell other people about what you have told them, so you give them only the kind of problem construction which you think they cannot use against you. You may be trying to protect someone or something else. You may not want people to think badly of your profession, or of your racial group, or of your class, or of your family. One of us was recently working with a student who experienced major problems with her course and her life. For a long time she did not want to talk about her problems. This turned out to be because she thought it would reflect badly on her parents. From our point of view it looked very different; we shall probably never meet her parents, we would not be likely to make strong judgements about them, and we could not see why her parents should care what we felt about them. None the less, within her moral code, she should not do anything that could reflect badly on them – even if the personal cost of that was to fail her degree.

Similarly, people may fear that to tell someone about a problem may hurt the person they are talking to: that it will damage the listener's grip on reason and meaning, or that they will be shocked by what they hear. If you are seen as a pillar of the community, you may try to protect the community from seeing how wobbly you feel. You will disguise from them the character of the problems you are constructing.

Perhaps it is best to acknowledge that problem constructions are never fully shared. In an organization, the different people who might be interested in some problem that one of them is experiencing will all have their own problem constructions, but they may still be able to help each other. It is often possible to find issues that will prove helpful to work on for two or more parties to a situation, even though none of them is working directly on the problem that they had to start off with. Think of the different groups involved in the example in Chapter 1, 'Organization and Organizing', who were organizing a party for new students. The new students wanted something to do; the member of staff wanted to be seen to be doing something for them; the older students wanted something to do a project on. They all had quite different constructions of the situation and different interests in it: that is, they had different problems, but the actions that resolved the problem for one group also helped resolve the different problem experienced by another group.

PROBLEM BUSTERS

All of this has implications for the activities of management consultants, whose main stream of activity is to help members of organizations with their problems. Very often the consultant will have some technical skill to offer, and there is a history in consultancy of being disappointed that clients are not as pleased as the consultant feels they should be with what is done for them. This may be because consultants take too straightforward a view of the problem they are trying to work on, and may ignore the way the account given subtly changes the view each time the problem is passed on. Sometimes, so many people have had a hand in editing the problem between the person who originally experienced a problem and the consultant, that the brief the consultant is given has nothing to do with the problem. The consultant then finds themselves solving a problem – perhaps with great skill and finesse – that no one has got. So however elegant the solution, no one is particularly pleased.

Consultants often find themselves being given the kind of problems that people think they would like: 'Whatever kind of consultant you are, I will tell you about the problems that would fit with it.' So the change consultant is given a different script from the quality consultant, and different again from the systems consultant. This also happens the other way around. If you are good with a hammer, you may go round looking for nails that need knocking in. If some of those nails have a groove cut across the top of them you will not let it worry you; screws can be hammered in too. People go around 'finding', or more accurately developing, the kind of problems they like to work with, and this applies very much to consultants helping others with problems.

This is not necessarily bad. Consultants have their own problems – including how to practise their skills, and how to stay employed. Ideally they will find, together with their clients, relationships which enable them both to address their respective problems constructively.

DON'T BRING ME PROBLEMS – BRING ME SOLUTIONS

This is a favourite phrase of macho management, and is a classic statement of what we might call the 'planned irresponsibility' school of management thinking. It has been around in books of 'tips for managers' for a while, with notions like 'get the monkey off your back on to someone else's back': that is, when a person feels that they have a problem in their organization, the first thing to do is to see whether they can 'pass the monkey on' – make the problem someone else's. There may be some problems that are worth keeping because they are fashionable, or because they fit the person's role. For example, many reputations have been made in health care by those who were early in the field to address the problem of caring for patients with HIV and AIDS, and made this problem their own.

It may be possible to delegate aspects of the work on a problem, while retaining its ownership and overall control. In some organizations, problem solution and construction are related to seniority. If a senior person needs a problem solved, they may use the bright young minds of junior staff. For problem construction, however, they may want to use all their own experience as a senior manager, and all their background knowledge and experience.

But what of the person who just wants to be brought solutions? If one is concerned with the survival of the organization this may seem worrying; what if no one picks problems up? What if everyone expects someone else to do the hard work of problem construction? But perhaps the individuals concerned have learned something important for individual survival in organizations, which is that you need personal boundaries, areas in which you do not hold yourself responsible. If someone tries to take responsibility for too much, they may not be able to handle any of it effectively. We came across one manager who lacked such boundaries. He was a charming, caring man. He had time for his employees, and was a mine of information about what was going on and why. To our surprise, some of his subordinates found him very irritating. One of them explained that:

> Whenever anything comes his way, whatever it is, he thinks it is his problem. If we are lucky he forgets about it, and someone who has time will pick it up instead. If we are not lucky, it gets bundled up with all the other problems that he knows about, and popped into the problem soup that's inside his head.

The person who tries to take responsibility for everything – to take all the organization's monkeys on to his or her back – is likely to drop them or to be dropped by them. Over-responsibility can have consequences just as serious as irresponsibility. In voluntary organizations, it has always been possible to see a few people who are taking responsibility for defining and working with too many problems. In so doing, they often feel that they are being heroic supporters of whatever cause the organization is devoted to; other people may just see them as clinging on to too much activity. We are seeing this increasingly with commercial organizations too, as some members work ever longer hours.

SUMMARY

Problems are not things. They are constructions in the minds of people. Different people construct different problems. When people talk about 'the real problem', they are often trying to influence others' views of **reality**. People often feel that they are judged by the problems they are seen with, and may wish to have big enough problems for others to take them seriously, and to be up with the fashion in their problems. There is not always a free choice in the problems we construct, and people may create problems for others, for example, through prejudice. Problems are not necessarily solved; they may be forgotten, or die of boredom, or be overtaken by events. People may nurture favourite problems. The problems that people actually care about and work on are not necessarily the ones that they are officially supposed to work on. It is difficult or perhaps impossible to tell another person all about a problem, but quite possible to negotiate with another person a new problem to work on together. This is what often happens when there is a consultant or some other person officially involved as a helper with a problem. There are strategies to stop oneself getting overloaded with problems; if someone is clearly underloaded or overloaded, other people may find this very irritating!

- Problems depend on the view that people take of a situation.
- There is no one 'real' or right way of seeing a problem.
- Some problems may be defined in such a way that the definer does not have to do anything about them.
- We need to have some problems, and people may have favourite problems that they would not want to lose.
- The problems that people care about are not necessarily the 'official' problems in the organization.
- When someone tells someone else about a problem, they always have to make choices about what aspects to disclose.
- People have different problems, but may be able to act together in ways which help several persons or groups with their different problems.
- People can become overloaded with problems.

THESAURUS ENTRIES

cognition	leadership
communication	learning
construct and construing	meaning
decision making	motivation
discrimination	objectivity
emotion	perception
identity	problems
impression formation	reality
informal networks	scapegoating
knowing	stress
language	

READING ON

Much of the early literature on problems concentrates on problem solving, and often in a quite mechanistic way. It very often offers stage models which reflect ideas about how a good problem-solving machine would go about its work. The assumption made is that good human problem solving would have the same characteristics, and should emulate such an imaginary machine. Classic writing in this area includes Maier (1970), Miller et al. (1960) and D'Zurilla and Goldfried (1971).

The constructivist approach to problems came to the fore in the work of Sims (1979) and Eden et al. (1983). This was taken forward both theoretically and practically by writers such as Bryant (1989), and in a brief but captivating and practical book, McCall and Kaplan (1990).

Some recent work has focused on the language of agenda shaping rather than problem construction: if you know what a person, group or organization sees as being on the agenda of things that they want to talk about and act on, you know what problems they have constructed. A good summary of this work can be found in Dutton (1997).

8

Learning the ropes

Much is written on **learning**, a topic with far-reaching organizational, educational and political implications. We spend a large part of our lives learning – in our families, at school, in the streets, at college, in organizations. Massive resources are spent on education, **training** and development. Is this money well spent? How do we learn? What stands in the way of learning? Are there right and wrong ways of teaching? Right and wrong lessons?

In this chapter we consider some of the ways in which we learn. We go on to look at different learning styles and different types of learning. We then look at certain types of learning and knowing that go beyond the individual, becoming parts of **organizations**. Can we talk of **group** or organizational learning as involving something more than the learning undertaken by their members? Is it true that some organizations, like some individuals, are good learners and others not? We conclude this chapter by considering the relationship between knowledge and **power**.

One of the difficulties with the word 'learning' is that there are many different things which we learn, many different ways of learning and many obstacles which stand in the way of learning. Some learning, like learning a football result, takes place almost instantaneously; learning to use a piece of software may take several days or months; learning to play the violin can take many years. Some of the things we learn are information (e.g. 'There are five divisions in this organization'); some are **skills** (e.g. learning how to drive a car or how to send an e-mail) and academic disciplines (e.g. medicine or engineering); some are stories, like the story of how a particular product ensured the survival of our organization. Learning is something that takes place in the head (knowledge, information, stories), but also in the rest of the body.

Juggling, skiing and playing the drums are skills which are located in the limbs at least as much as in the head.

SOME TYPES OF KNOWLEDGE

Common Sense

Sometimes we are aware that we know something. Sometimes it seems so obvious that we do not even think of it as knowing. This is referred to as common sense, or the taken-for-granted view of the world. Until recently, it was assumed that the earth's resources were effectively limitless as was the earth's capacity to absorb pollution. Today, such views are no longer taken for granted. Instead, what seems commonsensical is the view that we cannot go on indefinitely using the earth's resources without jeopardizing the welfare of future generations.

One of the fascinations of coming into contact with different organizations is realizing that things we consider absolutely unavoidable are in fact conventions which other organizations do without. We consider it inconceivable that an organization could function without a personnel department until we encounter an organization where 'personnel matters' are routinely handled by other departments, without the need for a special department.

We are bound to take some things for granted. We cannot be checking everything the whole time. Within organizations we constantly make assumptions about the behaviour of other people, about the functioning of machines and equipment, about the operation of different types of system. It is for this reason that we can easily find ourselves thrown off course if suddenly one or more of our assumptions fails – for example, if our colleague is so depressed that he only wants to talk about his divorce, if the electricity supply fails or if we discover that our boss has been sacked. Tacit knowing is both inevitable and useful, yet there are times when it stands in the way of learning. We can rely on existing routines and assumptions which served us well in the past, not realizing that the world is changing and that the time has come for new ideas, new skills and new ways of engaging with others.

Acquaintance and Description

One of the distinctions that has proved helpful for thinking about knowing in organizations is between 'knowing by acquaintance' and 'knowing by description'. A dog lover knows his or her dog by acquaintance. By contrast, a scientist or a historian knows his or her subject matter by description, that is through scientific theories or records and observations made by other people.

Most of us know about trench warfare by description; war veterans who lived through it had a very different type of knowledge of its meaning:

> I have read many books, I have seen films, I have been to lectures. Nothing but nothing can capture what it was like to be there. The horror of it. (Joe Laskem, First World War veteran, *Today Programme*, BBC Radio 4, 11 November 1998)

Those who 'know by acquaintance' often believe that nobody who has not lived through their experience can appreciate its meaning, no matter how many books, television programmes or films they are exposed to.

Knowing by description is sometimes referred to as *propositional knowledge*, while knowledge by acquaintance is known as *experiential knowledge*. Propositional knowledge is generally open to traditional forms of testing and proof – the validity of the propositions can be tested through experiments, observations or arguments. Experiential knowledge, on the other hand, is more difficult to test, or even to talk about. As Louis Armstrong said about jazz, 'Man, if you gotta ask what it is, you ain't never gonna get to know.'

The knowledge that people have of their own organizations is mostly experiential. When we join a new organization, we may be given a description of it – for example, through company prospectuses or corporate videos. These are unlikely to take us very far (see Chapter 2, 'Entering and Leaving'). As we become used to the place, we gain knowing by acquaintance – knowing individuals, knowing procedures, knowing past examples and likely outcomes – and we act with more confidence. Organizing is carried out on both bases, and could not be done on the basis of either one alone. This book, on the other hand, like all books, can only offer you knowing by description – this enhances and speeds up your learning from acquaintance with actual organizations. The two kinds of knowing are not totally distinct; a really good autobiography is a description, but the reader may come away from it feeling almost acquainted with the subject of the book. Knowing by description can be a help in gaining knowing by acquaintance.

Skills and Competences

Much of our learning involves 'knowing how' to do things rather than 'knowing that' certain things are true. Often, we find ourselves doing things perfectly competently, without knowing the principles that underpin them. We can speak a language without knowing its rules of grammar and syntax, we can ride a bicycle and play billiards without knowing or understanding the physics. To take an example that has more to do with organizational life, many successful entrepreneurs may know how to set up and run profitable businesses without being able to articulate the underlying principles. Knowing how ('know-how') is often tacit knowledge, passing unnoticed and unrewarded.

Much of the knowledge in organizations is knowledge by acquaintance and knowing how. This is the knowledge on which much organizing is based. It often amounts to a range of skills and competences rather than the application of scientific concepts and theories. Rules of thumb, intuition, past experiences, organizational folklore and tacit understanding can be more helpful than the latest scientific discoveries. One of our students wrote a dissertation in which he tried to show that, if only small businesses followed formal appointment procedures for their managers, they would make far fewer mistakes and be better able to compete with larger businesses. He investigated firms where an owner had started a business and later recruited a manager as an employee. He found that judgements which seemed to be intuitive, where the owner had followed 'gut feelings', were more successful than the ones where more formality and rationality had been attempted. It seemed that such owners knew how to choose a good manager for their business; the more they considered the 'knowing that', the factors they 'ought' to consider, the less likely they were to make a **decision** which turned out well.

One particular type of knowing how is knowing how to get things to happen. A lot of knowledge in organizations can go untapped, simply because people who possess it do not know how to make it work for themselves or the organization. An information systems manager said:

> I have been trying to get the board to take an interest in IT for years now. We are way behind most of the rest of the industry. But every time we get near to talking about it properly, the conversation slips off to somewhere else. I just cannot get them to focus on it.

What he was expressing is a common frustration. He has an area of expertise. It is almost self-evident to him that the company would do well to pay attention to that area, but he cannot get it on to senior people's agenda. Many managers are in a perpetual state of hurry, of trying to do more things at once than is really possible, and many issues compete for their attention. However well you know what you are talking about, getting something you care about on the organizational agenda requires a different kind of knowing – knowing how to time your attempt, knowing who to talk to in which order, and knowing how to get them interested. This requires a mixture of **communication**, **political** and interpersonal skills without which technical know-how can remain untapped.

Narrative Knowing

This type of knowledge has attracted much attention in recent years. Many statements in organizations may sound factual, but imply a story. Consider for example the statement: 'Since Jeff joined us, model 312 has really started to take off.' Such a proposition can go beyond a mere statement of causal connection between two facts. Instead, it may amount to a story, a very short one to be sure, since the teller of the story can assume that the listeners have the tacit knowledge to make sense of it. They may know, for example, that Jeff was lured from working for the customers' trade association with a big salary offer, and that he is a very personable character; they know the success of model 312 has been at the expense of model 314 which has declined; and they also know that the director who brought Jeff in reduced the chances of his decision being shown to be wrong by arranging a healthy price cut and a big advertising campaign for the 312 at the crucial moment.

Some psychologists are now suggesting that narratives are central to learning. Making sense of the world around us, understanding what is going on, is achieved by turning 'facts' into 'stories'. After a football match or an interview, we prepare ourselves to tell a story of how that match or that interview went. In presenting ourselves to others, we invite them to share our stories, to get to know us through the stories we tell them and to form their own stories out of meeting us. When we go for an interview, for instance, we do not only offer a list of our achievements and experiences – instead we weave them into a narrative, and usually one that will cast us in the best possible light. At the same time, we listen carefully to the stories told by others. A word or phrase can reveal that they see themselves as a hero struggling against enormous odds, or as a victim of circumstances. Narrative knowing consists of being able to spot the plots of such stories and making sense of them.

An Example

Consider the following story in a naval camp. The story was often told before the inspection which preceded the handing out of furloughs – the permits to leave the barracks. This was a tense period, when the recruits could be denied exit leave if their appearance was not up to standard. One officer, the story went, liked to torment the sailors by denying them their exit leaves on the most absurd grounds. On one such occasion, he had asked recruits to lower their trousers while standing to be inspected. He then proceeded to cancel everyone's leave. The navy, he had explained, went to great trouble and incurred substantial cost in providing each recruit with three full sets of underwear as part of the military uniform. But, he observed, the recruits had seen it fit to discard the regulation white boxer shorts stamped with their serial number, in favour of a motley assembly of briefs. This he regarded as a violation of the military code with disciplinary consequences. The recruits needed a reminder that a sailor was to be a sailor through and through, for instance by spending some more time in the barracks.

This story had an unsettling effect on new recruits, although more seasoned sailors appeared to find it amusing. As a piece of organizational lore, the story acted as a depository of important knowledge, though the precise nature of this knowledge would vary from person to person. Unlike a moral tale which has a simple message and a straightforward moral, this story could be read in many different ways. Its meanings existed in many different layers. In one sense, the story cast the recruits in the **role** of victims of sadistic officers. They could take some comfort in surviving such ordeals. In another way, the story suggested that underneath the blinding uniformity of army clothes, each individual could maintain a part of their individuality, symbolized by their underwear. In yet another way, the story acted as a warning for new recruits. Navy life, it seems to announce, is full of unexpected troubles and dangers. Surviving requires more than just compliance to rules – it requires fortitude and, even, a sense of the absurd. As such, the story makes its point in a far more telling way than would a mere admonishment: 'Be prepared for the worst!' In this way, narrative knowing offers us both a way of making sense of our experiences and a way of coping with the difficulties and problems we face.

LEARNING STYLES

Different people learn in different ways. In a classroom, a teacher may give pupils a question and then suggest that they carry out an experiment to find out the answer. Alternatively, the teacher may give them the answer directly. Is it a waste of time and resources to have students carry out the experiment, given that the experiment has already been done many times? Likewise, if pupils know how to solve a problem, is it necessary for them to know the abstract mathematical principles which underpin the solution?

Learning styles is a concept which seeks to capture the ways different individuals learn. Some people are referred to as *pragmatic learners* – they prefer to learn how to get things to work, relying on a mixture of intuition, instruction and trial-and-error. They are interested in results, not theories. Others are known as *discovery learners*, approaching learning as an adventure and learning best from the satisfaction of solving problems themselves. For them learning comes mostly from experience. Yet others are referred to as *critical enquirers*, approaching their subject in a systematic enquiring way, using analysis, reasoning and criticism as means of reaching the deeper principles.

Learning by instruction and learning by experience are both active processes. Learning by instruction requires active engagement with what the instructor says, asking questions, raising criticisms, exploring new applications, trying out different examples. Learning from experience can involve hard work. It can be mental work, reflecting on experiences and trying to understand the reasons for mistakes or disappointments. It can also involve physical work, as in the following example:

> Once upon a time an old man saw that his days were coming to an end. He called his three sons, blessed them and told them that he had hidden a treasure in the field. When he died, they should go and dig the treasure out – it would stand them in good stead for the rest of their lives, he said. The old man died. His sons mourned him and then started to dig the field. They dug every part of the field thoroughly but could find no treasure. Had the old man made a mistake? This is what they thought. Until harvest time came, when they reaped many times the usual crop, for they had dug the field so well. It was then that they realized that the old man had not lied to them.

The old man of the story wanted to teach his sons a lesson by experience rather than by instruction. Had he said 'Work hard, my sons, to earn your living', the message could easily have been lost. Hard work, the frustration of not finding the treasure and the final realization of what the treasure is were likely to leave a much deeper mark on the sons. You can see now why some of your best teachers were those who refused to spoon-feed you easily digestible pieces of knowledge, which are just as easily forgotten. Instead, they demanded hard work from you. Hard lessons are harder to forget.

Experience does not necessarily lead different people to the same types of knowledge. Two people can go through what outwardly appears to be the same experience and end up knowing quite different things as a result. Even the three sons of our story could draw different lessons from their experience. The first one, for instance, might have learned that hard work on the fields is the secret of a happy life; the second son that his father wanted them all three to work together; the third son that hard physical work was not for him and that becoming a watch-repair man was a better way of earning a living. Thus, our individual way of knowing, or **construing**, the world gives a particular spin to what we see happening, and therefore what experience we gain from events. People know things in very different ways. A painter and a policeman would look at a riot quite differently and could be expected to draw different kinds of knowing from their observations. A poet and a botanist bring different kinds of knowing to the observation of a flower, and they take different kinds of knowing from it.

If we now relate this to narrative knowing, we would expect people to differ considerably in terms of the kind of story they made out of what they had just seen. Suppose that you miss an important meeting in your organization. You ask two or three of your friends who were present what happened. You are likely to get different narratives or stories through which they make sense of what went on, and in which they cast themselves as characters. One may present the meeting as an arena of political and intellectual jousting, where he managed to outsmart an awkward adversary. A second one may report that the meeting was a complete waste of time, with two or three individuals on ego trips being intent on arguing through the most trivial points. A third one may report that while much argument took place over trivial matters, the really important decision went through 'on the nod', right at the end of the meeting when most people were too tired to notice. These accounts may or may not be incompatible – they each seek to turn the experience of the meeting into a story from which the listener can extract the essence of the meeting.

Knowledge and meaning change as they travel from person to person through stories or information. Even seemingly hard statistics, like unemployment or profit figures, can lead to different conclusions being drawn, as different people read different meanings into them. One form of knowledge that we do not expect to change as it travels from person to person is that of scientific theories. After all, in the natural sciences, we expect a theory to hold across time, space and **culture**. Yet, in the human sciences, theories are constantly confronted with new unpredictable realities which demand constant re-evaluation and rethinking.

Obstacles to Learning

What stops us from learning? Why is it that sometimes we seem entirely unable to understand something or find ourselves repeating the same mistakes over and over again? It is sometimes said that some individuals can have 25 years' experience, while others merely have one year's experience repeated 25 times. Some people are better learners than others or better able to adapt, update and fine-tune their knowledge to changing circumstances. Learning itself involves a range of skills, which some of us can master better than others.

Many factors can conspire to inhibit learning – poor teaching, lack of **motivation**, absence of resources, the apparent lack of relevance can all prevent us from learning. A very important obstacle to learning is old learning, especially when it has assumed the form of habit. Habits that were once valuable can be difficult to shake off when they become counter-productive. One may learn to smoke as a way of being socially acceptable and successful; it is very difficult to quit later. Having learned to pass exams by simply memorizing pieces of information, it is hard to abandon this approach, even when it is no longer adequate or appropriate. Likewise, having learned that success is the product of hard work, we may be unable to stop and think whether the work we are currently engaged in is the right work.

Sometimes, old knowledge becomes an object of great emotional attachment. We can almost fall in love with our theories. This is especially the case with primitive theories, like stereotypes (see Chapter 11, 'Judging Others') or theories which have served us well in the past. We are then quite reluctant to abandon them and replace them with new knowledge, just as an organization may be reluctant to abandon a tried and tested product that has brought it much success in the past, when the time for its replacement is ripe.

Maybe the most important obstacle to learning is the fear of failure, a fear that may itself be the product of earlier failures and disappointments. Learning is not nearly as comforting or as reassuring as habit. It can be exciting, enjoyable and life-enhancing but it inevitably draws us outside the comfort zone of what we already know. It can be a disorganized and unpredictable business. It generates many anxieties: Are we on the right track? Are we wasting our time and money? Are we going to get the answers we want? Are we going to survive the tests and trials lying ahead? Shall we be branded failures? Are we perhaps stupid or mentally disabled? Faced with such anxieties, it is often tempting to fall back on old habits and routines, 'stick to the knitting' and continue doing what we already know how to do.

The teacher's skill lies in keeping these anxieties in check, never neutralizing them completely, but stopping them short of disabling the learning process. A good teacher can help us cope with the disappointment of failure, not by denying it or preventing it, but by turning it into a valuable lesson in its own right. A great teacher can inspire us with a genuine thirst for learning, maintaining our sense of adventure which combines danger with achievement. We can then develop a wide repertory of learning styles and approaches which enable us to benefit and learn from subsequent experiences, positive as well as negative ones.

ORGANIZATIONAL KNOWING AND LEARNING

The last few years have seen a huge growth in the number of books and articles on organizational learning, the learning organization, knowledge management, and similar topics. It has become increasingly common to link these rather academic-sounding concepts with competitive advantage and profit margins. Recently too, there has been an emphasis on understanding intellectual capital as one of the most important resources that an organization can deploy. In addition to physical, financial and human capital, organizations possess a type of capital which includes ideas, memories, recipes, timetables, forms, systems, routines, tacit knowledge and lore: all such forms of knowledge are so valuable that they should be understood and valued as capital. An organization starting from scratch would have to invent them afresh, and this would cost much time and money. There are already commercial firms running courses in which stockbrokers and financial analysts train participants in recognizing and calculating the commercial value that should be put on such intellectual capital.

Does it make sense to speak of organizational learning or indeed of a learning organization? In a way, organizations do not know anything. They do not have brains or memories in any conventional sense, even if it has become commonplace to view computers as the organization's brains and accounting systems and databases as its memories. Words like 'knowing', 'learning' or 'memory' have to be applied with caution to any subjects that are not people. Yet both practising managers and academic writers find them quite useful in thinking about what is happening in their organizations. Organizations are attributed with capacities to learn (or fail to learn) and to develop (or fail to develop) in their own right, over and above the knowledge and learning of their members. How is this possible?

KNOWLEDGE SURVIVES STAFF CHANGES

One reason for believing that organizations learn over and above what their members learn is that a certain kind of know-how or lore survives changes in staff. Certain orchestras are famous for the unique quality of the sound they produce over many decades, irrespective of the conductor who happens to direct them or the musicians who happen to be playing in a particular concert. In a similar way, organizations are known to have 'ways of doing things' which are inherently right and proper irrespective of their staff at any particular moment in time.

How is such knowledge maintained within organizations even when the personnel change? Some of it assumes the form of folklore, which passes down generations. Some of the knowledge becomes embedded in routines, procedures and ways of working which are never questioned. Some of the knowledge becomes embedded in the ways that buildings, equipment and materials are arranged. In the same way, certain orchestras are reputed to produce a particular type of brass or string sound because of the musical instruments they possess, because of the positions the players occupy in a particular hall or, indeed, because of the acoustics of the hall itself.

As a new entrant to an organization you are likely to face a special situation. Your job description may say that you are to prepare spreadsheets which forecast the cash flow for the coming year, a job which you have already done in another company, a job in which you are already well trained. There will still be much that you need to learn in order to be able to do it right for your new organization. How do you know the things that are and are not taken into account in your new organization? Some of this knowledge will come from the other people you work with, who will fill you in on what is needed in the spreadsheet – thereby conveying to you some of the collective organizational learning. Some of it will come from the shape of the spreadsheet itself, its design being the result of past learning. Some of it will come from the feedback you will receive when you present your first set of figures.

Of course, changes of personnel may lead to some new ideas, but it is surprising how much stays the same. Bringing in 'fresh blood', trying to produce organizational **change** by introducing new staff, can work, but it is surprising how often the new staff find themselves drawn back into doing things the way they were done before. In effect, the attempt to introduce a new way of thinking about things is absorbed by the organization. The stock of organizational knowledge can sometimes overpower the individual attempt to influence it.

KNOWLEDGE IS NOT JUST IN THE HEAD

One of the recent developments in **cognitive** social psychology has been to understand that knowing and thinking are widely distributed in the body. We do not only know the ideas that are represented in our brain. We also know things because we know where to find them or how to generate them; for example, because they are in our diaries, or because we have set up a regular meeting to talk about them. Skills and competencies may be 'remembered' as much through other parts of the body as through the brain. Tennis players learn about their sport in many ways, including watching it and vividly imagining what it would feel like to produce that particular shot. Such learning and imagination seem to happen in the nerves and muscles of the arms, legs and back. A flute-player's skill may be embedded in the dexterity of her fingers, the sensitivity of her mouth or the speed with which her eyes can move along the score. Similarly, the skills of conducting a good meeting or inspiring colleagues to greater efforts may be based in physical movements, in facial expressions, in tone of voice rather than conscious ideas.

Similar phenomena can be observed at an organizational level: knowledge becoming embedded in different parts of the organizational structure. The departments of the American government were once described as 'monuments to past problems' (Schön, 1971). Most organizations show something of their accumulated knowing in their structures: each department indicates the existence of an old problem which was addressed by assigning it to a specific department. The spatial layout, the location of different offices, the structure of different forms, the timetables, the procedures and regulations and many of the other features of an organization similarly reflect acquired knowledge and learning. The Head Office is imposing because it was once found that a simple building was interpreted by customers as meaning that the organization was insubstantial. The Consumer Credit Department is there because it was once found that sales could be boosted by offering favourable credit terms. The Overseas Relations Department dates from the time when it was realized that the names and features of different models had to be adjusted for foreign sales.

LEARNING FROM MISTAKES

A large part of learning theory is dedicated to understanding how individuals and organizations learn from their mistakes. Recognizing a mistake is a first step involving the detection of a mismatch between the intentions behind an **action** and its actual outcomes. This recognition can be a difficult and painful process, since all kinds of excuses may be used to deny the failure or to offload responsibility on to someone else. Recognizing a mistake by itself is no guarantee that the mistake will not be repeated. In order to ensure that the same mistake does not occur in future we must change behaviour, habits or procedures. This is known as *single-loop learning*. It can be observed easily in animals that can learn different skills by a combination of punishment and reward. Avoidance is a typical form of single-loop learning: being close to fire is painful, stay clear of it. (Notice how this 'lesson' can actually disable learning: 'Learning is painful, avoid it.')

A deeper form of learning takes place when we assess not only the action which led to a mistake, but also the strategy for avoiding the same mistake in future. *Double-loop learning* aims not merely to fix or resolve a problem but actually to establish why the problem arose and why it was **constructed** as a problem in the first place (see Chapter 7, 'It's not My Problem'). Avoiding fire may be an adequate strategy to stop oneself getting burnt, but rather obliterates any possible constructive uses to which fire may be put. Double-loop learning enables us not only to avoid errors and problems but to take better advantage of the opportunities in our environment by exploring our own learning capacities. In this sense, it involves not merely learning but also learning how to learn.

Organizations too can be seen as engaged in single- or double-loop learning. Single-loop learning may be said to take place if repeated failure to launch a new product leads to a decision not to attempt it again. Double-loop learning would involve an effort to understand why such attempts were unsuccessful in the past, the conditions under which they may be successful in future and the reasons why they have taken place at all.

RIGHT AND WRONG LESSONS

Organizations, like other social phenomena, are complex. Relations of cause and effect are rarely direct. Failures and successes are rarely the result of a single factor. Profits might rise in the same year that the corridors were painted purple, without there being any necessary link. In the same year, there may have been an advertising campaign, a relocation of the warehouse, a change in the reporting relationships in production, a new accounting system, and a Total Quality Management effort. The managers behind each of these initiatives may do their best to suggest their action alone is responsible for the profit rise. With so many factors at play, how can an organization learn the right lesson? Indeed, is there a right lesson at all?

After the Second World War, there was a widespread belief in the USA that victory had been the result of American technical superiority. This was the 'lesson' the war had taught American politicians, military and the wider public. In the years of the Cold War which followed, the USA acted on this lesson by concentrating on further technological advance. This strategy was, of course, bolstered by the vast economic and political interests at stake in ever-expanding military expenditure. Recent historians have argued convincingly that America was not ahead of Germany in technology in the early 1940s, and that victory resulted from superior logistics, not technology. The lesson learned from the Second World War may have been at odds with evidence produced by historians. Yet the strategy which was adopted subsequently was not necessarily inappropriate: escalating military expenditure may have brought American success in the Cold War not by ensuring victory on the battle front, but by bankrupting the Soviet Union, which tried to keep pace with American military technology (Locke, 1996).

Under such circumstances, it is hard to know what is the right and what is the wrong lesson. At times, the 'right lesson' may lead to undesirable consequences, just as the 'wrong lesson' may lead to desirable results for entirely unpredictable reasons. The lessons which our organizations learn from past experiences often owe more to wishful thinking or political manoeuvring than to dispassionate analysis. Yet, such lessons are very difficult to alter. They become inscribed in the collective memory in very stable ways, through symbols, stories and social structures.

Organizational learning is a matter of maintaining these symbols, stories and social structures by ensuring that new recruits become thoroughly attuned to their meanings. New learning becomes encoded in fresh symbols, stories and structures, which modify, displace or complement older ones.

BUYING KNOWLEDGE AS A SUBSTITUTE FOR LEARNING

Learning, both at the individual and at the organizational level, is a slow process; it can also be an inefficient one. It involves the exploration of ideas which may turn out not to be good; and it involves costly mistakes, blind alleys, testing, implementation and practice. Calling a plumber, someone who already has the required knowledge and skills, prevents the need to learn how to fix one's leaking taps. Learning to play the piano in order to enjoy Beethoven's piano sonatas can be a lifelong project. How much quicker simply to listen to them performed by a great virtuoso at the concert hall or on compact disk.

For an organization, developing its own information system or even producing its own mission statement can be costly and time-consuming, involving many individuals, much argument and political posturing. It is not surprising that increasingly organizations seek to 'buy knowledge', making use of specialists and experts. The burgeoning of MBA education and the **consultancy profession** bears ample testimony to the fact that organizations seek to supplement their own learning with knowledge acquired from outside. Academic theories and techniques, concepts and buzz words, fads and fashions have colonized organizations, at times coexisting with, but often subverting, traditional forms of knowledge. Buying knowledge very often means buying the latest fashion to come out of a business school or out of a management guru's head.

The Lean, Flat, Agile, Right First Time Learning Organization

One of the current management fashions is the idea of the lean, flat and agile organization. There must be enough people to fulfil the required functions and no extras; there must be as few layers in the hierarchy as possible. The organization must be capable of very rapid change to meet new circumstances and must be able to get things right first time. Another current management fashion extols organizational learning as the key to competitive advantage and lasting success.

There is an inconsistency here. We argued above that organizational learning resides in part in the stories that members tell each other. Middle managers have been the most important repositories of such stories in the past, and they told these stories over lunch and at social times when story-telling was an appropriate activity. The tendency to right-sizing, producing a lean organization, means that the pressure to do the immediate work becomes too great to permit such stories to be told. The flattening of organizational hierarchies has particularly reduced the ranks of middle managers, thereby excising much of the organization's memory. Agility in an organization means that it responds immediately to circumstances. To achieve this it needs to be lean and flat. 'Right first time' means that there is no room for experimentation and error. But learning requires that you allow for the possibility that you might be wrong. The requirement to be right first time discourages originality, risky experimentation and learning.

THE POWER OF KNOWING, AND OF NOT KNOWING

'Knowledge is power', runs the old cliché. There is a very obvious sense in which knowledge is power. Like money, many kinds of knowledge are a currency that can be traded. This is especially true of one type of knowledge – information – which can be traded either directly (for instance by selling entire databases or banks of information) or as **gossip**, rumour and innuendo. A single piece of information (such as knowing where a 'millennium bug' is located in a piece of software) can sometimes command enormous value. This is also evidenced in the world of military and industrial espionage, as well as in the practice of blackmail. More generally, intelligence gathering by companies represents an important investment, and is aimed at giving them competitive advantage or denying this advantage to their rivals.

Within organizations, possessing the right piece of information on an adversary gives one a valuable advantage. For example, if I know more about the context of a decision than you do, I can ask questions in a meeting which will make your proposals look silly. 'Have you considered the implications for your proposal of the... [something obscure]?' This can undo all the hard work you have been doing in presenting your case. Information then becomes a valuable resource. The dissemination of inadequate or deceptive information becomes itself part of organizational politics. Subterfuge, lies and misinformation (information which, though not inaccurate, is designed to mislead by the omission of vital elements) are features of the political life of many organizations, in which individuals and groups compete for power by affecting to know more than they do.

But information is not the only form of knowledge which accords power. Knowing by acquaintance, knowing by description, knowing that and knowing how can all also translate into power. Knowing an important politician, a manager from a rival company or a supplier can enhance a person's political standing within an organization, as can their technical or political expertise, their social and communication skills or their procedural know-how. The value of knowledge increases in times of crisis or rapid change, when specific information or expertise acquires great value. Mental and manual skills enhance the market power of their holders and usually translate into better pay, job security and working conditions. A skilled craftsman no less than a lawyer may be able to convert their skills into earning capacity, so long as these skills are in limited supply. Conversely, as we will see in Chapter 9, 'Machines and Mechanizing', deskilling leads to a loss of job security, earning capacity and control over work.

There are times, however, when lack of knowledge – ignorance – can be a source of power. Consider a new manager who arrives in a company with very little direct knowledge of what has happened in the past. Such a manager may, of course, be easily outmanoeuvred by her scheming rivals who already know the ropes. Alternatively, she may be able to use her ignorance to her advantage. She has, after all, no axe to grind. She is not burdened by past failures and past successes. She is not tied to a particular brand or strategy. She is not disabled by the past as her predecessors were. She may also be given a 'honeymoon' period by her colleagues and subordinates, a period in which to prove herself. Under such circumstances, she may be able to succeed in initiating policies which would be doomed had they been initiated by someone with inside knowledge. We know an organization which appointed a new chief executive two years ago. He was brought in from outside, and from the start made a virtue of the fact that he did not know all the history of the company. He got away with a lot of actions which he could not have taken if he had been around for longer, and he would occasionally let slip a boast: 'They won't try to stop me, because they think I don't know my way round yet!'

CONCLUSION

In this chapter we have introduced a number of important distinctions regarding the nature of individual and organizational knowledge and have examined how knowledge within organizations is transferred through stories, symbols and structures. In this way, knowledge can be said to exist independently of the people who make up an organization, and survives staff changes.

We also examined how individuals and organizations learn and some of the obstacles they must overcome in order to learn. We made some reservations on current views which regard organizational learning as the key to competitive advantage and corporate success; we noted that in the area of organizations, it is hard to speak of right and wrong lessons, since such lessons are strongly influenced by wishful thinking and organizational politics.

Finally, we examined the view that power is knowledge and identified certain ways in which different types of knowledge can enhance an individual's or an organization's position. Information is a particularly useful prop for power, though other types of knowledge may readily translate into power. There are instances, however, when ignorance can free an individual from the burden of the past, enabling him or her and/or their organization to attempt actions that would otherwise have been inhibited.

- Knowledge is not always conscious; we may take a particular view of the world for granted.
- There are different types of knowledge, including propositional and experiential knowledge, know-how and narrative knowledge.
- Different people have different learning styles; some learn better by instruction and some by experience.
- Single- and double-loop learning are different ways of learning from discrepancies between desired and actual results of actions.
- Learning involves risk, danger and uncertainty; fear of failure and disapproval act as barriers to learning.
- Organizations may be able to learn over and above the learning undertaken by their members.
- Such learning becomes embedded in organizational structures, symbols and stories.
- Buying knowledge can be a substitute for organizational learning, though it is by no means sure that knowledge acquired in this way is readily assimilated.
- Generally, knowledge (of facts, procedures, persons, etc.) enhances an individual's power in organizations.
- There are instances when ignorance can strengthen one's hand.

THESAURUS ENTRIES

action	learning
change	motivation
cognition	organization
communication	politics
construct and construing	power
consultant and client	professions
culture	role
decision making	skill
gossip	training
group	

READING ON

The distinction between 'knowing by acquaintance' and 'knowing by description' goes back to the work of Russell (1946), whereas Polanyi (1964) distinguished between 'knowing that' and 'knowing how'. Narrative knowledge as a key to understanding human learning and remembering was discussed by Bruner (1990) among others; Weick (1995) has examined how story-telling functions as a means of sense-making; Gabriel (1991, 1998) has examined how we turn facts into stories and stories into facts.

The view that everyday knowing is not unlike scientific knowledge and that we should look at people as if they were scientists – developing theories, anticipating events, and trying to understand the world they are living in – goes back to Kelly (1955).

Management learning is a relatively recent discipline which developed out of the writings of, among others, Argyris and Schön (1974), who proposed the distinction between single- and double-loop learning; Mintzberg (1973) who identified the competences deployed by actual managers in their work; Levitt and March (1988), who discussed the concept of the competence trap; Senge (1990), who codified the features of a learning organization; and Pedler et al. (1997), who identified different types of learning. The concept of organizational learning as a key to competitive advantage has been explored by Moingeon and Edmondson (1996) and Probst and Buchel (1997), among others. Learning, under conditions of complexity and unpredictability, has been studied by Stacey (1995, 1996) who brings together insights from chaos theory and psychoanalysis.

Cook and Yanow (1993) offer a convincing image of organizational learning as something over and above the learning of individual members. Based on a study of high-quality flute-making firms in Boston, Massachusetts, their work argues that the specialist expertise which made each firm unique did not reside in individual members of staff. When craftspeople moved from one company to another, even doing apparently the same job, there was a whole lot they had to learn about how that job was done in their new company.

9

Machines and mechanizing

Man is a tool-using animal.... Without tools he is nothing, with tools he is all. (Thomas Carlyle, *Sartor Resartus*)

K woke up with a start; his alarm had not gone off. K looked at it accusingly and noticed that both hands were rigidly stuck on 12 o'clock. He jumped out of bed looking at his watch, but that too had stopped at 12 o'clock. He dressed himself in haste, remembering that he had an important work appointment that morning. He picked up the phone, thinking of suitable excuses, but it was dead. Over the next few minutes, K realized with rising frustration that his electric razor, the kettle, the radio, the TV, the fridge and all the machines in the house were not working. He slammed the front door and left his flat. As the door smashed shut, it set off the burglar alarm, whose shrill monotone pierced his skull. He woke up for real this time, the alarm buzzing noisily.

Life without machines has become inconceivable. Our age has been described as 'The Age of the Machine'. Machines dominate our physical landscape, they **control** our daily routines and affect every moment of our lives. Machines have enabled us to fulfil some of the oldest dreams of our species and have given us powers which our ancestors reserved for gods. With the help of aeroplanes we can fly, telephones help us to communicate across vast distances, and computers provide huge amounts of information at our fingertips. Jupiter's thunders look rather tame in competition with the weaponry available to today's warriors and Vulcan's magic bellows are pathetic compared with the robots that fill modern factories.

Alongside these visible, physical machines there are wider social forces working towards mechanization and routinization. Machines bring a repetitive orderliness to physical and mechanical tasks, and procedures and systems in organizations seek to do the same for other tasks. The internal mail system in an organization tries to treat pieces of paper and objects in as predictable and orderly a fashion as a telephone treats speech. With its regular collection times, its rules about what will and what will not be carried, its defined collection and delivery points, it attempts a similar level of efficiency to a machine by accepting similar limitations. In this respect, it is a machine, even though it does not involve mechanical or electronic components, and as such it may be replaced by another machine, such as electronic mail. On a personal level, organizing may be done with the aid of time management systems (a way of mechanizing time allocation). The appeal (if any) of the filofax and the electronic diary is that they offer some mechanization of difficult tasks that can be expected to require judgement and care.

HOW MACHINES MADE THE TWENTIETH CENTURY

There are three primary purposes that we hope machines and tools will fulfil for us: to protect us against our natural environment, to help us control it and profit from its resources, and to make our lives easier. Think of any domestic appliance: a dishwasher eliminates the tedium of washing up, a refrigerator extends the life of food, a vacuum cleaner speeds up the cleaning of a house, as well as removing dust which manual methods can only redistribute. Advertisers emphasize the labour-saving qualities of domestic machines, keen to portray the consumer as freed by their latest offering and able to pursue more pleasurable interests.

Not for nothing has our species been called 'a tool-making animal', an animal who seeks to fulfil needs not only directly by taking what nature offers, but also by using nature's own resources to control nature. Control over fire gave people some measure of control over the temperature of their ambient environment and opened the way towards control over metals, clay and glass. The watermill, invented in the first century BC, made the grinding of corn immeasurably easier, offering welcome relief for women (and especially slaves) who had spent the best part of the day grinding with pestle and mortar to provide for their families and masters. 'Stop grinding, you women who toil at the mill', wrote Antipater of Thessalonika in a poem dating from that time. 'Sleep late, even if the crowing cocks announce the dawn. For Demeter has ordered the water Nymphs to perform the work of your hands, and they... turn the axle which with its revolving spokes turns the heavy Nisyrian millstones. We taste again the joys of primitive life, learning to feast on the products of the earth without labour.'

Since the early days of humanity, however, machines have served another, less edifying purpose. This is illustrated in an early sequence of the classic film *2001: A Space Odyssey*, when the chiefs of two primitive tribes are about to attack each other. Suddenly one of them focuses on a bleached thighbone lying nearby, his face lights up, he grabs it and proceeds to beat his opponent senseless with it. A primitive instrument of war to be sure, but it proves to be an effective one.

As the ancestor of intercontinental ballistic missiles and nuclear submarines, the thighbone sums up two important features of **technology**. Firstly, it shows how a part of nature, something lying out there, is transformed into a tool through the power of an idea; it is the idea, eventually crystallized into know-how, which turns inert matter into technology. Secondly, the thighbone underlines the fact that fighting and the domination of one's fellow human beings are mothers of invention, on a par with economic necessity and the desire to dominate nature. War has spawned many new tools, new machines and new technologies. From the primitives' poisoned arrows to Archimedes' catapults and mirrors, and from Leonardo's prototype machine-gun to 20th-century developments in explosives, poison gas, nuclear and other technologies, warfare and destruction have acted as a stimulant of human technological genius.

Machines do not just help us go about our business, in peace or war. They also define our business. They shape not only our physical but also our social and psychological world. The lift, invented in the 1880s, did not just help people get from floor to floor; it genuinely revolutionized architecture by paving the way for 'vertical living', culminating in the skyscrapers of Manhattan.

If the lift was a major breakthrough in dominating vertical space, a machine, dating from the 13th century, whose central feature is a perfectly steady rotation of one or two mechanical hands around a central pivot, has revolutionized our perception of time. The clock, whose failure started off K's nightmare, arose initially from the need for time-keeping in medieval monasteries. The clock was not merely a means of keeping time, but a means of synchronizing people's actions. The marking of hours and, from the 17th century, of minutes and seconds, turned people into time-keepers, time-savers and eventually time-servers (Mumford, 1934).

In the Factory

It is not accidental that the mechanical clock, and the time-keeping and time-saving consciousness which accompanied it, emerged just as the growing European cities were calling for orderly routines. Neither is it an accident that it found its place of honour as the only 'decorative' item to grace the interiors of Victorian factories. In the factory, time is money; it is against the ticking seconds on the clock that work, machines, outputs and money are counted.

Not everyone liked this. In the 1810s, the Luddites, bands of workers who saw their livelihoods ruined as traditional cottage industries were swept aside by manufacture, had roamed the manufacturing areas of England breaking machines and destroying factories. A hundred years later French railway workers bequeathed the term 'sabotage' as they removed the shoes (sabots) holding the railway lines.

Philosophers too expressed profound reservations about machines. John Stuart Mill wrote that 'it is questionable if all the mechanical inventions have lightened the day's toil for any human being'. Instead of more leisure time for all, manufacture brought forced unemployment. Moreover, workers found that their role was to serve the machine: feed it with raw material, remove its product, always at the pace set by the machine, on the terms of the machine. 'The machine unmakes the man. Now that the machine is so perfect, the engineer is nobody', wrote Emerson, the American essayist.

With the rise of machines, production was detached from the **skills** and ingenuity of individual workers. The intelligence and craft which had hitherto resided in the operator were now incorporated in the mechanical process. The worker found that his or her specifically human qualities and creative capacities were no longer required.

> Owing to the extensive use of machinery and to division of labour, the work of the proletarians has lost all individual character, and consequently, all charm for the workman. He becomes an appendage of the machine, and it is only the most simple, most monotonous, and most easily acquired knack, that is required of him. (Karl Marx, *The Communist Manifesto*)

Mechanizing Management

While industrial machinery had already revolutionized production, a new management movement emerged in the early decades of this century, known as '**Scientific Management**'. Its chief exponent was F.W. 'Speedy' Taylor and its greatest achievement was the 'supramachine', Henry Ford's assembly line.

Taylor argued that managers had been unsystematic in their approach to production. Maximizing efficiency and rationalizing production were the proper tasks of management, and ought to be done in a scientific way. Taylor proposed his principles of scientific management, which included:

1 Remove all brain work from the shop floor; managers must plan and organize production and limit the worker to the task of implementation. 'We are not paying you to think.'
2 Standardize products, parts and production methods. Scientific methods should be used to determine the most efficient options.
3 Fragment the production process to elementary tasks, each of which can be optimally standardized.
4 Select the most appropriate individuals for each specified task, train them to work precisely according to rules and formulae and monitor them to ensure that they adhere to these.
5 Offer financial incentives to the workers linked to their output. Taylor believed that workers, as well as their employers, would benefit from the results of increased efficiency.

Taylor's theory was not about machines but the mechanizing of **organization**. His interest lay in the detailed study and design of often simple instruments, like shovels, and in the work activities themselves in the belief that small changes in the planning and organization of production and instruments of work can lead to great changes in output.

An apt illustration is provided by one of Henry Ford's assembly lines. One man took 20 minutes to produce an electrical alternator; when the process was spread over 29 operations, assembly time was decreased to 13 minutes. Raising the height of the assembly line by eight inches reduced this to seven minutes, while further **rationalization** cut it to five minutes. But more planning by management meant less control by the worker, who is now further reduced from being a servant of the machine to being a part of it. Like parts of machines, workers are interchangeable, their jobs require little or no **training**, the speed and quality of their work are easily controlled since no skill or thinking is involved. In the film *Modern Times*, Charlie Chaplin memorably captures and criticizes the spirit of Taylorist ideas and Fordist applications. The worker is seen being fed by a giant feeding machine while working on an assembly line, where his day is spent tightening pairs of bolts with two spanners. One hardly knows whether to laugh or cry as the feeding machine goes berserk, scattering bits of corn and tipping bowl after bowl of soup on the worker's face.

The history of 20th-century industry is inextricably connected with Taylorism. Highly sophisticated technological products are produced by workers whose skills took hardly more than a couple of days to acquire, who know virtually nothing about the products they are producing and, at times, do not even know (or care) whether the parts they are making will end up on washing machines or nuclear submarines.

Assembly lines became the established mode of industrial production, dominating not only manufacturing but also service industries and office work. One ingenious application was in catering, where fast food technology ensured the production of a consistent, standardized product and service with the help of virtually unskilled staff. The process is designed to ensure that the food will be prepared to specific standards by people who may be unable to boil an egg at home. The self-service principle transforms every customer into his or her own waiter.

The ingenuity of this technology, however, leaves the workers with few intrinsic benefits. In contrast to simple cooking technologies which allow cooks scope for initiative and experimentation, fast food staff are handlers of materials. Their experience resembles that of production line workers, with the additional pressures that direct contact with the customers brings. 'It is not an easy job, but it's very monotonous', said one who had worked for two years. 'If there was more variety and skill, people here would be less short-tempered. The staff would stay longer too; in this place I've met two or three hundred people who came to work and only five or six of us are still here.' As work becomes more routinized (unlike the work of professionals or skilled craftspeople), it becomes purely a means of earning a living, something to put up with for as long as one can.

INFORMATION MACHINES

The technological revolution of our time is that of **information**. This is not the first revolution in information handling. The invention of writing in the fourth millennium BC was seminal, permitting the keeping of accurate records and the development of accounting. In the 15th century, the invention of typography combined with the production of cheap paper revolutionized the dissemination of information. The mechanical clock itself is an information device. The invention of the telegraph in the 19th century provided a cheap and instantaneous method of communicating information across vast distances; previously, with the exception of smoke signals, semaphore and drums, information had travelled at the speed of the fastest horse.

Information technology consists of many instruments apart from computers (such as pens, paper and erasing fluid), machines (such as typewriters, adding machines, telephones, computers) and systems for gathering, storing, processing and communicating information. Taylorism in the office has sought to emancipate the processing of information from the personal quirks of clerks. Maximizing output and efficiency were pursued through the standard Taylorist recipes – fragmentation, standardization and control. This approach was suited to large bureaucratic organizations handling vast amounts of routine information. The issuing of passports or of electricity bills, the handling of insurance claims or of mortgage applications yielded easily to long paper-processing lines. Each individual received a set of documents in an in-tray, carried out one or two simple operations or simply signed them, and then placed them in the out-tray.

The shortcomings of this approach are familiar to all whose documents get 'lost in the system', whose special requests cannot be accommodated within the standard forms or who have to wait for ages until their cases are seen. Personal service to the customer is unknown; service of any sort rudimentary. The clerk becomes a 'pen-pusher' or a 'paper-shuffler', enjoying no discretion, variety or security, having little contact with fellow workers and almost none with the customer.

On the other hand, there are undoubted benefits to some people. The arrival of electronic office equipment has changed dramatically both the nature of information handling in organizations and also the nature of information itself. Instantaneous access to and updating of records, multiple access to them, processing and communicating capacities previously undreamed of, open new possibilities both for the service offered to the customer and for the planning, forecasting and organizing of production. The desktop computer, at best, enables clerical staff to process individual cases from beginning to end, offering a more personal and prompt service to the customer. Errors can be rectified more effectively, and controls can be introduced discreetly.

Mechanized Information at Work: An Example

One of us conducted a research project in which we interviewed 47 managers and clerical staff in a privatized utility. In the space of ten years, most of the office workers had made the transition from working with manual files, cabinets, typewriters and index cards to working with desktop computers or terminals. A mainframe system of customer accounts, enquiries and service records had been installed. The staff dealt directly with customer enquiries over the telephone and planned the work schedules of service engineers.

This is how one of the workers recalled the experience:

> We were computerized seven years ago. With computerization morale hit rock bottom, mainly because of the way they were brought in. People were worried about the changes and the machines weren't as easy as we had been led to believe.... A group of us were picked for our typing ability and were shown the computer. We had to input all the existing records into the machine. At least, in those days we worked in two-hour stints in front of the machine. It was thought that it is not good for you to stare at the screen any longer. Even later, there used to be a compulsory break every hour. Of course, it is no longer on offer.

While staff had come to terms with the computerized information system, numerous grievances were mentioned. A supervisor had looked forward to computerization:

> It meant less paperwork, less files, originally it seemed like a fabulous idea. As time went on, however, we realized that it didn't stop the paperwork, but actually increased it. We get reams and reams of tabulations, most of which are never read. ...The customer gets a better service; we can provide an immediate response to customer enquiries. If there is a complaint or a disputed account, I have the information ready at my fingertips. But most of the girls in the office would sooner go back to the old manual system; you could moan about that, but it was not bad. The computer makes the job more monotonous; it has decreased **job satisfaction** for the girls. They can't move around any more; they don't have to go looking for files, most of the time they are stuck at their desks. There is less variety, less time spent chatting by the filing cabinet.

Seventy per cent of those interviewed in that site said that they would happily revert to the old manual system. 'Service to the customer has improved but my job satisfaction has declined; mind you, the computer always gives you an excuse why you can't do something', said another member of staff. 'If in doubt, blame the computer', was a fairly common attitude. In spite of the improved service to the customer, the computer had not reduced the overall number of errors. Wrong bills were still being sent to customers or the wrong appliances delivered, engineers were still being sent to the wrong address, and at times two crews would be accidentally sent to do the same job. The clerk responsible for rectifying mistakes said:

> Work now is quicker and more efficient; there is less duplication, for example I can send bills out to the customer directly through the computer. The computer also covers some mistakes, like wrong sums, no bill goes out if the sums don't

add up. But generally there are more mistakes since computerization; there are omissions leading to disputed accounts, which means more work for me.

Managers too drew attention to some of the difficulties resulting from computerization. One of them said:

> Since computerization some operations have become more awkward. Travel by service engineers has increased; with the old card system, you could see at a glance how each engineer's day was turning out. This is now computerized, but we cannot get an overview of the jobs planned for each engineer.

A common problem was that the computer treated all engineers as interchangeable, whereas in fact each engineer had his preferences in terms of the type of work he did and the location of the job. Of course this *could* have been built into the system, but it had not; in reality there are always such extra factors that are important, that could in principle be built in, but so far have not been. It may sound unfair to the computer to complain about these, but it does seem to be an inherent weakness of a machine approach that it is insensitive to some of the complexities that can be handled by people. In this case, some managers kept an informal system of manual records on cards or loose pieces of paper, especially when jobs needed to be done urgently or a specific engineer was to be sent to do a special job. This informal system often overrode the computer, causing irritation to clerks who had assigned jobs through the system.

Several staff reported that they frequently resorted to 'cheating the computer' in order to assign a particular engineer to a job, or in order to give priority to an especially troublesome customer; to do so, the computer would be fed with one or two pieces of strategically wrong information, 'forcing it' to do as the clerk wished. The result was that some of the data in the system were not entirely reliable. One manager remarked:

> Much of the time, my staff try to find ways of working around the computer, outsmarting it. For example, when they are dealing with a dodgy case of a customer who complains about something, instead of entering their initials after the action they have taken, they enter the initials of the person who carried out the original transaction. In this way, when a mistake occurs, it is impossible to establish who is responsible.

Such findings do not support the view that new information technology necessarily liberates the worker from boring and routine tasks, equips him or her with new skills and gives him or her new powers and controls. On the contrary, they suggest that the computer can restrict the worker's mobility in the office, limit informal

communication and casual chatting, and if anything further dehumanize office work. While it gives more information to clerks, enabling them to accomplish tasks from beginning to end, it does not increase their overall control over the work process. To do so, clerks engage in all kinds of tricks and dodges, some of which are to help the customer, some to protect themselves and some to obtain the satisfaction that they can outsmart the machine.

The conclusion from this illustration is a mixed one. Technology itself is neither enslaving nor liberating. It is the **management** of technology that is important. Information technology, like earlier manufacturing technologies, was used here to replace human intelligence and skill and to increase the control over the individual. The worker, stuck in front of a terminal, sees the world shrink to a range of symbols on a screen and a sequence of voices at the end of a telephone line. Feelings of **meaninglessness**, boredom and **powerlessness** prevail. It is too early to generalize from this example. Nevertheless, it highlights some serious dangers inherent in current information technologies. In essence they are not so different from the dangers of technologies past, but their magnitude is even more alarming.

The desktop computer also offers a more restricted view of the world. One study (Weick, 1985) suggests that it is generally hard for people to make sense of what they are doing in front of terminals; there are five deficiencies which together lead to a chaotic understanding of the world:

1 **Action** deficiencies: the operator cannot see, hear or smell data from the outside world, but only see symbols on a screen.
2 Comparison deficiencies: the operator cannot walk around and look at things from a different angle, but has to rely on one, uncontradicted data source.
3 Affiliation deficiencies: people often work out what is going on by talking to other people, and working at screens discourages this.
4 Deliberation deficiencies: it is hard to see the wood for the trees, to tell the important from the unimportant, on a screen.
5 Consolidation deficiencies: material on a screen does not look like work in progress, and it is hard for people to go away and think about it, as they might with less imposing-looking information.

These five points apply generally to the world as mediated by a television screen. The limited world of the television viewer has been brought into the workplace.

THE MEANING OF MACHINES

But there is another side to machines. Some people like them; they even become addicted to them. Far from leading to meaningless-ness, machines enhance the lives of these people, filling them with meaning and anchoring their sense of identity. For such people, machines like cars and computers can become the focus of folklore, generating stories which are full of **meaning** and feeling. Some people may end up treating machines with greater care and affec-tion than their human companions. An analyst uses the following story as an opportunity to describe her own relation to computers:

> I never forget going to a party and there was one of the most eccentric pro-grammers that I've ever met in my life, sitting on a sofa with a bottle of gin, and he proceeded to tell me that he preferred computers to women because they didn't answer him back, and he was serious! He was totally serious. His whole life revolved around computers. I just think it's sad. It's funny but it's sad. And I think that a lot of people become obsessed with it, I think I was, when I first started learning about computers, oh I loved it! It was exploration – there was always something you didn't know, there were always things to find out, but it was always achievable, you'd get there in the end. Whereas I don't feel like that anymore!

This story expresses the feelings of many computer enthusiasts, for whom computers are a challenge, a source of satisfaction and a major part of their life. In our own research, we collected a number of stories featuring computers at the workplace. Three major types of plot were identified:

1   In some stories, the computer features as a *physical object*, as a machine, which gets stuck in lifts, falls off trolleys or 'crashes' to the basement. In these stories (some of which are extremely funny or unpleasant), the role of the computer could be taken by some other machine, like a photocopier, without drastically changing the meaning of the story.
2   In other stories, the computer is treated as a 'living being', whose strange and unpredictable behaviour puzzles, amuses, threatens and dismays. In these stories, the computer appears as a true character in the narrative, most frequently as the *villain* or the *fool* of the piece, occasionally as the innocent *scapegoat*, now and then as the *hero*.
3   In the largest number of stories, the computer features as a unique *resource* or *tool*, often a priceless one, which can be used or abused, which may be mastered, and whose control confers great *power* on its owner. In these stories, the computer functions

just like the magic rings or golden keys in folk tales. The commonest presentation of computers in stories is as a valuable but dangerous tool or resource.

Consider the following story, told light-heartedly, by an executive of a large computer manufacturing company:

> I used to work for a company where we had regular bomb practice. The security chief would hide a package with a sign saying BOMB, to see how quickly people got out of the building and how quickly his boys would locate the 'bomb'. They carried out this exercise many times and were pleased with their response times. Until eventually the bomb was hidden under the mainframe computer, where it proved impossible to locate; for hours they searched all over the building, but nobody thought of looking under the machine!

It is interesting to speculate why the security staff failed to check under the mainframe. Was the machine seen as being above suspicion or was it a taboo object? Did the men perhaps fail to see the computer altogether, regarding it as a fixed part of the building, in the same way that our untrained eyes fail to distinguish the dozens of types of snow apparent to an Eskimo?

The story was presented as an illustration of an earlier comment to the effect that, to the non-expert, computers are mystifying and threatening. The executive telling the story was seeking to have a little fun at the expense of security men, hardened men who will go after bombs and yet will not go near a computer. It is the computer which is the real threat in the story, rather than the fake 'bomb' of the drill. At the same time, the executive uses the story to cast himself and his expert colleagues as brave individuals at the cutting edge of a technology which mystifies lesser mortals. This view of computers as dangerous items acquired fresh meaning at the turn of the century, when most users were gripped by a blind panic concerning the 'millennium bug' – throughout the late 1990s forecasts of doom and gloom regarding the inability of software (often dating from the 1960s) to deal with the year 2000 abounded.

In our research, computers had different symbolic significance for different users. Different organizational participants recounted different types of computer stories. Four main types of participant were identified, each type characterized by its different feelings about information systems:

1   *Routine users* generally do not talk much about computers or incorporate them in their stories; for them, computers are symbolically insignificant, they do not form part of their identity and, provided that they have mastered the essentials, they do not

generate especially strong emotions. For such users computers can enhance feelings of meaninglessness, boredom and alienation.

2   *Creative users* have rather ambivalent feelings about information technology and computers. Many are apprehensive about the disappearance of traditional 'professional' aptitudes and skills as a result of computerization. At the same time, they enjoy the benefits of access, speed and range afforded by modern information systems. In their stories, they very occasionally laugh at experts, while more commonly they blame the machine for everyday difficulties and problems; at times they laugh at themselves for 'silly' mistakes which they make, and at others times they gripe at the complexity or rigidity of the systems they use.

3   *Managers* face different dilemmas from routine and creative users. In their stories, they laugh at the naïve user's blunders as well as at the expert's lack of common sense. They often disparage their subordinates for what they see as irrational resistance to computerization. Yet, they also express discomfort at having to control the experts and depending on them without always having their knowledge or expertise. Some seek to promote an image of themselves as computer competent or indeed as experts, yet in many of their stories information technology is a territory full of promise but also full of danger. Few of them feel very secure operating in this territory.

4   The *experts*, for their part, see themselves as the masters of this territory which they seek to mark and protect. Their stories, celebrating the naïvety of other users and highlighting their own indispensability for the organization, strengthen their sense of professional unity and of being special. Their stereotypes of 'users' are invariably disparaging. Some expert stories are at the expense of fellow professionals, but on the whole these tend to be part of what have been termed 'joking relations', i.e. relations in which mutual baiting and teasing are a sign of respect and affection (see Chapter 14, 'Serious Joking').

If in Doubt, Blame the Machine

Computer experts, in our research, often attracted negative nicknames from non-experts, like 'zombies', 'androids' or 'the zoo'. But they were rarely the direct target of stories. In most of their stories, it was the computer itself which was ridiculed or blamed for organizational failures. The non-experts enjoy computer failures almost as much as the experts are amused by the naïvety of ordinary users. In their stories, the computer emerges as 'a dumb machine, pretending to be smarter than it is', whose humbling is similar to that of the pompous and pretentious persons discussed earlier. In some of the stories human wit and common sense come to save the day when the machine fails to deliver the goods. For example, in the library of a large manufacturing firm, they liked to tell the story of a director urgently requesting a copy of an article that had appeared in a newspaper. No amount of on-line searches could identify the article until a seasoned librarian phoned up all the newspapers and eventually tracked down the article. It had been written by a freelancer who held the copyright, and did not feature in the computerized database. The point of this story seemed to be that old-fashioned librarian skills came to the rescue in a situation which the computer could not handle.

Similar stories of staff having to fall back on their traditional skills and use their cunning and experience every time the computer crashes or fails can be found in many organizations. Even in highly automated environments, such stories seem to proclaim that the computer doesn't have the last word. People cannot and must not become mere servants of computers; they must maintain their skills and aptitudes and remain in control of the machines. A few years ago, one of our students returned from a placement in a prestigious accounting firm with the latest word in information. He reported how the partners, having lost faith in the bug-ridden system, routinely asked for files to be manually retrieved by 'a little fellow buried in a basement stacked to the ceiling with files'. This person alone in the organization knew where each document was kept, and his imminent retirement was seen as the organizational equivalent of Doomsday.

To sum up then, stories about the computer in organizations reveal a variety of meanings that are vested in them – they are a source of power and advantage, a useful but dangerous resource, a baffling and mysterious force, a convenient excuse for every failure, a cause of much frustration, irritation and boredom. At the heart of many of these stories lies an unease; this combines a recognition that computers make our lives easier, more comfortable and more fun with a feeling that computers are already too clever to be controlled by humans. We have become far too dependent on them to be able to function without them.

BEYOND MECHANIZING

The effects of new information technologies on production have been far-reaching. Product differentiation and targeting of consumers, decentralization, the contracting out of products and services, globalization of financial services – all these were logistically impossible, but have now become possible thanks to the computer. Flexibility replaces standardization and routinization as the order of the day: flexibility of products and production methods, of working practices and labour markets, flexibility in geographic and financial terms.

Japan has been hailed as the prototype of the new industrial age, in which success depends not on churning out a uniform product cheaply, but on very fast adjustments to market and other external **changes**. 'Japanization' and its developments have now been imported into virtually all advanced productive systems. New computerized technologies require a new range of industrial skills and work attitudes. The worker must have an overall understanding of **systems**, must be able to switch from one area of production to another: from production to maintenance, from maintenance to service, and from service to information processing.

It is becoming popular to argue that the age of mass production is now giving way to post-**Fordism**, the era of the intelligent machine. While it may be too early to judge how current developments in information technology will shape tomorrow's organizations, certain trends are already apparent. A move away from the **hierarchical** pyramids of the past towards flatter, leaner organizational structures is widely regarded as essential for survival. While classical management theory recommended that each superior should be in charge of between five and ten subordinates (the number of people he or she could 'keep an eye on'), today's managers might manage a hundred or more subordinates, in different locations, with the help of computerized information processing. Henry Ford's own organization has seen its levels of management decline from more than fifteen to seven, a number which has proven adequate for the Catholic Church throughout its history, and which would still be seen as excessive by most Japanese companies. Middle management is squeezed out, as senior executives have instant access to information that would have been processed by numerous intermediaries in the past.

The optimists view this as an opportunity to bring the human factor back to the workplace, to restore meaning and dignity to work and to do away with the drudgery and monotony of much manual **labour**. The **alienated** mass production worker will be replaced by the expert information handler. Just as a very few farmers can provide enough to feed a nation, it is argued, in future a few manufacturing workers will supply most of the material commodities required. The rest will be engaged in managerial, service and information-processing work.

The pessimists take a different view. They regard the information technology revolution as yet another step in humanity's subordination to its own creations. It takes the process of **deskilling** to ever larger sections of the workforce. The supramachine of the present, the computer, threatens the last vestiges of privacy, freedom and independence. Electronic spies monitor our every move, huge databases maintain records of our every credit card purchase, computers decide where and how to commit vast sums of capital which sooner or later are translated into jobs lost and gained, livelihoods created or destroyed. This is not flexibility but perpetual insecurity and suffocating impotence.

- Technology is not just tools and machines, but recipes, techniques and know-how.
- While many tools and machines make our lives easier, technology has for a long time been linked to the requirements of production and warfare.
- The application of new technological methods in production has, under capitalism, led to some deskilling and degradation of work.
- Taylorist principles and Fordist mass production subordinated the worker to the mechanical requirements of production.
- This has resulted in alienation and feelings of powerlessness and meaninglessness.
- Technology, and especially information technology, can create strong dependency; people become unable to function without mechanical supports.
- Computerization may offer some relief from monotony at the workplace.
- But computerization often reduces people's control over their work and severely restricts awareness and understanding of what they are doing.
- Developments in information technology facilitate changes in organizational structures, notably towards greater flexibility and shorter managerial hierarchies.
- It remains an open question whether technology offers solutions to today's social and organizational problems or whether it is at the very root of these problems.
- But there is abundant evidence that machines can end up becoming the master of humans rather than their servants.

THESAURUS ENTRIES

action	management
alienation	meaning
change	meaninglessness
communication	organization
control	powerlessness
deskilling	rationalization
Fordism	Scientific Management
hierarchy	skill
information	system
information technology	technology
job satisfaction	training
labour	

READING ON

Lewis Mumford (1934) in his classic book *Technics and Civilization* offers a very insightful account of the impact of machines on our lives. Taylor's principles of Scientific Management are presented in his book *Scientific Management*, and critically reviewed in detail by Aktouf (1996). The argument that mass production technologies cause worker alienation was put forward by Blauner (1964), who argued that fully automated process production brings about a reduction of alienation. The view that Taylorism has been the dominant influence in shaping the modern corporation was first put forward by Braverman (1974), who argued that throughout the 20th century the working classes in industrial countries have been systematically deskilled through the application of Taylorist ideas. Braverman viewed Taylorism as a doctrine which bolstered management control over the productive process and reduced workers to mere extensions of machines. The concept of deskilling has been borne out by numerous field studies, including Beynon (1973), Nichols and Beynon (1977), Pollert (1981) and Gabriel (1988). Braverman's work generated a tradition of scholarship, referred to as 'labour process theory', which addresses issues of control over the workplace and the limits of management control. Increasingly researchers have focused on different mechanisms of worker resistance to management's attempts to control the work process. Several accounts of the resistance-control process are offered in the collection edited by Jermier et al. (1994).

The effects of computerized information systems on management are discussed by Zuboff (1988), while Weick (1985) has offered fascinating insights into the shrinking world of the employee who spends increasing parts of his or her time in front of a computer screen. The incorporation of computers in organizational language and folklore has been discussed by Bloomfield (1989) and Gabriel (1992). Numerous authors have discussed the Japanese phenomenon: the causes and nature of Japan's manufacturing success, and the extent of Japanization of the industries of other countries. Womack et al. (1990) identify the origin of Japanese success as lying firmly in its pioneering of radical manufacturing systems of lean production which mark a major leap ahead of Taylorist systems. Other authors, however, notably Kamata (1984), Wilkinson (1996) and Wilkinson et al. (1995) have challenged both these views and the culturalist views (which argue that culture is the secret of Japanese success); instead these authors believe that Japanese success is essentially due to an intensification of the disciplines and controls that are embodied in Taylorism.

10

Leading and following

So there is a boss, sitting in a comfortable chair, in a fine office, telling others what they should do. He (rarely she) is world weary, gets frustrated and stressed, and shouts a lot at people – because they often do silly things. This is a favoured, but predictable, image of organizational leadership amongst writers of television soap operas. It makes good drama. It is saturated with coercive **power** – the wielding of decisive influence over people's lives. Many of the early industrial barons were well practised at such leadership, as are some of their late 20th-century descendants. Lee Iaccoca, reflecting on his executive career in the Ford Motor Company, tells us:

> Each time Henry (Ford) walked into a meeting, the atmosphere changed abruptly. He held the power of life and death over all of us. He could suddenly say 'off with his head' – and he often did. Without fair hearing, one more promising career at Ford would bite the dust.

Pushing people hard, with threats, can certainly get them moving; but in what direction? It has not proved a very successful strategy for engendering commitment and creativity, or reducing **conflict**, being based on a very crude **psychological contract** between boss and subordinate. The boss is doing just that – bossing. This style of leadership still exists, although coercion today is usually presented with a more friendly face; it has been called 'tough love'.

WHO IS IN CHARGE, THEN?

As the image of the omnipotent boss fades, we sometimes have to search harder in the organization for the leader. The following is typical of recent conversations we have had with some of our management students when we visit them on industrial placement:

Tutor: Who's looking after you here?

Student: Well, no one, really. I suppose Bill is, officially.

Tutor: Yes, but who guides your work?

Student: Oh. Quite a few people. We all help each other.

Tutor: But the project you're on. Who's in charge of it?

Student: It depends what you mean by 'in charge'. As we work in a mixed team, there are several different managers who are looking after different bits – one on design, one on production, and one on marketing.

Tutor: OK, then, how do you get your instructions on what to do?

Student: It comes from several sources – I usually have to go and ask, and then make my own work.

Tutor: What happens if you can't do the work?

Student: I just say so. We then work out something between us.

What this student was trying to convey to her tutor was something about the quality of working in an organization which had little of the traditional **hierarchy** of **control**. She worked in a project team. Leadership was not the prerogative of a single boss; it was distributed across managers and team members, a typical picture of a **matrix organization**. She went on to describe how, in meetings, senior managers seemed to 'just chat' with them, after a lot of listening to their issues and **problems**. She could not remember many times when she was actually told what to do: 'It feels as if I'm being given space to draw my own conclusions and work schedule – which is nice. Sometimes I can even help others.'

Not everyone would feel as comfortable as this student with the kind of direction she was receiving, but she illustrates three important features of organizational leadership.

Firstly, it is a two-way process of mutual influence. What happens (and we shall come back to this) is often a subtle shaping of another's world. A major theorist on organizational behaviour made the important point that 'executives are essentially powerless until the time comes when followers grant their leaders the **authority** to lead'. In other words, if everyone refused to be led, then the leader would be pretty much disabled. A supervisor in a large chemical corporation told us of her shock when she first discovered this simple principle in her early career: 'I said "do this" and "do that" to someone and he simply said "No". I was stumped. I could have said "Well, I'll go to Personnel" or something like that, but what kind of atmosphere would that have created?'

Secondly, the effectiveness of a **leadership** act is evident in what others, on the receiving end, do and feel. In order to gain maximum commitment, the influencer somehow has to hit what is important and relevant to those involved, while also steering them in a direction that he, she (or 'the organization') desires. No easy task.

Thirdly, leadership, in some form or another, is an essential ingredient of social organization – but you do not have to be a designated leader to lead. Working relationships involve a myriad of leading–following interactions, often aimed at meeting different needs – **emotional**, task, organizational. Within groups or teams different people can play different leadership roles at different times; leadership is 'distributed'. In fact it is hard to imagine a social situation where there are no attempts at organization through leadership…but let us try:

> You are asked to attend a managerial training meeting. Around the table are six people you have not seen before, but you know that they work for your organization. A trainer (you have not met) is sitting there, the obvious leader, you think. But he does nothing, says nothing. There is silence; an extremely long silence. You feel uncomfortable. Others look uncomfortable too. Where is the agenda? What are you supposed to do?

This scenario is, in fact, not fictitious – it happens in 'T-groups' ('T' is for training), once popular in **management** training. They are events specially stage-managed to be free of obvious **structure**; free from formal leadership. They create a social vacuum which, like its physical counterpart, is very soon filled. Leadership just happens. People begin to talk, laugh nervously, get angry – anything to produce some structure and meaning out of the highly ambiguous situation. In doing so they reveal something of their own style and anxieties. Some will specifically try to influence the direction of affairs; others will gratefully fall into line. A few may protest, offering their own ideas about what everyone should do.

The effect of a leadership vacuum on people's desire for leadership is pervasive. Populations in countries which experience long periods without stable leadership will often look appreciatively – for a time – on anyone who is willing to sort out the mess (a fact not missed by opportunistic dictators). One of us took up a directorial position in his own academic department following a long period of organizational uncertainty. He was astonished to find how willingly people, well known for their recalcitrance, would respond to his requests for co-operation. His tale is worth recounting – in his own words:

> The department had gone through a long period without a head, and was now facing the prospect of no programme director (Dean of Studies) – a key role for the functioning of the academic programme. Normally, the position is filled from the ranks of academics, on a rotating basis. However there was no one who relished the prospect of the high administrative load, preferring instead to do their research and teaching. The department was at crisis point: everyone

acknowledged the need for a director, but no one wanted to be one. Staff were mysteriously unavailable when needed, and tension was high. Finally, the matter was resolved bureaucratically. Although I have only modest administrative skill and zero inclination in that area, I was nailed – following vague threats of the sort, 'we will have to look carefully at your contract of employment if you refuse'. The word got round fast that there was now a programme director and colleagues appeared, as if by magic, from their hiding places. I was heartily congratulated for my good fortune. Ha! Significantly though, for at least a year, not one of my actions, requests or initiatives was queried. Co-operation was amazing from a department usually full of divisions and conflicts. Colleagues were much relieved that someone was now in charge – and that it was not them personally.

THE GOOD AND THE GREAT

Will you make an effective leader? Have you got what it takes? There are many lists of desirable **personality** qualities reeled out by personnel specialists and psychologists which can make even a saint look suspect. Some can be found in job advertisements – 'reliable', 'initiative', 'self-starter', 'effective in groups', 'firm under pressure', 'good communicator', and so forth. Despite many studies which show there are no such things as universal qualities of leadership, many of us cling to the firm belief that we can spot a leader when we see one. But, it seems, different people spot different things, and it is not uncommon for 'experts' to disagree.

Leadership is a *process*, not a personal trait. That process takes place within a particular social context of which the people to be led are an obvious, but often forgotten, part. It does not make a lot of sense to analyse leadership without reference to what is going on between leader and led. For example, so-called 'leadership qualities', like charisma, are only detectable in their effects on *others* – such as in their blind trust and awe of the leader. After the Second World War, Winston Churchill's charisma faded – not because he had suddenly become a different person, but because he was perceived differently by a peace-time constituency who had peace-time needs.

But this is still only part of the story. Being influenced by a leader does not necessarily make that leader *effective*, or his or her actions **ethical**. Somewhere along the line a judgement of quality has to be made. Effective by what criteria and in whose terms? A manager may be regarded by his or her staff as delightful to work with and attentive to their needs. However, the manager's manager may see things differently: 'A nice person, but perhaps too nice; a low productivity section.' Different people can attribute different qualities to a leader, according to what *they* think is important.

TODAY'S HERO, TOMORROW'S FOOL

Audiences can, on one day, praise the leader and on the next casti-gate the person, branding him or her as fool or villain. This shows that leadership is partly a reflection of the social times. Politicians who say the wrong thing at the wrong time (or the right thing at the wrong time) can be fast eased out of prominent positions. National heroes whose words, wisdom and faces become immor-talized in books and stone, can face sudden obliteration when their message is no longer seen to be appropriate: tumbled effigies of Lenin now litter the junk yards of Eastern Europe. Clive Sinclair, the British inventor and entrepreneur, has, on a number of occa-sions, been the focus of intense media coverage and praise for his brilliant electronic innovations – from miniaturized radios and televisions to battery-powered cars and bicycles. Often, though, in just a short period of time, some of his products hit reliability, delivery or credibility problems – and sometimes all three. The news about him then switches quickly from praise to ridicule.

Again, we return to attributions – what people choose to ascribe to the leader, and how fickle a process it can be. As part of this, one burden for the leader is to carry the projected disaffections and inadequacies of organizational members. This means he or she is a visible focus for blame, as well as a source of balm. Organizational leaders will often find that they inherit a history of problems in working relationships, which they are expected to shoulder. In this manner we can dump our most intractable problems on the leader and pretend they are his, or hers, to fix. But they are rarely solved in this manner, because the difficulties lie within us, not with the leader. Many an energetic, but naïve, company director has enthusiastically re-structured the organization to improve its effectiveness – while old hands quietly look on. Sure enough, after a short period of time, the old patterns re-emerge. Sometimes this is because people gain a vicarious pleasure and power from helping them to reappear (see Chapter 7, 'It's not My Problem'); other times, it is because shifting the organizational pieces around does not touch underlying **cultural** beliefs and tensions. So the weary adage: 'The more things **change** around here, the more they stay the same.'

MANAGING PEOPLE OR MANAGING MEANINGS?

Followers, of course, do not do all of the work in creating leader-ship; the leader is the other half of the equation. How can we envisage the leader's role? Organizations comprise different **groups** of people with different beliefs and interests. People vie with each other for influence and power. In this environment few leaders can expect automatic compliance with what they personally think is important. Leaders need to know what is important and meaningful to the people they work with, and somehow shape their beliefs, or '**meanings**', in a direction which makes organizational sense. In other words, it is the world as seen through the follower's eyes that the leader has to appreciate – first and foremost.

The psychological logic here is fairly straightforward. We are more likely to be committed to actions which have been crafted and steered subtly by a leader than to ones that have been thrust down our throats; and the shaping starts with what we, not the leader, think is crucial. This involves an interesting reversal of the old maxim that power can corrupt; powerlessness too can corrupt, in that it leaves people weak and out of control of their own destinies. The paradox of the kind of leadership we are discussing is that the leader needs to turn his or her so-called followers into leaders; to 'empower' them to use their talents to serve themselves and their organization. The notion of **empowerment** is appealing, and it is a fashionable one in current leadership thought. However, it should be borne in mind that in re-setting the power balance the leader's hand is still firmly on the steering wheel – which leaves empowerment open to the accusation that it is but a subtle form of manipulation – where some people remain 'more equal' than others.

Nevertheless, powerlessness can be corrosive, and its effects can be observed in many organizations. Powerless people feel insecure, and one response is to cling to whatever fragment of control they can acquire. It is as if they are saying: 'Well, if I'm valued as no more than a cog in a machine, someone to be ordered around, then I'll show you how valuable I really am.' The janitor will make themself very hard to find when someone wants their services. The secretary will point to the backlog of work on his or her desk when asked to do an urgent job.

THE LANGUAGES OF LEADERSHIP

The shaping of what other people think and feel is central to the leadership process. It is accomplished through the skilful use of **symbols**: talk, stories, visual images, ceremonies, writings and rituals. These are the essential tools of the leader's trade. They are used variously to represent the leader's aspirations, visions and beliefs.

Talk

Organizational leaders appear to spend an inordinate amount of time talking. In meetings, in corridors, over lunches, at conferences, in cars, on trains, in planes and on telephones – they talk. Talk, and its words, is the most basic symbolic process through which leaders define, and re-define, their ideas, and those of others. For leaders, all this talk *is* their action, and their action *is* the talking. Effective leaders are able to combine listening and talking in a way that gently shapes a direction which offers mileage to both leader and led. We can eavesdrop on a (fictitious) conversation between a Chief Executive and her Marketing Manager to see the process at work:

> *Chief Executive*: So what you are saying, Joan, is that you would like a marketing strategy for our magazine which extends the age range of readers.
>
> *Joan*: Exactly! I've been feeling for a long time that we need to take into account the shifting attitudes of youngsters. Today's 15-year-olds think like 18-year-olds did when we launched this magazine in the 1980s. Their attitudes to sex, drugs, personal relationships, work, education, the family and so forth, are nothing like ours were!
>
> *Chief Executive*: Mmm. That's a good point.
>
> *Joan*: And I really would love to have a go at re-framing our advertisements and feature articles with a younger market in mind.
>
> *Chief Executive*: Joan, I really think you could be on to a winner. But first of all I need to get straight the financial implications. Our parent company is unhappy about our turnover and profit this year, and I'm keen to find a new image. Your idea could be the answer. I wonder if there's a way in which you could do a trial run to test the water first?
>
> *Joan*: I hadn't thought of that. I suppose we could do a supplement to our November issue – say one special feature with ads.
>
> *Chief Executive*: Fine. Go ahead. Meanwhile, I do need a long-term financial estimate to prepare my case for the board – as soon as possible. Why don't I arrange a meeting between you, me and Mark from Financial Planning? He can help us put the financial flesh on your idea....

In this exchange we witness the Chief Executive building on an idea suggested by her Marketing Manager in a way which (a) supports the Marketing Manager's initiative and (b) re-channels it in a form which meets the Chief Executive's own objectives. Notice that the Chief Executive shifts Joan's initial expectations to a rather more cautious position, while also setting up a structure to keep her involved in the development of *her* idea. And it is all done with the careful use of talk.

The way a leader crafts his or her words has much to do with **rhetoric**. By this we do not mean rhetoric in the pejorative sense of deception, pretence and bombast (although we acknowledge that many leaders, political and organizational, are well practised at those). Rhetoric, in its nobler form, is the refined art of persuasion – to some extent reflected in all social interaction. The skilled leader exploits the resources of ambiguity in language to suggest and steer meaning; *how* things are said can be as important as, if not more important than, *what* is said.

Persuasion, in a brasher form, is evident in the ethos of effective public speaking, a strictly one-way skill which is much valued in managerial circles. The effective leader, goes the argument, moves hearts and minds by offering stirring, polished performances. And some certainly do. In 1978 Jan Carlzon, president of Linjeflyg, Sweden's domestic airline (affiliated to Scandinavian Airlines Systems), made a stirring speech in a huge aircraft hangar to his assembled staff, an oration which signalled a turning point in his company's fortunes. Standing on a tall ladder he opened his speech, 'This company is not doing well...', and closed with, 'I have some ideas of my own, and we'll probably be able to use them. But most important, *you* are the ones who must help *me*, not the other way round.' The powers of oratory are mentioned by many high-profile business leaders. Lee Iacocca, Chief Executive of the Chrysler Corporation, claims that a public speaking course was instrumental in putting him on the right track. His faith in such training has been such that he has sent 'dozens of introverted guys' on courses, and 'for most of them it made a real difference'.

Evocative Imagery

Imagine being summoned to a key departmental meeting on the future of your organization. You get there, and one hour later it is all over. You have a headache and eye strain. It was a low-key affair. You have been listening to financial forecasts, peering at pages of statistics on the company's declining performance, and hearing a long diatribe from the Chief Executive about the poor effort everyone has made (which includes you). You feel depressed and overwhelmed. Now imagine a replay of this event, but with a new script. This time you leave the meeting fired with enthusiasm and motivated to do new things. Your Chief Executive has acknowledged 'everyone's extraordinary effort in keeping the ship off the rocks in these hard, recessionary times'. He talks sincerely, and confidently, of the 'talent in the company which has now got to face new challenges, and take new opportunities'. The competition is fierce, but he is 'convinced that everyone has something important to offer'. The company 'needs to work as a solid team to climb to new heights of excellence and quality'; and he will 'do all he can to build that team – with your help'.

The contrasting scenarios reveal the effects of using very different symbols in managing meaning. In the second setting the Chief Executive is using word pictures as a rhetorical device, especially **metaphors** (ships, climbing, building) to create a **reality** which looks attractive and possible. In the first case, the images are more rational (lots of numbers) and dry, and have a grey, punitive tone about them.

Writings

The written word is almost as prolific as the spoken one in the daily business of organizing. Some managers manage by memo. Each morning there can be a new flow of directives and suggestions on paper and/or electronic mail, for staff to collect, collate and consider. The actual flow can symbolize something about the manager's style (intentional or otherwise). A constant stream suggests a possibly nervous individual, desiring to exert control over affairs: it is as if to say, 'don't forget I'm here and I'm in contact with all key affairs'. On the other hand, rarity or unusualness of a written **communication** can signify the importance of the message – 'if the Chief Executive has taken the trouble to write, it must be something crucial'. Employees of a major British computer company told us of their special version of such missives – Stanograms. The label was coined whimsically from the name of the Managing Director, and they were yellow pieces of paper containing his cryptic thoughts or key messages. No one could miss them.

The style and tone of correspondence from a leader can be manipulated to set the psychological distance preferred. Does William Draycot receive messages from his boss addressed 'Dear Bill', 'Dear William', 'Dear Mr Draycot' or even 'Draycot'? Does the boss always feel impelled to write out his or her title in full – as if to reinforce the **status** of the position? Or perhaps be the only person not to do so, which ends up having a similar effect. Does the message invite a reply, and will that reply be acknowledged? Is it only the bad news and personal criticism which gets put in writing? Dismissal or redundancy are a case in point. Rather than face directly the shock or discomfort it can cause, a manager might choose to do it all in writing – regardless of the effects on the receiver of the news. For example, we know of a senior manager from an engineering company who received his dismissal notice by personal delivery at his home. What made the event particularly poignant was that the letter was carried by his boss's secretary in the very early hours of the morning; and up until that moment the man had felt perfectly secure in a job he had held continuously for 11 years (see also Chapters 2 and 5, 'Entering and Leaving' and 'Morals'). For some leaders, maintaining (or switching to) formal, impersonal relationships helps them cope with issues that otherwise would get swamped by feelings. Hiding behind the written word, or using others to deliver unpleasant messages, provide the leader with a protective screen.

These various manifestations of the written word are normally taken for granted in the daily mêlée of organizational life. To the student of organizations they are, however, small, but significant clues to the texture and health of the leadership process.

Physical Settings

Monarchs and dictators have long symbolized their authority by grand physical props: a palace, a throne, lavish furniture and décor, luxurious transport, expensive clothes...the physical setting speaks for itself. The corporate manager has followed suit. Sometimes the whole building does the job, becoming more luxurious as one moves up the floors. One company chose to construct its headquarters to resemble a vast set of steps, like a stairway. No visitor, or employee, could fail to know who was more important than whom. Divisions of corporate status have long been marked by what and where people eat – from works canteen to plush dining room. The very occupancy of a four-walled office amidst an open-plan layout can immediately mark out who is a leader. Gradations amongst those leaders are shown by the degree of opacity of the glass walls: the higher the manager, the more privacy they get.

All offices say something about their occupants; some ooze authority and **authoritarianism**: the huge desk, the thick carpet, the original paintings, the dark wood panelling, the carefully placed fresh flowers, and the throne-like chair behind the desk where the manager sits. Contrast the room which has light, bright colours, easy chairs and a coffee table in the centre; the desk is tucked away in a corner – all suggestive of someone who is comfortable with a relaxed, consultative style of management.

The acquisition of material symbols of power and status can turn into something of an obsession. The square-metreage of the room, the cubic capacity of the company car, personalized car-parking space, access to privileged dining areas, first-class air travel, are just a few of the outward signs of having 'arrived'. They are often jealously guarded by their owners, while envied by those without them. Likewise, they are carefully dispensed by the organization. A middle-grade civil servant arrived at his new office one morning to find a workman carefully snipping 25 centimetres off the perimeter of the fitted carpet. 'Sorry about this. This room was an assistant secretary's', explained the workman. 'Five grades higher than you. You're not allowed a full-size carpet.' The carpet, of course, not only speaks of the assistant secretary's status, but also of those who fall into order above and below her. We have a professorial colleague who was keen to remove the large executive desk from his office in order to create a more informal feel to the room. He asked his secretary to arrange this. The weeks turned into months, but nothing happened. His secretary offered all manner of administrative excuses, until, one day, the true reason dawned on him. She was very proud of his senior **role** in the department, especially because it offered her reflected glory and a certain authority. The 'important' desk symbolized this. To remove it meant diminishing her role – as well as that of her boss.

MESSAGES FOR SHOW, AND MESSAGES YOU BELIEVE

The symbols of leadership have to be carefully managed to convey the meanings they intend. A slip, an over-usage or a misusage can render them invalid. For example, we know of one company director who ends memos to his staff with the statement: 'If you have any problems or queries about this, do not hesitate to contact me.' At first this sentiment was well received; an indication of a person who would listen. After a time, though, it was presented ritualistically on all correspondence, on virtually every issue. It lost its impact. Some began to see it as a cover for the director's lack of consultation with them in the first place. This reaction runs close to the 'I've heard it all before' one. The leader makes a bold speech, full of fine sentiments and imagery – but fails to stir hearts and minds. The imagery fails to connect – because the previous fine speeches were seen to have come to nothing. 'It's all words', mumble people as they leave the conference room.

Those much-prized physical symbols of power can also backfire. How, for example, can the director whose office is full of fine objects and whose expensive car sits in the courtyard, preach on the virtues of austerity and economy to the workforce?

Perhaps the most powerful image a leader can create is a vision which others can identify with and carry forward. Such 'envisioning', the offering of a major creative idea, was what Jan Carlzon, mentioned earlier, was trying to do for his airline in the late 1970s. It is also the trademark of other high-profile executives, such as Anita Roddick of the Body Shop, Richard Branson of the Virgin Corporation and Lee Iacocca of the Chrysler Corporation. Each, in their own ways, has offered a vision of the shape and style of the company they want, presented in a form which aims to tap into the desires and values of the people who work for them, or simply to catch the mood of the moment. Anita Roddick, for example, has attempted to demonstrate – by personal example, by her products, and by her whole business policy – that ecologically sound principles should govern all aspects of her enterprise. Contrast a television interview with a senior director of ICI who, when challenged about his company's publicly declared 'green' credentials, stumbled when asked for his target for waste reduction. After an embarrassing silence he stated a generous-sounding figure – which later turned out to be untrue: no specific target existed. And contrast the Jan Carlzon of the 1990s who spoke of an ailing airline business and a demoralized workforce. He has talked of the difficulties in maintaining the 'big idea' – and in finding a new one.

Clearly, leadership credibility means that grand words have to be matched by grand deeds – and both can decay in plausibility and attractiveness as time goes by. Some leaders will catch the different moods of the time and create new images accordingly. Others will fail to read the signs of the times.

- Leaders now have to rely less on hierarchical power; there are other ways to manage people.
- Leadership involves managing with symbols and managing 'meanings': the skilful use of language, images, writings, physical settings and rituals.
- Leadership is an interactive process – followers have to grant leaders the right to lead.
- A vacuum in leadership soon gets filled.
- You do not have to be a designated leader in order to lead.
- There is more than one way to judge the effectiveness of a leader's efforts.
- What followers attribute to leaders is crucial – and fickle: today's hero can be tomorrow's fool.

THESAURUS ENTRIES

authoritarianism	matrix structure
authority	meaning
change	metaphors
communication	personality
conflict	power
control	problems
culture	psychological contract
emotion	reality
empowerment	rhetoric
ethics	role
group	status
hierarchy	structure
leadership	symbolism
management	

READING ON

Leadership, and to a lesser extent followership, has captivated organizational researchers for decades, symbolizing the importance placed on the role of the leader in many societies. Burns's (1978) classic study explores the 'transactions' between leader and follower – a two-way influence process – but distinguishes this from leadership which focuses on major 'transformations' in organizations. He argues that transactional and transformational leadership essentially require different leader characteristics. Some writers (Bennis, 1989; Zaleznik, 1977) regard leaders as separate from managers, the former doing 'right things' and the latter 'doing things right'.

The psychodynamics of leadership – such as the way subordinates use leaders as parental figures and become dependent upon them, as well as disappointed with them – feature in the writings of Bion (1961), Hirschhorn (1988) and Kets de Vries (1990). The charisma of some leaders is an intriguing issue: is it to do with the leaders themselves, their followers, or both (see Bryman, 1992)? Bryman (1986) also provides a good overview of leadership theories which have tried to predict leadership *effectiveness* from the characteristics of the leader's style – such as democratic or authoritarian. Contingency theories (e.g. Fiedler, 1967; Fineman and Mangham, 1978) regard this formulation as too simplistic; the leadership situation must be taken into account, such as how structured the task is, how well the leader is liked, and the relative power balance between leader and subordinates.

11

Judging others

We were there to meet Justin for the first time, our newly recruited technical manager and my new boss. He sauntered casually into the room. Tall, young, immaculate suit, gold bracelet on his wrist, clutching a mobile phone. He hardly looked at us before launching into a prepared speech in a really posh accent. 'Oh yeah', I thought, 'he's one of them. Dead keen, university type, a bit cocky and already has more money than sense.'

Snap judgements like this are part and parcel of organizational life. They can matter a lot or a little, depending upon how we feel about them and what we do with them. Such judgements may not be shared by others, but when they are we often feel more comfortable and reassured. Sometimes we change our judgements over time when we get to know the Justins of the world better. But we can also cling to our initial impressions, as if we *need* them to be right. What exactly is going on here? And what are the implications for organizing?

FRAGMENTS AND CUES

The event with Justin merits closer examination. The observer selectively picked out features of his dress, build, voice and possessions in ways that reflect what the observer felt was important or noteworthy. These are comments, or judgements, in themselves, but as perceptual fragments they can be augmented by our beliefs, attitudes and prejudices – such as about 'sauntering' people, those who have posh accents, or who wear gold bracelets. We are more comfortable if we can make a whole out of incoherent elements, what psychologists have termed the *gestalt effect* in perception. To do this we call on our **implicit personality theories**: what personal characteristics we believe go with what kind of person.

But filling in the gaps is not a dispassionate process. We are **motivated** to do it in a particular way. Our **perceptions** are coloured by our desires. We often see, hear and feel what we want to see, hear and feel. We give people characteristics we want them to have. Love is blind, goes the old saying, but so are hate, anger or jealousy. Justin, as a new boss, is clearly viewed with some disdain (a 'university type', 'cocky'), perhaps reflecting his subordinate's envy, or anxiety in the face of someone who will have some control over his work life.

The complexity of our perceptions, what we believe to be real, lies at the heart of judgements in organizations. Their accuracy is less of an issue because there is no absolute standard of objectivity in the social world, but there are areas of more or less agreement. There are classic everyday examples of this: arguments between friends on how good or awful the film was last night; differences of opinion on who was at fault in a traffic accident or near miss; squabbles between parents and their teenage children on exactly what their agreement was about staying out late. In organizations we can see highly experienced managers failing to agree on who is the best candidate from a shortlist of people they have just inter- viewed; an employee who judges himself as skilful and competent in conflict situations, while the boss comes to the opposite conclu- sion; an employee who accuses a manager of bullying when the manager says he was simply giving clear instructions.

In all these examples what were apparently the same event, circumstances or facts produced different judgements. Part of the explanation for this lies in the way we select cues that suit our purposes – sometimes consciously, sometimes unconsciously. For instance, if achieving good marks and ratings is extremely important to you, then you readily notice announcements in this area. On the other hand, *perceptual defence* can screen out cues that are disturbing or threatening, so if you are anxious about your poor level of perfor- mance you can block out, or not hear, critical or uncomfortable news. There are also **political** reasons behind many judgements. We might stick to a particular version of events because it helps us gain power or prestige, or helps us to avoid being censured.

Yet lingering behind many social judgements in organizations, sometimes with dramatic consequences, are two enduring features of perception – **stereotyping** and **prejudice**.

STEREOTYPING

'If students weren't so concerned about experimenting with sex and recreational drugs, then higher education might get us somewhere.'

'Accountants? Just about the most boring people you can imagine.'

'The British are OK I suppose, but none of them really want to work hard.'

'Environmentalists love talking about trees, bunnies and bull-frogs, but none of them have a clue about the real world of industry.'

These are stereotypical judgements. All the people belonging to a particular group are regarded as having the same characteristics. So, as a student, accountant, Briton or environmentalist, you are pre-judged, fitted into a category which already sums you up. Stereo-types massively condense the amount of information we need to know about someone in order to make a judgement. They are prim itive, often instant, categorizations, but they are widespread and enduring. Some stereotypes have survived for many centuries, espe-cially those associated with nationality, religious or ethnic origin. People are not easily argued out of their stereotypes, a 'don't confuse me with the facts, my mind is made up' type of response.

Write down a few words to describe:
    BMW drivers
    Police officers
    Social workers
    Nurses
    Heavy drinkers
What makes these judgements stereotypes?

Certain stereotypes can be self-confirming, in that people seek out and exaggerate a quirk or peculiarity in others to validate their own stereotypical views of them. Those who are stereotyped may even fit in, or play up, to others' stereotypes of them, so that they can feel more accepted – such as a 'fat' person acting 'jolly', an 'old' person being 'forgetful', or a French person being 'romantic'. Such action, when finely timed, can also be used ironically to mock the stereotyper. Indeed, mocking stereotypes often makes successful comic humour, such as the 'little old lady' who turns out to be a tough street fighter, the small child with an enormous vocabulary, the philosophical policeman, the gambling priest or the villain with the heart of gold. Such events surprise and amuse us because they challenge some of our taken-for-granted perceptions.

Stereotyping is no doubt socially and psychologically functional. It is a way of coping with much variability in human behaviour by reducing it to small, manageable categories. It is also a way of making ourselves look and feel better or superior by assigning negative characteristics to groups we choose not to like or approve, and positive descriptions to members of our own 'tribe'. The 1998 football World Cup was a setting where stereotypical allegiances fermented, some UK supporters aggressively chanting *En-ger-land* to proclaim their superior affinity, while picking fights with other national groups to 'show them who's best'.

SHOULD WE WORRY ABOUT STEREOTYPING?

The answer to this question is, 'It all depends'. Some stereotypes are benign, others less so. To think, for example, of all students as 'brainy', all scientists as 'serious' and people who live in the countryside as 'escapist' is a different order of judgement from extreme negative stereotypes, such as expressions of hate or disgust because of a person's sexual preference, race or religious belief. Indeed, many such stereotypes are deeply rooted in people's belief systems and **cultural** ways, to the extent that individuals who hold them are convinced they know what their targets (e.g. women, gays, blacks, strangers, skinheads, the old) are 'really like'. While firm company policies, and even legislation, may discourage some overt stereotyping, the underpinning opinions and feelings are less easily touched. They have a habit of bubbling to the surface in particular social conditions – such as during difficult economic times, and in periods of high unemployment. **Scapegoats** are sought to take the blame, such as 'foreigners', 'Jews', 'gypsies'.

To stereotype is to pre-judge. Some stereotypes we term *prejudice*, pre-judgements at the root of discriminatory practices in society and in organizations. The prejudice may be directed at women, 'not good drivers', older people, 'slow learners', the disabled, 'need too much special attention', blacks, 'good at sport' and so forth. Such beliefs are rarely explored or examined in depth by those who hold them because it serves their interest not to do so. The prejudices help buttress their own views of the world. In the hands of powerful people, this can be translated into discriminatory practices at work – such as excluding some people from promotion or recruitment. Ironically, sometimes the very hallmark of prejudice is its denial, classically expressed as: 'But of course, some of my best friends are....' Social psychologist, Roger Brown, points out the curiousness of such a remark:

There is a real phenomenon, a paradoxical one, behind the remark. People who are well stocked with unfavourable beliefs about group X do nevertheless make friends of individuals who are members of X. There is always in such friendships an almost unconscious trace of uneasiness on the part of the befriended one, which stems from his or her suspicion that, if they two were to fall out, the other would voice those things that are part of the culture. (Brown, 1986: 597–8)

In other words, some people are able to maintain and protect their particular prejudice about a social group, while making an exception for some members of that group. But that exception may not survive a severe test: the prejudice often wins out in the end.

Prejudice, while often having negative connotations, does not always have these. The **attitudes** – beliefs, feelings and behaviours – that prejudice embraces can be positive. We may hold favourable prejudices towards beautiful women, towards children, film stars, tall men, people who do charitable work. We may personally discriminate positively in their favour – we like them more, seek them out, give them more attention. Some organizations may institutionalize such prejudices – for example by offering more posts to attractive women or to privately educated job applicants. They may favour those who have education from a particular university, or who are family members of existing employees. Should we be concerned about this? Is this better or worse than negative prejudices? After all, if some groups are favoured, others, the less favoured, will be shouldering the costs.

What is judged as desirable or undesirable prejudice depends on the social time and place. Whereas prejudicial remarks towards women, different racial groups, the elderly and homosexuals were once tolerated, even encouraged, it is now far less so in many Western organizations. Social attitudes change because of a number of processes – the greater visibility, power and voice of discriminated groups; a better understanding of the perspectives and feelings of the victims of prejudice; vigorous moral debate in the media; laws against discrimination. Where prejudice creates tension and division in the workplace, it can be in management's interest to reduce it, if for no other reason than to maintain organizational efficiency and effectiveness. As organizations become more multicultural and multi-gender, there is some evidence supporting the 'contact hypothesis': that the more people mix with those they stereotype, the less likely they are to cling to their stereotypes.

However, social attitudes are not homogeneous. Prejudices seem to thrive in some organizational settings, while in others they are far less apparent. The social **norms, sub-culture, values** and traditions provide more or less oxygen for prejudices to survive. Moreover, the attitudes which form prejudices can be complex – some people will think and feel prejudice, but suppress it in their behaviour. Others will try and segment their prejudices; this is epitomized in a recent statement by a British politician: 'I have nothing against gays, but we can't have a gay minister, the country's not ready for it.'

Many organizations now claim equal opportunity, anti-discriminatory policies. Some such claims do not survive close scrutiny and are worth little more than the paper they are written on. Others are more substantial. For example, the British do-it-yourself company, B&Q, actively promotes a policy of recruitment which claims not to exclude older job applicants, or people beyond retirement age. Typically, such people find it hard to find employment. Encouraged by legislation, some firms have specifically allocated jobs to the disabled. But, as organizations representing the disabled point out, this often results in minimal compliance. An additional complication is that the best of intentions towards the disabled can become entangled in other layers of discrimination and prejudice within an organization. This point was made forcefully by one of our students, recounting her experiences working in a vehicle manufacturing company:

> The atmosphere in the company was very aggressive, very confrontational. It is a them-and-us type attitude. There is a fine line between workers and management. On the surface it is often quite polite and very jovial. Underneath there are many class undercurrents and prejudices which make it all the more menacing.
>
> The foreman of the stores, a part of the factory where supplies are kept, required two more workers for his stores. He wanted two able-bodied men to be transferred from the main factory. Management, however, did not really want anyone to go to the stores, and if they did, would only allow so-called 'restricted' workers, i.e. those with physical disabilities.
>
> The problem had been going on for a long time. Management had kept delaying a decision and the union and stores foremen were getting very frustrated. When I arrived, it was the perfect opportunity for management to find a scapegoat, someone to take the heat. I was given the task of finding two suitable workers for the stores. Not an easy job! On one side, I had management who did not want able-bodied men going, and on the other I had the union who only wanted able-bodied men.
>
> Things were reaching boiling point. One morning I was sitting in my office and there was a knock on the door. In walked four very angry-looking shop stewards, shutting the door behind them. I was trapped in a small office looking up at these four men who were intent on catching their prey. Gone was the politeness, gone was the jovial manner. In its place was a scheming, cunning, aggressive, menacing even, attitude. Behind closed doors the real company emerges.

The conversation consisted of them asking me questions, me trying to answer, and them twisting my answer. They would take it in turns to ask questions and would alternate quickly, trying to confuse me.

I managed to defend myself and didn't say what they wanted me to. After a few more minutes I had had enough and just made an excuse about a meeting. I asked them to leave. They did not leave in a jovial manner; the old façade was not quite back in place. I had frustrated their attempts to ensnare me in their web of words, and in so doing I had passed my first initiation test to life at the company. Not a pretty picture.... Trust seems to be the key. The shop stewards did not trust my motives or my actions. Being the naïve student that I was, I had actually been trying to please everyone – and not just the management. But the shop stewards could not see this. My first lesson, therefore, was: try as you may, you cannot please everyone and, so, please those who pay your salary or write your appraisal. The hard truth is that they are the only people who count.

Here we see disabled workers, euphemistically labelled 'restricted', or 'not able-bodied', the innocent pawns of the partisan interests of management and workers, separated, it seems, by a history of social difference and mutual suspicion. This difference was absorbed and then reproduced by the student, struggling to find her way in a tough job. In the end she takes on the 'they are not to be trusted' mantle, stereotyping the shop stewards, just as they stereotype her.

The stereotyping here conveniently draws lines of division which help position and legitimize people's feelings about each other, and **role** behaviours. The everyday surface joviality hides deep differences that surface when an issue of contention emerges: old ideological positions ('management', 'workers') and mistrusts are expressed. To the student, the shop stewards were 'scheming and cunning'. To the shop stewards, the student was there as a representative of management who, like other managers, was intent on frustrating their good intentions. An ironic twist in this tale is that, as traditional guardians of employee welfare and interests, the shop stewards were less prepared than management to grant their disabled colleagues access to certain jobs that they, supposedly, could do. Their prejudice towards management appeared stronger than their support for disabled colleagues.

LABELS MATTER

Do the labels and words we use to frame our judgements matter? If we changed the **language** and categories we use would stereotypes and prejudice melt away?

Those who espouse political correctness, saying things in ways which do not offend people by certain current social values, would argue that the language we use is distinctive in putting people into degrading, if not insulting, categories. So a first step in tackling prejudice is to redefine the labels we use. 'Physically challenged' or 'restricted' can replace disabled or crippled; 'ethnic background' can substitute race or colour. People should be described as 'large' rather than fat, and 'gay' now replaces homosexual. Even the two categories, 'men' and 'women' can, according to some observers, drive a wedge between the genders. The writer, Deborah Tannen, illustrates:

> A female executive at a large accounting firm was so well thought of by her firm that they sent her to a week long executive-training seminar.... Not surprisingly considering the small number of women at her level, she was the only woman at the seminar.... This did not surprise or faze her, since she was used to being the only woman among men.
>
> All went well for the first three days of the seminar. But on the fourth, the leaders turned their attention to issues of gender. Suddenly, everyone who had been looking at her as 'one of us' began to look at her differently – as a woman, 'one of them'. She was repeatedly singled out and asked to relate her experiences and impressions, something she did not feel she could do honestly, since she had no reason to believe they would understand or accept what she was talking about. When they said confidently they were sure that there was no discrimination against women in their company, that if women did not get promoted it was simply because they didn't merit promotion, she did not feel she could object. (Tannen, 1995: 129)

In this tale, being defined as different – as a woman – by a male majority ended up stifling the apparently laudable intentions of the latter part of the course. The very focus by men on the one 'woman' created an uncomfortable difference for her, placing her in a category that, hitherto, she had not felt in the meeting, a category she was asked to defend or explain – to men. Some labels make us very self-conscious, inhibit communication and create barriers; others can invite stereotypical responses in accord with label: 'Well, women think...'; 'I guess students are typically...'. So at one level the very use of a label creates a difference and distinction that may not have existed before, but how much that matters depends on the **meaning** of that label to those who use it, and to those to whom it is applied.

There may be some absurdities in politically correct approaches to labelling, yet the serious point, and one made by **discourse** theorists, is that stereotypes and prejudice are direct reflections of the form of language we use. Language, rather than being a transmitter of opinions, actually constitutes those opinions. The discourse we use – its signs, labels, grammar and expressions – is the very substance of our thinking and attitudes. Thus, if we take for granted that the male pronoun is to stand for all human beings, then male automatically gets privileged over female. It is a delicate issue understanding how the use of language can create categories which are, or are not, experienced as prejudicial. For example, as a mark of non-discrimination within an organization, management may studiously avoid direct reference to its black and Chinese staff in those terms. Yet this can sometimes backfire; it is seen by blacks and Chinese as an attempt to deny important features of their identity, to pretend their ethnicity and colour are not important.

JUDGING *WITH* OTHERS

It was a con. The salesman who had just given us his presentation was far too smooth for my liking, and too expensive. We definitely must avoid him. My boss, Alan, in the chair, asked for our opinions, round the table. 'Well, I was really impressed with that guy', he said, referring to the now absent salesman. 'I think we should go with it. What do you all think?' I thought to myself, 'I don't believe it – no way.' Then, George says he agrees with Alan! Eleanor chips in with a few reservations, but says she thinks we should take a chance. Oh dear. By the time Eric, Dave and Helen had their say I realized that I was alone. Amazingly, I then found myself saying we should chase up the offer and go with it. Why on earth did I say that? Maybe they were right after all?

Why on earth, indeed. The desire to **conform** can sometimes be overwhelming. Or, to put it another way, the psychological costs of being a nonconformist – feeling different from a colleague-group, embarrassed, having to defend your minority judgement, standing out from the crowd – can be too much to bear. In group situations such as this, the censure by others if we do not fall into line can generate huge pressure to conform, while also raising questions in ourselves about the soundness of our own judgements.

The power of the **group** over the individual has been demonstrated in classic psychological experiments, where people would literally deny the evidence of their senses. One of these was conducted by Solomon Asch in 1951. He simultaneously showed two large cards to six people sitting around a table. One card had a single vertical line on it, the other had three vertical lines of different length. He then asked each person, in turn, to declare which of three lines on a second card matched the first one. It was a very easy and obvious task. But the experiment was rigged such that five members of the group were pre-briefed to lie about which one was correct. The sixth member, the subject, did not know this.

Over a series of trials, with different subjects, three-quarters of the subjects went along with the majority view – often with visible anguish and incredulity. Asch also observed that subjects conformed even more readily when the group contained people of higher status than themselves. But, significantly, it needed only one ally in the group for the effect to be reduced, so we gain strength and confidence in the presence of a like-minded person. It is, perhaps, a sobering thought that if an extremely simple judgement like comparing lines can be so readily affected, what of the complex decisions and judgements that take place in work teams and on committees?

There are other things that happen to judgements when made with others. Feeling part of a secure and cohesive group can often lead us to make more extreme judgements than we would normally make – more extremely cautious or more extremely risky, depending on the kind of people in the group. This group polarization effect results, it is believed, from a cumulative roll-on effect as more people become more persuaded by new information for or against a position. Sometimes this can result in groupthink – where a group becomes so convinced of its superior judgement and strong identity that it shuts out any criticism or dissent – from within or from outsiders (see also Chapter 4, 'Dealing and Double-Dealing').

Perhaps the most dramatic form of groupthink is crowd behaviour. Some writers speak of the 'mind', as well as the mindlessness, of some crowds – such as at civil protests or football matches – when people get emotionally carried away to do things which, on their own, they would not even contemplate. Their usual criteria of judgement become suspended, or radically re-defined, in the excitement, contagion and flow of the crowd. Some crowds turn into mobs, creating their own moral order, licensing violence or victimization. This is partly due to anonymity – people feel less personally responsible and less visible in a crowd. Notorious white lynch mobs in 1950s and 1960s America were like this, yet contained some people who showed little obvious violence in the rest of their lives.

STICKING TO YOUR OWN JUDGEMENT?

The desire to conform, to be one of the crowd, can, as we have suggested, be very strong. We can additionally observe that some national, as well as organizational, cultures are built upon expectations of consensus; appearing to conform is an important expectation. But what of the person who resists such pressure? The individual in the meeting who proudly proclaims his or her difference of opinion and holds to it, regardless? The person who insists on wearing casual clothes in formal-dress meetings, or who always arrives later than everyone else, or who pushes to re-define the agendas of meetings?

These are all expressions of nonconformity: sticking to your own beliefs and judgements. But there are differences in nuance. Some nonconformist behaviour comes from an independence of personality, the person who 'does his or her thing' within a group. Often, these are people who have a clear image of their self-identity, a conspicuous absence of inferiority feelings; they can also be somewhat rigid. Nonconformists typically resist pressures to 'go with the crowd' for the sake of uniformity, or for the approval of others.

There are others who are anti-conformists, people who tend to be opposed to the majority, 'normal' response on all occasions. Anti-conformists in work teams can be a source of difficulty, even stress, to other team members. While teams do vary in the variety of views they permit, they can often respond by marginalizing, stereotyping, even ridiculing the extreme anti-conformist ('oh, here she goes again'; 'as predictable as ever'). Some anti-conformists take their stance from other, minority, community standards with which they identify – such as 'going back to nature', pacifism, or ultra-conservatism. But anti-conformists (and nonconformists) are not always bad news for the group. Some are tolerated, even celebrated, akin to the medieval court jester. The jester in the group has idiosyncratic views, 'sideways' judgements, on what he or she sees as important. They challenge taken-for-granted beliefs and uncontested agreements in provocative ways, but in a manner that is tolerated, if not enjoyed. Importantly, the jester is prepared to be laughed at as well as laughed with – and still continue the act.

This chapter has drawn attention to the importance of how we make judgements of one another in organizations. Judgement processes are often central to the tone, decision making and morality of organizational life, so we need to be aware of how we perceive the world and categorize others. In some organizations social divisions foment, encouraged by negative stereotyping and prejudice. In other organizations, deliberate attempts are made to soften such differences and encourage a more egalitarian culture. **Rules** alone are rarely sufficient. Education and training for understanding and tolerance are required, as well as leading by example.

The subtle effects of groups on individuals requires additional understanding and skill. Groups and teams often need care and management if they are to be satisfying and effective. At worst, the group can stifle the best of individual judgements as it presses for conformity. And well-meaning attempts not to exclude anyone's views can result in mediocre, even absurd decisions, as reflected in the adage, 'A camel is a horse that was designed by a committee'. Being aware of how such influences operate, allowing for all views but still judging and shaping their overall quality, addressing the use of language and stereotypes, are all part of the challenge of organizing.

- Judgements of others are often partial and instant.
- We select cues that fit with our motives, needs and prejudices.
- Stereotyping is pervasive and inevitable in many judgements.
- The acceptability, or otherwise, of stereotypes reflects the social times.
- Prejudice may be positive or negative in intent, and lies at the heart of discriminatory practices in organizations.
- Labels matter – they capture the slant, or discrimination, in the way we categorize others.
- Judgements in groups are subject to conformity and polarization effects.
- There are nonconformists and anti-conformists who are able to maintain their own judgements, regardless of group pressure.

THESAURUS ENTRIES

attitude	perception
conformity	politics
culture	prejudice
discourse	role
group	rules
implicit personality theory	scapegoating
language	stereotyping
meaning	sub-culture
motivation	values
norm	

READING ON

There are classic experiments on conformity by Asch (1951) and Sherif (1936) which are still well worth reading at source. For a recent summary, see Buchanan and Huczynski (1997). Other noteworthy landmarks on the effects of groups on judgements are Janis's 1972 book *Victims of Groupthink* and Keisler and Keisler's *Conformity* (1969).

Discussions on stereotyping, prejudice and discrimination at work cross a number of literatures, ranging from social psychology to social policy. Helpful accounts may be found in Tajfel (1981) on how we socially categorize and Dovidio and Gaertner (1986) on prejudice and racism. For more basic discussions on the nature of the way we perceive, consult Jones (1990) and Luthans (1992).

Judgements are hard to separate from attitudes, on which there is considerable literature. Accounts of extreme, rigid attitudes can be found in the seminal work of Adorno et al. (1950). A traditional view on the different components of attitudes, and how they may be more or less in tune with one another, is described by Ajzen and Fishbein (1980) and by Festinger (1957). Festinger's classic work on 'cognitive dissonance' attempts to explain how attitudes may change; this is also well explored by McGuire (1985).

12

Feelings

Feelings can be a nuisance. We get fed up at work, angry, stressed, bored. We can feel malicious, vengeful, embarrassed, fearful or hurt, especially if we are judged negatively. We can feel torn between the demands of our career and family. These sorts of feelings can gnaw away inside us – before, during and after work. They can be exhausting. Other feelings hit us rather differently, more positively. There is the happiness, joy, love, excitement, pride or elation – the up-side of working life when things are going well, such as when we are praised or complimented (see also Chapter 19, 'Working and Living').

Sometimes people seem to want to talk candidly about their feelings – perhaps quietly in corridors, coffee rooms, pubs and dinner parties. In other settings, however, talking about feelings takes the form of an oft-repeated, but hollow, ritual:

> Alice's boss strides purposefully up to her desk:
> 'Morning Alice, how are you today?'
>   Alice replies quickly, with a broad, confident smile:
> 'Oh, I'm fine thanks John. It's a great day isn't it?'

What John did not know (and did not want to know) was that Alice did not feel at all fine. He would have been more than confused if Alice had said what was really on her mind, which would have been this:

> 'Well John, I had a terrible time last night with my boyfriend. I think we're going to break up. I feel shattered. I feel really pissed off working here too, especially the way you treat me John; how you seem to take me for granted.'

The exchange of pleasantries is just that. They are designed to mask, not reveal, our inner feelings; to create certain **impressions**. Why should this be the case? What happens to our feelings when we become 'organized'?

'BE COOL!'

Exhortations to be calm, to think things through, not to get upset, run deep in the education and training of most of us. They are strong social **values**. We may harbour strong feelings – fears, passions – but they are to be kept under **control**, and carefully managed. Here we may draw an important distinction between *feelings* and *emotions*. Feelings are essentially private, 'internal' experiences, which often have both psychological and physical manifestations – such as the stomach churning and sense of apprehension before an examination. They provide an essential, personal, read-out on how we are doing, how we are relating to the world as we deal with it. We may have feelings about feelings – such as being angry that we feel upset, or anxious that we feel attracted to someone. Emotions are the outward presentation of our feelings through learned social codes. We may, for example, express our feelings of anger in very restrained or 'acceptable' ways during a meeting at work, more openly at home, or not at all in the presence of an authority figure, such as a police officer. Our emotions may be entirely faked, such as appearing relaxed at a party because that is the thing to do.

The different ways of disguising and shaping feelings are essential features of human **socialization**. They mark out contrasting national cultures and contribute to mutual understanding and social control within those settings. Travellers switching cultures – such as from emotionally 'closed' Northern Europe to more open Latin or African countries – are often well aware of these differences and the problems they pose for their own communication. Does the smile and nod mean pleasure, acceptance or just recognition? Is the 'angry' face serious or playful? Is the touching a sign of intimacy and sexual attraction or a more routine acknowledgement? Organizations are microcosms of such processes; they contain their own emotion rules and codes. Some, such as theatre groups and social clubs, have more open emotional climates than others. It is easier to show what you feel; indeed, it is expected – but only within the range of codes appropriate to the sub-culture. Others, such as the military and civil service, pride themselves on their stricter control over feelings. There is a narrower band of feelings which are legitimate to express. The emotion codes are firmly set within the formal hierarchical culture and its different operational settings – when, for instance, it is appropriate for a soldier to display fear, grief, anger or pride.

One's position and gender can also make a difference. For example, top managers often have to demonstrate they are clear, decisive thinkers, not simply victims of their feelings. Female leaders who show 'decisive' characteristics win a certain ironic praise – such as the 'iron lady' descriptions of Prime Minister Margaret Thatcher in the 1980s. While women may be permitted to be rather more emotionally expressive than men, they are to contain their 'unreliable' feelings in public in the interests of logic, **rationality** and decorum. If they do not they risk confirming the negative **stereotype** that people, especially men, hold of them (see Chapter 13, 'Sex'). This becomes crucial in public events, like conferences, or major speeches. Important politicians and organizational leaders often plan carefully their presented image, sometimes down to minute details – gestures, tone of voice, dress, words. It can make all the difference to the way they are **perceived,** such as emotionally sensitive or firm, and to the kind of emotions mobilized within the audience.

The social veneer we place on our feelings is most evident when we are permitted a backstage glimpse at the private worlds of our heroes and heroines. They are rarely the cool, clear-thinking souls they seem. They have rows with their partners, they have mental breakdowns, they have depressions, they have fears and jealousies, they have anxieties about their jobs. They are, after all, real people. The most publicly respectable of 'rational' scientists can be ruthlessly competitive, vain and anxious, to the extent that they may resort to faking results to win attention and praise. The media's preoccupation with stripping away public masks of famous people is seductive, and can make compulsive reading or viewing. Why? Maybe it says something about our own emotional lives. Even the great and glorious can be confused and mixed up, like we sometimes feel ourselves. We can safely peer at their distress, and in doing so acknowledge some of our own messy feelings.

Inside most work organizations, though, the controlled act – in one form or another – must go on. The essence of organization, as laid down in the traditional texts and much current practice, is the creation of **structures** and lines of command to ensure that A leads to B leads to C leads to D. Material and effort go in one end, and a product comes out the other end. In the strictest **bureaucracies** there is little room for doubt, anxiety or passion. Reliability and predictability are all-important, the mark of good machines and good workers alike. Feelings get in the way of reliability and predictability, so keep them to yourself (see Chapter 9, 'Machines and Mechanizing'). Alice knows that her work role would be untenable if she told her boss what she really thought about him. Similarly, John cannot afford to care too much about Alice's (or anyone else's) doubts and worries. If he did he would be unable to function effectively – or so he believes.

There are organizational procedures and terms which help people to manage their feelings: crisp job descriptions which lay out the demands of the job; rules, objectives and targets to keep us on track; and then the statistics – on profits, growth, sales, share values, waste – to tell us how well we have done. After a while the whole activity can take on a momentum of its own, to the extent that feelings become blurred, or largely forgotten, in getting through the day. We may fumble when trying to express them. At the extreme we become emotionally illiterate: 'I don't really know what I feel about my job; I just do it', is a phrase one hears from people who have worked at the same activities for years on end. At first glance some jobs, such as firing people, could not look more emotional. But a senior personnel officer from a large car manufacturer put it to us thus:

> I have had to handle literally hundreds of layoffs personally. To tell people face to face that their livelihood is going to end. At first it used to tear me apart. Now it's just part of my job. I've seen all the reactions; I know exactly what I've got to say. I know their rights and our rights. Of course I try to be sympathetic and helpful, but in the end it's something that just has to be done.

THINK, DON'T FEEL

There has been a long tradition of separating feeling from thinking, or *affect* from *cognition*. The processes that distinguish us as problem-solving, intelligent beings (cognitive) have been distinguished from the supposedly more primitive and uncontrollable forces of feeling and emotion. Both philosophers and psychologists have been intrigued by our reasoning abilities. Measuring them, such as through intelligence testing, has found its way into many walks of life – educational assessment, personnel selection, training. Feelings are often regarded as an interference with good thinking and wise judgement – the 'higher' faculties.

Recently, however, this view has been turned on its head. Feelings do not interrupt or side-track decision processes, they *make* them. Indeed, without feelings we cannot make choices or decide on what is right or wrong. Cognitive processes and feelings are inextricably entwined, and this can be demonstrated in careful studies of human behaviour and clinical studies on the workings of the brain. From this the notion of **emotional intelligence** has been coined. Rather than strip away feelings from organizational processes and **rational**

action, we should be cultivating emotionally intelligent action. This means special help and training to enable us to see and express feelings in ourselves and in others. Dealing with **decisions**, **problems** and organizational relationships quite properly involves 'gut feelings', hunches and anxieties, and these are key in shaping where we go and what we do. Rational decision-aids, such as step-by-step guides or statistical modelling techniques, cannot *make* decisions. *We* do this, guided by our feelings.

PUTTING FEELINGS TO WORK

In the late 1950s managers began to acknowledge that trying to engineer jobs so that people could do them completely automatically, without thinking, was not altogether appropriate. Simplifying, routinizing, mechanizing and supervising work certainly rationalized production; but it also left people with boring, monotonous, meaningless tasks. For some employees it did not seem to matter, as long as they had money to spend as a result of their efforts. Others, though, became dissatisfied and depressed, and showed it by staying away from work, demanding ever higher financial compensation and fighting the management. That state of affairs spawned much social science research aimed at seeking ways of enhancing job satisfaction – from playing music while you work, to splitting assembly lines into 'autonomous working groups'. Jobs became 'enlarged' and 'enriched'. Volvo, for example, broke with the traditions of mass car production, permitting their assemblers to work in teams around separate workstations. Together team members could decide how much they would produce and in what way. **Participation** was seen to be key to increasing worker satisfaction. And it did for some workers – for a time. For others it did not.

While jobs can be enriched in the manner described, this rarely touches the essential meaninglessness of the task; it just rearranges the pieces. Other than in special cultural conditions, such as in Japan, it is unusual to find mass-production workers strongly identifying with the product. Overall design, control and supervision still, typically, rest with management. What employee participation provides, however, is an opportunity for workers to come out of their social isolation (standing at a workstation on a long production line) and enjoy the emotional release of chat with colleagues.

There are **ethical** and psychological issues to face when we manipulate working conditions in order to raise employee satisfaction. Ethically, it is open to accusations of deception if the prime managerial interest is increasing profit and production and this is not declared. Psychologically, there are questions about what **job satisfaction** is. Satisfaction is a complex phenomenon which cannot simply be produced, or induced, at the turn of a managerial key. For a start, most of us experience a range of different feelings as we work; satisfaction may or may not be an appropriate description for what we feel. More crucially, though, our satisfactions are likely to be ephemeral, and fluctuate in quality and degree as the day passes. So your high satisfaction at 11.15 a.m. (you have met a deadline) may drop to mild dissatisfaction at 12.20 p.m. (you cannot contact a key customer), to deep dissatisfaction at 4 p.m. (your report has been rejected by your boss). Satisfaction is deeply embedded in the subtleties of our relationship to our work and organization, distinctly coloured by our personal needs, background and non-work life. Attempts to manage it by simple structural means are likely to be unsatisfactory – in part, or in total.

SELLING EMOTIONS

> First we practise a friendly smile at all times with our guests and among ourselves. Second, we use friendly courteous phrases. 'May I help you?' 'Thank you....' 'Have a nice day....' 'Enjoy the rest of your stay', and many others are all part of our working vocabulary.

That is what Walt Disney World demands of all its employees. Similarly, McDonald's 'Hamburger University' tells its managers to ensure that 'all American traits' are displayed by its counter staff – 'sincerity', 'enthusiasm', 'confidence' and 'a sense of humour'.

Here we witness an extreme form of commercialization of emotional display. You have to express the right emotions in order to survive in the job – it is 'emotional labour'. The **rules** about what to express, and how to express it, have been decided in advance by executives in a boardroom, and you have to **learn** them by heart. Effective restaurant waiters and salespeople have long had an intuitive appreciation of the importance of displaying the right 'interest', 'concern', 'understanding' and 'warmth' if they are going to clinch a sale or get a good tip. What has changed, however, is the extent of corporate control over what an employee should or should not feel.

The point comes over strongly in a study by American sociologist, Arlie Hochschild (1983). She studied what happened to flight attendants in a major American international airline. The flight attendants are pushed very hard by their company to practise an 'inside-out' smile. They need to believe the act, and take it inside themselves. In this way they should really feel OK about the crowded, hectic life in the cabin of the aircraft, and they really should not mind whatever a passenger throws at them – literally and metaphorically. Flight attendants are taught to perfect their emotional performance, which is kept up to par by regular refresher courses. In this way, as superheroes and heroines of the aircraft, they receive and re-process adversity and abuse with a smile and a kind word. For the airline, it makes commercial sense. If customers feel good about the nice-looking people who serve them, they will (it is believed) be more likely to use the airline again. The flight attendants' emotional performance is thereby linked with the company's profits.

The required emotional performance can be achieved more subtly than via smiling lessons. It can be part of a deeper cultural change in the whole organization where top management offer a vision of the emotional atmosphere they wish to create (see Chapter 10, 'Leading and Following'). In the 1980s a major British airline attempted just such a programme, with some success. However, this did not prevent private feelings bubbling to the surface when the reality of sustaining the emotional performance took hold. A senior flight attendant, with 19 years' flying experience in the airline, explains:

> You try saying 'Hello' to 300 people and sound as though you mean it towards the end. Most of us make a game of it. Someone – probably a manager – said, 'This business is all about interpersonal transactions.' He was wrong. It's all about bullshit. If life is a cabaret, this is a bloody circus. (Hopfl, 1991)

Her colleague, equally cynical, describes her economy class passengers as 'an amorphous mass of inconsequence'. Over time, and under pressure, the constant strain to keep up the emotional front leads to an ever widening gap between inner feelings and outward display. Sometimes, the mask slips:

> A young businessman said to a flight attendant, 'Why aren't you smiling?' She put her tray back on the food cart and said, 'I'll tell you what. You smile first, then I'll smile.' The businessman smiled at her. 'Good', she replied. 'Now freeze and hold that for fifteen hours.' (Hochschild, 1983)

Getting by in such work means keeping up the act, but not taking it too seriously.

EVERYDAY EMOTIONAL CONTROL

Organizations which are out of the direct eye of the consuming public are less concerned with these very obvious forms of emotional control. Control still exists (as Alice and John show, at the start of this chapter), but the processes are more subtle and implicit. We learn the social rules of appropriate emotional display by trial and error, revealing too much or too little, in the various settings and circumstances of organizational life. We learn where humour, seriousness, anger, despair, joy and so forth can and cannot be expressed, and the verbal and non-verbal displays that are acceptable. The settings are particularly important. What is right for the coffee room does not necessarily work in the committee meeting. What can be said in your own office cannot always be said in your boss's. An unburdening of worries in a car ride with a colleague cannot necessarily be repeated elsewhere. After a time we take these things for granted, and it can come as something of a shock when we find ourselves confused as to the correct emotional response for the situation, and feelings of embarrassment begin to show. One of us was faced with just such an event:

> What do you do when a policeman takes his trousers off in front of you? I was with this police superintendent in his small, well-ordered, office – a first meeting – conducting a research interview with him. He was in full uniform. He was a very formal man, and quite proper in his style. After about an hour and a half he invited me to go to lunch with him at a local restaurant. I was pleased to accept. He said he would have to change out of his uniform, and made as if to go to another room. Instead, he stopped at a large wardrobe in the office, took out his civilian clothes, and slowly started to change in front of me, removing his trousers first of all. I was suddenly struck by the absurdity of it all. This sober, authoritarian man silently performing a fairly private act in front of a relative stranger – and in a work office. I felt embarrassed, but I did not want to show it. I stumbled for something to chat about, but I just couldn't continue the interview while he was standing there in his underpants. It felt like a sketch from Monty Python! I tried to hide my embarrassment (he wasn't the slightest bit ruffled) by getting up, talking about the weather, and then strolling as casually as I could into an adjacent room – until he had finished changing.

Fear of embarrassment is an **emotion** which, in many cultures, controls social behaviour. It is learned fairly early in life; only very young children do not get embarrassed. Looking socially competent becomes all-important in itself; gaffes or cracks in one's social poise have to be disguised with face-saving routines. Thus we see people in boardrooms, committees, coffee groups or classrooms trying to look and perform the part. To avoid the embarrassment of ridicule or censure they may sometimes over-perform, deflect attention with humour, self-justify, or simply say or do as little as possible.

OFF-STAGE

Playing our emotional parts in organizations involves knowing what not to express, as much as knowing what to express. But what happens to Alice's dislike of John, her boss? What do flight attendants do with their distaste about their false smile? What does the calm-looking waiter do with his frustration at pernickety and critical customers? How do production operators handle their long hours of boredom, or anti-management feeling at work? And how does a person handle feelings of sexual attraction to someone else at work?

As a rule, the direct, up-front expression of any of these feelings could seriously compromise a working relationship. Typically, therefore, the feelings are suppressed, kept to oneself – at least in the work setting. Some will be too sensitive to share with anyone else. Others will surface and be re-worked outside the organization – with a partner, friend, doctor or therapist. But the very need to express hidden feelings can also spur the growth of informal organizational processes which help give indirect voice to feelings. For example, stories and **jokes**: the telling and re-telling of tales about the 'utter incompetence of management', 'that dreadful speech by the Chief Executive', 'the sales department where no one answers the phone' or 'Bill, the engineering foreman, who can't fix his own car'. Stories can carry, in coded form, people's worries, disaffections, desires or ignoble thoughts, which otherwise could not be expressed. They can, symbolically, compensate for the **power** imbalances in the organization. So the secretary who feels put upon by her powerful boss vents her feelings by telling tales which demonstrate how awful and insensitive he is (see Chapter 14, 'Serious Joking').

Off-stage relief can also be seen in games (see also Chapter 3, 'Rules are Rules'). Not the conventional ones like sporting activities (although these no doubt play their part), but creating games out of the everyday tedium. Production workers may compete with one another to produce the most unusual rogue product – like a cake which is extraordinarily deformed, or a misshapen package. The organization's communication technology is ripe for fun: computers on which one can load absorbing games; telephone systems where colleagues' calls can be mischievously diverted (to the elevator, in one company we know); faxes and e-mails through which friends can be sent silly messages. While providing emotional relief, some of these games become a strong part of working **culture**. For example, one organizational researcher (Child, 1977) describes the cosy atmosphere of a patient-records office in a hospital where, for years, clerks had contributed to an office 'doughnut fund' each time a paper pellet they threw missed a target bin. This practice had to stop when the department was streamlined by management – and morale plummeted.

Sometimes games have a sharper edge, aimed punitively at the person to whom one's feelings cannot be directly expressed. For example, creating a recurring breakdown which a supervisor has to keep correcting, or deliberately arriving late for a meeting – which prevents a boss starting on time. Some **games** can be at the expense of the weaker members of a work group, especially the novice. On joining a steel company one of our students received a phone call from a major client, asking for 'special steel with a pink and green speckled surface'. The student expressed puzzlement at the request, whereupon the customer snapped angrily at him for his equivocal response. Frantically, the student called all the managers he could find to get an answer to the query. What he did not know was that the colour was absurd, and the 'client' had been put up to the hoax. The student's embarrassment was his colleagues' delight.

Some organizations have clearly demarcated settings where the public courtesies of emotional control can be relaxed. The school staff common room, the restaurant kitchen, the nurses' rest area, the works canteen, the galley on an aircraft are all no-go areas for the public. There the pupil, customer, patient, manager or passenger can be chided, cursed or reviled – with impunity. The professional mask is dropped for a while and private feelings can spill out. There is usually a willing audience. The switch from public mask to private, and back again, can occur many times in a working day. The waiter epitomizes this as he or she criss-crosses the boundary between restaurant and kitchen – calm, cool and collected at one moment; shouting for orders the next. Similarly, a police officer can show restrained politeness to an abusive motorist whom he has just caught for speeding, but then 'return' the abuse in the privacy of his patrol car – to the eager ear of a colleague.

Now and again we witness some remarkable, accidental, off-stage revelations – cracks in the mask – such as the private and confidential tape recordings of President Nixon of the USA in the 1970s. We hear his anguished words as he struggles desperately to cover his tracks on his own illegal activities. More whimsically, a television broadcast a few years ago showed another ex US president, Ronald Reagan, very jittery and roundly cursing his audience. Someone had inadvertently thrown a switch, transforming a private rehearsal into a national live broadcast. The emotional import of these events was accentuated by the 'real' public performances of the presidents – which were calm and reassuring.

CHANGING THE EMOTIONAL RULES?

Can work organizations operate with more emotional freedom? Greater emotional intelligence? Should they? Some practitioners have asserted that what employees feel, and how they can express those feelings, must be very much more than an add-on feature to the economic or management purpose of the organization. However, the most influential force for change has come from **feminism**. Feminist writings are now part of most business school curricula (reaching student audiences comprising around 50 per cent women), and they regularly feature in the national press. Questions concerning the interests of women at work have been debated at national level, especially the poor representation of women (and ethnic minorities) in senior posts in corporations and government.

From an emotional point of view, feminist thought draws our attention to the contrasting socialization of the sexes, and different ways of valuing and showing feelings. The meaning and expression of feelings such as care, pain, love, sensitivity, aggression and anxiety are massively influenced by **gendering** – what is regarded as appropriate for a man or a woman. The differences can be found in statements such as: 'the sweet smiles of women'; 'women should be demure; men should be forthright'. Women can reveal their pain and distress; men should hide it. Women can cry (only to be judged by men as 'emotional', which they often resent); men should not show tears. Arguably, such gendering of emotion impoverishes both men and women, and encourages occupational stereotyping: 'women's jobs' and 'men's jobs' divided according to supposed emotional and skill requirements. Indeed the latest surveys of job attitudes reveal a persistent belief that women are more suited to occupations such as nursing, personnel work, domestic work and secretarial activities, while men should be the mechanics, commanders and engineers. There is no biological or emotional necessity for such gender divisions; however, it may be convenient for men to believe that they are more temperamentally suited to jobs which happen to have the most power, pay and prestige in our society.

Typically, corporate success for women has meant learning male-type behaviours and male emotional expression: competing with men on men's terms. A female middle manager in a dominantly male, and macho, car retailing organization, described her position to us as follows:

> They call me 'dearie' or 'young lady', even those who are much younger than me. If I'm ill or a bit off colour my manager keeps asking me whether I'm pregnant. They have reluctantly agreed to pay for me to study for a part-time MBA, but only if I sign a pay-back clause in case I leave the firm within two years. The interesting thing is that no male manager has ever been asked to do this. I need to swallow all this stuff, and meet them on their terms. I have to show that I'm one of them even though I feel I'm not. So, for example, I've taken to putting on overalls, going down to the car service bay, driving on to a ramp, and saying to the boys there, 'OK, I want to learn to service it; show me'. They're amazed – and it works a treat.

There is evidence that, to be taken seriously, women have to be demonstrably better than men at the same level. Alternatively, women may conform to the female stereotype and, by sheer force of **personality** and shrewd political judgement, steer their way through the corporate networks. Furthermore, women, more than men, will have to cope with the conflict of split loyalties between job and family – which can be perceived by an employer as evidence of their potential unreliability (see Chapter 19, 'Working and Living'). The woman (or man) who wants to create an open emotional climate, with bonds based on care and concern for the organization as a community, usually has to stand alone – and experiment.

- Feelings and their control are intrinsic to human organizing; organizations have rules of emotional display.
- Many jobs involve the creation of the 'right' emotional expression for the right situation.
- Some jobs and roles require more personal effort than others to control one's private feelings. This involves continuous acting, which can be stressful.
- Some organizations systematically manipulate employee feelings for commercial gain.
- We learn the rules of emotion display – according to our culture, our gender, and our work organizations.

- Many organizations develop informal rituals through which private feelings can be more easily expressed.
- Social changes, especially from feminism, have challenged traditional assumptions about feelings and rationality in organizations (but male ways still prevail). There are also other reasons to believe that we should no longer separate what we feel from what we think.

THESAURUS ENTRIES

bureaucracy
control
culture
decision making
emotion
emotional intelligence
ethics
feminism
games
gender
impression formation
job satisfaction
jokes

learning
participation
perception
personality
power
problems
rationality
rationalization
rules
socialization
stereotyping
structure
values

READING ON

Emotion has recently become of special interest to organizational researchers. Major reviews of the field can be found in Ashforth and Humphrey (1995) and Fineman (1993, 1997). These writings trace the history of emotion and feeling in organizations, look at different academic and gender perspectives on emotion, and offer case descriptions of emotional life. They also show how emotions can be understood as social construction, part of the culture, structures and rules and roles of social life.

Arlie Hochschild's (1983) study of flight attendants is a seminal work on emotion management: the way companies train employees to 'smile' and the psychological costs of such regimes. Hochschild has developed the notion of 'emotional labour', now explored in a variety of service occupations – see Waldron (1994).

The way emotions are 'performed' in sales and related settings has been researched by Rafaeli and Sutton (1987, 1989).

Organizational culture shapes and is shaped by emotion – see Van Maanen and Kunda (1989). Conrad and Witte (1994) and Fineman and Sturdy (1999) discuss the wider ideological significance of emotion control in the power and economic structures of society.

13

Sex

'Well, I'll sit here to look at Vanessa's legs', announced the director of a manufacturing firm as he sat opposite the student trainee at the start of a meeting. Vanessa was not impressed. 'Before I worked at Powertech', she said later, 'I did not have much sympathy with women who complained about sexism in the workplace as I really did think it was a thing of the past. I was absolutely unprepared to deal with all the comments and attitudes I encountered on placement. Many of these attitudes are very subtle. Many of the offenders do not understand that they are being sexist, they just feel they are "having a laugh", or being friendly.'

The issue of sexual harassment has lately placed sexuality in the centre of discussions about organizations. For a long time, sexuality in organizations has been a non-topic. Try looking at the index of any Organizational Behaviour text. It is as if people lock up their sexual thoughts and desires the minute they walk into their workplaces. After all, workplaces are not places for pleasure, romance or sensuousness, let alone sex. Most people see sex as a private matter, not as public business (see Chapter 5, 'Morals' and Chapter 19, 'Working and Living').

SEX TALK

Looking at organizations purely as places of work is almost as naïve as looking at sex purely as sexual intercourse. Men and women are sexual beings. Our sexuality is a central part of our personality. We all have sexual desires, anxieties and **fantasies** and we spend some of our working time talking, joking and thinking about sex. The frequently quoted statistic that on average men think about sex every three minutes, or 40 seconds, or whatever, does not have any authority that we know of. But the graffiti in toilets and lifts, the pin-ups in lockers and workshops, the sex gossip and casual conversations provide ample evidence that sex is very much on people's minds during their time at work.

In some organizations, sex talk goes on incessantly. Its variety is enormous, ranging from the subtle to the explicit, from the friendly to the hostile to the downright nasty. Consider the following two examples:

> I had been doing consultancy for the launch of a US software product called Soft-tool. With a name like this you don't stand a chance. I told the manufacturers, you have to change the brand-name. No luck, it was company policy to use the same name in all its geographic divisions. My job was to come up with a logo for this product; imagine now, 'Buy Soft-tool to increase your performance'. When they realized their gaffe, they changed the name to...Hard-tool!
>
> (Computer executive)
>
> I think it's mainly me really they tease, about the postboy. Because he's so sweet, you know, I say he is my toyboy, and the others ask me 'Have you seen your toyboy today?' Silly things like that, it just lightens the day up.... Or the gentleman across the corridor, I notice him because he is always working, he's such a nice gentleman, such a nice character, and I always say 'I just met him on the first floor, I think he's madly in love with me!' Silly things. We just laugh about them.
>
> (Office worker)

It may come as no surprise that the first story was told by a man and the second by a woman. In their distinct ways, both narratives could be seen as revealing sexual anxieties – the man's worry about masculinity and the woman's concern about being loved. They both suggest fantasies: the first a fantasy about sexually inadequate men, the second about an innocent postboy and a romantically inclined 'gentleman'. Both stories court embarrassment as they shake some taboos and use potentially risky words. Told in the wrong way to the wrong audience, they could lead to stony silence and embarrassed glances. Told in the right way to the right audience, they generate a unique kind of pleasure, strengthen the sense of intimacy among those present and bring femininity and masculinity into the heart of organizational life.

Wholly male and wholly female work environments spawn distinct brands of sex talk. Yet, sex talk is not confined to groups of the same **gender**. In some mixed offices continuous sex teasing goes on between men and women. Men may tease women about their appearance while women may tease men about their virility. In two district offices of a privatized utility, sexual banter and obscene jokes were traded endlessly across the genders in apparently good humour. Not one of the 47 people interviewed by one of us admitted to being upset about them. For Andrew, fresh from university, the office had been a **culture** shock.

> *Andrew*: When I first came here, I just couldn't believe the language people used. Gossip about who's going out with whom, who fancies whom, it's just like school. The jokes! Not down to the level of whistling, but about how people look.
>
> *Interviewer*: Do the women mind about it?
>
> *Andrew*: I'd say they enjoy it. I've got to be honest, the difference between here and college is huge, people could no way get away with some of the jokes. The attitude here is totally different. It's horrible saying this but most of the women seem to enjoy it. Totally sexist thing to say. But it goes on and on and on. Like the story about two people who are having an intimate situation, this is how it started, and people just constantly crack jokes about them. It's become like a serial. Probably none of it is true.

Nicky, a 21-year-old clerk who had joined the company as a trainee four years previously, said:

> I don't mind sexist jokes, I make them myself. Men tease me about the size of my backside but it's all in good spirit. Mind you, I have taken down the nude calendars. I wouldn't like nude men on the walls either, in fact, I'd rather have the women!

OFFICE ROMANCES

Much of the sexual behaviour at work takes place at the level of talk and fantasy. Nevertheless, physical display and contact are not entirely absent. Touching, hugging or kissing may not be much in evidence in most workshops or offices, but many have apocryphal tales, such as what went on at the Christmas party, or during the residential conference, or behind the closed doors of the office. In the organization above, in the interest of better understanding between clerical and technical staff, once a year each clerical worker accompanies a service engineer on house calls. On a different day, each engineer sits in the office paired with a clerical worker. The joint house calls fed a constant stream of innuendoes. Eventually, one of the women in the office married 'her' engineer, providing a happy ending to another local soap opera.

Sexual fantasies are an escape from the ordinariness of work. Sex talk breaks the monotony, introduces a playful element and brightens up what can otherwise be a rather boring day. Sex talk also reminds people that their bodies are not just labouring instruments hiding inside uniforms and suits, but are also sources and objects of pleasure and **desire**. Nor are their feelings tied exclusively to the demands of their work.

This is half the story; the other half is less agreeable. Sex in organizations goes far deeper than being a mere diversion from the monotony of work. Discrimination, AIDS and harassment remind us of some darker aspects. The rest of this chapter explores some of the ways in which sex cuts across and strengthens the **power** relations in organizations.

SEXUAL HARASSMENT

Increasing awareness of the dark side of sexuality within organizations has coincided with an explosion of concern about sexual harassment in the United States and Britain. Sensitivities, **attitudes** and feelings are changing. On the one hand, there is an increasing recognition that **sexual harassment** is not an exceptional occurrence but a routine phenomenon in many workplaces and that large numbers of women (and to a lesser extent men, especially gay men) suffer in silence. On the other hand, there is a sense that forms of behaviour which used to pass as 'innocent' and 'well-intentioned' involve a covert attempt to humiliate women, to bolster negative stereotypes and to preserve organizational forms in which men generally occupy superior positions to women.

The norms of permissible and abusive sexual behaviour are changing. What used to pass as 'innocent banter' is rapidly being re-classified as offensive behaviour. 'Friendly' compliments are frequently resented, either because they are perceived as implied propositions or because they are seen as devaluing other qualities. Many women now feel that they tolerated such behaviour in the past, pretended not to notice or feel ashamed about it, instead of recognizing the hurt that it caused and fighting back. At the same time, many women and men are debating the boundary between harassment and the inevitable and even pleasurable sexuality of much organizational life. The 'sexless' organization which was seen as the safe option to aim for in the 1980s was found to be too dull to survive. But the problems of sexual activity or attraction between people of unequal power that it was intended to solve, remain.

Sexual harassment comes in many forms. At its worst it amounts to nothing less than rape, or the demand for what some call 'sexual favours' in return for promotion or other material benefits. This is sexual bullying, the abuse of power to exploit, humiliate or hurt and the pleasure of doing so. Sexual harassment may, equally, assume more subtle forms. Persistent compliments can be irritating, as can excessive familiarity, exaggerated intimacy or physical closeness. One of the commonest forms of harassment lies in sexist remarks which either reduce people to sex objects or reaffirm unpleasant **stereotypes**. This puts them, especially women, in a rather invidious position: if they express disgust or disapproval this tends to reinforce the stereotypes ('women lack a sense of humour', 'they are emotional', and so forth), while if they bottle up their feelings they offer tacit encouragement to their aggressor.

One of our students reported three incidents that took place in quick succession between her and her manager in a bank.

> I came to work in a smart trouser suit and Paul greeted me with 'Did you forget to take your pyjamas off, Suzie?' (He knows I hate being called Suzie.) A little later I was trying to print some documents and said 'This printer is so temperamental!' and Paul quipped 'It's obviously female'. Eventually, the fault was found to be in the computer and he said 'Have you broken it already?' Me: 'No.' Paul: 'Ah! that's what happens when you let women near machines.'

Susan tolerated this type of put-down for several days. The worst thing, she explained, was not knowing whether these comments were meant as friendly teasing or as serious criticism. She put on a brave face, hid her feelings and tried to 'rise' above this baiting. One day, however, she felt especially annoyed and when Paul told her that he planned to take a three-week holiday, she quipped: 'Why, visiting your Spanish sweetheart again?' before she had time to check herself. 'Don't be cheeky!' said Paul. 'I can remember experiencing mixed feelings about what had happened. Perhaps I overstepped the mark, the fine line between what an employee can and cannot say to a manager. As a result I told myself off for not checking myself, I blamed myself. But I also felt that it didn't seem fair that I had to take his jokes in good humour, no matter how bad they were, while his position meant that I couldn't give as good as I got.'

How certain can we be that this is a case of harassment? Surely this kind of unequal rights (for instance, the right to joke at someone else's expense) is common to interactions between senior and junior members of staff. But for women this raises extra difficulties. Are they being laughed at because they are young, because they are junior or just because they are women? It is sometimes hard for women to know. The suspicion of harassment remains and this shapes their experience.

THE AMBIGUITIES OF HARASSMENT

When does a well-meant joke or compliment become sexual harassment? This is a thorny issue. A joke which in one organization may
cause amusement, may cause offence in a different one. During a
workshop run by one of our colleagues, a participant told of his
plans to tour the Far East, 'just three men, without women to complicate the party or disapprove'. Challenged to say what they
intended to do, he casually remarked 'Oh, a little bit of rape and
pillage!' The comment outraged many of the others and led to a
heated debate in which men and women were sharply polarized.
What seemed like an innocent joke to some of the men was felt to
be a vicious sexist and racist comment by the women. Whether or
not by the teller of the joke had meant it as an abusive comment to
the women present, this is exactly how they experienced it.

In most circumstances we rely on social **norms** to guide us
through what is acceptable and what is unacceptable social behaviour. Tact and sensitivity alert us to the needs and feelings of others.
In the area of sex, however, norms vary enormously and leave a lot
of ambiguity. They have also been changing very rapidly – and not
necessarily in an obvious direction – over recent years. To make
matters more complex, being on the edge of what is acceptable
seems in itself to be an almost sexual pleasure for both genders –
but perhaps with different views of what is pleasurable about it.

What problems does this leave us with? For men, sexist innuendoes are often presented as 'innocent jokes' with no intention to
offend or hurt. All the same, the excuse 'I didn't mean to hurt you'
sounds highly unconvincing in most cases. Nor does the word 'innocent' seem altogether appropriate for some of the obscene graffiti in
male lavatories or some all-male conversations in bars. This suggests
that hate and scorn are sometimes as much part of men's feelings
towards women as are attraction and love. The jokes and the graffiti
may be less prevalent than they were a few years back, but their continued existence points to a lasting anti-women undercurrent.

Men's **emotions** towards women are often ambivalent. Their feelings are often in conflict with each other. They frequently stereotype
the women they meet in one of a few basic categories, like mother
figure, iron maiden, witch, whore, or defenceless 'pet'. Men idealize
'the virgin' while denying that the 'mother figure' has any sexuality
at all. Women with independent sexual desires are often typecast
as 'tarts' or 'whores', at whom large amounts of male lust and
aggression are directed. Unless perceived as virgins or mothers,

women are often said to be bringing male violence upon themselves through provocative or flirtatious behaviour. 'She asked for it' becomes the stock defence of perpetrators of male violence against women. Instead of blaming the wrongdoer, it is the victim who gets the blame.

SEX AND ORGANIZATIONAL POLITICS

Blaming the victim by turning women into deserving targets for male violence presents sexual harassment as a purely personal matter. But sexual harassment would not have become a major issue if it amounted to nothing more than the actions of a few male chauvinists, let alone the experience of a few over-sensitive females. One of the reasons it has become a major political and management issue is that sexual politics is closely related to organizational **politics** and **conflicts**.

Sex is a feature of many organizational **games**. As Susan noted in the earlier story, men and women rarely enter these games as equals. In competing for jobs in the labour market, women have faced many visible and invisible barriers, **prejudice** or **discrimination**. If direct discrimination is rare these days (women being paid less for doing the same jobs as men), many more or less subtle forms of discrimination prevent women from rising to positions of great power or influence (see Chapter 17, 'Career-ing'). What are these forms of discrimination? If you are a woman, you will probably already know. If you are a man, you may know; if you do not, ask a woman who trusts you not to respond dismissively to her answer.

In most organizations, women tend to occupy subordinate positions, either directly 'servicing' male managers and bosses or coming into direct contact with the organization's customers as sales staff, telephonists, air stewardesses, waitresses and the like. Feminists have pointed out that women's sexuality is far from peripheral in most of these jobs. On the contrary, it is harnessed either to lure the customer, or to boost their boss's ego and image or to project a glamorous image for a company or an industry. **Femininity** and sex appeal are virtual prerequisites for employment in many such jobs. In many organizations, an attractive secretary is still seen as indicative of the **status** of her boss, while glamour is part of the image cultivated by industries, such as cosmetics, airlines, advertising and the mass media.

But women's sexuality is also harnessed by organizations in subtler ways. In jobs involving direct contact with customers, consumers or employees, the 'feminine touch' is deployed to defuse awkward or dangerous situations and to maintain a discreet form of social control. Female telephonists, sales staff, receptionists, cashiers, nurses, teachers and police officers are all expected to exercise their delicate interpersonal skills on behalf of their organizations, preventing things from getting out of hand. Of course the same may be expected of their male counterparts, but a feminine presence in most organizations is seen as a civilizing influence and a balancing counterpart to male aggression.

In some organizations, management maintains a low-level sexual 'simmer', placing great emphasis on women's appearance and demeanour, encouraging smart dressing, make-up and so on. One of our students worked for a pizza restaurant which placed high emphasis on the appearance of the waitresses; it also paid minimal wages. Result:

> Some of the waitresses would do anything to earn a tip. Some of the younger ones wore black bras which were clearly visible underneath their pink blouses. Some deliberately shortened their skirts. Some compared this to prostitution, selling yourself in order to make money. I have to agree with them.
>
> Other waitresses adopted their own tip-making strategies. For example, Elaine in her spare moments would go over to the customers and start up a conversation. She would often tell customers about any personal problems that she had. It appeared as though she was begging for a tip.
>
> I swore I would not sink to this level. However, I did, and developed my own strategies. One of these was to ask customers with relatively young children whether they would like a bowl and a spoon for the children to use. This was actually quite successful and I believe that it encouraged customers to leave tips.

'USING SEX'

This astute account illustrates one of the linkages between sexuality and power in organizations. The waitresses gained money and sometimes power by adopting sexual and emotional tactics, which could then be used against them (and women in general) to stereotype them and disparage them. It also illustrates both the distress that having to adopt such demeaning forms of behaviour causes women and the pleasure which successful use of such tactics can bring to the performer. Jo's story illustrates this:

> I went along to the product launch with Marianne, my assistant. She's very young, and she thought she could charm her way around the directors on her own and not rely on me for her power base. But she doesn't have either the shape or the experience. I thought 'I've been doing this for ten years longer than you matey, and I'm bloody good at it', so I put all my lights on, drew the directors into a group around me, and left her invisible. It was great. Now that's what I call girl power.

Femininity, encompassing physical allure, warmth, tenderness and subtle interpersonal skills, is part and parcel of how some of women's work in organizations gets done. Women are placed in a 'double-bind' or no-win situation. The same work environment which encourages femininity, and even seductiveness, chastises women for using their 'feminine charms' to gain personal advantage and influence. On the other hand, women who suppress their **sexuality** and seek to confront men as equals are often branded 'iron maidens' or lesbians. Women frequently feel that they are treading a dangerous ground of permissible and non-permissible displays of femininity, between being 'too sexy' and 'not sexy enough'.

There is little evidence that women gain personal advantage against male colleagues by using their sexuality, although they are often accused of doing so. If anything, there is some evidence of the opposite. To the extent that certain jobs emphasize attractiveness, they are seen as requiring little in the way of intellectual abilities, qualifications and motivation, although it is also the case that more attractive people are usually assumed to be more intelligent than is justified by their intellectual powers alone. Attractive women in positions of genuine power are often accused – even if they are not genuinely suspected – of having risen on the basis of their physical attributes, and become a target of male hostility and sexual harassment.

MALE SEXUALITY

While sexual harassment and discrimination have forced us to look at female sexuality in organizations, it would be wrong to imply that male sexuality is excluded from them. To be sure, the stereotypes of men in organizations tend to underplay sexuality, just as those of women emphasize it. Think of grey-suited businessmen, rational, tough, analytic, and you would be forgiven for imagining that they are pure brain and will, detached from bodies and desires. As we saw earlier, however, sexual fantasies and wishes are rarely far from men's minds and frequently feed organizational sex talk.

Physical appearance is a central ingredient of male sexuality as it is of female. A computer analyst in a large firm prided himself on his bulging muscles, the product of long sessions spent in the gymnasium. 'I had an office', he recounted not without self-irony, 'next to the girls in the legal department, and they were talking about the sexiest man in the building, and they were coming up with all these men I'd never heard of before. So I went into their office and said "Sorry about this, ladies, I thought that I was the real star, the hulk".

They cracked up laughing and said "We had a vote and you were voted the most boring old fart in this place".'

Sex teasing in organizations can be good-humoured and benign, but relations between men and women are asymmetrical and unequal. A woman entering an all-male office saying 'Sorry about this, lads, but I thought that I was the sex sensation here', would doubtless elicit a very different response from the witticism of the earlier story. A man who prides himself on his sexual exploits may attract a well-deserved taunt but may secretly be admired as a 'stud' or a 'ladies' man'. A woman doing likewise may still be derided as fast, promiscuous, or worse.

While women have to tread a precarious line between 'not sexy enough' and 'too sexy', displays of masculinity come under more lenient controls. Even when it assumes the distasteful shape of sexual harassment it often goes unpunished. There is, nevertheless, a taboo in most workplaces on **homosexuality** and, more generally, against men's displays of physical closeness or affection. Hugging and kissing among Mediterranean men give rise to great anxiety in many Anglo-Saxons, who regard them as a possible blot on their masculinity.

One of us was attending a conference in Italy, in the company of two close colleagues from our university department, and remembers vividly the following incident:

> There was Roberto, an old associate, who I met about once a year. He threw his arms around me and gave me an affectionate hug. I was pleased to respond to his warmth. My two British colleagues gave me 'knowing' glances. I was a little embarrassed and they teased me. I laughed it off. Throughout the day, the teasing continued – jokes, quips and innuendo about my 'relationship' with Roberto. I still smiled. After all, I could take a joke, couldn't I?
>
> The teasing, as I recall, resumed the next day. They seemed to be having great fun at my expense, while I felt increasingly uncomfortable. It was now beyond a joke. It seemed curiously childish behaviour, insensitive, silly. Then it was one remark too many. 'I am not enjoying these remarks, could you please stop?' I snapped at Chris. He seemed surprised. Chris communicated my comment to Geoffrey. There was a slightly uncomfortable feeling between us, and then it stopped. A couple of years later, Chris and I discussed the incident. We both agreed about the 'facts'. As for the meaning of the incident, there seemed to be a gulf dividing us.

With few exceptions, Western organizations are neither kind nor permissive towards gays and lesbians, who often become victims of vicious sexual harassment. Gays and lesbians find themselves in especially invidious situations, looking for strategies of **survival** while constantly suppressing their sexuality. Denial, over-compensation, avoidance or straight lying are strategies which take their toll emotionally. Having to laugh at your colleagues' anti-gay jokes (or even initiating them yourself), not disclosing the gender of your partner, keeping constant vigilance over what others know of your desires and fantasies, 'splitting' your sexual self from your work self: these are all psychological ways of coping, which exact their price in anxiety, stress and guilt.

But male sexuality at the workplace is not limited to displays of **masculinity** and bravado. It is also revealed in very masculine styles of **management**, sometimes referred to as 'macho management'. Confrontation, ostentatious use of force and intransigence, contempt for compromise and compassion became the trademarks of this style of management. Its champions included 'hard men' who introduced new tough regimes in their companies which broke all other forms of power base. Talking tough and acting tough is a matter of masculine pride for those who see it as their mission to restore 'managers' right to manage'. Television and film images of tough managers present them as exploring heroes – perhaps the modern equivalent of cowboys. Cowboy movies were less misleading, however, because not many of the cinema audience were going to take up careers as cowboys. Films portraying macho managers may have a disproportionate influence on audience behaviour as people look forward to trying out the strong tactics they have seen on screen. In many organizations this is dealt with by gentle mockery (see Chapter 14, 'Serious Joking') as young staff are gradually mentored away from the film images to something gentler and more effective. In other organizations, particularly if the manager is the son of the boss, or if the organization is very small or under threat, behaviour learned from films is allowed to persist.

Whether macho management has become the norm or not is debatable, as is its success in restoring order and peace in many organizations. It appears, nevertheless, that macho management has now gone out of fashion, at least in its brashest manifestations. Yet aggression, competitiveness, rigidity and hardness are all qualities which are not only accepted but encouraged by organizations which find them as useful as they find the feminine qualities we discussed earlier. The essential difference lies in the fact that while masculine qualities enhance **career** prospects, feminine ones, though indispensable for many organizations, are frequently an impediment to personal success.

SUMMARY

Sexuality plays a large part in how men and women relate to each other. Whether among colleagues or rivals, superiors or subordinates, friends or lovers, gender is ever present. Our ways of looking at things and relating to others are shaped by our identities, and our identities are sexual. It is not surprising, therefore, to find sexuality in most episodes of organizational life. In this chapter we have argued that sexuality is not just incidental to organization, but of the very essence.

Organizations harness the sexuality of both men and women, mould it and frame it. The women's and gay movements must claim the credit for demonstrating how sexuality becomes entangled in organizational politics, revealing its ugly side in incidents of sexual harassment and intimidation. Women's femininity are more severely manipulated and controlled than masculinity, with stereotypes from wider culture conveniently invoked as excuses for discriminatory and unequal treatment.

At the same time, we have argued against the view which automatically equates sex in organizations with oppression and exploitation. We have suggested that sexual joking, banter and innuendo are welcomed by the majority as a break from the impersonal routines of organizations and as a reminder that inside every overall, suit or uniform there is a human body, which is not just an instrument of labour, but also the source and object of pleasure and desire.

- Sexuality is expressed directly and indirectly in organizations, ranging from sex talk, innuendo and office romances to stereotyping, harassment and discrimination.
- Gender issues and sexuality often become enmeshed with organizational politics in which, almost invariably, men have greater power than women.
- Sexual harassment can take many different forms, including exaggerated compliments, offensive language, sexist jokes and sexual blackmailing.
- Sexual harassment tends to reaffirm gender stereotypes and frequently puts the victim in an invidious no-win situation.
- Men's attitudes and behaviour towards women are often conditioned by naïve stereotypes of women such as 'virgins', 'pets', 'mother figures' and 'whores'.
- Organizations mould both masculinity and femininity, though in different ways.
- On the whole, the controls placed on female sexuality and homosexuality are tighter and more inhibiting than those placed on what are seen as 'traditional masculine' traits.

THESAURUS ENTRIES

attitude	management
career	masculinity
conflict	norm
culture	politics
desire	power
discrimination	prejudice
emotion	sexual harassment
fantasy	sexuality
femininity	status
games	stereotyping
gender	survival
homosexuality	

READING ON

The area of sexuality at work has only recently become part of academic study. The work of Hearn and Parkin (1987) and Hearn et al. (1989) is especially relevant in exploring the contexts and social construction of sexuality at work. These authors criticize previous analyses of organizations (most of which are by male authors) for not acknowledging gender issues. Hearn et al. speak of sexuality as associated with the 'politics of the body' and the negotiated expectations between the genders. Sexuality is embedded in the pattern of emotions and language of the organization.

Gardner (1995) also develops a number of similar themes, but more broadly in various social settings. Sexual harassment and its link to power and gender is discussed by Gutek (1985). Harassment can include offensive language, sexist jokes and negative stereotypes, and frequently plays on the power differences between the harasser and the harassed. Collins and Blodgett (1981) offer an everyday business perspective, while the different national–cultural and perceptual issues are explored by Brant and Too (1994). Important here is how different cultures and sub-cultures define appropriate sexual display, reminding us of the cultural relativity of sexual, and other, organizational behaviours.

14

Serious joking

Most organizations are serious places. People go about their business with deliberate seriousness. They fill in forms seriously, they answer phones seriously, they write letters seriously, they tap in on their computer terminals seriously, they attend meetings seriously, they discuss strategy seriously, they bargain seriously, they operate different types of machinery seriously. An air of no-nonsense fills organizational spaces.

From time to time humour makes a tentative appearance. A joke in the middle of a stuffy meeting or a cartoon on an office wall lightens the atmosphere and raises a smile. But books on management and organizations have not paid much attention to such phenomena, which were not seen as a part of the serious business of organizing, but merely as decoration.

To the outsider, organizations tend to present a uniformly serious front: entering a bank, a hospital or a government department, reading company reports or sales literature, telephoning the local office of the gas or electricity company, one finds little that could be described as amusing. But if, with an innocent eye, we glance backstage in these organizations, a rather different picture is revealed, a picture which may combine the ridiculous, the absurd and the funny. For example, there are people being incredibly serious about matters which look utterly trivial, such as a group of executives discussing at length the precise phrasing of a strategy document which they know will have little impact on anybody. Or people carefully filling in forms in triplicate, for no apparent reason other than they have 'always done it that way'. And there is a middle-aged clerk, in a suit that was once smart, complaining bitterly about the plastic cups in the coffee machine, while a group of younger office workers giggle and smile....

In addition, unlike the official visitor who sees the serious front of the organization, the insider in offices may share a **joke** about the latest fiasco (10,000 Valentine cards delivered 'as promised' on 15 February), gossiping about the latest come-uppance of the brash young executive ('you should have seen the state of that Porsche after he reversed into the garage wall') or recollect a practical joke played on an awkward colleague ('do you remember the scream he gave when he opened the box and the severed hand dropped out all covered in blood?').

It does not take long to discover that the air of seriousness in the majority of organizations is only paper thin; underneath, a continuous humorous banter goes on, providing an unofficial commentary on organizational life. People joke, laugh, play tricks on each other and generally try to have a good time. Often, the mere mention of an individual or a group, like 'the inspector', 'personnel' or 'the lawyers', is enough to generate a funny story. 'The computer's gone down again; it must be the director pouring another whisky soda on his terminal!' 'No, it's the computer boys trying to wipe out the last three years' accounts!' 'More likely, someone unplugged the server to boil the kettle.'

JOKES AND SURVIVAL

Workers who have recently joined an office may find many of the jokes unfunny or incomprehensible. For a time, they may smile to show that they too are in on the joke, but soon they will start trying to chip in. Not being able to share a joke, however unfunny, makes one feel excluded; a person without a sense of humour quickly becomes the butt of many jokes.

Sharing a laugh and a joke is an important **survival** mechanism, especially for those people who feel stuck in mundane and repetitive jobs. Laughter and humour make light of the many injuries that we sustain in organizations, physical injuries as well as injuries to our pride and dignity. Fred, who has lost part of his finger in an apple-pie-making machine, becomes the target of many good-humoured jokes a mere few days after the accident. The women checking the beans on a continuously moving conveyor joke about management's attempt to replace them with pigeons, trained to pick the dud beans, only to find that the Royal Society for the Prevention of Cruelty to Animals has ruled that the task is too cruelly repetitive for the pigeons. Such jokes seem to celebrate survival against the odds.

Jokes and laughter defuse tense situations, break the monotony and let the weak turn the tables on the strong. 'You have to have a sense of humour to survive in this job' is a statement one hears often when talking to people doing jobs that would not test the intelligence of pigeons. 'You don't have to be mad to work in this place but it helps' proclaim signs in innumerable workplaces, expressing what many people must feel. The joke was taken one stage further when the Royal College of Psychiatrists used the phrase as a title for a course they were running for prospective entrants to the profession.

Above all, humour gives people licence to say things that could not be said otherwise. Organizations require people to keep their mouths shut a lot of the time and keep their opinions to themselves. Criticizing superiors to their face is not a recipe for promotion or success. A joke, however, with people sharing similar views, permits the venting of emotions, such as fear, hostility and contempt, that loom under the surface, and you can do it all while still being ambiguous about whether you seriously mean the criticism or not (see Chapter 12, 'Feelings').

In a computer company, one of us was told the following joke which clearly expresses the staff's disparagement of the board of directors. 'Our Chairman meets the Presidents of America and France in an international conference. "My problem", says the American President, "is that I have 12 security advisers. One of them is a foreign spy, but I don't know which." "Funny you should say this", retorts the French President, "my problem is that I have 12 mistresses. One of them is unfaithful, but I don't know which." "Your problems are nothing compared to mine", says our Chairman. "I have 12 directors on the board. One of them is competent, but I don't know which."' Alternatively, there is the joke you hear in many different organizations about the little boy who wanted his daddy to buy him a cowboy outfit for Christmas, and the generous dad bought him...(fill in the name of whichever company the story is being told in).

Jokes enable people to test the water and say things that would normally be prohibited or taboo. To exclaim directly, 'The manager is a lazy so and so' may cause embarrassment even if several people in an office recognize it as true. Saying instead, 'Our boss is an extremely ambitious man; his greatest ambition is to draw a salary without doing any work' camouflages the hostility and allows the teller to see if others share the same opinion. A joke then offers an amnesty to the teller, enabling a particular view and a range of **emotions** to evade organizational and moral censorship and find expression. In the last resort, it offers the escape route 'I was only joking'. But if it generates great laughter, both the teller of the joke and the listeners have discovered that they have something important in common.

Laughter bonds people as tightly as a shared secret. One cannot tell oneself a joke or a secret, just as one cannot tickle oneself. Jokes and secrets require a social relationship, a shared understanding based on a common **language** which excludes others. Most organizational jokes are also secrets; some people are in and some people are out of these secrets: 'If only the Chairman knew what we say behind his back....' A joke strengthens the sense of trust for those who share it. Having shared a joke, especially one that is directed against a party excluded from the group, generates a tremendous sense of 'usness'. In this way, the joke unleashes two types of emotion: affection for those who share it, and **aggression** for the target (see Chapter 15, 'Us and Them').

Few incidents generate as much hilarity and pleasure as the humbling of a pompous person in a position of authority. Such misfortunes are invariably celebrated by their subordinates and turned into jokes, generating the same type of laughter as pies in the face and banana skins. A manager whose tie gets caught in the office shredder will provide much amusement, especially if he places great store by his appearance. Likewise an executive who always insists on punctuality and time-keeping when he/she turns up late for a meeting. The greater our hostility towards the victim of misfortune, the greater our enjoyment. The undeserved suffering of our fellow human beings may trigger in us feelings of sympathy and compassion. Yet, no amount of suffering provides protection against ridicule, so long us we can convince ourselves that the victims brought it upon themselves with their arrogance or their foolishness. As Erasmus said, 'The mad laugh at the mad; each provides mutual enjoyment to the other'.

IN-GROUP HUMOUR

While much of disparagement humour is directed outwards, towards members of other social **groups**, some of it is reserved for a group's own members. In particular, individuals who persistently deviate from group **norms** may find themselves on the receiving end of cutting or ironic remarks from their colleagues. Social norms guide our behaviour and shape our expectations of other people's behaviour. Much psychological research has gone into showing how we become **socialized** into the norms of the society and the groups to which we belong, so that the norms eventually become part of ourselves. Norms affect most aspects of our life, from relatively minor matters of etiquette to major aspects of our **personality** and life choices, like sexual preference or career choice. Our moral **values** themselves, our sense of what is good and what is evil, depend to a substantial degree on the values of the groups of which we are members (see Chapter 5, 'Morals'). Most of the time, social norms guide our behaviour without our being aware of them. Eating with a knife and fork, for example, becomes second nature to us, so that we cannot appreciate how difficult little children may find the mastery of these implements. If one of our work colleagues chooses to eat with their hands, or to eat a particular food at a time of day that we find surprising, or to eat something that stinks the office out, we will probably make jokes about it rather than seriously investigating this interesting difference.

Within organizations, as in society at large, our behaviour is regulated not only by written rules and regulations but also by unwritten norms. Not all groups impose their norms with the same severity, but generally deviance from group norms is discouraged. Humour is crucial in both reaffirming groups' norms and enforcing **conformity**; it is a type of sanction relying on embarrassment to pressure the offending individual back into conformity.

An office worker who dresses in an unorthodox manner, a pupil who rushes to answer each of the teacher's questions, a worker who consistently works harder than the rest, a manager who 'crawls' to his/her superiors soon begin to attract disparaging remarks, frequently dressed up as jokes. This acts as a first reminder that such behaviour threatens group cohesion and undermines the group's accepted standards of behaviour. It is surprising, at times, how tiny details of appearance or behaviour become extremely important symbolically for different groups. The college student who drinks half-pints of beer while his/her mates are downing pints will soon be picked on, as if he/she had violated an important group taboo. If sarcastic remarks are the group's first attempt to pull individuals back to the norms, exclusion, verbal abuse or physical violence may follow.

Humour then usually provides the first indicator of the line between acceptable and unacceptable behaviour. It acts as a mechanism of group **control**. People who persistently break group norms face two possibilities. They may be marginalized and ultimately rejected from the group. Alternatively, they may become accepted as 'eccentrics', in other words as exceptions which reinforce the norms: they are figures of fun whose tolerated existence is taken to show the strength and confidence of the system from whose detailed prescriptions they are allowed to deviate.

JOKING RELATIONS

Not all in-group humour functions to chastise deviance and force people to conform to group norms. Much of the humorous banter that can be heard in offices, building sites and other workplaces takes the form of friendly teasing. Individuals are routinely teased for their appearance, their accent, their **ethnic** origin or their tastes. Such teasing can be quite coarse but is generally good-natured, a sign of trust and intimacy. Targeting an individual, in this case, can be a sign of affection and esteem – the assumption is that the target 'can take it' without offence. But it is also quite possible for there to be two different ways of understanding this situation which are not mutually exclusive: the teasing is good-natured – no offence intended or taken – but it has the potential to turn sour. The bullying form of teasing that is practised in school playgrounds is often perfected in organizational workgroups.

Proving that 'you can take a joke' is often important in order to be accepted as a full group member. New recruits in military or police academies, new boarding school pupils are often subjected to bizarre tests, known as **rites** of initiation or passage, which will later provide the material for jokes. The new police recruit may be asked to go and arrest a supposed criminal hiding on an island in the middle of a lake in the park. A new computer analyst may find that his/her terminal has been tampered with, pretending after a while to delete precious files in front of his/her very eyes. The medical student will be invited by the lecturer to join in tasting urine to detect diabetes – only for it to be revealed later that the lecturer did not taste the finger that he dipped in the urine, and that you cannot detect anything this way. The Chairman's new chauffeur may be asked to go and pick up the Chairman from an address in the red-light district in the middle of the night. The individual who successfully survives these initiation ordeals is then accepted as a full member of the group and as fit to take part in joking relationships (see Chapter 2, 'Entering and Leaving').

Anthropologists have used the term 'joking relationships' to describe relationships which are built around continuous teasing, horseplay, ridicule and jocular repartee but without resulting in offence. Such relationships have been studied in factories, offices, department stores, hospitals and shipyards as well as in informal gatherings. Obscenity, cursing, insults and vicious pranks are part and parcel of joking relationships yet, in a curious way, the coarser the insult, the greater the affection, warmth and respect it is meant to **communicate**. St Thomas Aquinas went so far as to argue that a lack of mirth is sinful because someone without a sense of humour is burdensome both in failing to offer the pleasure of playful speech to others and because their dourness stops them from responding to the humour of others.

THE UGLY SIDE OF HUMOUR

Humour cements group bonds, builds up trust and humanizes **impersonal** relations. Yet the line between friendly teasing and brutal bullying can be very thin. What passes as an innocent joke may to its target amount to abusive racial or **sexual harassment**. We saw earlier how the weak and exploited members of organizations use humour to symbolically turn the tables on those who dominate them. The reverse of this happens when the dominant party of a relationship forces his/her tasteless or abusive humour on his/her subordinates and invites them to laugh at grotesque wisecracks. Under the mock trust of a joking relationship, black employees may be invited to laugh at **racist** jokes and women at **sexist** jokes. Such jokes are expressions of aggression and can be the first step of racial or sexual harassment, which may then escalate into more disturbing forms of abuse (see Chapter 5, 'Morals' and Chapter 13, 'Sex').

Sexist and racist jokes are especially humiliating types of harassment; the target is put in a no-win situation. Laughing at the joke (while secretly despising themselves for doing so) reinforces the joke and makes it socially and morally acceptable. Refusing to laugh, on the other hand, automatically excludes the target from the group and turns them into a legitimate target of sarcasm, apart from anything else, for lacking a sense of humour. Both responses may be adding fuel to the fire and encouraging further insulting jokes.

In such situations it may be best to retort to the joke with a joke: one that twists its meaning and turns the aggressor's ugly innuendo on its head. One of us was once interviewing clerical staff. The atmosphere in the office was relaxed and jocular; many of the disparaging jokes were targeted against the central headquarters.

(Example: 'What is the difference between HQ and a bag of manure? The bag.') The local managers were in on most jokes, being no mean wits themselves. Much of the banter and teasing in the office was overtly sexual; people's appearance, their secret crushes, the engineers' exploits on house calls were the source of continuous joking. After Jenny, a young and outspoken office worker, had been interviewed, Brian, one of the managers, asked her tongue in cheek in the presence of several bystanders: 'Did you spill the beans, sweetheart?' 'Sure', she replied. 'I told him that you are a dirty old man.' 'Me, old?' he retorted, without a moment's hesitation. Everyone listening to the conversation burst out laughing.

These three short phrases are charged with danger, innuendo and risk. Each seems to break a minor organizational taboo and threaten the established order. The first two generate tension; the third resolves it and in doing so defuses the situation and leaves an atmosphere of goodwill and effervescence.

Jokes and joking then can be liberating and subversive but they can equally be oppressive and humiliating. They can question assumptions and express unpalatable truths or they can reinforce crass **stereotypes** and perpetuate **myths** and untruths. They can provide a soothing ointment for the scars of organizational life or can be a prime cause of such scars.

JOKES AND THE IRON CAGE

To regard humour and jokes as a superficial phenomenon of organizational life, as has been the custom, misses the rich undercurrent of **meanings** present. Jokes that people tell at the workplace can reveal as much or perhaps more about the organization, its management, its **culture** and its **conflicts** than answers to carefully administered surveys. If anything, under the moral smokescreen supplied by humour, people can express deeper feelings and views. Even more, they can express the ambiguity that they feel – simultaneous respect and frustration, oppression and freedom; if you are feeling two inconsistent emotions at once, jokes are often the only way of expressing this.

Even the scarcity of humour can be extremely revealing about an organization. Joke-free zones have been said to exist, both at the level of countries and organizations (some religious or political sects), though we are not sure that we have ever found an example that stands up to examination. People's sense of humour wanes if they are brutalized into quiet resignation or if they take themselves and the organization terribly seriously. The majority of organizations, however, can neither control their members to such an extent, nor persuade them of the incredible seriousness of their objectives.

Moreover, we suspect that even the most serious work environments may not altogether lack humour. Instead they may control rigidly those targets of humour regarded as legitimate. One simply does not joke about certain issues, they are taboo. Nevertheless, the wit in the organization will sooner or later find a target which is at least tolerated or even encouraged. If joking about internal matters is severely frowned upon, joking about the organization's rivals may provide an alternative outlet.

Humour thrives as a way of killing boredom, creating solidarity and scoring symbolic points against internal and external opposition. For these reasons, the different types of jokes examined here seem perfectly suited to the exigencies of organizational life. There is, however, one type of joke which best captures organizational humour and this is the joke against the organization itself. It is the type of joke epitomized in satire, such as that directed at military organizations or at the bureaucratic regimes in what used to be the Communist bloc. The organization, satire proclaims, is an absurd farce. Instead of trying to make sense of it, let us have a good laugh at its expense. Satire celebrates the little and large chinks in the armour of those impressive organizations which dominate our society. It shows that behind the formidable administrative, technical and financial resources of these giants, there are people messing about and making mistakes. Behind their **rationality** there are absurdities, foul-ups and blunders. However hard organizations may try to eliminate individuality by turning us into extensions of machines and by controlling our behaviour through ever more precise procedures, they can never be fully successful. A whole tradition of satirists, from Erasmus up to the present Dilbert cartoons, have helped people to oppose pomposity, self-aggrandizement, greed and malice (Harries, 1998).

Organizational satire can be seen as a protest against the 'iron cage of bureaucracy' and all those who are eager to provide their services to it. **Organizations** themselves, for the greatest part, do little to discourage it. To be sure, a practical joke that results in serious loss of production or the wiping out of the company's records will not go unpunished. However, so long as the work gets done and the orders are obeyed, most organizations are willing to tolerate humour and satire, even if they themselves become the object of ridicule. While offering no prizes to the quickest wit or the most original prankster, they recognize that even defiant humour is a protest, not a rebellion. Its victories are **symbolic**, not material.

SUMMARY

Humour and jokes, far from being inconsequential, are important features of organizational life. They break the organizational routine and enable people to cope with boring or **alienating** jobs. They generate trust and affection for those sharing a laugh and a joke and permit the venting of unacceptable views and emotions (like aggression or contempt), by offering a moral amnesty which permits the breaking of taboos.

The targets of organizational jokes are varied, but most work-groups have an individual or another group which serves as the butt of disparaging humour. When directed against superiors or outsiders, jokes strengthen the solidarity of a group and enable the group to score symbolic victories against their psychological adversaries. When directed against members of a group, jokes may be part of joking relations, highlighting the intimacy and trust between the group's members, or they may serve to reinforce group norms and force compliance.

Finally, the target of jokes may be the organization itself, whose foul-ups and absurdities are celebrated because they undermine the façade of rationality and seriousness. Such jokes, for a brief moment or two, explode organizational order and give rein to anarchy, disorder and disorganization. In this way, they restore the human factor, in its fallibility and unpredictability, at the heart of organizations.

- Under the veneer of seriousness, jokes, irony and humour play an important part in most organizations.
- Jokes offer a way of saying things and venting emotions which could not be otherwise expressed.
- Humour can provide a way for the powerless to turn the tables on the powerful; having a laugh at their expense. It therefore functions as an important survival mechanism.
- Laughter bonds people, generating feelings of solidarity, intimacy and trust.
- In-group humour establishes the boundaries between acceptable and unacceptable behaviour and provides a way of testing group norms.
- Jokes and mockery can act as a group sanction against those who violate group norms.

- Jokes offer a way of expressing mutually incompatible ideas, of showing a complex mixture of feelings towards the object of the joke.
- Racist and sexist jokes tend to rely on crass stereotypes; when addressed at a member of the stereotyped group, they can be seen as a form of harassment.

THESAURUS ENTRIES

aggression	myth
alienation	norm
communication	organization
conflict	personality
conformity	race
control	rationality
culture	rite of passage
emotion	sexism
ethnic groups	sexual harassment
group	socialization
impersonality	stereotyping
jokes	survival
language	symbolism
meaning	values

READING ON

This is a very difficult topic to read on about; little has been written on it, and the material available is often anecdotal, where some successful manager is saying, in effect, either 'Everyone told me I had to be serious but I found it worked OK when I was not' (e.g. Brandt, 1996), or 'Humour will make your organization more healthy' (Abramis, 1992). Analysis and research are rather more difficult to find. Conferences about humour are notorious for the seriousness with which they are conducted. It is difficult to write about humour because the readers expect to be amused, and this often does not work when the context is changed. Paralysis by analysis seems to be the rule here – and not the paralysis of uncontrollable laughter, but the paralysis that comes from trying to catch the wind, from destroying the very life of what is being examined.

Rodrigues and Collinson (1995) comment on the functionalist perspective of a lot of the literature that does exist on humour in organizations; that is, a lot of it argues one of the following: 'If you make people laugh, they will work harder for less money'; 'If you make people laugh, they will buy your product'; 'If you allow yourself to laugh you will be more effective.' By contrast, their article emphasizes the more subversive use of humour in an organization where other forms of resistance are not available. Duncan and Feisal (1989) have attempted a typology of humour in the workplace, along with a set of recommendations for managers. Their approach is in many ways the converse of the Rodrigues and Collinson one, not because they disagree with each other's points but because the assumptions they make and the values they claim are so different, and it would make for a good balance to read the two together.

Hatch and Ehrlich (1993) take us beyond the instrumental use of humour. They are interested in the rather different theme that organizational life is full of contradictions and incoherence, and humour can be a way for people to handle this for themselves.

The use of humour for expressing serious matters is discussed by Yarwood (1995). Although his research is based in the American public sector, there is no reason why the points made should not apply equally to other sectors. Yarwood's analysis includes relating the topic to humour about organizations as found in novels and the like, which opens up another whole interesting discussion that we have not given space to above.

The importance of humour for acceptance is discussed in a very brief summary by Fisher (1996): this considers recent research which suggests that women are held back by not being adept at the use of humour in organizations. The suggestion from the study is that managers who use humour get rated more highly, and that the women managers in the study were seen as less humorous, possibly because they were holding themselves back from bringing humour into the serious business of managing.

15

Us and them

The director of an engineering firm attended a 'Team Building' course and came back to his office fired up with new ideas. **Team-work**, he had heard, is the key to success; everyone within the organization must be made to feel that they are a member of a winning team. From senior executives to part-time clerical staff, everyone has a contribution to make, everyone counts. The director decided to start by holding a Christmas dinner for his staff to strengthen team spirit. Unfortunately, he was embarrassed when all the workers crowded around one table, while he, his wife and the managers had the second table all to themselves. He commented, with irony, how successful he'd been in fostering team spirit among his workers, only he had been stuck in the opposite team!

Social divisions in organizations, as this director found, can run deep. The idea, or ideal, of bringing everyone together, unified in purpose, is often bedevilled by two social factors. Firstly, that people often feel more comfortable in one social **group** than in another. Secondly, they will resist attempts to bind them to groups with which they feel no particular affinity. From an organizational point of view this is important. People will behave in tune with those with whom they identify most – and this can shift according to place and time. So you might feel one of 'us' when in a committee meeting with colleagues, but a different 'us' when having coffee with your immediate team members. You may see management as 'them' – except when you are invited on to a working party which has a mix of managers and other employees.

Although there is a tendency to formalize certain us–them divisions – managers/workers; staff/hourly paid; blue collar/ white collar; professionals/unskilled – the lines of them and us in organizations rarely follow the orderly patterns that their **leaders** would wish. Within each organization, different **sub-cultures** may coexist. Sub-culture is an important concept in that it describes the special understandings, bondings, shared backgrounds and beliefs of particular groups within an organization. They are *sub*-cultures because they exist beneath the wider organizational culture. While the *overall* **culture** of an organization may be shared by everyone (they are 'M&S' people, 'IBM' employees or 'university students'), significant sub-cultures will bind, say, just all women within the organization, all the older staff, all the black employees or all the smokers who meet outside the building regularly for a cigarette break. These people may feel that, irrespective of rank or department, they are emotionally bonded through their particular common experience, background or heritage. Alternatively, different departments may develop their own sub-cultures and end up seeing other departments as 'them'.

Some of these organizational sub-cultures may challenge the **values** promoted by management. For example, one of our students returned from her placement with a large accounting firm, the product of a recent merger. The merged company produced a glossy brochure extolling its values – the fundamental beliefs which supposedly underpinned its whole way of working: 'excellence, dedication, team work, decisiveness and integrity'. These values, according to our student, carried little credibility with the staff:

> The merger had produced a company in which people refer to themselves as ex-A or ex-B; different paperwork and different procedures are still in operation. As far as decisiveness is concerned, after nine months of negotiation, no decision has been made by the two rival camps about which computer system should be used. As for integrity, who can forget that the man who masterminded the merger, and who now stands behind the 'values campaign', had told the financial world that there would be no merger, just three months before the event?

Another student who had worked for the same organization reported:

> The tension in the office was only lightened by making fun out of the values booklet. 'Value shifting' became the joke phrase. The booklet was likened to something from the fast food world, and someone suggested that our work should be graded on the McDonald's star rating. The five star award would go to the person with the best values joke.

Values are important to psychological functioning, defining the things in life that we treasure most, which we are unlikely to compromise on, and which are worth fighting for. But, as we see, when values are lifted into the corporate arena their meaning can be easily trivialized or debased. In these instances we can talk of the emergence of 'counter-cultures', which define themselves through their opposition to the dominant value system – or at least to the values of those who dominate.

Sub-cultures and counter-cultures complicate the lines between us and them in organizations. My boss, as one of the managers, may be one of them, yet as a woman she is one of us; as someone who has her own marked parking space she is one of them, as a mother she is one of us. At times, the **identity**-switch can be sharp and dramatic, such as when someone turns whistle blower, a shop steward accepts promotion to become a foreman, or a woman testifies in favour of a man in a case of sexual harassment. Such shifts can attract great hostility from erstwhile companions.

Scapegoating

Even greater hostility is reserved for those members of a group who are ceremonially and emotionally cast out as unworthy of being one of us. This is the phenomenon of **scapegoating**. In the biblical ritual, the sins of the people were symbolically placed upon the head of a goat which was then cast out into the wilderness. Scapegoating is familiar within organizations, especially in the aftermath of major disasters when 'heads must roll' and must be seen to roll. By placing all the blame or the guilt on a single person or group, the rest of the organization can cleanse itself and maintain its unity and integrity. The scapegoat can be a manager, a group of employees ('trouble-makers', 'traitors', 'saboteurs') or a convenient third party, such as a consultant, a large shareholder or the government, which becomes the target of hostility. The scapegoat is usually presented in stereotypic negative form, to ensure that no one can doubt the person's evil, or errant, ways. Such a process can be observed in high gear during the run-up to a national election. A bemused electorate will watch as candidates aggressively, and sometimes desperately, attempt to scapegoat each other (or a third party) for failings in national social or economic performance. A similar ritual takes place to explain the failure of 'our' sports team, or army at war.

Shared Languages

Looking more closely at the nature of the bonds that define in-groups and out-groups we notice that they also involve a **cognitive**, or thinking, dimension. A shared interest (economic or political), a shared body of knowledge, a shared understanding, a shared **language**, bond us to each other. Consider, for example, the jargon used by computer experts. It can act as a barrier to the non-expert and clearly differentiates us, as those who understand the lingo, from them, who do not. A senior executive from a leading computer manufacturer recounted an incident which occurred during the demonstration to a government department of a system called DRS-PWS:

> The presentation went very well, and the department officials said they were impressed with the system, but they couldn't understand who this woman Doris Pughes was, whose name kept cropping up. They had misunderstood the acronym of the system DRS-PWS, for the name of a woman. Obviously they hadn't understood anything, but pretended to have been impressed with the system.

The ability to understand a jargon, a language or a joke which excludes others is a powerful bonding device. You can observe it among audiences at avant-garde concerts, who 'understand' the artists' idioms and are amused by the baffled incomprehension of the uninitiated. In organizations it is 'old hands' who know every three-letter acronym, every bit of jargon and every bit of obscure procedure or regulation. A kind of smug satisfaction, or self-admiration, is a common characteristic of this bond, which others often find irritating.

In this form a shared language is also a source of **power**; the more difficult and esoteric the language the more protected the power. Consider the computer expert's confession:

> DOS [once widely used by personal computers] is, I wouldn't say part of a conspiracy, people are not organized or intelligent enough to perpetrate such a large conspiracy. But I think that it conspires in a way that gives people power. Because it is difficult to operate, difficult to understand and difficult to work with, those people who can work with it have power, influence, and they are respected for their knowledge. I personally don't find it particularly difficult because I am an adaptable person, but now having used a Mac computer, where I don't need any of that DOS nonsense, I realize that it's a far superior tool. I think that DOS proponents believe that Mac computing is Mickey Mouse computing, not serious computing; it's not difficult, so it can't be serious.

SOCIALIZATION

The computer expert illustrates that, within an organization, **learning** the local jargon is an important part of 'learning the ropes', of becoming 'one of us'. In short, it is part of becoming **socialized** (see Chapter 2, 'Entering and Leaving'). Socialization goes through many phases. In early life, we each undergo a drastic transformation from our early uncomprehending, impulsive and spontaneous actions into being a member of society. We learn to tame our impulses, to distinguish what is permissible and not permissible behaviour, and to understand the meanings of different gestures and utterances. Within organizations, socialization enables us to make some sense of what is going on, to understand what we may and may not do, what is rewarded and what is looked down on, what is taken for granted, what is 'dangerous' or 'sensitive' territory. Through socialization we learn where we belong. This often involves a change in self identity where our self gets fused, to a lesser or greater extent, with those with whom we now feel we belong. The tell-tale signs of this are when people start making statements about what 'we' are doing at work; 'our' latest project; the way the government fails to understand 'our' way of working...and so forth. The point here is that 'I' is not used; it has become part of a greater whole.

All socialization involves hidden curricula. Just as many school-children absorb (some would say they become indoctrinated in) the values of time-keeping, politeness, deference to the teacher and so forth, the employees of a work organization learn a profusion of things that do not form part of any set of rules or written curriculum. In some organizations, for example, he or she may learn that referring to women as 'girls' is deprecating, that wearing blue jeans is frowned upon, and that mixing in the canteen with manual staff is 'not on'. In becoming part of a new 'us' we must learn a whole range of new words, **assumptions** and values and must adopt a new repertoire of **actions**. We must also unlearn some of the products of past socializations, assumptions and values.

ORGANIZATIONS AND SOCIETY AT LARGE

Organizations are part of wider society. They continuously engage with the customs and social divisions of that society. Inequalities of **gender, race** and class are not forgotten once people enter the worlds of their organizations (see Chapter 17, 'Career-ing'). In fact, the odds are that most people see many of these inequalities recreated and amplified in their workplace. Black employees can find themselves ghettoized in low-income, dead-end jobs. Women can find themselves 'serving' male bosses, or working in the 'caring' industries in conditions that almost replicate their subordinate role at home. Working-class people can find themselves patronized by middle-class managers, perhaps half their age. Pretending that such inequalities do not exist at work, and that everyone is in the same boat, is unlikely to be credible to people who have already experienced very real discrimination or injustice because of their race, gender, class or other attributes. Allegiance to these groupings is not easily shaken, as the director of our opening example discovered to his cost.

Many middle-class managers, faced with the minefields of class, race and gender, prefer to keep themselves to themselves. Embarrassed to socialize with people they do not understand, they shut themselves in their offices, following a policy of avoidance which is often taken as arrogance by the other side. The lines between us and them harden. Some, however, manage to transcend these lines, effectively bridging the divide. In spite of driving a Porsche, the manager of a team digging holes in the road was definitely 'one of the lads'. Talking their language, sharing their breakfast as well as their **jokes**, he was not averse to lending a hand with the spade, or to sharing a wisecrack at the expense of the pen-pushers at Head Office.

One strategy for handling **ethnic**, gender and other divisions in organizations is to pretend that they do not exist. Everyone is dealt with as an individual in matters of hiring and promotion, reward and discipline, being judged on their merits rather than on other criteria. Admirable in principle, this strategy fails to recognize subtler forms of **prejudice** and **discrimination**. Even if they are not directly victims of negative **stereotypes** (like 'blacks are underachievers', 'Greeks are unreliable', 'Poles/Irish are stupid'), members of ethnic minorities often fail to live up to the criteria of 'merit' laid down by dominant social groups. For example, academic qualifications may be used in hiring the 'best' person for a job (see Chapter 2, 'Entering and Leaving'). This generally handicaps members of already disadvantaged groups and communities, whose lack of expensive schooling and supportive home environment has limited their academic achievement.

Some organizations adopt more active policies for countering the effects of prejudice and discrimination, like 'affirmative action' or 'positive discrimination'. Such policies usually stipulate that certain quotas from particular groups should be hired/promoted, irrespective of their paper qualifications. These policies have been controversial. Undoubtedly, they enhance the prospects of disadvantaged groups, yet they perpetuate some of the racist and sexist myths which fuel prejudice of the sort: 'No black/woman/member of ethnic minority would be employed here if it wasn't for the "affirmative action" programme. They are just not good enough! What is worse, they keep good men out of this company.'

It would be wrong to conclude that managers can do nothing to overcome divisions rooted in wider social inequalities and to foster bonds that are stronger than them (see Chapter 16, 'Managing Differences and Diversity'). There is evidence that Japanese organizations in foreign countries have succeeded where local firms failed. People were sceptical as to whether Sony technical staff would agree to wear the Sony jacket as worn by manual employees. They did, when they saw the senior executives and even the chairman wearing the same jacket.

Such changes are often most successful on greenfield sites – when the organization, and its new values, can be built up from scratch. Long-established organizations, with very deep us/them divisions, are less malleable. A young, ambitious plant manager in a large, traditional, confectionery manufacturer, explained:

> I look enviously at companies where the main atmosphere is one of trust. Where people work in groups or teams, are well informed about all aspects of the company, do not clock in, organize their own hours, and above all welcome, and contribute to, change. Where I work the production line grinds on. Management literally had to force a quality programme – contradiction in terms – because the workers were so suspicious of us. And somewhere between us and them are around a dozen unions and their officials – who seem not to communicate with their members, or with each other. The directors of the company are driven by the latest, short-term, sales figures; if these are down people are laid off. So that doesn't exactly ease tension. But the main problem is that it has been like that for many years, so it's very hard to instigate change.

SYMBOLS, EMOTIONS AND CULTURE

In talking about values in an organization, we have shifted somewhat from the *cognitive* aspect of the bonding process. Values bond us, not just cognitively, but *emotionally* (see Chapter 12, 'Feelings'). Becoming socialized implies that the groups to which we belong, and the physical settings and objects about us, will acquire a special emotional significance. They come to symbolise, or stand for, something important, inaccessible to the uninitiated eye. They will evoke special feelings.

Symbols are powerful bonding devices. People have sacrificed their life to defend a piece of patterned rectangular cloth fastened to a long pole – called a flag. Of course it is much more than this. A national flag can, for some, stir deep **emotions** of pride and belonging. Symbols come in many varieties; think of the cross and the swastika, the BMW and the VW Beetle, the designer jacket or the blue jeans. They all stand for something else, something larger than themselves. Words themselves are symbols conveying emotionally charged ideas and values. This is obvious in the case of words such as 'dictatorship', 'justice', 'democracy', 'freedom' and 'success'. Dictionary definitions do not convey their emotional resonance; that requires an understanding of the culture within which they are used.

Cultures organize clusters of beliefs and attitudes. They turn simple words into vibrant ideals and innocent images into powerful emblems. Culture infuses everyday events with **meaning** and directs our emotional responses to the world around us. The study of culture, as anthropologists and sociologists tell us, reveals how many of the phenomena that we come to regard as 'biological' may in fact be culturally *learned*. Anthropologists, goes the legend, like to throw spanners in the works of academic conferences. Whenever someone mentions something they have regarded as a timeless truth, the anthropologist will say, 'Ah, you haven't heard about the Marquesan islanders, who...', showing that there are exceptions to every rule of social behaviour.

ORGANIZATIONAL CULTURE AS 'US'

Why has the concept of culture become of interest to the study of organizations? Since the early 1980s, culture has emerged as a dominant concept in understanding patterns of usness and themness. In trying to comprehend the great success of Japanese organizations in the 1970s, many Western theorists turned to the concept of culture as the key. Japanese organizations and Japanese society, it was argued, foster those values of co-operation, loyalty, innovation, flexibility and sheer hard work which account for their success. Above all, Japanese companies have *strong cultures*, which bond their members into highly cohesive and effective teams (although under fairly paternalistic management). In sharp contrast to many Western companies, they are part of a bigger 'us'. People are inspired to great feats of productivity, seeing themselves as heroes. A British, an American and a Japanese car worker are asked what they do, by a slightly naïve sociologist, runs the story. 'I am fitting hub-caps', says the British worker; 'I'm making profits for Henry Ford', says the American; 'I am a member of a team who make the best cars in the world', says the Japanese worker.

In spite of the subsequent problems of the Japanese economy, Western management has continued to look at **corporate culture** as the key to organizational success. Leadership in organizations is not merely the technical decision making, but the strengthening of organizational culture, that is the generation of commitment and the **management of meaning**. Resourceful leaders have a profound impact on people's perceptions, through the skilful manipulation of organizational **symbols** (see Chapter 10, 'Leading and Following'). In the hands of some leaders, symbols (especially words) can have tremendous power. Senior managers can strengthen organizational culture, manipulate it and control it to generate commitment, unity and meaning, by using symbols. For example, when Lee Iacocca took over the ailing Chrysler Corporation in 1979, he gave himself a salary of $1 for his first year. This was meant to tell the employees that everyone would have to make sacrifices in order to save the company, and that sacrifices started at the top. Similarly, new corporate headquarters, a new corporate logo, company awards to loyal employees, a luxurious restaurant and an imposing lobby, are organizational symbols intended to communicate meanings about the organization and its culture.

The management of meaning is far from simple. When Sir John Harvey-Jones took over ICI, he faced a situation similar to Iacocca. With staff being reduced and their salaries and wages being frozen, he felt that the Chairman's 'Rolls-Royce should be dispensed with, as another symbol of all being in it together' (Harvey-Jones, 1988: 292). However, the Chairman of Rolls-Royce phoned and told him that if ICI was to break with tradition, then Rolls-Royce's total business would suffer as other companies cancelled their orders. With a degree of guilt, Sir John changed his mind and ordered the traditional new Rolls. He was relieved some time later, when talking to some shop stewards, to be told that 'they were glad I had decided to buy it, as they did not want to have the feeling that they belonged to a company that was in such a poor way that it couldn't afford a Rolls-Royce for its Chairman'.

CONCLUSION

In this chapter we have examined the cultural dimensions of organizations, identifying the extent to which culture can generate a collective identity and feelings of 'usness'. We identified some of the factors which have brought culture to the centre of discussions of organizations in the past 20 years. We noted the importance of leadership in shaping the culture of an organization through the use of symbolism, but also pointed out that the management of culture can be unpredictable and even self-defeating.

- Emotional bonding, a sense of unity and belonging feature prominently in most organizations.
- Within organizations people continuously cross different mental boundaries between 'us' and 'them'.
- 'Us' may refer to all members of a particular department or trade union, to all female employees, to all members of a privileged sub-group or even to nearly all the members of the organization.
- Bonding is both cognitive and emotional; sharing an interest or a language is strengthened by feelings of solidarity and togetherness.
- Symbols are very important in cementing social bonds; they can be manipulated by leaders to motivate, inspire and strengthen people's commitment to an organization.
- Experiences of 'usness' and 'themness' are sustained by organizational cultures and sub-cultures which encompass shared values and assumptions.
- 'Strong cultures' (cultures with powerful shared values, ideals and symbols) have been hailed as the secret of organizational success.
- Yet the management of culture is full of dangers and pitfalls, especially if subordinates suspect their leaders of insincerity or dishonesty.

THESAURUS ENTRIES

action
assumption
cognition
corporate culture
culture
discrimination
emotion
ethnic groups
gender
group
identity
jokes
language
leadership

learning
management of meaning
meaning
power
prejudice
race
scapegoating
socialization
stereotyping
sub-culture
symbolism
team-work
values

READING ON

The wish to belong to cohesive workgroups has been extensively discussed by social psychologists since the pioneering Hawthorne Studies (for an extensive account, see Huczynski and Buchanan, 1991). The specific role of groups and social pressures in the process of socialization is explored in social psychology texts by Brown (1986) and Myers (1994).

Culture and symbolism became major areas in the study of organizations in the 1980s. Pascale and Athos (1981) and Ouchi (1981) were among the first to look for the 'secret' of the Japanese economic success: their findings suggested that culture is as important in organizations as it is for the wider society. Subsequently, in what became international bestsellers, a number of authors, notably Peters and Waterman (1982), Deal and Kennedy (1982) and Kanter (1983), stressed the importance of culture and symbols, including myths, logos and artefacts, for organizational success. A strong culture, according to such authors, was the key to corporate excellence.

Enthusiasm about culture as the single key to efficiency and success had subsided by the late 1980s, to be replaced by other supposed management panaceas, such as lean production or the learning organization. Huczynski (1996) has explored in detail such management fads. In recent years, culture and symbolism have remained areas of interest in the study of organizations, though there is a far greater recognition of the importance of subcultures and counter-cultures. Instead of considering organizations as having uniform and shared cultures, many current authors prefer to approach them as having overlapping and often contradictory cultural and symbolic layers (Frost et al., 1991). Most authors now recognize that culture and symbolism cannot be 'managed' using uniform formulas and that to some extent they may be 'unmanageable' (Gabriel, 1995).

16

Managing differences and diversity

It is said that 'variety is the spice of life'. The differences between people, from physical characteristics to the views they hold, are endlessly fascinating. So why are we not simply celebrating the idea that we are different from each other? Ask a group of students what they would like to do if they had enough money, and the answer is often that they would like to travel. Why? Not just for spectacular scenery or historic buildings; they want to be able to meet different people and see how they live. Ironically, sometimes students will tell you this while sitting in a lecture hall in partly segregated groups, avoiding sitting next to people from different **cultures**. Perhaps many of us are happier with the ideas of difference and diversity than the experience.

There are certain differences in which we can all take pride. Most people who read this book will at some time have been praised for being cleverer and more effective in their work than some others of their age. There are many other ways in which people are pleased to be different from their peers – they may kick a ball further, they are better looking (at least in their own eyes), they play the guitar better, they support a better football club, they possess some characteristic or other which in their own eyes makes them stand out from the crowd. We use differences as part of our way of understanding ourselves, of defining and declaring our **identity**; we also use sameness for this purpose – identifying some people who we see as like ourselves, 'one of us'. We see ourselves as a particular kind of person, and find ways of letting others know that this is who we wish to be taken to be. For physical characteristics, think of a time when you were meeting someone new, and had to describe yourself so that they could recognize you. The descriptions which people give under such circumstances can be very revealing about their sense of their own identity. Then when you meet that new person, another round of self-presentation may start to take place, as you selectively demonstrate to them various characteristics that you think will make you stand out in their mind – your sense of humour, your knowledge, your aggression, your cleverness, or whatever you pride yourself on that you wish to display to this particular audience.

Not only do we enjoy showing the ways in which we are different, we may also delight in the ways other people are different. A new person in the office may be seen as quite different from all the others, and may be welcomed for this. 'At last we have got someone who can finish jobs off/do the accounts/reach the top shelf', or whatever the special characteristic. Affectionate statements made about a colleague usually tell you about some way in which that person is different: 'she is wonderful, she is a really good listener', or 'he was always asking the difficult questions, so we really miss him'.

But almost everyone has experienced the other side of this: the feeling of being different, but feeling uncomfortable about it. You may feel isolated, on the wrong side of some difference which makes others dislike or misunderstand you. Many of us have found ourselves in an uncomfortably small minority at some time, a minority that does not seem to be valued by others. We may feel, for example, that we are the only member of our race, religion, sexual orientation, style of upbringing, moral persuasion, hobby group or age. Often this produces nothing more than a mild feeling of loneliness and frustration. But the universal character of that experience means that we should be able to empathize with those who are made to feel pain, or at least extreme discomfort, because of their differences. As one of our students put it:

> It was very obvious that I was the only Asian in the section. No one was rude, but they seemed to expect me to smell of curry the whole time, and they did not think I would be house trained – you know, I wouldn't know how to behave with customers. And the funny thing is that most of them were odd in their own way. It just wasn't so obvious to them.

The truth, however, is that we often fail to show much empathy for those who are different from us. Instead, we enjoy our status as members of the majority or of a privileged minority. But not all minorities are privileged. When members of a minority display their disaffection and **alienation**, we may then blame them for failing to make an effort to blend with the majority and abandon their difference. Invisible psychological lines are then drawn. The majority seeks to disregard the plight of the minority by asking it to forget its difference and act 'like everyone else'. The minority, for its part, responds by focusing on its difference as its source of pride and identity, since it is this difference which accounts for its subordination. This, in turn, invites further marginalization and lack of empathy from the majority. In this way, the experience of difference may involve both being cast in the role of being different and accepting that role as the only way to maintain one's self-respect and dignity.

Privilege itself may have its drawbacks. Individuals who have great wealth or those who acquire sudden riches and fame may feel cut off from their peers. They may be excluded just as effectively as those who are disadvantaged, ending up by feeling cut off and alienated. As one student said of another:

> The trouble is he's got so much money and he's either embarrassed about it or he thinks that everyone else wants to sponge off him, so he ends up with his only relationship being with his horse.

DIFFERENCES THAT MATTER

Language and Differences

Differences are closely associated with labels (see Chapter 11, 'Judging Others'). We may be aware of a difference, but before we can remember how we are differentiating among things and before we can carry attitudes from one object to another we have to work out what to call it, or in other words how to label it. The words that people use to describe differences do not simply describe; in a very real sense they *create* and maintain the difference that they relate to. You may have a generalized dislike or suspicion of someone, but it is only when you have used the label 'cheat' for them, or heard someone else use it, that your feelings turn into hostility or contempt. Some of the words we use to describe people have emotional overtones, positive or negative, whereas others appear to be more neutral, so the choice of word can generate a significant difference with positive or negative overtones or, alternatively, may contain or neutralize the difference. Consider, for example, the difference created by using words like 'spastic' and 'disabled', 'dyslexic' and 'dumb'. What these terms suggest will also vary between different people, and according to the situation in which the words are used. If I describe someone as lively that may be a term of approval for me, while it might fill you with foreboding.

Why do we take some differences to be very important matters, while regarding others as trivial? Why are we sometimes totally unaware of differences that another person might regard as very important? We have seen how our own difference from others can be part of our identity, while the difference of other groups may mark them as objects of envy or derision. But why do some differences become the focus for individual identity, assuming enormous **symbolic** importance, while others remain trivial matters of detail? Why do some differences become the focus of political activity? How are differences manifested in organizations and to what extent do they require management? Can difference be managed at all?

Differences and Identity

When you joined your university or college, you probably had to listen to several speeches from senior staff who told you how proud you should feel as a new member of that organization. They wanted to impress on you that your status as a student of that particular institution must become a part of your identity. Not everything we do becomes part of our identity. Watching television may not be part of our identity, though being a fan of a particular programme like *Star Trek* can become part of it. Wearing casual clothes may not be part of our identity, though a much-loved item of clothing or a certain way of dressing can become part of who we are. Our identity is composed of numerous **meanings**, images and ideas which enable us to think of ourselves as distinct and integrated entities. Not all features of our identity are conscious.

The same is true of our identity as members of organizations. When university staff visit students on placement in companies they often find that absence has made the heart grow fonder; the student's status as a member of the university has started to mean a lot more to them. Students who seemed quite hostile or indifferent when they were at university greet their lecturers like long-lost friends, and enquire eagerly as to what has been happening in their absence. You see the same thing in many expatriate working communities: people who would have found little in common in their country of origin spend a lot of time together. As a company club manager at an expatriate centre told us, 'If we said that this evening's activity was that everyone would come up to the club and walk slowly round the swimming pool behind each other, they would come. There is nothing that these people would not do so long as they are together.'

Identity Kits

We give each other clues to the differences that are important to us. Some people literally wear their old school tie to identify themselves or keep drumming up some sporting or other achievement in the distant past which is important for them. The central hero of the film *Requiem for a Heavyweight* kept reminding himself and others that he had been the '*fifth*-ranking contender for the world heavyweight title'. This is what sustained his identity throughout his years of hardship and made him somebody, at least in his own eyes if not in the eyes of those who saw a washed-out man. Alternatively, our identity may be based extensively on objects, people or institutions that we love, on beliefs, hobbies or behaviours that are central to our sense of self, or experiences that are part of our past or on dreams which we have for the future.

In presenting our identity to others, we normally adopt different strategies bearing in mind their interests and identities. To present yourself as a person with a voracious sexual appetite may go down well with friends of your own age, but not with their parents. To suggest that it is your nature to be a particularly tough manager might be seen by the interview panel as the best qualification for a job, but not gain much enthusiasm among your new subordinates.

Identities are neither easy to form, nor easy to change. Many of us go through periods of identity crisis when we are not sure what are the important things about us and what we need to shake off. We may then experiment with different beliefs, lifestyles, accents, friends, jobs and careers, until we discover those in which we feel most comfortable. Smoking, drinking and drugs are initially all forms of experimentation which we may try in seeking to leave behind what we characterize (often with the help of those who wish to sell us something) as our childish identities and construct our new adult ones. We may try new hairstyles or fashions, we may tattoo or pierce our skin, we may affect new attitudes or ideas, entertain different fantasies about the future and make different plans. These are periods which psychologists call 'identity moratorium', when different and sometimes conflicting identities fight it out for predominance. Eventually, a more or less coherent identity emerges, which sets over the years until it is threatened again by a new identity crisis. Identity crises often accompany the major life transitions like adolescence, parenthood and retirement or great traumatic and testing periods in our lives, like those surrounding the death of loved people, redundancy or serious illness – these are periods when new identities must be negotiated out of the old ones. This often involves the discovery of new differences and the obliteration of old ones.

Differences which become embedded in our identity may call for a different type of management. They are certainly not easy to change, even if we suffer in order to sustain them. Taking drugs may be an important act in forming an identity which rebels against the conformity of childhood or the conservatism of our parents; admonishments regarding their harmful consequences may then fall on deaf ears. Eventually, 'having a drug problem' may itself become part of our identity. We are not arguing here that all of life's problems become part of our identity. But, as we pointed out in Chapter 7, 'It's not My Problem', to solve a problem that is part of someone's identity may amount virtually to robbery. If someone sees themselves as a nervous person, it is going to require much more effort to help them stop being nervous than if they happen to be nervous about a particular issue. In bringing about change in a person's identity, including our own, it is often less effective to frontally assault our existing identities than to enable new identities to grow out of old ones.

Differences with Symbolic Importance

As an experiment, an American school teacher separated her class into those who had brown eyes and those who had eyes of any other colour. She then started treating the brown-eyed group as superior to the other, explaining that they had to carry the other group, which was not as good as their own, while being quite abusive to the children whose eyes were not brown. The following day, she reversed the prejudice, with the brown-eyed group being blamed for everything that went wrong.

The object of the teacher's experiment was to show her class how easily symbolic differences could be set up and reinforced in organizations. Eye colour may not be a difference automatically loaded with symbolism, but it only takes a small amount of **discrimination** to set it up as one. Race, gender and physical capacity, on the other hand, are readily recognizable as having symbolic significance, associated with privilege and supremacy over centuries. Why are some differences seen as having greater symbolic importance than others?

The answer to this is unclear. Particularly puzzling is race. Race is often associated with fixed genetic or biological features. But it is also a social construction in that people invest often small differences in appearance, language or belief with special meanings.

Historically, the importance of race has been propped up by different ideologies. Early European explorers in South America engaged in correspondence with the Pope to discuss whether the local inhabitants should be thought of as human beings at all – whether, in other words, they had souls liable to conversion and salvation. Request for a papal ruling was typical, especially for Iberian culture at that time. In Germany, in the 1930s, a violently racist policy was given an economic foundation; the 'Zionist conspiracy' was presented as the explanation for the financial woes of the country. In South Africa in the time of apartheid the Dutch Reformed Church justified racist policies on the basis of their readings of the Bible. In recent years there have been various attempts at 'scientific racism': some psychologists have argued for the superiority of specific races, especially in terms of attributes such as intelligence.

The number and absurdity of different ideas used to justify and maintain **racist** beliefs and attitudes highlights the symbolic character of this difference. Race lives on as an important symbolic difference, even when the arguments for its importance crumble. As the experiment by the American teacher illustrates, it is the reality of discrimination and privilege rather than presumed superiority or inferiority of racial characteristics that sustains the belief in difference. But there is a fundamental asymmetry between the symbolism of race for dominant groups and that of subordinate groups. Dominant groups believe in racial characteristics as inherent and immutable in order to justify their own supremacy and privilege. Subordinate groups, on the other hand, believe in racial characteristics as explanations for their victimization and suffering.

It is puzzling that some of the worst racial violence in this century has been committed by people who are physically difficult to distinguish from their victims. Psychoanalysis has noted the phenomenon it calls 'narcissism of small differences' – groups that are most similar may in fact perceive each other as the gravest threat to their identity and pride. In order to defend this identity, they exaggerate the importance of minuscule factors, investing them with massive symbolic significance. This may apply to rival football clubs in neighbouring parts of a city, which keep their greatest hate for each other. Similar exaggerations of small differences underline the hostility between rival urban gangs, similar organizations or similar groups within organizations. What the narcissism of small differences suggests is that individuals and groups tend to exaggerate the importance of the tiniest differences which set them apart from those closest to them. This has implications for the management of differences in organizations. We may have the best intentions of making light of individual or group differences; we may be very open minded to the different world views of others. We may laugh at the unimportance of the colour of ink a person uses, or the meanings they attach to physical build. But we have to recognize that there are some differences which, however small and insignificant they may seem to us, produce especially powerful emotional responses from people; seeking to deny or neutralize these differences may have the contrary effect, that of exacerbating them.

MANAGING DIFFERENCES

How can differences be managed so that they do not undermine the cohesion and unity of organizations?

In answering this question, it is important to appreciate that no management technique or method can permanently silence difference or prevent it from turning into **conflict**. On the other hand, disregarding differences and treating all members of the organization as though they were copies of each other, having identical concerns and interests, priorities and sensitivities, can be a recipe for resentment and disharmony.

Difference cannot be Ignored

It is sometimes tempting to think that we only have to ignore a difference for it to go away. For example, why can people not just behave in a 'colour-blind' way on race? Why can't each employee be judged purely on his/her merits, independent of race, gender or age? Unfortunately, ignoring such differences has a very poor record as an organizational strategy. Indeed, claiming to pay no attention to them has often been used as a means by which more powerful groups ignore the needs and demands of the less privileged. 'We're all one big family here', says the Managing Director of a small company, but if you talk to some of his workers you find that they think this is just an excuse for not paying them much.

Disregarding differences obscures the special needs that different groups may have. Some employees may benefit from the provision of crèche facilities or flexible working hours, dyslexic students may require special examination conditions, younger employees may require career development guidance, older employees may require re-training and re-skilling. Failing to observe and honour differences within an organization tends to act as indirect discrimination against all those individuals whose beliefs, lifestyles or physical characteristics do not conform to those of the assumed 'normal employee'. But the normal employee is a fiction which violates individuals' and groups' sense of identity and specialness.

Organizations taking a proactive stance on the management of differences recognize the special needs of different **groups** of people. They recognize that providing for these needs can be a source of strength for the organization as a whole, enabling the organization to draw on the talents and skills of those who would otherwise be disenfranchised or alienated.

Differences can be Positively Valued

Differences and diversity do not make life easier, but they do make it richer, and the more we can accept and even celebrate the diverse people around us, the more creative and productive we are likely to be. Yet, many people find diversity more attractive in the abstract than in practice. Proactive organizations in this area do not merely preach equal opportunities for all employees and prospective employees; they actively seek to promote them and to be seen to be doing so. Equal opportunities involve a variety of proactive measures aimed at enabling all members to develop their full potential and thrive within the organization. These may include recruitment policies, for example ensuring that advertisements for posts are constructed in such a way as not to discourage applicants from different groups; and they include the elimination of artificial barriers (usually the specification of attributes which are unnecessary for the conduct of an office) which *de facto* filter out less advantaged social groups; and they include the presence on promotion or appointment panels of a diverse group of people (including women, members of **ethnic** minorities and less senior employees) who will not automatically opt for appointing the candidate most like themselves.

In order for these measures to be effective (rather than lapse into meaningless ritual) organizations must constantly proclaim their commitment to diversity and their tolerance of difference. Awareness and sensitivity training programmes, in which members of different groups are brought together for the express purpose of identifying and sharing their concerns and worries, can make considerable contributions to the acceptance and even appreciation of the unique qualities that different groups of employees can bring to the workplace. They can undermine negative stereotypes (see Chapter 11, 'Judging Others') and build solidarity out of diversity and difference.

Avoidance of Tokenism

Disadvantaged groups within organizations are not easily fobbed off with token appointments of specific individuals to positions of power or responsibility. The token woman or black on a board of directors will merely reinforce the experience of underprivilege and inequality, unless there is also a visible attempt to address these issues at a general level. Token individuals have the tendency to become outspoken defenders of the status quo ('If I could make it to the top, why can't everyone else in my position?'), – yet to their ethnic or gender groups they become symbols of collusion and betrayal. In short, tokenism is highly counter-productive because it is perceived as rubbing salt into the wounds, compounding discrimination with deception.

Language is Central

Marshall McLuhan's famous phrase that 'the medium is the message' seems never more true than when applied to the most straightforward of media – words. **Language** does not simply describe differences, it constitutes and in a sense creates them. People differentiate in words. Words are not simply an innocent medium for conveying something which already exists in the mind; they are part of what keeps some things in the mind and some things out, as well as shaping what is in the mind. They also support and perpetuate political and power structures in organizations and in society.

Combating racist or **sexist** language, or more generally language that offends, entraps or marginalizes particular groups within organizations, is central to building a climate of trust, and overcoming division and suspicion. Changing ways of expression, however, will not by itself eliminate discrimination and prejudice unless accompanied by other measures.

The Management of Difference is not the Exclusive Preserve of Managers or Equal Opportunities Officials

However well the management of differences is conducted by managers or equal opportunities officials, its effectiveness will be limited unless it permeates the value structure of an organization, and unless most employees regard equal opportunities, fairness and equity for all as their business. Managers and equal opportunities officials will easily be dismissed as zealots or tokens unless their efforts are supported and reinforced by the whole organizational hierarchy, by

unions and by other stakeholder groups. In fact, making equal
opportunities the specialist field of a group of appointed officials or,
worse, consultants, may be the most effective way of neutralizing
calls for genuine reform and for proactive management.

Unfortunately, as soon as special needs of minority groups are
debated (crèches for parents of young children, provisions for disabled employees), those not directly affected tend to withdraw to
the safety of the majority, at best granting lukewarm support for
special measures (especially if large amounts of resources are
involved), at worst remaining bored or apathetic about the plight of
these groups.

Putting Resources to the Service of Diversity

However important words, procedures and **values** may be in combating discrimination and promoting equality of opportunity, organizations which are seen to hesitate or begrudge the commitment of
resources to achieve these ends risk generating the impression that it
is all rhetoric and tokenism. Unless organizations are seen to be willing to commit money and employee time and effort to promoting
equality of opportunity, members of minority groups receive the
direct message that they are acceptable to the organization only to
the extent that they are prepared to act as though their minority
status does not matter.

By contrast, organizations which seriously seek to promote an
atmosphere of tolerance, respect and freedom of opportunity
among their employees are seen to be willing to put resources at
the service of these objectives. To be sure, money alone cannot
undo the effects of **prejudice** or mistrust; on the contrary, it may be
nothing more than part of tokenism and defensiveness ('Racism in
our organization? Only last year we spent $100,000 on sensitivity
training for our managers', for which read '$100,000 to a firm of
consultants who ran an ill-attended workshop in an expensive
resort'). Without resources being visibly committed, equality of
opportunities can often remain at the margin of political and symbolic debates in organizations.

Leadership Matters

The behaviour of leaders gives vital clues to the rest of organizational members about the true priorities of an organization, its commitments and its values. It is important that leaders should provide

an example of understanding, honouring and managing differences. Leaders who can mix with different cultural and occupational groups, who make an effort to understand how the views and priorities of these groups differ from those of others, who are seen to take a proactive stand against prejudice and discrimination encourage their subordinates to do the same. By contrast, leaders who regard differences as an inconvenience and seek to minimize them or ignore them are liable to fuel resentment and conflict.

IN SUMMARY

Difference is a vital aspect of organizations, especially those which operate in a complex, multicultural society and those whose operations stretch globally. Difference is an important part of identity formation for the individual and the group and acts both as a source of solidarity and as a source of hostility, conflict and **aggression**. The management of differences in organizations requires personal skill and sensitivity, and also the setting up of institutional arrangements which address the concerns and interests of particular groups, especially those which have traditionally experienced prejudice or discrimination, and ensure that people have equal opportunities of reaching positions of privilege and power.

- Most people value variety but find it hard to mix with people different from themselves.
- Differences among humans can be psychological, cultural or physical. However, the meanings assumed by differences are products of different cultural traditions.
- Differences become embedded in the identity of individuals and groups.
- Differences which seem important to one group or individual appear unimportant to another.
- Language is not merely a tool by which differences are expressed; language can actually construct differences and similarities, and is instrumental in whether differences are positively or negatively experienced.
- Sexist, racist or offensive language cannot be justified on grounds of convention, convenience or amusement.
- Ignoring differences in organizations does not make them melt away.
- The management of differences in organizations requires both institutional support and the development of personal skills.

THESAURUS ENTRIES

aggression	language
alienation	meaning
conflict	prejudice
culture	race
discrimination	sexism
ethnic groups	symbolism
group	values
identity	

READING ON

A wide-ranging account of equal opportunities in organizations is offered by Legge (1995). Wilson (1995) presents the arguments of numerous researchers on gender in the workplace, visible and invisible barriers which inhibit women's career progression. Much of the discussion on women's careers has revolved around the metaphor of the 'glass ceiling' which stops women from reaching the top of organizations (Davidson and Cooper, 1992; Marshall, 1984, 1995).

Race in organizations has been approached from several different angles (for an overview, see Nkomo, 1992). Gordon et al. (1982) and several other economists have explored dual labour markets, and the benefits accruing to capitalist organizations by a workforce divided along race lines. The study of mechanisms of workplace discrimination has been pursued by American theorists since the 1960s. Alderfer et al. (1980) sought to go beyond issues of discrimination and prejudice and identify the meaning of race for majority groups in America. Omi and Winnant (1987) and Anthias (1982) have explored how the meanings of race become part of identity formation. Thomas (1993) has explored how race boundaries in American organizations may be burdened by intergenerationally transmitted emotions, rooted in the experiences of slavery and racial exploitation.

17

Career-ing

Try responding 'Well, nothing', or 'I eat a lot' to inquiries at parties about what you *do*. The notions of job and **career** reach deep into our childhood experiences. 'And what are you going to do when you grow up?' is a challenge put to most children, long before paid work has any remote significance in their lives. But that soon changes. At school your parents' occupation becomes part of your own social **identity**, and there are pressures from teachers, relatives and friends to state your future job. Thereafter, things move fast. Although the prospect of a lifelong career in the same organization, industry, or even profession, may not be as strong as it was, subject choice at school, college and university still get firmly pinned to future work. At job interviews they ask about your career plans, and 'where you expect to be in five or ten years' time' – despite the increase in zigzag career pathways, periods in and out of work and breaks for re-training or further education. There is little escape for those who are uncomfortable about being job-labelled or who are simply not sure.

We soon **learn** that we *ought* to have job or career ambitions (see also Chapter 19, 'Working and Living'). This point was forcefully brought home to one of the writers of this book when his nine-year-old son was enticed on to the stage of a professional theatre during a Christmas pantomime. The little fellow was interrogated by an ebullient compere: 'And what's *your* name sonny?' 'Where do you live, Daniel?' 'Now, tell me what job are you going to do when you're grown up?' To the astonishment of his parents, Daniel grasped the microphone and firmly asserted, 'I'm going to be an archaeologist'. There were roars of approval from the audience. In a post-pantomime debrief, Daniel said he had no idea what archaeologists were, nor what job he would do, but he felt he ought to say something that sounded good.

Daniel's response is part of the story-telling about careers. Despite the many advice books and supportive techniques that speak strongly about *planning* one's career, events tend not to unfold that way. We usually have hazy ideas about the future, and rarely can we predict the way a particular job, or our life and relationships surrounding that job, will work out. Often we do not know what we want out of a job until we have tried it. And then we can be left with a sharp image of what we do not like, but still be confused about what we want next. More often than not our **decision** 'choices' are determined by expediency and chance.

So why hang on to the notion of career? Maybe we should abandon the idea? This could be difficult. We often feel more comfortable about the future if we believe that our past was coherent and logical. This is nowhere more strongly symbolised than in the curriculum vitae – a document in which carefully selected academic qualifications, prizes, jobs and civic duties are assembled to show just how planned, and glorious, was our past. Career gaps are camouflaged: we need to convince others, and ourselves, that we know where we are going. Careers, in this form, are constructed and constant *narratives*. We create meaning and consistency by providing accounts – stories of progress, moves and decisions – that give the impression that we are in charge of events and moving onwards and upwards. Such accounts reflect highly prized values in industrialized, competitive societies. Indeed, to be perceived as a victim of circumstances, as indecisive, or simply as opportunistic, is often a recipe for failure in job interviews. The fact that many people survive and prosper in exactly this manner has not yet undermined the myth that we all are, and should be, in charge of our destinies. Only those who are secure and have 'made it' can publicly declare otherwise. Indeed, it is often worn as a badge of honour by celebrities who claim it was only because of 'good luck', being 'accidentally discovered', that they have got where they are today.

Full control over one's destiny may be a fiction, but it is one that dovetails with the traditional image of the organizational career: a succession of challenging steps within and across organizations. With each move there is an increase in power and status, and most rewards are reserved for those who reach the top of the pyramid and attain **leadership** positions. But does this image stand up to close examination?

CLIMBING WHAT?

Firstly, we need to appreciate that the concept of an occupational career is somewhat rarefied, even elitist. There are some 30 million people in industrialized countries where the idea of a career, or even a job, would be regarded as absurd. The majority of these people are **unemployed**. They are unskilled or semi-skilled, and seek work, any work, simply to survive. There has been a movement of these people from poorer, high-unemployment communities looking for jobs in richer neighbouring countries. None of them are helped by economic recession, which has taken its toll even of those who have traditionally expected to walk into jobs – newly qualified graduates and professionals. In the recession of the early 1990s, like that of the decade before, it was not uncommon to find taxi drivers and waiters with PhDs.

Those starting their careers in the new millennium are likely to face very different types of organizations and working patterns from their parents. Once, an employee traded his or her loyalty for security and lifetime employment. Now employers tend to regard themselves as very vulnerable to international market forces, and less able to protect their workforce from recessions and takeovers. Ownership, and managership, of organizations can **change** rapidly. People get knocked off the corporate ladder in this process, which can be catastrophic for those whose career and identity have been wrapped up in a company for many years. A 56-year-old chief engineer describes what it feels like:

> I *never* considered I'd be out of work. I was really shocked when I learned I'd have to go. The more people sympathized with me the worse it got. I was there 14 years, and most of this period I enjoyed the job. I've been trying virtually everything to recover my self-respect and status – but people just walk over me. Yes, I'm feeling bitterly disappointed.

A works director, also in his mid-fifties, is even sharper in his summing up:

> After 28 years in an enjoyable job, what on earth can replace it? A damn big part of your life, just gone.

Historically secure, stable enterprises, such as major banks, can now undergo structural changes where people's jobs and careers are thrown into disarray. One of our students gave this first-hand account:

> I had quite frequently heard people say 'they have sent the axeman in' and 'have you heard about so and so, he has gone to the block'. Such jokes were told

with relief that the axe had not fallen on them. Following the break-up [in the bank], many people I had known and dealt with in my job were made redundant. There was one particular day in my department when no one did any work at all. They all sat there waiting to be called to a meeting and individually told what their future would be. What I failed to realize fully at the time was the extent to which their livelihoods depended on their jobs. This sounds a bit dramatic, but in today's economic climate it is very hard to get another job in banking as all the major banks are making people redundant.... Careers become linked to the fate of an empire [in the bank]. Obviously, being good at your job is a factor in deciding promotion, but it was certainly not the only reason. Unless these people were noticed by another empire head they could find themselves side-stepped.

These accounts reveal the unplanned, often idiosyncratic, twists and turns of careers. They are also consistent with studies which reveal the anchoring effects of employment in our lives (Jahoda, 1982). Apart from providing us with a livelihood, employment gives us something to get up for in the morning (the unemployed soon find themselves disoriented in time). It offers us people to be with, beyond friends and family. It confers social status (try approaching a bank manager, finance house or new employer when jobless). Most of all, perhaps, it gives us regular activity (the unemployed soon run out of ideas about how to pass the time). Employment is woven deep into our social and psychological life, and is part of our self-**perception**. But the old formula of a job for life, or a career practising one particular kind of expertise, no longer applies. Indeed, skills can date fast so that people who start climbing the corporate ladder can soon find that their ladder rests against the wrong wall – other skills are getting rewarded, not theirs. The trick now is to become sufficiently qualified and flexible to be *employable*, rather than just being *employed*. There is now talk of the 'protean' career, where people rely on themselves more than on employers; where flexibility, new learning and the self-creation of opportunities are the hallmark of the late 1990s worker.

CHANGING SCENES

How does one become employable, and for what? To answer these questions we must pull together a variety of technological, **cultural**, and societal changes, and see how they are affecting the organization and availability of work. One British city, Birmingham, serves as an excellent illustrative case.

In the 1970s the famous engineering factories of Birmingham were booming, and the region's unemployment was amongst the lowest in the country. By the mid-1980s unemployment soared to 20 per cent, some communities having up to 90 per cent of people without work. The huge factories which provided their, and often their fathers', livelihoods lay silent and derelict. Famous names in Birmingham, such as Lucas, Leyland and Land Rover, were struggling to survive a combination of recession and fierce international competition. As we write, the scene looks very different. New warehouses have replaced many of the factories, places equipped to automatically store and retrieve goods. Few people are needed to work them. The surviving manufacturers have become ultra modern, with computerized **technology** at virtually every stage. The time to change the design of a product has been reduced dramatically – from years to months or even weeks. More is being produced by far fewer people, and managers now talk openly of 'quality' and 'customer service'. Such companies employ relatively few permanent staff. Those who are permanent enjoy the status of being 'core workers' – high grade, high tech staff. The less skilled labour are 'peripheral workers' supplied and contracted by employment agencies, as and when required. Many of the companies have reduced their overheads to a minimum by shedding departments such as personnel, **information** technology and public relations. They can buy in those services from specialist consultants when they need them.

Some of the old buildings around Birmingham have become refurbished as huge open plan offices, 'call centres' owned by the financial services industry – banks, building societies and insurance companies. Hundreds of keyboard operators provide 24-hour telephone service to callers from anywhere in the country. On other old sites we now see new leisure developments – multiplex cinemas, health clubs, bowling alleys and restaurants.

Walking into Birmingham's city centre it is hard to miss the proliferation of banks, building societies and fast food outlets – amongst the first institutions to grab prime city space as it has become available. Many small high street shops have closed, unable to compete with the supermarkets and superstores, often based in American-style malls. Family-owned greengrocers, butchers, tailors and clothes shops have given way to country-wide chains run by professional managers and owned by huge financial institutions. Point-of-sale tills hint at the massive investment in information technology. They automatically provide an instant flow of information direct to local and national managers – on what is selling and what needs re-stocking and how an employee is performing. The managers can then issue appropriate instructions on their own VDU screens, taking charge directly of stock control, once a labour-intensive task.

The Birmingham phenomenon is observable across Britain and, to varying extents, across the industrialized world. As machines take over the manual work, flatter, leaner organizations require people with specific complex skills and knowledge. Labour-intensive work still survives, but mainly in countries or regions where labour is cheap. The new factories are not greasy; they employ people who wear suits or white coats: computer experts, systems engineers, accountants, professional managers, sales and marketing executives, designers and researchers. In Britain the revolution in manufacturing has made what remains of this sector of our economy more 'efficient' – and it contains far fewer jobs. In contrast, jobs in the services have expanded, especially in banking, accountancy, insurance, management, security, the health professions, and fast food. Basic information processing skills are now considered as essential as 'reading, writing and arithmetic'; the industrial heroes of the new century are likely to be the computing and software whizz-kids.

Loyalty to the company, once the fulcrum of the organizational career, takes on a different complexion in the new organization we have described. Allegiance is more to the project of the moment and the work team; but that can dissolve when the project is completed. Where there is a **matrix** organization different work teams can come together for different purposes at different times. In such enterprises self-management is emphasized, as there is unlikely to be a structure of many layers of managers to refer to for help. Some of these organizations have been termed '**learning organizations**' because of (a) the large amount of training and learning support they offer to their employees, and (b) their flexibility in changing their working practices to meet shifts in business circumstances (see Chapter 8, 'Learning the Ropes').

...FROM A DISTANCE, WITH BUTTONS

We have, so far, spoken almost exclusively of organizations to which people *go* to work. But changes in the technology of handling and conveying information have also created a new kind of work opportunity – **teleworking**. This involves working partly or wholly from home, offering a service which can be transmitted to a client through computer and telecommunications technology. It is the technology which makes this new, not the principle. Working from home has a long history, reaching back to the Industrial Revolution when the weaver produced cloth at home, to be collected by the wool master.

The most glamorous, and most publicized, teleworkers are highly skilled professional programmers, software engineers and systems designers. But teleworking is also used for word processing services, travel reservations and ticketing, market research, and fault-advisory services for computer users. Given that physical distance is no barrier to telecommunicating, it can provide some unusual, if not bizarre, opportunities – such as the consortium of medical practitioners in the USA who get their medical notes collated and word-processed by workers in Indonesia. They find it cheaper and quicker that way.

Teleworking needs only a room, or a bit of a room, with space to plug in a computer, telephone and fax machine. This has been attractive to companies such as IBM and Rank Xerox who wish to save on city centre overhead costs (offices, travel, pensions, insurance) but retain essential support services. It is also attractive to workers who do not want to, or cannot, physically commute to work. It has offered employment opportunities for single parents, part-time workers, and the disabled. It also offers opportunities for appropriately skilled people who fail to get 'normal' employment because of their age or the stigma of redundancy.

HIGH TECH WORK – SOME CONCERNS

Tales from teleworkers, and from others who are employed to work from home, reveal that the opportunities and freedom provided by their kind of work can be exploited by big companies, some of whom regard them as cheap labour. There are home workers, for example, who will do sewing and knitting for minimal pay; they have little choice. As part-timers, in the UK, they have poor legal protection concerning their conditions of work. Telework favours those who have good childminding facilities and some private workspace at home. A proportion of teleworkers find it impossible to get the conditions and balance right, especially if they cannot afford to hire a minder for their pre-school children. Teleworking, by its very nature, is socially isolating. There are no work colleagues with whom to share problems or gossip. The daily time structure of organizational life is missing, which means that considerable self-discipline is required about when, and when not, to work. The common complaint is about overwork – there is always something important do 'just upstairs'. There are now a few 'telecottages'. These are local community centres packed with information technology equipment where teleworkers can hire a workstation. At the same time they can meet others and experience some of the social routines of more conventional employment.

Stresses

As microchip technology penetrates more deeply into our careers and lives, we can see the first signs of 'technostress': people who feel lost without their computers. Their constant interaction with computers shows in their emotional flatness and low tolerance for people – their feelings and uncertainties. Logical thinking, like their computer, is valued highly. If we couple this with the veritable explosion of information that swamps these, and other, professionals we can detect the prototype of a new, skilled technology worker: he or she has a brilliant, but short-lived, work life – rather like a firework. The other side of the technostress coin is the feeling of inadequacy amongst those who are computer illiterate, or who find learning computer ways just too baffling.

The strong influence of technology on careers means that many people have to contend with a work environment which is progressively shifting away from people to working with, or on, high technology machines. Traditional craft skills are being replaced by new skills – such as those of the computer technician and the software programmer. Careers are beginning to be shaped around periods *out* of direct employment, when re-training or new learning takes place. Also emerging are careers which include significant sabbatical breaks, part-time employment, job shares and earlier retirement. At first glance this looks like providing a more interesting mix of career opportunities. In practice, though, it can also bring insecurities – such as an irregular income flow, not knowing when the next employment will occur, difficulties in filling time, status problems, and poor support for family care.

Tricks and Traps

Teleworking, small organizations and self-employment offer significant work opportunities. However, 'orthodox' employment is still mainly the province of large private and public corporations. To get on in such enterprises is often more idiosyncratic than it seems, each organization having its own particular career logic, or logics – as indicated in the student's story of life in a bank. One writer has suggested that it is a bit like facing a climbing frame, the shape of which varies from company to company (Gunz, 1989).

Career climbing frames are not apparent to the unattuned eye. They are not to be found neatly illustrated in company brochures, nor will they necessarily match the organization chart. They are to be found in the reward, power and **political** arrangements of the organization. People soon get a feeling as to whether they are at the centre of things, or peripheral to their department's affairs. They also know how high up, or low down, they are in the organization. But moving within or across the organization's invisible lines requires an especially keen sense of the unwritten climbing-frame rules. For example:

'It's not What You Know Here, it's Who You Know'

Personal expertise is essential to organizational functioning, but it does not always get you promoted – if that is what you desire. It can often help to have a powerful friend or **mentor** in the organization who can speak well of you to other powerful people who make promotion decisions. Winning friends and influencing people has a long tradition in public and corporate politics. It can be a remarkably effective way of getting on – while being equally effective at putting the wrong person in the wrong job. Most of us can spot people who are progressing rapidly in organizations, yet who seem to display extraordinary incompetence. The *realpolitik* of organizational life has, it seems, little to do with natural justice. But mentoring can backfire. High-profile mentors can use their protégés to mask their own shortcomings: the mentors get all the good publicity while their assistants get little or none.

'You've Got to Be Seen, Really Noticed, to Get on Here'

People who perform well may not progress because their job has low visibility; they are not noticed. A key administrative **role** can require much hard work and dedication, but because it is in the back room the results are not seen; they are taken for granted. Other roles are more visible – such as those associated with company rescues or product launches. If successful, the person is remembered: a recognizable face in the crowd. We here see, once again, that appearances seem to matter a lot. Like theatre, pulling off a good performance in front of an important audience can make one's career. The stars are remembered; the walk-on parts are forgotten.

'If You're a Woman Here, Watch out for the Glass Ceiling'

It is still relatively rare for women to reach top management posts. Organizations offer a host of reasons for this, such as: they do not apply for top posts; they do not have suitable qualifications; they are not likely to want the pressures of senior positions; they are more likely to leave because of family commitments…and so forth. While these statements may contain a grain of truth in particular circumstances, rarely do they survive close examination – because, more often than not, they are rationalizations or defensive positions constructed to preserve male prerogatives and empires. Fear, prejudice and **stereotypes** are often at the root of such judgements, not unlike those applied to different ethnic groups. The frustration for an ambitious woman is that there are no visible barriers preventing her progress. Often she knows she is being blocked but is uncertain why: she hits an invisible ceiling. To break through it usually requires exceptional courage, ability and political skill. If we look at the informal **power** networks of men – their clubs, golf courses, lunches, locker rooms and mentors – it is soon apparent what women are missing. They are not connected to the 'helpful' networks of influence, and they are excluded from entry. There is also a more primitive **gender prejudice** of the sort: 'Would you really like to work with, or be bossed around by, a woman?' The 33-year-old male general manager of an expanding company of 500 employees put it as follows:

> Working with men is cosy. You can eff and blind, and if they don't like it, tough. Blokes are like that. One of the things that would make me uncomfortable about having a woman on the team is that if somebody picked on her, I'd feel it was bad form.

This manager did have one woman in his department who, he acknowledged, was 'indisputably better' than a man of similar status. But the manager could not bring himself to promote the woman over the man: 'I owe him a lot. If he hadn't been working with me, I probably wouldn't have been able to move on. He would take great exception to working for her and I feel I would be letting him down enormously.'

There are, of course, women who have made it to the top – in national politics and in corporate life. Ironically, it has been noted that these people often do not go out of their way to help other women into senior posts. It is as if they are jealously guarding their own hard-won positions and pulling up the ladder behind them.

'You've Got to Move Fast, Early on, if You're Going to Get to the Top'

In some cultures an employee with wisdom accumulated from many years of experience is much valued. People in their fifties, sixties and upwards are regarded as key personnel. In many Western organizations there is a reverse ageism. Professions such as advertising, marketing and publishing are known for their 'if you haven't made it by 30...' ethos. It is rare indeed to spot an advertisement for a senior industrial position aimed at the over-forties. Those on the fast track get there at an early age. Not, it seems, because they have planned things that way, but more by recognizing and capitalizing on opportunities, with a sense of timing about when to move and when to stick. Like good poker players, their game improves fast with practice. Most make a number of rapid job changes in early career, maximizing their visibility and network of contacts. Because of this they are more likely to be 'head-hunted' – approached by another company, or by a consultant employed to find talented executives for client organizations.

Things are changing – slightly. Demographic shifts have meant fewer youngsters entering the workforce, while some occupations have become less popular than they once were. Employers have had to look elsewhere for now scarcer **skills**. This is seen for example in school teaching where some employers have offered financial and childcare inducements for trained, older people to return to their professions on a part- or full-time basis. Other organizations, such as retail stores, have 'discovered' older workers as people who are generally more reliable, more flexible in working hours, and often more knowledgeable than younger employees.

CAREER INTERFACES

Career-ing is intimately interconnected with what happens in the rest of one's life (see Chapter 19, 'Working and Living'). Where our careers take us, and our feelings about them, is not totally determined by the organization. We are, for example, better able to move job locations when we have no specific ties to family or community. If we have children at school and in a neighbourhood we enjoy, the psychological and social costs of moving to a new job at another locality can be considerable – a point often underestimated by companies who assume 'total mobility' of their employees. For single parents, especially, whatever support network is available locally – friends, neighbours, family – is a precious resource, not to be squandered. People who have felt forced to move (the alternative is unemployment) have pointed to their difficult period of adaptation, and sometimes the long resentment of their children, who have had to uproot friendships.

A compromise solution for some is long-distance commuting. Many early morning and evening trains, planes and cars are packed with commuters making expensive journeys to and from their place of work. Some choose to avoid the hassle of the longest journeys by setting up a weekday home near their place of work. Other commuters with families will claim that their shifting life-style in fact allows them to spend more 'quality time' with their partners and children, as well as use the travel time to do work. At best this is possible. But the reality for most commuters is often very different. Apart from being a financial strain, long hours of often unreliable, pressurized commuting can be exhausting, leaving little capacity to devote to important relationships in the evenings and weekends. The internationalization of business has accentuated this issue. The glamorous image of the jet-travelling, multilingual, 'briefcase' executive should be set against the stresses of global travel, the executive's much-reduced opportunities for developing stable personal relationships – and a place to call home. Such difficulties are compounded in **dual career** relationships, where both partners are trying to balance career demands with those of their own relationship and family pressures. Let us look at this in a little more detail.

Balancing Demands

Highly career-oriented people find it difficult to manage their jobs and family in parallel – they spill emotionally into one another. In traditional marriages the woman at home has supported the bread-winning male, absorbing his work anxieties and managing the household and children. There has been a considerable shift away from this structure, with a significant growth in two-career families – either from the outset of a partnership, or when a woman returns to work after a career break to raise children. The balance varies – from two full-time careers to combinations of part time and full time. This new equilibrium in work roles has had far-reaching con-sequences for the organization of careers.

Domestically, it has left a question mark over who is going to manage the household and children. Traditional beliefs about male and female roles overshadow the new liberalization of work arrange-ments. Many women find themselves returning home from work to then take on most of the domestic chores and child managing: in effect, they are working an extra shift (Hochschild, 1989). Even in 'new man' families (he does the shopping, vacuums the floor and cooks some of the meals) the woman still finds herself shoul-dering the responsibility for planning these events, while con-stantly having to anticipate the needs of her children. If they can afford it, some dual-career families will buy in help for household and child management. In some countries this means the employment of people (usually women) who, ironically, have to leave their own children unattended: it is the only kind of work they can obtain.

Organizations, in the face of an increase in dual careers, have had to reflect on their employment policies. People are more reluctant to relocate, and desire greater flexibility to accommodate the needs of children – maternity/paternity leave, crèches, child minders, time off for sickness, school holidays and emergencies. Furthermore, the heightened profile of women in the workforce (now over 50 per cent in the UK) adds to pressure for career compatibility with men. There has, however, been no rush by companies to adapt to changing career needs, and the United Kingdom noticeably lags behind many of its European counterparts. Most working women are part time. They are a more malleable, and vulnerable, work population than their full-time counterparts.

'What was Once Important isn't so Important Now'

Finally, we should stress that career-ing ebbs and flows as the events of life unfold. What seems important at 21 feels less so at 41, and perhaps quite irrelevant at 51. In later career, pensions and security become psychologically real, if not crucial, in ways that many young employees find almost incomprehensible. Career **motivation** rarely maintains an even course or force. There are peaks and plateaux. The **mid-career** plateau, or crisis, is much discussed – so much so that people who do not experience it can feel guilty or embarrassed. The 35–45-year-old, goes the argument, is having to come to terms with what she or he has achieved, and what has been missed. Or, perhaps, having made it, 'it' does not seem nearly as interesting or rewarding as it once did. What new challenges are there? Do I have the energy or ability to do something new? And if I do not do something, might I get stuck for the rest of my working life?

The most serious form of plateauing is **burnout**, where high initial expectations of what one can achieve at work are gradually thwarted – to the extent that one gives up, withdraws, or offers just about the minimum to get by. Some jobs are more prone to burnout than others. Helping professions, such as nursing, social work, medicine and school teaching, have more than their fair share of burnout. These jobs all deal with human problems, often have very limited financial resources and are emotionally demanding. The professionals who work in them can face big and difficult failures along with their successes. After a time all this takes its toll, leaving them exhausted and disillusioned.

The end of an organizational career opens what has been termed 'third age' opportunities. For example, further paid work is possible for some professional or skilled people whose expertise is still in demand – such as offering consultancy services to a network of personal contacts built up over the years. Formal learning and re-training can continue through special courses which are aimed at the retired population. But this optimistic image of post-career activity is not the typical one. Not everyone has skills to sell or the inclination to pick up formal education. Without special preparation and contingency plans the organizational careerist can find retirement a shock. The switch from organizational routines to domestic ones can be confusing, especially if the person's **status** and identity were shored up by his or her position and earnings in the organization. Outside the context of regular work, holidays, do-it-yourself activities and gardening can lack lustre. A lifetime's career, or sequence of jobs, leaves a legacy of habits, routines and social expectations which do not disappear suddenly after the final farewell to one's work colleagues, at 65 years of age (see Chapter 2, 'Entering and Leaving').

- A career, or job, becomes part of our self-image at an early age.
- There are many people for whom a career or job seems unattainable because of age, sex, ethnicity, infirmity, lack of skill or chronic unemployment.
- Career patterns are changing. A job for life is now rare; employability is more important.
- Matrix and flat organizations are replacing traditional hierarchies.
- Politics, personal connections and private networks influence many career paths.
- Women are less likely to be part of the informal (male) power networks and they can hit a 'glass ceiling', blocking their career progress.
- New technologies are producing new styles of working – such as teleworking. They have significant drawbacks along with their benefits.
- Work and non-work interrelate and can produce highly conflicting demands.
- Career motivation fluctuates considerably over a lifetime.

THESAURUS ENTRIES

burnout	mid-career crisis
career	motivation
change	perception
culture	politics
decision making	power
dual career	prejudice
gender	role
identity	skill
information	status
leadership	stereotyping
learning	technology
learning organization	teleworking
matrix structure	unemployment
mentor	

READING ON

A traditional view on how careers develop within and across organizations can be found in Schein (1978) and Hall (1986). Herriot and Pemberton (1995) and Arthur (1994) talk of the change in psychological contract between employee and employer as organizations become 'boundaryless' – personal choices that people make in search of self-fulfilment, a 'contract with one's self' rather than with an organization. Hall (1996) echoes this point, claiming that the 'protean' career has come of age. Is this now the common form of career? Fletcher and Williams (1992) feel not: they maintain that it prematurely states the demise of traditional organizational careers. Kinsman (1987) makes an extensive, and up-beat, case for teleworking.

In a highly original article, Grey (1994) has argued that career can become part of an organization's disciplinary mechanism. Individuals pursuing careers adapt their acting and thinking to ways which will enhance their prospects, in this way complying unconsciously with deeper organizational controls which function at the level of language.

Lewis and Cooper (1989) discuss the challenges of dual-career couples, while Hochschild (1989) gives graphic descriptions of different career arrangements amongst American couples. The extreme stresses and burnout in some occupations are discussed by

Pines and Aronson (1989). Levinson (1979) gives an account of how life stages, or 'seasons', interact with career and self-identity.

The 'glass ceiling' is one of a number of issues faced by women in organizations, and there is a lively debate on whether women have a unique style of managing compared with men – see Powell (1993) and Rosener (1990).

18

Producing and consuming

'The customer comes first.'
'We pride ourselves on the close relationships we have with our clients.'
'A world class service to consumers.'
'Quality, Quality, Quality!'

It is rare to find businesses which do not proclaim such slogans, as central ingredients of their **culture** and philosophy. The consumer reigns supreme in our time. Most organizations seem desperate to please their customers, pander to their every demand and delight them with new choices, new products, new services. Increasingly, government organizations, from social services departments to universities and prisons, are asked to address their constituencies as customers and consumers. In the United Kingdom, the Citizen's Charter in the early 1990s was an attempt to make state employees (including tax officers, social workers and clerks in job centres) accountable to the average citizen, in the same way that business organizations are meant to be accountable to their consumers.

In this chapter we shall examine how the consumer, this big outsider, shapes what goes on inside organizations. We will examine how consumers affect the work experiences of organizational members who deal with them directly or indirectly. We will also look at how we all reconcile our experiences as workers with those as consumers. We must not forget that the same people who busily try to satisfy an organization's consumers are themselves the consumers that other organizations seek to attract. Finally, we will examine the consumption that takes place within organizations themselves, in diverse forms, ranging from corporate hospitality and business travel to company accounts and perks at work.

WHO IS THE CONSUMER?

We all consume, as humans have done throughout the ages. We consume food and water, we consume electricity, we consume cigarettes, we consume services like education, we consume the air we breathe. Clearly we could not stay alive without consuming; nor could other animal or plant species survive without consuming those natural resources that are necessary for maintaining the delicate balances of life. To consume is necessary for life; to be consumed signifies the drawing of life out of something. An old, though still current meaning of the word 'to consume' was 'to use up' or 'to destroy'.

If consumption has remained a necessity for human beings throughout the ages, the **meaning** of consumption has changed dramatically. Today, we live in a society often referred to as a 'consumer society', a society in which we do not consume in order merely to stay alive, but we consume for pleasure, we consume for adventure and for excitement. From a very young age, we experience the power of choosing how to spend our pocket money and learn the important differences between the objects through which we may fulfil our desires. As children, most of us are exposed to alluring advertisements for toys, images and experiences which stimulate our imaginations and the demands we make on our parents' purses. From this young age, we learn to distinguish between different badges, different brands. In this way, we invest the commodities we use, those we buy ourselves and those given to us by others, with meanings. The meaning of a Barbie doll or an electric train may change as we grow older, but the idea that objects, commodities, carry meanings is one we will never grow out of.

Later, we learn to identify the meanings carried by particular brands of watches, holiday destinations or pieces of designer clothing. In our consumer society, commodities become important **status symbols**. By displaying expensive clothes, glamorous cars and other trappings of wealth individuals can earn the esteem of others. **Success** is often assessed in terms of how much money people have to spend and how they spend it. After all, commodities are there for all to see, unlike a person's family lineage, school or university. Commodities promise to infuse our lives with meaning, happiness and pleasure. By being the proud owners of a prestigious brand, we appropriate something of the brand's glamour and make it part of our own image of ourselves. The house we live in, the car we drive, the watch we wear thus become part of us, almost like extensions to our bodies, parts of our history and **identity**.

In Western and increasingly in other cultures, consumption has become a prolific source of meanings and identities, meeting needs which in earlier times might have been fulfilled by religion or politics. Some scholars are arguing that consumption has even supplanted **work** as the source of our images of ourselves. Who we are does not depend so much on the job we do, our **career** or the organization which employs us, but rather on our consumer tastes and the extent to which we can support them. In our work we may be bossed about, frustrated and dependent; but as consumers we can be kings, choosing what we like, experimenting with different products, services and lifestyles, controlling our bodies, our images and our destinies. While in our work many of the decisions are already made for us, in our consumption we can exercise choice. What is more, our choices and preferences as consumers matter, as indicated by the desperate efforts of advertisers and marketers to entice us to their products. Consumer choice, then, is one of the chief values of our culture; its emblem is the supermarket or, better still, the shopping mall in which we explore new fashions, compare the merits of different styles and products, and make the two gestures which epitomize our sovereignty as consumers – we pay for the things we choose and offer no explanations for the things or suppliers we reject.

The social and economic institution which forms the basis of the consumer's sovereignty is the market; the market is also what most organizations keep their eyes firmly on. In the market, they compete to attract the attention and the favour of the consumer. Earlier generations of entrepreneurs competed for the favour of the consumer, mainly on price. Henry Ford's great achievement was his ability to turn cars into a mass-produced, mass-consumed commodity, cheap enough to be within the budget of many American families. Many of today's consumers would not put up with Ford's arrogant 'They can have it any colour they like, so long as it's black'. (His model T Ford was available only in black.) Consumers today want choice, or at least the feeling of choice: they want difference. The right to choose among alternative products was one of the four fundamental consumer rights proposed by John F. Kennedy in his classic statement to the American Congress in March 1962 (the others were the rights to information, safety and representation by government regulators). What is more, today's flexible manufacturing technologies have enabled many industries, from woollen sweaters to cars, to move away from mass-producing identical products to turning out short runs of highly differentiated goods. Niche marketing, where specific segments of consumers are targeted with specialist products, has replaced much of the mass marketing of old.

This necessitates a great degree of flexibility in working practices. Companies must be able to employ, lay off and re-deploy staff at very short notice in very different positions. It also necessitates constant vigilance to trends in the market, new consumer fashions and styles, new niches and new ideas. From an organization's point of view, then, the consumer does not exactly look like a king, more like an unpredictable child, whose fickle desires must not only be met but anticipated, shaped and guided towards what the organization can offer. Even more than quality, service and value for money, many companies seek to mollycoddle their customers, feeding their fantasies, their vanity and their search for individuality and meaning.

Consumers, for their part, have become quite suspicious of the claims made by manufacturers and advertisers. They often resist suppliers' attempts to lure them towards new products or they use products in unconventional, unusual ways, creating a distance between the meaning which products have for them and those advocated by the producers and the advertisers. Consumers' suspicions can escalate into total mistrust and rejection, as has been the case with numerous products tarnished by health scares or when products become targets of boycotts.

IN THE LINE OF FIRE

Meeting the customer face to face is what Jan Carlzon, former President of Scandinavian Airlines Systems, calls a 'moment of truth'. It is a company's opportunity to impress customers, to convince them that they matter, that their needs and loyalty are vitally important.

> Last year, each of our 10 million customers came in contact with approximately five SAS employees, and this contact lasted an average of 15 seconds each time. Thus, SAS is 'created' 50 million times a year, 15 seconds at a time. These 50 million 'moments of truth' are the moments that ultimately determine whether SAS will succeed or fail as a company. They are the moments when we must prove to our customers that SAS is their best alternative. (Carlzon, 1989: 3)

SAS, like many other companies, spends much time and money selecting and training staff responsible for handling these moments of truth. Looks, manners and above all 'attitude' are essential – they are not mere attributes of employees but attributes of the organization, an integral part of the service the customer obtains. An alluring and responsive employee, radiating competence and responsiveness, can create a far more satisfied customer than a harassed, bad-tempered one, even if the latter is offering an identical product or service for a fraction of the price.

To the individual employee who has found shelter in the back office, being exposed to the critical eye of the customer for the first time is an important trial. Like actors who have only performed in rehearsals, they are suddenly exposed to a whole new experience, an experience of operating without a safety net. In the following description, Sandra, a student trainee in a large accounting firm, describes her feelings, as she finds herself having to explain some rather intricate tax procedures to a client.

> My manager received a letter from one of the clients, a supermodel, requesting that in future her husband should do her tax return – could we explain to him the process. John (my manager) asked me to write a letter instructing him, but I suggested that it would be much quicker to run through it with him in person. John agreed. Up until this point I had not been allowed to come into contact with clients face to face, so I was looking forward to the opportunity to attend a meeting, although I believed that I would be playing rather a passive role. John began his usual jokes, this time the theme being that I was going to be thrown in the den of the lion alone. For a moment I panicked, but my other colleagues reassured me that he was only teasing me.
>
> The day was approaching and still John continued his joking. Taking precautionary measures, I briefed myself on the whole issue, producing handouts and examples, just in case. The meeting time finally arrived, and I cannot express the relief I felt when John put on his suit jacket, following the phone call from reception informing us of the client's arrival. I went up to the meeting room and John arrived with the client. He introduced me as his colleague who specialized in VAT...and promptly left, closing the door on exit.
>
> It took me a few seconds to regain my composure, and I then proceeded to carry out the hour-long meeting. John arrived just as I was winding up the final details, and said that he had a few other matters to run through with the client. I shook hands with the client, and left.
>
> I feel that I learned more about myself and my position in the firm in that incident than perhaps I learned throughout my placement. I felt valued, especially with so many colleagues congratulating me, and John's praise when he returned from the client. John also told me that he was pleased that I had never really believed that I would be doing it on my own, or I would have panicked. It was surprising that John was so perceptive, as I thought that I was the only person in the firm to have the time to put together a set of assumptions and perceptions about the people I worked with.

Sandra's experience is not unique. Meeting the customer is a moment of truth in many organizations. After two decades of 'customer orientation' programmes and initiatives, employees in many organizations have internalized the significance of those moments. In some organizations, this has the effect of creating two categories of employees: a front line in contact with customers and back office servicing the front line with information, materials and resources. It is not uncommon for the former to be lionized, leaving the latter with a sense of being less appreciated.

In a privatized utility, which one of us studied in some detail, 20 clerks were dealing over the telephone with customer queries, requests and complaints. The office was buzzing with activity. On a wall, an electronic panel informed everyone how long the customers were waiting before their calls were answered. The clerks were busily trying to arrange for visits by service engineers, meter readings and appliance deliveries. They never saw the consumer and the consumer never met them – but talk about the consumer, with his/her complaints, irritation, impatience and demands, was everywhere in the office. Furtive conversations could be heard about Mrs Merton's order being delayed yet again and Mr Parsons's car being rammed by one of the company's vans. Most of the clerks appeared to have the interest of the consumer at heart, even when their organization's red tape and interest in cost-cutting made it hard for them to respond quickly and efficiently. Margaret Benton, a senior clerk, said:

> When you are trying to help a customer, you sometimes come up against a brick wall. The customer needs an appliance fixed, the house is freezing, you can see the problem and you do all you can to help. Then, you get the attitude from above, 'No it can't be done, no I haven't got an engineer to send'. And I'm thinking, if only I was near the [engineering] depot, I would get an engineer and say you go and do this job right now. It makes me go mad.
>
> When all the odds are against me, you know, I'm trying to help this consumer and everybody is saying 'No you can't have the engineer', in the end I won't let go – I go on and on up the line, higher and higher, and eventually somebody will listen and then the job gets done. And then the customer rings up, and she says 'I'm happy, thank you' and then I put the phone down and I think, hurrah, we've done it. But then why is it necessary to go through all this trouble? For me, it is a challenge when this happens and I get more excited; but, in the end, it shouldn't be like that.

Another clerk reported her anger about the way that customers are divided into groups – the rich ones who pay for the services and the poor ones, those living in public housing, whose problems seem not to matter.

> What makes me cross quite often is how the customers are treated, which is disgusting. The classic one is, if you are a council tenant, you are beneath the lot as

far as I can see. When a job comes up the computer tells you whether it is a council property, and whether or not there is a service contract; three-star contract is the best one. Three-star contract, we are supposed to send someone at once. Council tenants, on the other hand, are left to wait. 'We will endeavour to call today' – this is what we are meant to say, which doesn't give them a yes or no. In reality, their job number goes to the bottom of the pile and they may be kept waiting for days.

The division of customers into different classes mirrors the divisions of the employees themselves. The office staff who speak to the customers are subordinate to the true elite, the engineers who serve the customer directly, but superior to the other office workers, referred to as 'admin'.

My job is very much where you are at everybody's beck and call; it is the nature of the job, admin basically covers so many things, menial-type tasks: photocopying, stationery, equipment. When front-line staff want something, you are the one to find it for them. In that respect my job is responsible, because people need that equipment to perform their jobs properly. But I would prefer to deal with the customers and what is actually going on out there rather than what is going on in the office.

In this way, many organizations create 'internal' consumers, whose requirements derive from the fact that they service the external consumers. If these internal consumers require resources, information or anything else, their claims take precedence. Being in the front line of contact with customers gives employees a distinct sense of purpose and also considerable power within the organization.

'Serving the customer' becomes an excuse for virtually any type of behaviour. A major computer company held a weekly early-morning meeting of its senior executives, a meeting known informally as the Holy Council. At one such meeting, one of the executives failed to arrive, something that had never happened before. He eventually got there breathless in the middle of the meeting; he might have expected a rough reception, but he told his colleagues, 'I was with a customer'. Order was at once restored.

A CAST OF THOUSANDS

As industrialized countries move from manufacturing to service, an ever-increasing proportion of employees take their place in the front line. As we saw in Chapter 12, the emotional tone that these employees adopt becomes an integral part of the service they provide. Nurses must show care and concern, sports coaches enthusiasm and drive, funeral directors dignified respect, and professional wrestlers anger and hate. Managing one's **emotions** is a key feature of many front-line jobs. Equally important is managing the emotions of others. A waiter must diagnose whether a customer's anger is serious and justified and use his own emotional techniques for defusing the situation. A sales assistant must sense the needs of the potential customer in order to effect a sale.

One of the central features of our consumer society is that the act of working itself is often camouflaged. The consumer does not wish to be reminded of, let alone see, the sweaty faces of the workers who produce the gleaming objects he/she buys; nor does he/she want to see the bored expressions of the workers who service him/her, impatient for the moment when they can pack up, go home and become consumers in their own right. A screen is brought down between work and consumption. And the workers who service the consumer at the moment of consumption must cease to appear as workers. They must appear as props, livening up the consumer's experience, as performers of admirable routines, with their smiles and emotions: as artists in their own right.

Disney, a pioneer in these matters, is a company that has managed to persuade consumers of the incredible fun they will have, notwithstanding having to wait in interminable queues or to resist their children's constant pleas for yet more memorabilia. The theatre of Disney has gone the whole way by referring to its employees as the 'cast'. In this way, road sweepers, burger tossers, machine operators and lavatory cleaners are no longer workers, but actors; artists even. While sweeping roads, tossing burgers, operating machines and cleaning lavatories, they must sustain the consumer's fantasy of being in a fabled world where dreams come true. Other companies in the retailing, catering, travel, tourism and leisure sectors have also adopted Human Resource Management techniques aimed at enhancing the customer orientation of their employees – it is no longer enough to provide an efficient and competent service; they must supply a personalized, caring and flattering one.

An interesting implication of this organizational trend concerns the employee's sense of identity. This has two distinct facets, as many employees are also consumers of the industries that employ them. As more and more young people spend some of their time working in fast food restaurants, it is forecast that in 20 years, the majority of customers of these restaurants will be former employees of fast food companies. A growing number of individuals have experiences from both sides of the counter. How does this shape their expectations and their experiences of being served? Consider the importance of the company uniform that employees are requested to wear. Uniforms are now worn by an increasing number of workers, from airline staff to sales assistants and from chartered accountants to fast food employees. They are meant to connote professionalism, uniformity and a corporate ethos; 'we are all here to serve you', they seem to proclaim to the customers. And yet, the uniformity denies the very individuality which staff, in their capacity as consumers, have come to expect.

The ambiguities, even confusion, generated by uniforms are illustrated by a sales assistant interviewed by Paul du Gay. Much as she disliked wearing the uniform at the workplace, out of work she felt even more resistant:

> They said we can wear this uniform on our way home and I said 'I wouldn't be seen dead in this, man'. I tell you one time I was late out so I thought to get home in time I better leave my uniform on instead of wearing my own clothes. And I get to the bus-stop and everyone starts laughing. One of my friends said 'What happened, man? You had a fight with your trousers?' And the man on the bus he says 'That shirt, man, it looks like someone been sick on you'. And I thought, 'Oh thanks man'. So since then I haven't ever worn that uniform home or from home to work. (1996: 172)

The identity of young people like this is put under constant strain: as employees they are part of their employers' visual identity, marked by the company uniform, even though as consumers they are constantly looking for individuality and uniqueness. Recognizing this tension, some companies now allow their employees a degree of freedom in the way they dress or speak. Some personalize their uniforms, as when a waiter at a pizza restaurant serves customers wearing a bowler hat. Some companies, notably those flirting with a youthful, rebellious and daring image, may tolerate or even encourage such behaviours, in the belief that they increase their popularity with young customers. Most companies, however, have come to the conclusion that such individualism alienates the majority of their customers and undermines their image of professionalism and customer-centredness, so they insist on standard uniform.

The example of the uniform is typical of the general dilemma facing many members of organizations in their efforts to reconcile their experiences as employees with those as consumers. Some develop virtually split selves, where their opinions, emotions and even personalities as employees are quite different from those as consumers. Others try to integrate the two experiences by treating one of the spheres, mainly the work sphere, as a game – their behaviour at work is not a reflection of who they are but of how they perform in the game. Yet others may manage to identify with the consumers to such an extent that it justifies every personal sacrifice and hardship; they work uncomplainingly, delivering diligent service, believing in the deeper sense that they are providing for others, their customers, what they expect to receive themselves as consumers. Some of us seek to harmonize our experiences as producers with those as consumers, using them to forge our precarious and ever-changing identities.

CORPORATE CONSUMERS

We saw earlier that employees in the front line of contact with the consumers are themselves internal consumers of the services and products provided by their back-office colleagues. Employees, however, engage in another very important type of consumption. This is a form of consumption which places them in a very different type of dilemma from that described above – the consumption which they carry out *as members of the organizations which employ them*, and it includes products and services ranging from subsidized meals to company cars and corporate hospitality.

As members of their organizations, many employees get a taste of consumption considerably higher than outside the workplace. Consider, for example, the case of Harry. Harry, a 55-year-old man, the son of a Yorkshire miner, has a self-made career as a manager of a British food wholesaler. Harry lives in a comfortable house and drives a comfortable though unostentatious car supplied by his firm. His clothes are modest. He chooses his holidays carefully for the best bargain in a comfortable but hardly flashy resort. Yet, twice every year, Harry lives the life of a millionaire. He travels club class making ample use of the complimentary champagne and caviare on offer. Attractive stewardesses hover over him, ready to pander to his every desire. He is driven by limousine to expensive resorts guarded by special security forces. His commodious room is equipped with a jacuzzi and an almost limitless supply of drinks. By night Harry visits the local hot spots, by day he splits his time between the golf course and the boardroom. What accounts for Harry's metamorphosis from a member of the parsimonious middle class into a jet-setter? Simple. As a result of an accident to his superior, a few years back, Harry had to replace him at short notice on a trip to the Far East to negotiate with tea suppliers. He enjoyed his time out there and made sure that he became the man for the job. Twice a year, Harry travels to the Far East, where local businessmen compete for his custom and are willing to offer lavish entertainment in exchange for the hope of a deal.

Harry's experience as a corporate consumer may be extreme, but it is not exceptional. Many company employees these days find themselves consuming in their capacity as members of their firm, at a far higher level than they do in their private lives. Expensive meals, opulent hotels and other hospitality services, extravagant entertainment, corporate gifts and perks, company accounts, foreign trips, conference attendances, costly taxi drives, to say nothing of the ubiquitous company cars – these are all consumption opportunities which are enjoyed as long as they serve their company. One need not be a senior executive to enjoy these privileges. Accountancy trainees are regularly flown to foreign resorts for training residentials, successful employees are rewarded with luxuries beyond their individual budgets, and even the entire workforce may occasionally be entertained in glamorous hotels. But even beyond this, many people work in buildings which are more opulently decorated, more spacious and better air-conditioned than their homes. They make use of expensive facilities and resources from stationery to computers and telecommunications. In this way, many organizations lavish resources on the employees, allowing them glimpses or more extended experiences of expensive lifestyles, while at the same time they draw them into a deal. In exchange for these, the organization expects, and sometimes gets, loyalty, hard work and, more importantly, an internalization of the company's identity as part of the employee's own identity.

Corporate consumption is a mechanism through which some organizations seek to generate commitment on the part of their members. As a benevolent parent who lavishes presents and affections on his/her children, the company brings itself to the centre of the emotional life of its employees. In exchange, it asks that the employee should serve it properly, presenting the right front to outsiders, keeping any unpleasantness inside the family and serving the organization's customers in any way that is required. Many employees, in such situations, tend to idealize their companies, whose power, glamour and wealth rub off on to their own sense of identity and self. As individuals, they may be vulnerable, needy and ordinary; as members of an organization, on the other hand, they can feel important and powerful. Others may resent their company's opulence and splendour, especially when it is juxtaposed to cutbacks, redundancies and wage cuts. They may grab the company's largesse without feeling any reciprocal obligation, becoming more cynical and disenchanted.

CONCLUSIONS

The study of organizations cannot disregard the world of consumption and the consumer. Consumption is not something that happens at the boundary of organization when it sells its output to impersonal markets beyond its control; it is something that happens within every organization. In order to do their jobs properly individuals must consume resources; workers are consumers in their own right. Finally, organizations themselves offer special opportunities for consumption to their employees, as incentives or rewards aimed at strengthening commitment and loyalty. In our consumer society, the demands of consumers have a direct impact on how organizations are run.

We have examined the responsibility resting on the employees who come directly into contact with the customers and have argued that they, in turn, become customers for the services provided by back-room staff. We then examined the dilemmas facing individuals who, as employees, are driven to increasing uniformity, while, as customers, they are accustomed to searching for difference and individuality. Finally, we examined the experiences of employees as consumers of their own organization's wealth. These different experiences influence the way that individuals fashion their personal identities and shape the nature of their commitment to their company and its customers.

- Consumption takes place both at the margins of organizations and at their centres.
- Consumption is an important source of meanings and identities in contemporary society.
- Most individuals construct identities which try to accommodate their experiences at work with those as consumers.
- Contact with consumers creates special pressures for 'front-line' employees.
- Direct contact with consumers is also a basis for internal divisions within organizations, typified in the 'front office'/'back office' divisions.
- Corporate consumption is a mechanism through which some organizations seek to generate commitment on the part of their members.

THESAURUS ENTRIES

career	**status**
culture	**success**
emotion	**symbolism**
identity	**work**
meaning	

READING ON

Consumer studies have emerged as a major area of academic theorizing in the past 20 years. Many disciplines, including psychology, cultural studies, economics, social anthropology and political theory, have studied contemporary consumption, its meanings and implications. Above all, consumption lies at the heart of postmodern theorizing on contemporary society; many postmodern writers, including Baudrillard (1988), Bauman (1988, 1992) and Fiske (1989), view consumption as the sphere in which individuals construct meanings and identities, experimenting with different images and experiences.

Some of the discussion in this chapter is drawn from Knights and Morgan (1993), du Gay (1996) and Sturdy (1998) who have examined the implications of consumption for the behaviour of people in organizations. Gabriel and Lang (1995) offer a complex picture of the contemporary consumer and examine the views of the consumer adopted by a wide range of theoretical approaches. They argue that, contrary to most contemporary approaches, consumption has become fragmented, driven by numerous conflicting forces at the same time.

The later parts of this chapter have been influenced by the arguments of Schein (1980, 1988) and Schwartz (1990), who have explored the ways that individuals form emotional and moral attachments to their organizations. The emotional aspects of labour, when the worker comes face to face with the consumer, have been explored by Hochschild (1983) and Fineman (1993).

19

Working and living

'I come here and work my shift; I don't trouble them, they don't trouble me. People do sometimes get into trouble; I haven't got into trouble yet. I come here to do my job. I don't need much help. My private life is my private life.' These are the words of Mrs Vickers, a hospital cleaner. No one has difficulty understanding what 'My private life is my private life' means. It separates the world of work and organizations, the public sphere, from the world of the family and the home. The division between work and home has become second nature to most of us, although it makes less sense to people like farmers, the self-employed shopkeepers, sailors or soldiers, who either work 'from home' or whose organization *is* their home.

'Work is a four-letter word', says a poster. 'Thank God it's Friday', says another. The 'Monday morning feeling' is not one of excitement and joy at the prospect of the start of a new week. In the world of work, our time is generally someone else's time, the tools and machines we use someone else's, the premises we occupy someone else's, our **actions** determined by someone else's **decisions** and directions.

In the private world, the world of the family and the home, we do not feel accountable to an employer: our time is our own, our business is our own. Mrs Vickers was not just expressing what most of us take as a fact. She was also erecting a fence: 'You may ask me questions about my work. My boss gave you permission to do that. You may *not* ask me questions about my life outside this hospital. What I do there is my own business and does not concern you.'

To many people, the separation between public and private lives has the cast iron appearance of a 'fact'. Yet it does not take much probing to make the distinction disintegrate. **Work** does not take place exclusively in the public sphere, nor does play only take place in the private. Looking after a young child is work, whether you are doing it in your own home and the child is your own, or at a nursery and the child is someone else's. Some people play golf or drive fast cars for a living, while others mop floors, change nappies and cook lunches for nothing more than gratitude. What separates the work we do in the public sphere from that of the private is neither its quantity nor its quality. It is whether or not we get paid for it.

There is no denying that the two types of work, paid and unpaid, enjoy vastly different **status** in our **culture**. Looking after your infirm grandmother who lives with you requires effort, skill and application, but ironically is not seen as 'proper work'. Looking after other people's grandmothers in an old people's home is, on the other hand, proper work. Washing up at home hardly makes you anybody; washing up in a restaurant makes you an 'employed person'.

Some people have found it helpful to distinguish between work, the activity involving physical and mental effort, and employment, the means whereby the majority earn a wage or salary. The public world can then be seen as the time which we spend in 'gainful employment', in contrast to private life, essentially the rest of our time. Organizational theory, since Weber's pioneering theory of **bureaucracy**, has drawn a sharp line between private and public. On one side of the line lies the supposedly clean, predictable and orderly realm of organizations, of **rationality**, efficiency and **impersonality**. On the other side is the messy and unpredictable world of emotions, of personal and family life. Organizational theory has concentrated on the former, leaving people's private lives alone. The leading British and most American textbooks on organizations say very little about people's home lives or 'leisure' activities. They generally disregard the fact that people have other **roles**, apart from those assigned to them by organizations. But as we all know, people eat, sleep, go to the movies, participate in amateur dramatic societies, have children, support football teams, look after sick relatives, suffer from neurotic attacks and so on. Have these things no bearing on our behaviour in organizations?

One of the central assumptions of this book has been that the private and the public are inextricably linked. We take our work back home and, conversely, we take our home out to work. **Attitudes** and **values** formed within the family, the school or the wider culture remain part of us when we cross the boundary of an organization, as do our **sexuality**, sense of humour and **emotions**. Equally, our experiences inside organizations inevitably colour our personal and family lives. Our lives outside organizations and our lives in them cannot be studied apart from each other, even though some of us like to keep different parts of our lives in rigid compartments, while others manage to integrate them. Very few can develop totally split **personae**, one for work and one for home.

NIGEL'S STORY: WHEN HOME DISRUPTS WORK

Nigel prides himself on being a 'good' father. Ever since Emily and Alex were born, he has taken an active interest, spending as much time with them as his busy job as a senior advertising executive will allow him. Nigel loves the long summer evenings when he can spend time playing with the children in the garden. The children are both at school now, and Anne, Nigel's wife, has decided to resume her own career, as a hospital administrator.

Monday, 27 May was an important day for Nigel. It was the day of two crucial events: a presentation to a major customer and a meeting with the Customs and Excise over a disputed VAT return. It was also a significant day for another reason. This had been the first weekend that Nigel had spent alone with the children; Anne was on a three-day residential course, due to end today.

The weekend had been a terrific success. Safari park on Saturday, splashing around the garden Sunday, the kids had loved it and Nigel was happy. Nigel had some apprehensions about Monday morning. Taking both children to school, then dashing off to the office for the 10.15 presentation was going to be tight. But it could be done and it would be done.

Monday morning. Nigel wakes up and cheerfully calls the children. No answer. He goes to their room, where they seem to be sleeping soundly. 'Alex, Emily, quick, time to get up', he shouts, but his voice has no effect. It takes some more calls (his voice now has developed an edge) before Nigel realizes that the children's bright red cheeks, the bleary eyes, the sullen expressions tell their own story. Both children are running a fever.

Now, Nigel is nothing if not a man who loves a challenge. 'Problems don't exist, only challenges' is a favourite motto of his. For once, however, Nigel has a problem. He quickly appraises the options. The children must clearly be seen by a doctor; someone has to be found to take them and look after them during the day. But who? Anne perhaps; she could come back early from her residential; oh God, she will be so disappointed. What is more, Anne couldn't be back in time for him to make it to work on time.

The children are now awake; they need care, they need reassurance, they need affection. And Nigel needs someone to give them all this and to take them to the doctor. The minutes are ticking away and Nigel is no nearer to meeting his challenge. He looks out of the window into the street. All these women inside all these houses, all with masses of free time, and yet he cannot think of one, not one, he could turn to. Nigel is getting desperate and what's more, he is getting furious with himself for getting desperate. He, the champion of dozens of bruising campaigns, the winner of apparently lost causes, the master problem solver, is coming apart with the simple task of having two sick children looked after for say eight, ten hours at most.

He feels angry. He knows it; he should never have let Anne go to her wretched residential. Look at the mess she has left him with. Besides, what the hell did she need the residential for? Isn't it just an excuse for drinking, anyway? The children are now crying but Nigel can only think of his own chagrin, his own problem. Strange thoughts come into his head. Perhaps one of the girls from the office could come and spend the day with the children. Or, perhaps he can stuff them solid with medicine, take them to school, let the school sort it out...good God, what a thought. If only his parents lived a bit nearer! If only...Nigel thinks of the client, all the top brass, getting ready at that very moment for a decisive day. He is covered in cold sweat.

Then Nigel thinks the unthinkable, he thinks a thought that makes all other taboos seem like kids' play. *He* is the 'someone' who will have to take the children to the doctor, *he* will have to look after them, to comfort them and soothe them. They are still *his* children, just as they had been his children the day before, when they were playing happily in the garden. He is still their father. His mind is made up at once. A quick nagging question – how will he present his absence to the office? Surely, he can't say that he is staying at home to look after his sick children. What will they think of him? To hell with it, *he* is a man, *he* is not a child, *he* needs no excuses.

He picks up the phone. Good old Shirley, she is already there to answer the phone, a good 20 minutes before the office opens. 'Oh, Nigel, glad you phoned', says Shirley as soon as she hears his voice. 'Mr Wilmott called just a minute ago, from United Cereal, to say that they can't make it to the presentation today, any chance of re-scheduling it for next Monday?' Nigel feels a surge of elation. Had Shirley been in front of him, he would have kissed her.

For an instant, Nigel thought he might squeeze out of his resolution to devote the day to his children. Take the kids to the doctor, call Anne, make sure she's back in time for him to meet those Customs and Excise clowns: the thought crossed his mind like a flash. But no, Nigel had understood something and there was no going back.

'Thanks, Shirley', he said. 'That's funny, because something has cropped up here, and I was phoning to say that I can't make it to the office today.'

'I hope it's nothing serious', said Shirley.

'No, no, it's just...I need to take my children to the doctor', said Nigel. He felt vulnerable, saying this, exposed. 'Would you please phone the Customs and Excise and ask to rearrange our meeting, for another time?'

'Yes, of course, Nigel, don't worry at all about it, I'll sort it all out', said Shirley.

She too was aware that an important barrier had been crossed, and was pleased to be reassuring and businesslike. What's going on in Nigel's life, she wondered? I should try and find out discreetly.

Nigel's story is a true story. If you see nothing exceptional in the incident, you are quite right. Most working women would regard his 'problem' as boringly familiar, accustomed as they are to juggling work and family commitments, to being in two places and to thinking of four things at once. 'Who's picking up Liz from school?' 'When can I nip to the shop to get James's Scout uniform?' 'Ought to quickly phone Janet to see if she could pick up the dry cleaning.' These are ordinary thoughts, the like of which are rarely far below the consciousness of a large section of the population, and yet rarely trouble the minds of people like Nigel, who have been sheltered from the painful **conflict** between the demands of work and the demands of the family and home.

What makes Nigel's story interesting is that an ordinary experience should have an extraordinary effect. Nigel is neither an insensitive nor an inconsiderate person, as a father or as a husband. Yet his work had until that Monday morning been 'sacrosanct', untouchable. Nothing could be allowed to interfere with his important appointments. What his children's sickness forced him to confront was the double standard he had always employed in evaluating man's work and woman's work. It forced him to confront his own responsibilities as a father and to re-assess his priorities. It also forced him to question one of his assumptions about his colleagues and subordinates at work – the assumption that people should leave their homes behind them when they go to work, and should devote themselves wholeheartedly to their work and their organization. Finally, it forced him to question what he had always taken for granted: that people should not grumble when asked to work late, or to take a bit of work home over the weekend.

Nigel realized that to the extent that some men are able to devote themselves, spirit and body, to their work, it is because of an army of women, supporting them and their children, nurturing them and working for them. By assuming the **gender** role of 'main family breadwinner', these men have abdicated the responsibilities created by other roles, leaving the painful conflicts, the messy compromises and the juggling to their wives. And yet they have been the first to criticize women for lack of commitment to the organization. Nigel himself had not been above the odd dig at Shirley for 'abandoning him' in the office to sort it all out, long after all the other secretaries had left for home.

ORIENTATIONS TO WORK AND WORK ETHICS

Many working mothers would find Nigel's story unexceptional. Yet many workers would find it difficult to appreciate the leap of imagination that it took for Nigel to decide that he would not go to work. What is the big deal about taking a day off work, when whole industries run on four-day weeks? An American car worker was asked why he only turned up to work four days each week and his answer is legendary: 'Because I can't earn enough to make a living on three days a week.' His attitude is a universe apart from Nigel's, who thought that the world would grind to a halt if he missed a single day in the office. The American worker works to live; he expects little satisfaction or fulfilment from work, only a comfortable standard of living. The **meaning** of his life, his **identity**, are not linked to his job. For Nigel, on the other hand, work is a very important part of his life. He lives to work and work fills his life, his time and his identity. It is when the demands of his role as father come into conflict with those as a member of an organization that he is forced to evaluate some of the sacrifices that he has been making and some of the consequences of his attitudes towards his work.

Attitudes towards work vary widely. In the Bible, work is God's punishment for disobedience; it must be endured with grace. The ancient Greeks, on the other hand, considered work a base activity suitable for slaves, unworthy of cultured free men. The free Spartans did *no work at all*, occupying themselves with things martial, while the free Athenians preferred intellectual and aesthetic pursuits. The Trobriand islanders of the Pacific, in contrast, worked hard on their gardens and harvested many times the amount needed to sustain them; the quantity and quality of their product were seen as signs of their worth as members of their community.

The attitudes we bring to the workplace are partly shaped by the wider culture of which we are part. In trying to understand the development of capitalism in the West, it has been suggested that a crucial role was played by the 'Protestant **work ethic**'. This is an orientation towards work which grew out of the emergence of Protestant religion, especially Calvinism. Hard work was seen as a sign of godliness. Wealth and profit, far from being derided, were seen as signs of God's favour. Saving money, living frugally, refraining from the pleasures of the flesh and sheer hard work are the key ingredients in this type of the Protestant ethic (Weber, 1958).

Views of the Protestant ethic differ. Most people would agree, however, that nowadays its meaning has been stripped of its religious association. It has come to mean 'a sense of duty to work hard', and it is by no means restricted to Protestants. A friend told one of us about his Chinese Buddhist father:

> He used to keep his shop open until 10.30 every night. No one came in after 8.30, but it is part of the Confucian culture that you should keep your shop open whether anybody wants it or not, because they always *might* want it. And even if they don't, you have to do your best for everybody.

Much has been written about the weakening of the Protestant ethic as a source of economic decline in the West. Conversely, it seems that the Japanese have raised the work ethic to new heights, voluntarily cancelling their holidays and working overtime for no extra pay. Yet arguments which equate the wealth of nations to hard work fail to stand up to close scrutiny. Individuals and nations may work very hard and enjoy little economic prosperity if they lack **technology** or organization, or if they each work hard at undoing the other's work.

The Protestant ethic hardly explains the prosperity of nations; it does, nevertheless, describe a distinct set of work attitudes and work **motivation**, like Nigel's. In the 1980s it became common to brand as 'workaholic' people whose commitment to work creates a dependence, similar to that of an alcoholic or drug addict. This adjective underlines the fact that Nigel's orientation to work is not shared by everyone else, such as the car worker quoted earlier.

ALTERNATIVE WORK ATTITUDES

An important study conducted in the 1960s, *The Affluent Worker* (Goldthorpe et al., 1968), found that a majority of industrial workers saw work purely as a means of earning a living. Many had given up more interesting jobs to take better paid employment. They did not expect satisfaction and fulfilment from work, nor did they see hard work as a moral duty. *Leisure* was seen as the sphere of enjoyment and fulfilment. The Protestant ethic certainly had no grip on these workers, whose orientation to work is described as instrumental, that is, they saw work as a means to material well-being. By contrast, people who prize the interest and variety of their work above all else have an *intrinsic* orientation. Those who value workmates and the social aspects of work are described as having a social or solidaristic orientation. Such orientations distinguish different groups of employees, affecting the meaning they attribute to work and the way their work becomes part of their identity.

Even within a group of students taking the same university course there are variations in work orientations. On leaving, some will choose a more interesting job over a better paid one; some will choose one which gives an opportunity to socialize; some are attracted by jobs which 'look good on paper'. These orientations have been shaped by earlier experiences, role models, parental influences, careers advisers: they act as a powerful link between work and the rest of life.

WORK AND CLASS

In spite of such individual variations, work attitudes, like many other types of attitude, are linked to social *class*. The same study which established the instrumental orientation of manual workers, found that clerical workers were more concerned with the work itself, its status, and chances of **career** advancement. White-collar or clerical workers have traditionally been seen as having middle-class lifestyles and attitudes, emphasizing style, status and individual effort. They speak with middle-class accents and have middle-class tastes.

Class divisions in society account for a wide range of attitudinal differences, a fact well known to opinion pollsters, who divide the population into five categories: A ('high professions' and senior management), B ('low professions' and management), C1 (clerical) and C2 (skilled manual), D (semi-skilled) and E (unskilled), based on occupational status. Our consumption patterns, voting behaviour and opinions on a wide range of social matters display a degree of correlation with these categories. More generally, our class background affects ways we think and talk, our attitudes to work and leisure, our understanding of 'success', our views on society, crime, education and so forth.

Class and work often reinforce each other. Many of the misunderstandings, breakdowns of communication or trust and conflicts at the workplace which seem bizarre or irrational to an outside observer become understandable when the class barriers that divide people are taken into account. A comment which may have gone unnoticed in most cases can make a person feel deeply hurt if it is interpreted as a class insult, just as a **joke** can go very badly wrong if it is seen as a sexist or racist jibe.

ALTERNATIVE WORK AND NON-WORK ETHICS

Work ethics change. They change with changes in the class structure of society, they change with technological innovations as well as with broader economic and cultural developments. There are some who argue that the Protestant work ethic is disintegrating under the massive changes currently affecting our societies. Instead of work, individuals turn elsewhere in their search for meaning and identity; they turn to family life, hobbies, 'style' and material possessions.

In the early 1980s, young people with limited hopes of permanent work and even fewer opportunities for careers were seen as espousing a 'welfare ethic', content to live off the state and refusing to feel degraded or shamed by unemployment. The rich and the upwardly mobile are now rediscovering a different type of ethic: a 'wealth ethic'. Wealth, according to this view, is to be attained less through hard work than through clever deals or inheritance, and is to be enjoyed rather than copiously saved and invested. The wealth ethic merges with a 'hedonistic' or 'leisure' ethic which places great emphasis on pleasure, and paradoxically unites the 'idle rich' and those 'on the dole'. Enjoying life becomes more important than having a good job. **Success** is to be measured not through achievement but through consumption (Furnham, 1990) (see Chapter 18, 'Producing and Consuming').

Arguably, neither the rich nor large sections of the working class, at least in Great Britain, have ever been ruled by the Protestant work ethic. What is more surprising is the decline of this ethic among the achievement-motivated middle class. One of our friends was recently head-hunted for a job which carried with it a very smart 'compensation package', as the financial terms were euphemistically called. He was flattered and excited to be offered the job. However, as he thought about it, he decided that the phrase 'compensation package' was all too apt. In terms of how much of his identity he was expected to hand over, and how many week-ends he was expected to work, 'compensation' was exactly what he would need. He did not wish to give precious hours out of his life to something which was going to require compensation. He already had a satisfactory job. He turned down the offer.

As the Protestant work ethic is waning, it has been suggested that even the middle class is moving to different ethics. These include the 'narcissistic ethic' centred on self-admiration, the 'body ethic' based on lavish care for the physical body, and the 'spirit ethic' focused on self-development and self-actualization. What unites all these ethics is the shift away from *hard work* as a source of value and meaning. Yet the importance of work as a dimension of identity is unlikely to be supplanted in the near future. The time has still to come when people introduce themselves as avid readers of Proust, as owners of a Golf GTI, as 'being in analysis', or as proud fathers of two delightful children, rather than by referring to the work that they do.

Instead of disappearing completely, the Protestant work ethic may be about to undergo yet another radical transformation, just as it earlier shed its religious connections. And so long as work provides our main means of livelihood, most of us will have to reconcile the demands it makes with demands made by our homes, our families and friends, as well as our own desires.

CONCLUSION

The separation between home and work serves **organizations** well enough. The conflicts and worries of people's personal lives are not *their* problem or responsibility, but private concerns of the individuals involved. This separation, as Nigel discovered in our illustration, creates a set of double standards, justifying or even encouraging **discrimination** against women. It fosters the stance that employees should, for the duration of the working day, cut themselves off from emotional and moral attachments to their families and friends and commit themselves wholly to their organization.

Several chapters of this book have taken the view that this separation, though generally taken for granted, does not withstand close scrutiny. The line between work and home is fictional, it is part of the fiction of *order* perpetuated by organizations and their gurus. Our lives in organizations cannot and should not be studied in isolation from the rest of our existence. Organization itself, as we have studied it in the pages of this book, is not a separate, distinct universe of human activities, isolated and cushioned from the forces of disorganization and chaos.

- 'Home' and 'work' constantly interact.
- Work as well as play takes place both inside and outside of the home.
- Our attitudes and values, shaped within the family, the school or wider culture, influence our actions at the workplace, as do our family and other commitments.
- People's orientations to work vary enormously, across individuals and cultures.
- The Protestant work ethic is a set of attitudes towards work which stress self-reliance, hard work and frugality.
- There is some evidence that the Protestant work ethic is in decline in the West, though the work that people do is an important dimension of their identity.
- Work orientations (for example whether work should be a means towards an end or whether it should be enjoyable in itself) differ across the social classes.
- Traditionally working-class attitudes towards work were instrumental.
- Middle-class and clerical attitudes, by contrast, have emphasized other aspects, such as status, career or self-actualization.
- The separation of work from home severely disadvantages women, whose responsibilities are still predominantly seen as lying within the family, and whose careers are hampered as a result.
- Men's undivided commitment and loyalty to their organizations frequently rest on the sacrifice of women's career prospects and their confinement to the home.

THESAURUS ENTRIES

action	meaning
attitude	motivation
bureaucracy	organization
career	persona
conflict	rationality
culture	role
decision making	sexuality
discrimination	status
emotion	success
gender	technology
identity	values
impersonality	work
jokes	work ethic

READING ON

A lot of important research in this area has addressed the ways in which women's responsibilities at home interfere with their work lives and inhibit their career development (Cockburn, 1991; Marshall, 1995; Sharpe, 1984; Wilson, 1995). Du Gay (1996) offers a theoretical account backed with empirical case material of the fashioning of contemporary identities out of both work and domestic experiences. The relationship between consumption and work, especially in connection with issues of identity and selfhood, is discussed by Gabriel and Lang (1995). The classic work on identity and identity crisis is Erikson's (1968). Willis (1990) has offered one of the most insightful accounts of identity formation among adolescents.

The Affluent Worker study (Goldthorpe et al., 1968) produced extensive research material about the domestic and industrial attitudes of workers in Luton in the 1960s. While somewhat dated, the work provided influential theories on work ethics and the relation between work and the domestic sphere. A wide-ranging discussion of the Protestant work ethic is offered by Furnham (1990), while Maccoby (1976) and Lasch (1984) provide accounts of emerging ethics which are currently displacing the Protestant ethic.

The classic studies on achievement motivation, in juxtaposition to affiliation and power motivation, were carried out by McClelland (1961, 1971). The phenomenon of addiction to work or workaholism has been studied by Oates (1971) and Machlowitz (1980). David Stall (1994) offers a wide-ranging discussion of different sociological and psychological approaches to work.

20

Learning and organizing in uncertain times

As you reach the end of this book, it is tempting to think that you have concluded your learning on the subject of organizations. You have followed our arguments, familiarized yourself with various theories, and become aware of some of the main issues involved. You may have some good ideas of your own on how to apply this knowledge in practice. We hope that from now on, when you enter a shop, when you start a new job or when you think about the administration of your university, you will do so with more inquisitive eyes: you will be able to read and understand some of the processes which may have remained opaque in the past.

The deeper message of the book, however, is that learning about organizations can never end. Even if you learn all that there is to know about the subject, organizations do not stand still. In fact, many of them are undergoing important transformations, which call for different types of understanding and different management and practical skills. The organizations of tomorrow, those in which you are going to work and which you are going to be part of, may not be like the organizations which have inspired the theories and ideas present in this book. Theory does not stand still either. New ideas, new ways of looking at things and new concepts emerge which cast new light on what now seems tired or familiar. Thirty years ago, studying organizations through their symbols or their stories may have seemed bizarre, yet today it has become routine.

Two things about the future are certain. Firstly, organizing will continue to occupy the time and minds of people, on an increasing scale. Secondly, learning as a lifelong process will continue to support, inform and enhance our organizing activities. Organizing and learning will absorb increasing amounts of resources, time and effort, as information proliferates and as times and distances shrink. Lifetime learning has become a political cliché, yet it captures an important idea: the idea that learning is impermanent, it never stops. Or better, that when learning stops, knowledge and understanding can decay into dogma and routine. And this is the paradox which is often concealed by political cliché – old learning and old ideas can act as a hindrance to new learning and new ideas. This is especially true if the learning has been acquired with a lot of effort, pain and sacrifice – giving up old ideas can be anxiety-provoking and even painful, especially if these ideas have served us well in the past. But this is often the price we have to pay for new learning. A famous world chess champion was once asked whether it was possible to improve his game further. 'Yes', he answered, 'I only wish I could unlearn all that I know about chess, and start from scratch.'

Unlearning is a condition for learning – unlearning theories, unlearning habits and unlearning lazy shortcuts which stand in the way of new understanding. Unlearning takes courage and requires the ability to drag ourselves out of our comfort zone, the zone we create with the help of our existing stock of concepts, ideas and theories. At times, learning takes us precariously near uncertainty and chaos. 'Without "chaos", no knowledge', argued Paul Feyerabend, the philosopher of science, in what now seems less like iconoclasm and more like common sense. Chaos is a term that is used more and more frequently in studies of organizations. At times, the word 'complexity' is preferred, which sounds more scientific and less threatening.

Chaos and complexity theories emerged in the natural sciences in the 1960s, drawing on the study of non-linear dynamic systems, such as the weather or the turbulent flow of fluids. They have found many applications in other fields, including the study of organizations. Complex systems are systems which do not return readily to a condition of equilibrium; nor, however, do they suddenly collapse into utter disorder. In this book we have avoided the view that organizations are systems, because much traditional systems theory disregarded those vital meaning-creating processes that are central to our concerns. Complexity theory, on the other hand, presents a view of systems which is unpredictable, uncertain and even unmanageable. It views the future as inherently unpredictable and accepts that small causes, including accidents, can have disproportionate effects. In one famous image, a butterfly flapping its wings in China causes a hurricane in America. Managers try in vain to plan for the longer term, since the longer term for most organizations is unknown and unknowable, like the weather. A new range of metaphors for understanding organizations is now emerging – organizations as precarious entities, whose success and survival may be jeopardized at any moment by entirely unforeseeable factors.

Under such conditions of unpredictable change, successful organizations are those whose leaders and members do not seek to predict the future and control it; instead they can rapidly change course, redefine themselves and learn to live with uncertainty and even chaos. These organizations must be prepared at times to be wasteful, destructive and conflict-ridden in order to be creative and innovative. Looking for targets to apportion blame or give credit for successes may appear to be organizationally expedient, but has little justification: single individuals are not responsible either for success or for failure, these phenomena being the products of a multiplicity of chance and systemic factors. Seeking to repeat success by applying a 'winning formula' can be futile; organizational learning has little to do with learning formulas and much to do with experimentation, reasoning by analogy and an ability to question underlying assumptions and existing patterns. Learning in such organizations means essentially being prepared to operate without the safety net of received wisdom and knowledge, taking risks and never standing still.

At the same time, in a period of transition it is tempting to follow fads and fashions, prematurely discarding practices and ideas that still have life in them. This is a form of premature obsolescence of ideas – simply because they are no longer new they are assumed to be counter-productive. Here we encounter another facet of the learning paradox – the need to maintain old learning in new learning, knowing how much of the old to preserve and how to modify it and use it. Learning must both preserve the old and identify when it is time to discard it.

Unfortunately much of university education does not help us in this type of learning. Knowledge, all too frequently, comes to be equated with who said what, definitions and lists. The **authority** of the lecturer, both as a source of all **knowledge** and as a final arbiter of learning in the judgement game of examinations, is rarely questioned. The authority of the printed text, the book, is taken for granted. Students' minds are assumed to be blank pieces of paper, with no knowledge, no understanding of their own. Clarity is extolled above all other virtues in academic writing, disregarding the possibility that learning involves a movement from what is more precise to what is less clear. But the emphasis on clarity tends to close enquiry prematurely, as does the preoccupation with definitions and completeness. It is not surprising that business schools are coming under increasing criticism for producing conservative, tame and uncritical intellects, ill suited to the challenges facing managers in the real world.

In this book we have adopted a different approach. We have viewed knowledge as part of all organizations. Knowledge can be implicit or explicit, incomplete, confused or temporary. It is sometimes transferred passively from one individual to another, but then it tends to become impoverished and irrelevant. By contrast, knowledge which grows out of human action and interaction stays lively and dynamic, subject to development, criticism and correction. Ideas are continuously juxtaposed to experience, each supporting and enlightening the other. In no way do we seek to undervalue the great theories of the past to which the study of organizations owes its existence as an academic discipline. These theories must be a source of questioning and inspiration rather than a recipe offering easy answers to the burning questions of our era.

We hope that as you went through the pages of this book you made connections between concepts and ideas we presented and your own experiences of organizing or of being organized. Some of these experiences will have provided support and illustrations for our arguments; others may have qualified, modified or even contradicted what we have been saying. We have stressed throughout that **meaning** and making sense of things is personal as well as corporate. What makes sense to one person does not always make sense to another. It is not just that different people wish to say different things about organizing; the aspects of organizing about which they think it is worth saying something are different too. One person is especially concerned with order and control while another is fascinated by change and uncertainty; one is interested in gender and power relations while another focuses on team-work and groups.

The meaning of organization varies from person to person. Different individuals, working side by side in the same organization, may be working in organizations that are in effect different – one person may experience the organization as a hostile and malevolent force, while a second experiences the same organization as a model of everything that is good and right and a third 'is only doing a job' and does not care one way or another for the organization. Likewise, different academic traditions highlight different aspects of organizations: some their impersonality, some their hierarchy, some their goals, some the preoccupation with efficiency and rationality. They have defined organizations accordingly. We, in this book, have accepted the plurality of views and experiences of organizations. We will not try to define them as *abstract concepts*, but will accept them as *social constructs*, ideas which have different resonances with different people. Each one of our readers may come up with a personal statement of what organizations mean to him or her – organizations in general, and specific organizations like club, university or employer.

BEING IN THE DRIVING SEAT: ACTING WITH SENSE

In the early days of space exploration, monkeys and dogs were propelled into space in 'capsules'. Later, as human space travel became possible, space capsules were renamed space*ships*. Why? One reason was that astronauts were not content to play the part that animals had played in earlier trips. Nor, if they were trapped inside 'capsules', could they be presented as heroes exploring a new universe. Astronauts had to be given some **control**. Unlike the dogs and monkeys of the early trips who had been just physical bodies surviving extremes of speed, acceleration and gravity, astronauts were given buttons to push, instruments to read and levers to pull. This made them captains of ships whose fate seemed to be in their own hands.

Of course, astronauts had limited choices. They could hardly decide to go out for a walk, change direction and fly off to Mars. They could, however, manoeuvre their spaceships and actively participate in their missions. They could make sense of their experiences as participants in meaningful collective expeditions. They could share these experiences with other people. They, as well as others, could learn from these experiences in ways that were not possible as long as space capsules carried passive passengers.

We are hoping that this book will enable you to accomplish a similar change in your journeys through organizations. We are hoping that you will understand more about your missions and the ways in which your organizations function, with better chances of being pilots of your ships rather than passive passengers. It would be absurd to suggest that reading the book will take you to the top of your organization or that it will free you from all the organizational pressures and constraints. We do, however, hope that the book will help you better understand what is going on around you and better appreciate the choices which you do have and the demands which you can make.

A word sometimes used to describe this relation between an individual and an organization is **stakeholder**: a stakeholder is someone who has a claim on the way an organization is run, its goals and directions; it is someone with *some* choices, *some* power and *some* responsibilities as opposed to a bystander, a pawn or a *customer*. A customer enjoys the privilege of choosing how to spend his/her money without having to offer explanations to anyone. In exchange, the customer must accept the vagaries of the market. A stakeholder, on the other hand, has a say in the meaning and goals of an organization, becomes involved in its governance and has rights as well as responsibilities. Unlike customers, stakeholders are bound to their organizations with ties of mutuality and respect. We are hoping that our readers will emerge from this book with an understanding that enables them to decide when and how they may participate as stakeholders in their organizations and when it is desirable or inevitable to sit on the sidelines. Understanding organizing and organizations does not make a person immune to occasional powerlessness or dependency. But it does reduce the chance of their needing to resort to statements such as 'I was only obeying orders', or 'This doesn't sound right but it must be – I'm only a small cog in the machine.'

MOVING ON

We have written about the aspects of organizing, being organized, and living in organizations that seemed interesting and important to *us*. Numerous questions, themes and chapter headings, after discussions, were left out. You may emerge from this book with a whole host of different questions and themes of your own.

For those who want to continue developing their learning, a good starting point is to compare the arguments, ideas and examples which we provide with your own experiences. Thereafter, different readers will pursue different paths, crafting their own questions, addressing their own interests. Here, to conclude, are a few hints that may help:

- Criticize our ideas, qualify them, revise them, fashion them in a way that makes sense to you. How do *you* find that **organizations, bureaucracy, leadership, emotions** and so forth work for you?
- Identify those gaps in our arguments or in our charting of the terrain of organizing and organizations which need filling. What fits and does not fit between the various topics? How, for example, are sexual and moral issues linked? Do machines dictate our life? How do we resist their influence?
- Focus on the paradoxical, the out of place, the irregular in your own experiences of organizing. Frequently, one unusual observation is worth more than large volumes of uniform data. What happens during a crisis, such as a breakdown, resignation, personality clash or redundancy programme? Often, the organization's colours are revealed when, normally, they are obscured.
- Mistrust jargon, clichés and the use of **language** in general. If you think that the answers to numerous problems lie in a single concept (for example '**motivation**', 'leadership', 'organization'), test out whether that seems fair and true. Often we like to give slick and simple labels to issues which are basically complex and can be analysed in various possible ways.
- Mistrust simple cause and effect explanations of human phenomena. It is unlikely to be 'all a **personality** problem', or a 'just a matter of changing the leader' to sort out the organization. Organizations are the products of many factors, systematic and accidental; change one part and others are affected in unexpected ways.
- Try using **metaphors**, similes and models to make sense of your observations. If you see the organization as a machine, madhouse, brain or battlefield, does it bring some things into perspective?
- Whenever you make a generalization look at the exceptions to check it out. Do *all* students, women, lecturers, civil servants and so forth do what you think they do? If not, how useful is the generalization?

And finally, there is little to be gained by prematurely closing discussions and debates in the interest of order, certainty and organization. Some of the best ideas in organizations (and in science) have resulted from accident, misunderstanding and error. Others have emerged from doing exactly the opposite of what intuition, good sense and methodology dictated. Enquiry, understanding and action will not always be in step. Do not try to be *too* organized.

THESAURUS ENTRIES

authority
bureaucracy
control
emotion
knowing
language
leadership

meaning
metaphors
motivation
organization
personality
stakeholder

Thesaurus

CONTENTS

INTRODUCTION

This Thesaurus is not meant to provide an exhaustive treatment of each entry but to introduce some of the main academic arguments surrounding these concepts. Thesaurus entries are **bold** in the book's main text, though the match is not always perfect; for example, **ethnicity** and **real** are not listed as such in the Thesaurus, but **ethnic group**s and **reality** are.

You may find that a topic which you wish to examine does not have an entry in the Thesaurus at all; try to think of a related concept and see if there is a relevant entry. For example, there are no entries for 'humour' or 'objectives', but there are entries for **'jokes'** and **'goals'**.

References to books and articles in or at the end of each entry can be found in full in the Bibliography. In some cases, secondary sources have been suggested because they are more readable or more easily accessible than original writings. Where books are given as references, you are encouraged to look first in the book's table of contents to see if there is a chapter matching the entry in the Thesaurus or, failing that, look in the book's Index for references to the entry topic. For example, under **'sabotage'** reference is given to Beynon's book *Working for Ford*; looking at the index of that book identifies the pages where the author deals with the issue of sabotage.

action

In contrast to behaviour, action suggests purpose and **meaning**. Unlike physical entities, like electrons, which only behave, human beings act. Placing a ring on somebody's finger is more than just a physical movement resulting from the expenditure of energy. It is meant to **communicate** something, it has a meaning. Human beings act towards each other and towards things on the basis of meanings which they attribute to the objects and to the actions. Sometimes meanings are shared and sometimes not. There are different schools of thought regarding action. Some sociologists tend to regard all action as social, stemming from relatively fixed **norms** and **values** within any particular society; symbolic interactionists, on the other hand, view the meanings behind action as precarious and unstable, constantly being negotiated among the interacting parties. One school of psychologists, known as behaviourists, tend to disregard the meanings that people attribute to their actions altogether and focus on behaviour itself. Yet another school, known as depth psychologists, question some of the meanings people claim for their actions, suspecting that these are **rationalizations** or excuses; they argue that the motives of many actions are unconscious.

See also **desire, motivation**

aggression

Aggression, as an overt physical attack on another person, is regarded as one of the most socially undesirable forms of behaviour in work organizations. Strict sanctions (often dismissal) are normally brought to bear on the perpetrator. However, aggression may be expressed in more culturally acceptable forms, such as through 'aggressive' bargaining, 'tough, uncompromising' **leadership**, and raw **competitive** behaviour. The *way* aggression may or may not be expressed has much to do with the **culture** and **gender** balance of the organization. So in a 'macho' production organization it is not uncommon to hear people loudly and angrily swearing at each other. In the more genteel atmosphere of white-collar organizations, such as the civil service or academia, aggression can be disguised as sarcasm or sniping. The psychological basis of aggression can be frustration – from feeling cheated, underrated, exploited or blocked. Some people will channel their frustrations into indirect channels – such as through political activism, and even **sabotage**.

Deaux and Wrightsman (1984), Luthans (1992)

alienation

An important concept in sociology, following its central position in the works of the great German philosopher and revolutionary, Karl Marx (1818–93). In his early writings, Marx used the concept of alienation to describe the condition of humanity under capitalism, a condition which is summed up in Brecht's phrase 'man can only live by forgetting that he is a human being'. The root cause of alienation for Marx is capitalist production, which separates workers from the

products of their **labour**, from the activity of labour, from their fellow humans and from what Marx called man's 'species being', that is, those features which make humans a unique species. Through the sale of their labour and through the production of commodities, workers surrender their productive capacities (which is what makes them distinctly human) to alien domination. A part of themselves is separated from them: it becomes estranged from them and confronts them as an oppressor. The alienated beings can be thought of as animals separated from their essential nature, animals which have spent their entire lives in captivity. They are discontented, oppressed and unfulfilled, but more importantly are not aware of the causes of their condition: their consciousness is systematically distorted. While Marx envisaged everyone under capitalism (including the owners of capital) as alienated, he conceived of the possibility of human emancipation and freedom in a society in which the **control** of the productive process is restored to the workers. As the concept of alienation has passed into everyday use, its **meaning** has shifted: it has come to mean frustration and separation. The sociologist Robert Blauner argued that alienation at the workplace comprises four emotional states: **powerlessness, meaninglessness**, isolation and self-estrangement. He found that increasing automation leads to increasing alienation, though very highly automated chemical plants were seen as having low alienation. His theory was that as industries move from craft to mass production, alienation increases, but as they move further to fully automated process production, alienation declines. His optimistic conclusion that in the long run alienation will be resolved by the very factors which fuel it, **technology** and automation, has been criticized as reflecting the optimism of the 1950s; his arguments, however, that link technology to the individual's experiences at the workplace and the degree of **job satisfaction** have proven influential.
Blauner (1964), Marx (1975)

anomie

A state of collapse of social **norms** and social **controls**. The concept was developed by Durkheim (1858–1917), one of the founding fathers of sociology, who argued that the cohesion of social groups and societies is achieved through two social mechanisms, which exist over and above the individuals making up the groups and societies: (1) social integration, the product of strong social bonds, unites groups like families, clans, military and religious groups;

(2) social regulation controls the individuals' needs and **desires**, bringing them into line with the means available for their satisfaction. In Durkheim's view social regulation is accomplished through the internalization of norms. Anomie occurs when such norms are weakened, especially during periods of rapid economic change or social transformation when aspirations and desires grow disproportionately. Their inevitable frustration leads to feelings of injustice, unfairness and disorientation. Durkheim argued that anomic societies display an increase in suicide rates and all kinds of manifestations of social deviance. Like **alienation**, anomie has had a long career in academic discourse and its **meaning** has lost some of the sharpness which Durkheim bestowed on it. Like alienation, it has assumed an increasingly psychological quality, indicating a state of being rather than a social phenomenon coming to signify a generalized condition of **meaninglessness**, normlessness and disintegration which affects numerous social **groups** and individuals. For example, the industrial working class as well as the 'yuppies' are seen as experiencing anomic tendencies, for very different reasons. The former have seen their expectations of a 'job for life', something they had come to regard as a right, obliterated by technological developments and the arrival of mass unemployment in the 1980s. By contrast, the young whiz-kids commanding vast salaries for speculating in the world markets saw their expectations soar out of all control in the 'culture of greed' of the United Kingdom and the United States in the 1980s. Both groups are seen as experiencing anomic tendencies, the results of which may range from fatalism and deviance to **stress** disorders.

Durkheim (1951), Howe (1986)

artificial intelligence

The use of computers to simulate human intelligence. Whether it is possible for computers to imitate human **intelligence** and achieve any genuine originality of thinking and **problem** solving is the topic of intense debate. What is certain is that the use of computers (and their formidable 'accomplishments' in playing chess, conducting 'conversations' or proving mathematical theorems) has forced philosophers and psychologists to re-assess their notions of 'intelligence'. The most significant outcome of research on artificial intelligence lies in what the efforts to simulate intelligence have told us about intelligence as it is found in human beings. Indeed, the origin of artificial intelligence lay in attempts to understand human intelligence

by asking, 'What would we have to do to simulate this?'
Lawler and Elliot (1996), Weizenbaum (1976)

assumption

Taking a fact, an idea or a principle for granted. Assumptions are widely used in all human thinking and **discourse**, and we can say little without making some assumptions. Assumptions are made in **decision making** (where it is impossible to account for all the uncertainties or background factors affecting a particular decision), in model construction (as in Weber's ideal type **bureaucracy**) and in general argument and theorizing. Some assumptions are integral parts of **culture**, for example 'people marry for love', or 'people work for money'. These assumptions may be shared by different individuals, enhancing their **communication**, which becomes very stilted when all assumptions have to be checked out. By contrast, members of different departments in the same organization may make different assumptions about the organization's priorities or **goals**. While assumptions are an inevitable part of thinking and knowing, we are not always aware of making them. This may lead to unpredictable or even catastrophic results. The assumptions that people and groups make are sometimes referred to as their 'world taken for granted'. Economists have a reputation for working from massive and improbable assumptions, for example 'Let us assume perfect competition', which, nevertheless, are 'good enough' for particular purposes.

attitude

A tendency to respond to people, objects, ideas or events in particular ways. Attitudes have traditionally been regarded as being comprised of components to do with **cognition**, feelings and tendencies to action. Katz and Kahn studied why all people seem to need to have attitudes, and concluded that they had four functions: they help people adapt to what is around them, they enable people to feel better than others, they are a way of expressing values, and they help people to form some sort of order out of the world. **Prejudice** is an example of attitude, and has inspired much of the research on attitudes and attitude change. It has been found that attitude change depends on the perceived status and probity of the person communicating the change message, on whether a conclusion is drawn, on whether both sides of the argument are put and on which is put first. One of the most interesting theories of attitude change is 'cognitive dissonance' (Festinger and Carlsmith), which suggests that if individuals behave in ways which are inconsistent with their attitudes, they are likely to change their attitudes to fit their behaviour. Recent work on attitudes has emphasized their function in bracketing out threatening questions about ourselves. It has also become increasingly popular to argue that attitudes emerge through **discourse** rather than that they exist independently in the mind of the person.

Festinger and Carlsmith (1959), Giddens (1991), Katz and Kahn (1978), Potter and Wetherell (1987).

See also **prejudice**

attribution

Defined by Buchanan and Huczynski as 'the process by which we make sense of our environment through our perceptions of causality. An attribution, therefore, is a belief about the cause or causes of an event or an action' (1997: 59). Many events have several contributory causes. Different people will attribute causes differently, particularly when talking about complex social issues. Many of the **political** acts in organizations centre around attribution; how do I get my colleagues to attribute the **success** of this action to me, and not to attribute the failure of that project to me? To what do I attribute the fall in sales – staff incompetence, poor training, or market conditions beyond our control? Attribution thus becomes one of the critical components in how people make sense of their situations, and is crucial to problem construction and decision making. It is the core process of human judgement, and is thus involved in almost every topic considered in this book.

Brown (1986), Buchanan and Huczynski (1997), Kelley (1972)

authoritarianism and authoritarian personality

Some people are more prone than others to believe that those in authority positions should be obeyed unquestioningly because of their position. Others would emphasize other bases of **power**, such as expertise or charisma. Research on authoritarian personality suggests that authoritarians tend to be mild and deferential with more powerful figures, and relatively imposing and inconsiderate with subordinates. Authoritarians tend to take **structures** and **hierarchies** very seriously, they like order and predictability and tend to be

rigid and intolerant. Seminal research by Adorno et al. linked the authoritarian personality with **prejudice**, notably with anti-Semitic and **racist attitudes**.
Adorno et al. (1950), Ray (1990)

authority

A concept generally identified with legitimate **power**, or an unequal relationship in which the right of the superior party to order others is recognized by the subordinate as legitimate. Weber (1864–1920) elaborated on Machiavelli's view that people obey orders either for fear or for love; he distinguished coercion when the superior's orders are obeyed unwillingly by the subordinate, because of fear, from authority (or domination) in which the orders are obeyed willingly. He then identified three sources of authority: charisma, tradition and a rational system of **rules**. Charismatic authority is based on the extraordinary qualities of the **leader** which command unconditional respect and loyalty. Traditional authority is based on the sanction of custom and practice; the leader is seen as the rightful heir of old lines of authority. In both of these, personal and **emotional** commitment to the leader are central to the legitimation process. Weber's third type of authority is rational–legal authority based on a system of rules which command respect because of their **rationality**. Orders are obeyed inasmuch as they are consistent with these rules. Unlike the previous two types, rational–legal authority is based on calculation rather than **emotion**, and is **impersonal**, i.e. it does not stem from the person but from the position which the person occupies. Weber saw charismatic leadership as essentially unpredictable and turbulent and argued that there is a gradual shift towards the rational–legal type; he referred to this process as **rationalization** and identified its principal **institution** as **bureaucracy**. Most contemporary organizations involve combinations of all three types of authority as well as a variable measure of coercion and force.
Mouzelis (1975), Weber (1948)

behaviour

See action

bureaucracy

A form of administration conducted by appointed officials. The theory of bureaucracy is one of the fundamental elements of the study of **organizations** and derives from the work of the German sociologist

Max Weber (1864–1920). Contrary to its pejorative colloquial meaning as equivalent to red tape, slowness and inefficiency, Weber saw bureaucracy as the epitome of administrative **rationality**. He developed a model or 'ideal type' of bureaucracy based exclusively on the **assumption** of rational–legal **authority**. This type of authority is founded on a rational system of **rules** and regulations and is essentially **impersonal**. The ideal type bureaucracy is a hypothetical organization, involving no other type of authority or relationship, no friendships or enmities, no informal cabals or cliques, no collegiate bodies or committees, but merely individuals giving and receiving commands underpinned by a rational system of rules. Weber identified a number of defining characteristics of this type of bureaucracy which include:

1 A strict hierarchy of offices in which superior offices control lower ones.
2 The appointment of individuals to offices on the basis of their expertise, certified by written qualifications.
3 The conduct of each office on the basis of precise rules and regulations.
4 Divorce of ownership from **control**, with **power** deriving entirely from the occupation of an office.
5 Free contractual relationship between the organization and its officials.
6 Written records of all important transactions.
7 The complete separation of official activity from the private, personal and emotional life of the officials.
8 A system of promotion and careers based on a combination of seniority and achievement.

Weber argued that ideal type bureaucracy is a formidable tool of administration, its attributes including precision, speed, unambiguity, discretion, subordination, lack of friction, economy, continuity and unity. While deploring the effects of bureaucracy on humanity, which he likened to an 'iron cage', Weber felt that organizations would inevitably move in the direction of his ideal type in search of greater efficiency. 'The decisive reason for the advance of bureaucratic organization', he argued, 'has always been its purely technical superiority over any other form of organization. The fully developed bureaucratic mechanism compares with other organizations exactly as does the machine with non-mechanical modes of production.' While Weber's bureaucracy has been criticized for a wide variety of reasons, it remains one of the foundations of organizational theory. Many of the criticisms have focused on his apparent disregard of the 'human factor' in organizational life. Weber would dismiss this and related criticisms for failing to appreciate the sheer magnitude of bureaucratic impersonality and for exaggerating the importance of the human factor. Another battery of criticisms have been directed at Weber's insistence that bureaucracy represents maximum administrative rationality; some of these criticisms too can be refuted by pointing out that they are directed at existing bureaucratic organizations rather than at the ideal type.

In recent times, bureaucracy has come under renewed criticism as a model of effective organization. In a highly volatile, changing world, where markets, technologies and political climates change rapidly, organizations which approximate the bureaucratic model are seen as too rigid to take advantage of opportunities and repel threats. They are doomed to be overtaken by leaner, more flexible organizations which have a greater ability to learn from experience and change their strategies and tactics accordingly.

Morgan (1986), Mouzelis (1975), Weber (1948)

See also **authority, contingency theories, environment, learning organization, oligarchy**

burnout

People who have high expectations and strong ideals of what they can achieve in a job, especially if it is one where they work with people in emotionally stressful circumstances, run the risk of burnout. The burned-out worker is exhausted and disillusioned by the constant frustration of failure: the social worker whose clients relapse after many months of painstaking work; the doctor who finds he or she is unable to offer sufficient care to patients because of the unremitting workload; the new teacher whose fresh ideas are fast rejected by pupils and colleagues. Such people can soon lose **motivation**, and their inspirational spark dies. The burned-out become cynical about the very people they once cared about, and will perform in a way which is only just about sufficient to get by. Burnout can be detected in many different occupations, and can occur at any stage of a **career**. Burnout can be regarded as an extreme form of **stress** reaction.

Edelwich and Brodsky (1980), Fineman (1985), Pines and Aronson (1989), Schaufeli et al. (1993)

career

Career, literally, refers to a pathway through life. However, it has become commonly associated with a planned occupational progression. As one's experience and formal qualifications increase, so do status, salary and hierarchical position. Traditionally careers were mainly for the clergy, the military, civil servants, doctors, lawyers and academics. Now we talk of managerial careers, political careers and careers in occupations as various as nursing, engineering, social work, marketing and accounting. Careers are sometimes contrasted with jobs, the latter involving less long-term commitment, less accumulation of skills and knowledge, and usually less security. Many companies still offer the prospect of a career to their new employees. However, as organizations become slimmer and flatter and more temporary (see **structure**), the traditional career progression in, and up, a single company is being replaced by a less predictable scenario: a number of moves across different projects in a range of organizations. Careers are becoming more fragmented, often less secure and less predictable.

Brown and Brooks (1990), Hall (1986), Schein (1995)

See also **professions**

change

Change, and resistance to it, is an important part of organizational life. Not all change is deliberate, nor can it always be safely managed and controlled. Nevertheless, some change may be necessary for the economic survival of an enterprise, and very much in the interests of its owners and managers. However, others in the organization may perceive change as threatening their position, **status**, relationships, competence or security. It is for this reason that change is often accompanied by some **conflict**. Change within an organization may be seen to occur at two different levels. *First-order* change (the most common) concerns small adjustments to work methods – such as having more team meetings to solve a communication problem. *Second-order* change looks more deeply at the beliefs and **assumptions** behind existing work practices – why exactly are team members failing to communicate? Second-order change is about changing the way in which future changes take place. Change is often engineered by **consultants** who employ a bewildering array of techniques. They range from 'quick fix' first-order methods, such as intensive **training** for top **management**, or the redesign of the organization's **structure**, to more profound second-order attempts to change the whole organization's **culture** through workshops, courses, counselling, and employee-feedback from questionnaires. It is now common for organizations to employ specialists in change management, or 'organizational development', an expertise which has developed over the past 20 years from our growing appreciation of how individuals and groups operate in organizations.

Cummins and Worley (1993), Goodman (1982), Smith (1991)

cognition

The activity of thinking. One way of looking at people and their actions is that there are (a) cognitive aspects, which may be thought of as the relatively cool, calculating parts of life, (b) affective or emotional aspects, which are full of feeling, and (c) conative referring to the will to carry things through. In practice the separation between different aspects of the human being is more complex, and these divisions reflect poorly the thinking and being of humans as we know them. We know, from theories such as that of cognitive dissonance (see **attitudes**) that **emotions** can affect subsequent cognition. If you fall in love, your cognitive opinions about the person you love may be affected by this emotion, as well as your cognitions about other aspects of your world. Similarly, some writers have argued that there is a strong cognitive element in emotion, as emotion cannot be sustained without some thoughts to keep it going. 'She should not have said that to me' is the kind of sentence which a person repeats in their heads in order to stay angry, or sad. Even such activities as chess or laboratory research, which may appear purely cognitive to the outsider, are described as richly emotional by those who are really good at them. Cognitive approaches to organizations have often been characterized by an 'information processing' approach, where the computer is taken as the basic metaphor for understanding people. As with all such metaphors, this highlights some features such as **decision** processes, while placing little value on others, such as the emotion and unpredictability of organizational life.

March (1997)

communication

It has become almost a cliché in organizations to attribute all sorts of difficulties to communication. To say that something is 'a communication problem' can be a catch-all phrase. Communication may be verbal, that is, to do with the words used, or **non-verbal**. Some communication research has used an **information** processing model, looking at the inputs, outputs, 'noise', and numbers of channels. Leavitt looked at the effect of different communication networks on the performance of tasks, and found that a star shape, where one central person can communicate with everybody else, is most effective for simple tasks, but the central person gets overloaded if the task is complex. All-channel communication, where anyone can talk to anyone, is slow but most effective for complex technical tasks, and so on. Should communication provide both sides of an argument to be persuasive? Should it make an appeal to people to act in a particular way if it is to affect what they do? What are the merits of one-way communication, like a lecture or a book, compared with those of two-way communication, like a discussion? Hovland and Janis, among others, have been studying these questions over the years. Much of the work is summarized by Clampitt. More recent work in communication has broadened into a whole field of 'communications studies', where the effects of different media of communication, different **cultural** contexts and so on, have been considered more fully. There has also been much recent interest in electronic communication and its merits relative to face-to-face communication, as well as in the communication processes within virtual organizations (Weick).

Clampitt (1991), Hovland et al. (1953), Janis (1972), Leavitt (1951), Phillips and Brown (1993), Weick (1985).

competencies

Recent moves towards establishing whether **management** development programmes were good value for money, and towards trying to develop a qualification for the **profession** of management, led to questions about what managers actually needed to be able to do. What competencies did they need to have? It seemed that in law or medicine the competencies which you would expect of the professional were clear, and the same could be expected of managers. In a pioneering work, Mintzberg argued that management competencies fall into three broad categories, interpersonal, informational and decisional. Others have questioned the validity of trying to establish management competencies on three grounds. Firstly, management is not one activity, but is different in different organizations, for different functions in the organization, and under different economic and social conditions. All of these will make a difference to the competencies required. Secondly, it may be that the mixture of competencies, and the ability to make use of others' competencies, are more important than the manager's own competency. Thirdly, management writers have not agreed sufficiently among themselves about how to describe particular activities or the competencies required for them. The labels are not yet well enough developed; to speak of 'competencies' sounds as if we all know what 'effective communication' or some such phrase means, and this is misleading.

Mangham and Pye (1991), Mintzberg (1973)

competition

A form of conflict, in which different parties are vying for the same resources or rewards, while usually agreeing to abide by a set of **rules**. Economic competition between buyers and sellers of commodities is the principal foundation of capitalist markets. Free market advocates argue that competition ensures efficient matching of supply and demand for goods and services and acts as a stimulant for efficiency and innovation. Its critics point out that competition frequently leads to duplication of effort, disregards the wider social and environmental welfare and leads to a preoccupation with short-term profit at the expense of long-term planning. In organizational studies, competition among departments has been identified as one of the dysfunctions of **bureaucracy**, although some writers will distinguish between 'healthy' and 'unhealthy' competition, suggesting some degrees of competition are energizing and productive while others are not. For example, Handy notes that argument, competition and conflict are types of *difference*; argument and competition which are perceived to be open and fair are beneficial for the organization, while closed competition and conflict are damaging. Kanter has observed that internal competition, such as between research teams researching the same product, can act as a stimulant to entrepreneurship.

Handy (1976), Kanter (1984), Porter (1985)

competitiveness

An **attitude** that predisposes to **competition**. This concept is used both organizationally and individually. For organizations, the issue may be how to gain more sales, a better reputation or higher profits than other organizations in the same sector. For individuals, competitiveness may mean trying to outshine their colleagues and catch the eye of those in authority. At both levels, it is generally assumed to be a good thing, reflecting a particular ideological position on how to succeed in business or even in life. But this needs to be questioned. In some industries (e.g. engineering in the UK), the competitiveness of the different companies can mean that none of them generate sufficient profit to finance research, or to pay salaries to encourage people to enter their profession. At the individual level, competitiveness may lead to lack of co-operation, secrecy and even sabotage. Paradoxically, effective competition usually requires a high degree of co-operation among participants.

conflict

This is common to virtually all societies and organizations and is especially acute in periods of **change**. Conflict may be constructive or damaging, depending on whose interests are being served and the situation in which it occurs. Conflict can be productive in stimulating change and innovation. It can force **organizations** to address chronic inefficiencies and dysfunctions. Otherwise, it is likely to be damaging. The last person to mobilize in a conflict is usually at a disadvantage, so many conflicts arise because people want to 'launch' a pre-emptive strike. Schein says that during a conflict, groups close ranks against the enemy; members of the conflicting groups listen out for negative information about the other group. The winners tend to become complacent, and stop working; the losers become more tense, and either learn a lesson or turn on each other. Pondy suggests five stages of conflict: *latent*, where the background conditions for conflict exist; *perceived*, where the individuals or groups concerned know that there is a conflict, but nothing has been publicly declared; *felt*, where one or more parties feel tense or anxious; *manifest*, where there is observable behaviour designed to frustrate others' attempts to achieve their goals; and the *aftermath*, which is the relationship between the parties after the conflict has been resolved or suppressed.

Kolb and Putnam (1992a and b), Pondy (1967), Schein, (1980)
See also **aggression, competition, institutionalization, politics, power**

conformity

There are classic psychological experiments which powerfully demonstrate that people are prepared to disbelieve the evidence of their own eyes in order to come into line with the views or behaviour of other people. We conform to social pressures because of the discomfort and embarrassment of looking different, or standing out from the crowd. We gain comfort and security from feeling we belong, so we often suppress some of our individuality in order to be accepted by the group. Through this, **group norms** and **values** grow which regulate group conduct. Paradoxically, many groups will also tolerate some nonconformists, perhaps one or two people who are allowed to be eccentric, like the traditional fool or jester. The nonconformist offers an emotional release for the group's worries and uncertainties; he or she is also given licence to criticize the group. Organizational **rules, hierarchies** and **bureaucracy** are features of formal, managerial, **structures** designed to bring about a measure of conformity in work behaviour. However, the more restrictive these are, the greater the likelihood of loyalty and conformity to the informal **organization** – with its particular freedoms and satisfactions.

Buchanan and Huczynski (1997)

construct and construing

Within Kelly's 'personal construct theory', a construct is composed of a pair of psychologically opposite words or phrases which together describe a dimension in a person's thinking. Thus 'bright...stupid', 'attractive...unattractive', 'like me...not like me', might be constructs. Kelly used **repertory grids**, among other methods, to discover personal constructs. The word 'personal' betokens the fact that we all have different constructs which, taken together, are as personal as a fingerprint. A construct is not simply a verbal tag, according to Kelly, but goes deeper than that in our thinking. Constructs are personal not only in the words that describe the constructs, but also in the way those constructs are organized. Within one person's own construct system 'bright...stupid' might be linked with 'employable...would not want to employ', whereas within another's it might be linked with 'competitive...not a threat'. It is also possible for two people to have constructs with the same first word or phrase but different second words or phrases; one person might pair 'bright' with 'stupid', while another might pair it with 'quiet'. As Kelly put it, the second pole of a construct is a psychological opposite, not necessarily a logical opposite. That is, it is an opposite in the thinking of a particular person, whether or not it seems sensible to someone else.

Bannister and Fransella (1971), Dalton and Dunnett (1992), Kelly (1972)

consultant and client

In recent years management consultancy has grown into a major industry, and at the same time the term has changed its meaning. A consultant is a person who is contracted to work for a client company on a specific project or activity, and usually for a specified time, as opposed to an employee whose expectation will be that his or her **career** is with the company. Consultants have usually been hired to do some specialized work which either requires a specific **skill** or expertise which is not available in the company, or requires more time than any appropriate specialist already employed can give it. Some companies which are trying to reduce the number of full-time staff, or do not want to risk the potential cost of making a specialist redundant later, hire consultants as and when needed. Some organizations employ 'internal consultants' – people operating as advisers or specialists from within the organization, and sometimes acting as intermediaries for external consultants. In recent years resentment has grown towards consultants from some employees: 'They come in, borrow your watch, tell you the time, walk off with the watch, and charge you for it.' 'You know they have arrived, because their Porsches are parked in your reserved bicycle space!' However, consultancy services have grown as part of the tendency in recent years to outsource activities that are not seen as being part of the core business process. As companies have downsized, making many senior and middle managers redundant, they have been forced to assign their functions to those same managers, working on consulting contracts.
Eden et al. (1983), Egan (1990), McLean et al. (1982)

contingency theories

Two types of theory are referred to as contingency theories: theories of organizational **structure**, and theories of **leadership**. Contingency theory grew out of an impatience with classical management approaches which seemed to prescribe universal solutions to all **management problems**, irrespective of different local circumstances. For example, Burns and Stalker argued that Weber's ideal type of bureaucracy does not represent an ideal structure for all types of real **organizations**. A structure which may serve one organization well may turn into a recipe for disaster when forced on another. Burns and

Stalker pointed out that organizational **environment** affects the type of organizational structure most likely to be adopted by successful organizations. Woodward argued that optimal structures were contingent on the production **technologies** employed by different companies. Yet other researchers have noted that optimal organizational structure is contingent on the size of the company. Contingency theories of leadership argue that no single leadership style is effective in all circumstances, but that leadership styles are contingent on the organizational and situational context. Fiedler has developed a technique aimed at assisting leaders in their diagnoses of this context and enabling them to adopt a style which is likely to prove effective. Burns and Stalker (1961), Fiedler (1967), Woodward (1965)

control

One of the central features of organizations and one of the main functions of **management** identified by classical theory. Controlling resources and outputs, controlling processes and machinery, controlling information and the environment, are all part and parcel of organizational life. In particular, organizations control individuals, to ensure reliable, predictable and consistent performance of organizational **roles**. This involves the monitoring of performance, its assessment against some stated standards, the provision of feedback, rewards and sanctions. Examination procedures, **performance appraisal** and organizational audits are all control mechanisms, aimed at ensuring that certain standards of individual and organizational performance are achieved. Physical violence was the main control mechanism of slave-drivers. In some early capitalist factories, workers were physically chained to their benches, as a way of ensuring that they put in the required number of work hours. Later, more discreet forms of control emerged. **Rules** and regulations gradually became the foundation of **bureaucratic** control, while Taylorism (see **Scientific Management**) sought to incorporate control in the technical process itself. The moving assembly line, the paperwork chain set the pace and control the activities of those who work. More recently, the importance of **culture** is emphasized as a mechanism whereby control is internalized by the individual as self-control. The organization's **values** and **norms** help to ensure that its members will behave in a certain way, not because they are forced to, but because it has become second nature to them. Generally, lack of control, or **powerlessness**, is seen as a major dimension of **alienation**. In recent years, the study of control has been complemented by increased interest in different types of employee recalcitrance and resistance. Different types of workplace resistance have been identified; these include sabotage, absenteeism, pilfering, restriction of output as well as symbolic defiance, cynicism and disparaging humour and jokes.

Austrin (1994), Collinson (1994), Edwards (1979), Gabriel (1995), Jermier et al. (1994), Thompson (1990)

corporate culture

A popular concept in organizational studies since the 1980s. Organizations, like nations, it has been suggested, have or 'are' cultures, composed of shared **values, norms** and **meanings**. Some organizations have cultures which enhance efficiency, productivity, innovation and service while others have cultures which tend to fragment initiative and are less managerially efficient and productive. Corporate cultures develop incrementally through the history of the organization, often reflecting the values and prescriptions of its leaders. Some corporate cultures are deliberately engineered by leaders to promote innovation, teamwork and commitment – seen to be the secret behind the success of some major corporations. In their highly influential bestseller, *In Search of Excellence*, Thomas J. Peters and Robert H. Waterman argue that successful companies are those which have *strong* cultures, that is, a strong commitment to a shared set of values and norms, which both unite and **motivate** organizational members. The forging of a strong culture, the strengthening of norms and values, the creation of meanings are all major functions of managers: 'Good managers make meanings for people, as well as money' (1982: 29), claim Peters and Waterman. Similar conclusions are drawn by Kanter, who believes that most Western organizations have developed **bureaucratic** cultures that thwart innovation and entrepreneurship by emphasizing adherence to rules and procedures. Deal and Kennedy suggest that, in future, successful organizations will have to generate cultures in which every employee has a sense of being a hero. Such arguments have encouraged the view that managers can manipulate organizational culture at will to produce a winning cocktail, through the use of symbols, stories, myths and **metaphors**. This has proven an oversimplification. There is evidence that people will resist such manipulation when it is seen to be at odds with their own self-image and personal aims, and employees fast become cynical about new 'fashions' in organizational culture. Furthermore, **sub-cultures** and counter-cultures may spontaneously grow and prosper to complement or undermine the official values. Even the strongest-looking cultures can hide significant cracks beneath the surface and many of them have not proven to be the long-term recipe for corporate success that was initially claimed.

Brown (1995), Deal and Kennedy (1982), Kanter (1984), Martin (1992), Peters and Waterman (1982)

culture

A concept mainly drawn from anthropology, which has acquired considerable currency in the study of organizations. (*See* **corporate culture**.) Culture can be thought of as the material and spiritual heritage of a community, the stock of myths and stories, artistic and craft artefacts, buildings, tools, laws, **institutions**, rituals and customs. It is frequently argued that culture is the cement that holds communities together by establishing shared **meanings** and **values**, which enable them to communicate with each other, taking many things for granted. Schein (1985) refers to these as 'basic assumptions'. For example, in many Western cultures it is taken for granted that people marry for love, a notion which would seem highly alien to numerous other cultures. Likewise many of our values and **attitudes** towards work, leisure, **authority**, **career**, happiness, success, death, **sexuality** are shaped by culture. Culture becomes internalized, it becomes part of us, influencing us without our conscious awareness. It is only when we are confronted by an alien culture that we appreciate the values and assumptions that are strong influences on our life. Harrison and Handy have argued that organizations fall into four types according to their culture: (a) *Power culture*, in which orders emanate from the organizational centre and are unquestioningly observed. Political organizations, the Mafia and many small businesses have this type of culture. (b) *Role culture*, dominated by **rules** and regulations, as in classic **bureaucracy**. This is common in the civil service and in large bureaucratic organizations. (c) *Task culture*, in which getting a specific job done by a strict deadline is all-important. This can be found in publishing and consultancy organizations where deadlines have to be met and, in general, in organizations where project work is common. (d) *People* or *support culture*, in which the development of human potential and well-being is paramount; this may be found in some voluntary organizations, partnerships, religious or academic organizations.

Handy (1976), Harrison (1972), Hofstede (1991), Schein (1985)

decision making

Commonly regarded as a major activity in organizational life, decision making is a rational-sounding phrase for an activity which is often more multifaceted and untidy. There are many 'stage' models of decision making, showing how it might be done in a sequence of rational steps. This does not necessarily fit with how human beings actually make decisions. People are capable of handling complex and uncertain information or ideas, of scanning situations for things that should be taken into account, or possible answers that could be taken up opportunistically. Many decisions that people have been happy with have been made by informal means. Even those (possibly few) people who follow logical steps, and work through all the possibilities they can think of, may then see whether the answer 'feels right'. If it does not, they may trust their feelings more than the rational procedures they have followed. Many techniques have been introduced to assist decision making, such as 'brain-storming', 'quality circles' (see **participation**), 'cognitive mapping' and 'mind mapping'. Recent years have seen the development of techniques for decision support and group decision support. Decision making has been one of the duties and rights attributed to managers for a long time, but some have pointed out that it may be a misleading label; it is very hard ever to see any direct evidence that a decision is being made, but we see actions being taken, and infer that a decision has been made.

Eden and Ackermann (1998), Eden and Radford (1990), Harrison (1981)

See also **emotion**, **rationality**

desire

A term used to explain human **motivation** which, unlike the concept of need, seeks to incorporate a social and a psycho-sexual dimension. One may need shoes for warmth and comfort, but one desires a pair of designer trainers because of what it stands for. Whether directed towards a physical object, a human being, an activity, or a state of being, desire is driven not merely by instinct or need, but by the **meanings** attributed to them. Desires may be fulfilled either in practice (for example, by buying the desired pair of trainers) or in **fantasy**, by imagining that the wished for object or state has been achieved. Alternatively, desires may by frustrated, in which case they may mutate into desires for different objects, which may be easier to fulfil, or they may be repressed into the unconscious. Three major traditions in the study of desire can be identified: (1) Sociologists have argued that desires are culturally constituted, as individuals learn to desire objects and states of being valued by their **cultures**. Consumer societies, for example, are said to place enormous value on material commodities and identify happiness with escalating material possessions. (2) Depth psychologists have emphasized the connection between desire and pleasure and have argued that most desires are modified residues of earlier desires, mainly stemming from childhood; these were originally repressed and later seek fulfilment in new incarnations. For example, belief in God is traced back to the child's desire to be protected by a loving father. (3) More recently, **discourse** theorists have argued that desire is an element of the discourse on sexuality, in other words, the complex and interconnected ways of thinking and talking about things sexual as against things unsexual (Foucault, 1979). The very **language** and words which dominate the sexuality discourse, (**gender**, **sex**, sexual **identity**, orgasm, body and even desire itself) are historically constituted as interconnected elements, in constant interaction with other discourses, like the discourse of power and the discourse of political economy.

Foucault (1979)

deskilling

In *Labor and Monopoly Capital*, Harry Braverman argued that, contrary to commonsense notions, throughout the 20th century, workers have been stripped of traditional **skills** and **competencies** by the onslaught of Taylorism and **technology**. Traditional skills of artisans, like printers, potters, engineers, machinists, cooks and clerks, have been eliminated, either by being absorbed into the production process itself or by being overtaken by new technological processes. The deskilled worker loses not only much of his/her bargaining power, but also **control** over his/her work, and pride and dignity in his/her work. Braverman's theory has sparked off a controversy. Especially vital has been the question of whether computerization of work processes and clerical work leads to deskilling. Empirical studies have documented strong deskilling tendencies in numerous industries, one finding that the majority of workers use more skill in getting to work than in doing their job. Nevertheless, there is also evidence of the emergence of a new range of skills, in response to the demands of new technology. More recently, there has been much greater appreciation of processes of employee resistance in the workplace and a recognition that deskilling is challenged and contested by those whom it affects.

Beynon (1973), Blackburn and Mann (1979), Braverman (1974), Jermier et al. (1994)

discourse

The way in which things are discussed – the language, grammar, argumentation and **rhetoric** that form what we say. More generally, discourse is used to describe our **assumptions** and evasions. Discourse analysis has become an important research method in recent years (Potter and Wetherell) which examines the structure of discourse as meaningful in itself, rather than signifying hidden meanings. Words do not merely reflect what is being talked about, they actually construct or even constitute that talk. This may lead to a focus on the **language** used. Conversational analysis (Beattie) has had a different, but closely related, emphasis. It stresses precise measurement, taking note of pauses in speech, changes of intonation and other non-verbal aspects of discourse. The uses of discourse analysis have expanded considerably lately; it has been applied to texts such as advertisements, poems, theoretical treatises or snippets of conversation.

Beattie (1983), Manning (1992), Potter and Wetherell (1987)

discrimination

Giving preferential treatment, notably with respect to employment or promotion, to an individual or a group on the basis of characteristics like **gender**, age, **ethnicity, race** or religion. Direct discrimination, for example the hiring of a man over a better-qualified woman purely on account of his gender, is illegal in both Britain and the United States. It is, however, very difficult to prove, especially if an **interview** is used as part of the recruiting procedure. More importantly, there are a wide range of discriminatory mechanisms resulting in unequal opportunities. The structure of the job market itself acts as an obstacle to equality. Child-bearing and child-rearing are serious impediments to women's career chances, the location of jobs and educational prerequisites inhibit the chances of ethnic minority groups, the requirement for job experience disadvantages young people and, conversely, limited training opportunities disadvantage the elderly. The way a job advertisement is phrased can dissuade particular groups from even applying; for example, specific requirements, like long hours or foreign travel, will automatically exclude many women. Gender, racial and other **stereotypes** and sheer **prejudice** can equally fuel discrimination. Finally, harassment at work can act as a discriminatory mechanism, by placing victims on the defensive, contributing to their character assassination or forcing them out of employment.

dual career

In the past decade the growth of dual careers has been a noteworthy contrast to the traditional one breadwinner (usually male) per family. In dual **career** relationships both partners have, usually, full-time occupations, and each occupation requires considerable commitment in time and energy. Dual career couples will give a high priority to career satisfaction, which can conflict with domestic and child-rearing responsibilities. This is rarely resolved without family **stress** – and a measure of guilt. Despite some marked shifts towards equality in gender roles in and out of work, it is often the woman who picks up the responsibility for housework and childcare, in addition to managing her own career – and perhaps, ultimately, giving way to her partner's career interests. Some organizations have acknowledged the special needs of dual career couples and offer more flexible working arrangements and support. There are some variations in dual career patterns, such as two people sharing part-time careers, or a job split – both partners sharing a single job. Hochschild (1989), Lewis and Cooper (1989), Schein (1995)
See also **career**

emotion

Emotions are the outward display of feeling, appropriate to a particular societal culture or situation. Thus we learn how and when to display grief, anger, jealousy, envy and so forth. The social nature of emotion can be contrasted with *feelings* – our subjective experiences. Our feelings tell us something about the quality of our interactions and performances in the world. Sometimes our emotional display matches our feelings, other times we choose not to reveal what we feel: we will disguise or fake our emotions because of how we believe we are going to be judged by others. Some writers contrast emotional and feeling processes with thinking/problem-solving ones ('**cognitive**'), although in practice the two are closely linked. A number of emotions, such as shame and embarrassment, play a significant part in social control and moral behaviour, and their meanings are culturally specific. There are organizations which specialize in regimes of emotional **control** for their employees (the ever-smiling waitress; the air hostess who looks cool all the time; the receptionist's 'have a nice day') to the extent that some employees can become cynical about their 'act' while others, in contrast, become confused about what they are 'really' feeling. **Corporate culture** can often reflect 'rules' about how employees should feel about their company, and some corporate leaders are adroit at mobilizing 'good feelings' amongst their employees. The expression of emotion is gender-linked. Women who try to move up organizations in competition with men often find they have to suppress their own feelings and adopt male norms of emotion display. The study of emotion also involves an appreciation of society's structures of **power** and **status** which broadly shape emotional display; the organization's sub-culture which more specifically determines what employees should or should not express; and finally the individual's own personality, which accounts for his or her particular interpretation of the world, history and emotional sensitivities.

Fineman (1993, 1996a), Hochschild (1983)

emotional intelligence

Emotional intelligence is a relatively recent notion, put forward to describe the perceptiveness involved in the ability to read other people's emotional cues. It is proposed that emotional intelligence is a separate process from traditional concepts of cognitive **intelligence** (IQ). People may be of high IQ but poor in emotional intelligence – and vice versa. Emotionally intelligent people are said to be skilled at knowing and managing their own, and others', **emotions**. The concept has attracted interest in both popular and academic management literature, especially how it might be measured.

Goleman (1996), Greenspan (1997)

empowerment

Empowerment has become a popular notion in **leadership** theorizing. It is based on the idea that, given the freedom, scope and resources to achieve organizational **goals**, people will be able to contribute to leading themselves – if it is in their interests to do so. Leaders, therefore, do not tell others what to do, or attempt to sell their ideas to them. Rather, the leader's **role** is to help others achieve their own ends creatively by helping them to discover their own potential, and clearing a pathway for them. The leader, in this way, gives **power** to his or her followers: the leader is a facilitator of other people's action. Empowerment is an extension of democratization in management, and the fading of the authoritarian leader. However, it has also been seen as a paradoxical and sometimes false process. There is something strange about management taking action to 'empower' others – when that is itself an exercise of power. Empowerment could also be a useful term for managers to hide behind when they do not want to take responsibility for their own actions.

Srivastva (1986)

environment

The social, economic, political and cultural context in which organizations operate. Closed **systems** theories have focused on organizations as time capsules or black boxes isolated from the effects of what goes on around them. While suitable for the study of a few organizations which operate in highly inert environments, such theories, which include Weber's classic theory of **bureaucracy**, have severe limitations when applied to organizations where the environment is a constant source of threats and opportunities. In a pioneering study, Burns and Stalker (1961) argued that firms operating in stable environments tend to adopt *mechanistic* **structures**, with rigid **hierarchies, rules** and regulations. By contrast, organizations operating in changing environments tend to adopt *organic* structures enabling them to respond flexibly and rapidly to environmental threats and opportunities. This was an early example of the use of **contingency theories**. While the organizational environment has assumed pride of place in management literature (see, for example, Peters and Waterman, 1982), it is not an unproblematic concept. In the first place, the perception of what constitutes the organization's environment may differ across different individuals. A chemical company's environment looks very different to a public relations officer who seeks to allay fears about the company's record on the environment, to a production worker threatened with redundancy, to a research scientist and to a financial expert concerned with the company's standing in the securities market. Equally, in a collective way, the environment cannot be defined unless there is a shared sense of what the organization is all about. Is Ford to be seen as a car-making company (in which case the competitors' cars are a central feature of its environment) or is it a money-making organization (in which case the competitors' cars are less important as long as Ford can find new ways of making money, for example by trading in the currency markets)? This has led to the concept of the 'enacted environment'. Instead of 'given' environment 'out there', enacted environment is based on the continuous trading and juxtaposing of **meaning** and interpretations about the organization and its purpose.

Burns and Stalker (1961), Morgan (1986), Peters and Waterman (1982)

ethics

Ethics concerns the rules and principles which shape moral (good/bad) **actions, values** and **decisions**. Ethics in organizations can be seen in three main areas. Firstly there are the organization's social responsibilities – the harm or benefit that results from its products or services. For example, there is much debate about the ethics of producing and selling cigarettes, cars which could be safer, or using materials which deplete or damage the natural environment. The second area is that of the everyday decisions which affect those working in an organization: is it ethical to promote a particular friend over a more competent person? Is it ethical to fire someone without warning or good reason on 'personal grounds'? And is it ethical to exclude **ethnic** minorities from a shortlist of job applicants? The third area of ethics concerns the relationships between organizations and societies. Is it ethical to choose the cheapest third world supplier for a product, to negotiate the lowest possible price with them, and to ignore questions about their employment policies and practices? These questions involve principles of fairness and justice and standards for judging what is right or wrong. The standards will usually derive from the religious, social or professional codes that guide our lives, although moral philosophers point to two major principles – utilitarianism and formalism. Utilitarianism looks for the greatest good for the greatest number of people. A good decision is one where the aggregate benefits outweigh the aggregate costs. Formalism is less pragmatic: it measures the worth of a decision by the extent to which it meets certain fundamental liberties and privileges – such as the right of employees and customers not to have their lives or safety endangered, not to be intentionally deceived, and not to have their privacy invaded.

Brady (1990), Parker (1998), Walton (1988)

ethnic groups

Communities or collectivities usually based on a sense of shared origin, shared traditions and shared fate. Ethnic groups may be culturally, territorially or historically based. Their members have a sense of 'belonging' to the **group**, sharing many **cultural assumptions** and **values**. Ethnicity does not necessarily imply that the group concerned has a sense of superiority over other traditions, although the term 'ethnocentrism' is generally used pejoratively to signify a group's assumption that its culture and values are superior to those of others. Ethnocentrism may, therefore, fuel **prejudice** and **discrimination** against members of other ethnic groups.

See also **prejudice, race**

experiential learning

Learning which is initiated through, and seems largely to stem from, experience. Most theories of learning involve experience, but experiential learning begins with experience which the learner then tries to make sense of; it emphasizes that the experience is core, and not just a means of testing or practising the learning. This is in contrast to propositional learning, for example, where the learner starts with an idea and then may seek to test the idea in relation to experience. Kelly (1955) pointed out that experience does not necessarily produce learning; learning is to do with how much a person is changed by experience, not simply with the number of events they collide with. The concept of experiential learning is sometimes criticized because it is difficult to verify that learning has actually taken place; it is also difficult for the person who has learned experientially to articulate precisely what they have learned. The concept has been taken further with the notion of 'self-organized learning' (Harri-Augstein and Thomas), which argues that effective learners are those who take responsibility for learning experientially how to become better learners, that is, they learn how to learn.

Harri-Augstein and Thomas (1991), Kelly (1955), Kolb et al. (1979)

extrinsic rewards

When used in connection with employment, this concept refers mainly to rewards unrelated to the nature of the **work** itself. Although extrinsic rewards have been used as incentives to hard work through the ages, they became a central feature of **management** philosophy deriving from Taylorism. According to this philosophy the worker does not and cannot expect to derive intrinsic job satisfaction, so his/her **motivation** to work hard must be spurred by the expectation of extrinsic rewards, like pay, bonuses and performance-related benefits. Goldthorpe et al., in a pioneering study in the 1960s, found that manufacturing workers, working in three factories in Luton, had an instrumental orientation to work; work was seen mainly as a means to an end or rather to a range of ends related to material well-being. These workers did not expect intrinsic job satisfaction and many of them had swapped more intrinsically rewarding work for more highly paid jobs. This finding has not received unanimous support. Other studies, like Beynon's investigation of workers at Ford or Gabriel's study of catering workers, have indicated that workers may adopt instrumental **attitudes** only because they feel that intrinsic satisfaction on the job is denied to them.

Beynon (1973), Gabriel (1988), Goldthorpe et al. (1968)

See also **motivation**

fantasy

Imagination plays an important part in our lives. People daydream, run events through in their minds, muse and imagine. This can be an involving, powerful process as if the event were actually taking place – a fantasy. Fantasizing envelops the whole person and has been shown to influence later **actions**. Some fantasies are surrogates for action, while others are rehearsals. **Skills** may be practised as fantasy, 'envisioned', to improve physical performance, such as with gymnastic and sports skills. Many of the activities of organizing will be tried in the imagination before they are acted out. Fantasy has also been related recently to **leadership** studies. Some effective leaders convey a clear and attractive fantasy of how things might be; followers are then inspired to turn this fantasy into a reality.

Bennis and Nanus (1985), Sims (1985, 1986)

See also **desire, sex, sexuality**

femininity

A term used to describe equally the major components of female **sexuality** and the **role** attributes of the female **gender**. Feminist theory in the 1970s and 1980s has drawn attention to distinct features of early childhood and **socialization** which mould the **personality** development of boys and girls and prepare them to assume different gender roles. The social construction of femininity explores how different 'agents' in society – men, magazines, story books, films, television, photographs, **discourses** – mould images of femininity against which women (and men) measure themselves and shape their identities. Also revealed is how patriarchal capitalist societies place greater constraints on female sexuality than on male, turning it against women and using it to perpetuate male privilege and domination. Psychoanalytic approaches take a different tack, focusing on early mother–child relationships. For example, Juliet Mitchell, in *Psychoanalysis and Feminism*, argued that a girl's femininity undergoes a traumatic transformation 'from the active wanting of her mother to the passive wanting to be wanted by the father' (1975: 108).

Chodorow (1978), Mitchell (1975), Wolf (1990)

See also **gender, masculinity, sexuality**

feminism

The feminist movement, which began in the 1960s, draws attention to the dominantly male **values** which have determined the shape of our political, institutional and organizational **structures**. Feminist writers have argued that there is a deep imbalance in societies which systematically undervalues women, relegating them to **stereotyped** roles in the home, family and work. The unequal distribution of **power** features prominently in this analysis. In organizations, the feminist case is supported by evidence of relatively few women in top positions, the disproportionate number of women in lower **status** jobs, the poorer pay of women compared to men, and the inadequate support offered to women who wish to work and have children or to take career breaks. Feminist theorists must be credited for introducing into academic studies issues which had gone unnoticed, notably relations between public and private lives, and between work and sexuality. The 1990s has been described as a 'post-feminist' era when many younger people have been exposed directly or indirectly to feminist thought. While some of the most rigid sex demarcations have begun to soften in the UK and America, most observers believe that there is still a long way to go. The shift has also been marked by some backlash from both men and women, disenchanted with more radical forms of feminism and for whom the simple association of 'feminist equals good' have broken down.

Greer (1970), Marshall (1984), Spencer and Podmore (1987)

See also **femininity, gender**

fiddling

An array of illegal operations going on in many organizations, at times with the tacit or active involvement of **management**. These include pilfering and stealing, the illicit use of company property, tampering with records (for example for the purpose of clocking additional overtime), the making of false expense claims and the use of company accounts for private ends. Some organizations have virtually **institutionalized** fiddles as a job benefit, and in some cases the proceeds increase the longer an employee stays and the more loyal he or she proves. Fiddling can be collective, in which case it serves to bind together those involved, or individual, engaged in especially by those who feel powerless or excluded, and who consider this a way of 'getting their own back' on the employer who is causing them to feel like that. The frequency, scale and scope of fiddling varies enormously across different organizations, but in the food wholesaling industry, for example, most companies make provisions for 'shrinkage'. People rarely regard their own fiddling as a criminal, illegal or immoral activity and see it as a **norm**-guided behaviour, with its own **rules**, **ethics** and limits.

Gabriel (1988), Mars (1982), Mars and Nicod (1984)

Fordism

A system of mass production based on standardization of products and processes pioneered by Henry Ford (1863–1947). Stretching Taylorist principles to their extreme, Ford initiated the production of motor cars on assembly lines, substantially cutting production costs and improving overall quality. 'They can have it any color they like, so long as it's black', he said about his famous Model T, which was, all the same, the first affordable car for the mass population. While paying his workers substantially more than his competitors, Ford experienced rates of labour turnover up to 400 per cent, resulting from the **deskilling** and **alienation** of his workforce. 'We expect our men to do what they are told. The organization is so highly specialized...that we could not for a moment consider allowing men to have their own way' (1923: 11). While Fordism dominated the world of manufacturing industries for 60 years, its domination is now virtually over. New **technologies** and new management and manufacturing techniques, notably those pioneered by the Japanese, have undermined the equation of volume, standardization and efficiency. Instead, flexibility, customer-centredness, corporate **culture** and

concern for **quality** have assumed major significance. These new production systems are sometimes referred to as post-Fordism.
Doray (1988), Ford (1923)

games

This is used in at least three senses in organizing. A style of individual and group training called transactional analysis was made popular by Berne in *Games People Play*. The games he identifies have names like 'Wooden Leg' – a game in which a person seeks sympathy – and many other 'games' have been identified in which people treat each other in more or less inauthentic ways to achieve some undeclared end. Games also refer to game theory, in which the **strategy** that a person adopts in dealing with colleagues can be understood by thinking of what they are doing as a game, with rules, moves, possibly a referee and so on. Radford has described a number of game approaches to organizational analysis. Allison pointed out that in organizations the players are usually involved in many different games at once, and the progress of one game will affect play in another. The game that is going on in the New Products Committee will affect the Chief Engineer and the Finance Director when they are both also players in the quite different game going on in the Policy Committee. To make matters more complicated, in organizational games you may use one of your 'turns' to try to change the **rules**, rather than to play within the rules. This is called a 'hypergame', and is often indicated by phrases such as 'I wonder if we could just check on how we are going about this task…'. Thirdly, the **political** and illegitimate activities of organization members are often referred to as 'game-playing'. This has something in common with both meanings of 'game' above, but implies the similarity between much of what takes place in organizations and the school playground, whose more or less intense, determined and possibly hurtful or damaging activities may be seen by teachers as 'just games' but are considered matters of great importance by some participants.
Allison (1971), Berne, (1964), Radford (1986)

gender

The division of humanity into men and women has, since the 16th century, been assigned the term **sex**. Sex, in other words, marks the physiological differences between the genders. Gender, however, is used to distinguish between the culturally specific patterns of behaviour or **roles** attached to the sexes (Oakley). Thus while one is born a particular sex, one is socialized into one's gender. **Socialization** prepares individuals to perform roles consistent with their gender **identity**. Such roles may include sexual roles, family roles and work roles. In organizational settings, gender acts as a formidable divide, with women being concentrated in lower echelons of organizations, in generally low-pay, low-status industries. Even in high-pay, high-status industries, women are concentrated disproportionately in low-skill grades, mainly clerical and sales. This is partly due to old structures of **prejudice** and **discrimination**, which inhibit women's progress and **career** opportunities. More subtly, gender **stereotypes** presenting men as rational, tough, aggressive and task oriented and women as emotional, soft, caring and process oriented have further disadvantaged women. Women's skills, notably in clerical, sales and service jobs, are often taken for granted (Crompton and Jones) and lead to neither material nor **symbolic** rewards. Nevertheless, it is becoming increasingly accepted that **femininity** offers organizations a powerful though subtle mechanism of **control**; organizations like supermarkets, airlines, restaurants, media groups and banks find it desirable to maintain a low-level sexual 'simmer', the key to which is femininity, to promote their sales, enhance their image and lure customers.

Crompton and Jones (1984), Oakley (1972), Tancred-Sheriff (1989)

goals

Many authors regard 'goals' as a defining feature of **organization**, and speak of 'organizational goals'. At first, this appears unproblematic; the goal of a firm is to make profit, of a university to educate people, of a hospital to treat sick people. On closer inspection, however, it seems that the goals of an organization will differ in the view of different organization members. The Marketing Director may believe that the goal of her organization is to produce the most prestigious product in the market, and that profit will naturally follow. A lecturer may place 'research' above 'teaching' in his or her list of goals for a university, an administrator the balancing of the books. Thus, the goals of an organization appear different from different angles. Moreover, even specific goals, like 'making profit', may mean different things to different people: are we talking about long-term or short-term profit, what accounting decisions have been made about the allocation of costs, and what social or personal damage may or may not have been taken into account in calculating that profit? Traditional theory, following Weber (1864–1920), saw organizations essentially as tools for the achievement of more or less fixed goals in a rational, businesslike manner. Michels (1876–1936), however, pointed out in his Iron Law of Oligarchy that goals are constantly displaced in accordance with changes in the organization's environment, to ensure organizational survival. A political party dedicated to a particular cause will change its objectives if they turn out to be unrealistic or unpopular. Much current management theory has sought to re-emphasize the concept of goals by subsuming it under concepts like mission or vision, which are forged by the leaders and espoused by all organizational members. Mission statements are often used as a test of goals; if your goals are inconsistent with the mission statement, you will probably keep them to yourself. Sims and Lorenzi have argued that goal setting is a crucial part of **leadership**. Michels (1949), Sims and Lorenzi (1992), Weber (1948)

gossip

The act of sharing stories with other people. Gossip is traded in most organizations; people exchange stories with others, or tell their stories for pleasure or in order to be seen as someone in the know. Sims found that some managers will go out of their way to be in the right place to gossip with other people, believing this to be one of the most reliable ways of gaining **information** about what is going on. The problem is that there is very little quality control on gossip, and that those who engage in it will be motivated as much by their wish to entertain as by any desire to inform. The way gossip gets passed on means that there is no chance for the person being gossiped about to challenge the accuracy of the things being said about them. It is relatively easy to set a rumour going, and once you have heard a rumour, even if you mostly do not believe it, the suspicion lurks. People will make some allowance for the source of gossip, but by the time it has been through several hands, and each person has reframed it a little to fit their interests, it may have taken on a life of its own. Gossip can sometimes be done as a virtuoso activity, for the sheer joy of spinning a good story, or to see what you can get away with. There is a related body of research, summarized by Rosnow and carried forward by Difonzo, Bordia and Rosnow, on rumours in organizations.

Difonzo et al. (1994), Rosnow (1980), Sims (1992)

group

Much work is undertaken by groups in some form or another. These may be formal, such as committees, project groups or teams; or informal, 'unofficial' relationships and cliques which influence the pace, quality and output of work. The study of formal groups has focused on the way different sizes, **structures** and compositions of groups affect productivity and satisfaction, and the kind of **roles** that people play. The dominant research in groups had been in the area of 'group dynamics' – why and how groups form and change over time. The now classic 1930s study of workers at the Hawthorne Electric Plant in the USA first revealed that the groups' informal allegiances, **norms** and pressures to **conform** could far outweigh managerial attempts to manipulate productivity. One more recent application of this type of thinking can be seen in Volvo's attempt in the 1970s and 1980s to replace the long car production line with autonomous working groups of assemblers. Informal groupings often emerge as a way of meeting social, emotional and security needs which cannot be addressed in the formal organization. Groups can be highly cohesive, to the extent that they will resist changes which disturb their pattern of relationships. Likewise, they can freeze out or eject members who break the informal codes of practice – such as on levels of productivity or time-keeping. Groups often go through discernible stages of development, from an early 'sounding out' of members, through to a surfacing of differences and personal agendas (hidden desires, anxieties or aspirations), to ultimate consolidation or collapse. When groups are able to creatively combine the strengths of their members, 'synergy' is said to occur: the total product is greater than the sum of the individual efforts of the members of the group. On the other hand, groups can get trapped in their own cohesiveness. Studies of major decision-making teams have revealed the tendency to '*groupthink*', where individuals feel invulnerable, quickly dismiss opposing ideas, and take wild risks. Groupthink can be seductive – and dangerous – and has been thought to be behind some of the biggest mistakes in decision making at national and international levels – such as Britain's do-nothing policy towards Hitler prior to the Second World War, and the unpreparedness of US forces at Pearl Harbor. Janis has described groupthink as 'deterioration of mental efficiency, reality testing and moral judgement that results from in-group pressures' (1972: 9). Typically, people who try to resist the group are **stereotyped** as weak, stupid – even evil.

Champoux (1996), Douglas (1983), Janis (1972), Smith (1991)

group cohesion

See **group**

groupthink

See **group**

harassment

See **sexual harassment**

hierarchy

A feature of organizational **structure**, usually referring to a **system** of **control**, in which higher offices control the lower ones. Weberian **bureaucracy** forms a strict hierarchy of control, essentially like a military command structure, with no horizontal lines of **communication** across levels. While most organizations have hierarchies, they deviate considerably from Weber's model, by incorporating horizontal lines of communication and appointing collegiate bodies, task forces or committees which cut across the hierarchy. Organic organizations (see **environment** and **contingency theories**) permit individuals to communicate across levels of the hierarchy with scant regard for the ceremonial. Classical **management** theory envisaged each officer as capable of controlling no more than about ten subordinates. The result was that large organizations tended to have numerous levels: their structure was tall and thin. The fashion now, following Japanese practices, is to move towards short and flat hierarchies, eliminating most middle levels of management.

See also **matrix structure**

homosexuality

A sexual preference for members of the same **sex**. While seen as a sin, a crime or a (possibly transmittable) disease by some **cultures**, it is condoned or even encouraged by others (like the ancient Greeks). Homosexuality seems to be normal and natural for some men and women. It has been studied in numerous different cultures and societies, where it often merges with heterosexuality in a bisexual orientation. Psychologically, there is evidence of homosexual **desires** even among heterosexuals, although such desires may remain repressed or may be sublimated in feelings of camaraderie and friendship. In

spite of the decriminalization of homosexuality in the US and Britain, it is still viewed with hostility by some, whose sexual **norms** it undermines or threatens. Within organizations, many gays and lesbians prefer to conceal their **sexuality** rather than face the intolerance and bigotry of their superiors, peers and subordinates. Gay and lesbian liberation movements are fighting to eliminate **prejudice** and **discrimination** and to ensure that people's opportunities and freedom are not restricted by their sexual orientation.
Hearn and Parkin (1987), Hearn et al. (1989)

Human Relations

One of the early influential **management** theories. Human Relations emerged in response to **Scientific Management** in the 1920s and emphasized the importance of the social and **group** factors in explaining **motivation**. Elton Mayo (1880–1949), widely regarded as the father of this approach, argued that through work, people try to fulfil social needs. They generally work harder when they feel part of cohesive groups, rather than in response to financial incentives and **extrinsic rewards**. Each individual's output is tied to a group **norm** to which people tend to conform. While the Human Relations approach dominated business schools and management theory for over 60 years, its impact on industry is arguably smaller than that of Taylorism and **Fordism**. As a generalization, it might be said that many managers preached Human Relations and practised Scientific Management.
See also **group**, **norm**

human resources

A term now taken for granted in most organizations to suggest, in economic-type language, that people are a 'resource' to be used with skill and care. What was once personnel management is now, in the main, human resource management (HRM), and there are signs that 'human capital' will be the next terminological change for this area. Such labels **symbolize** different ways in which people are seen and used in organizations. They also represent different philosophies of management. Personnel management, for example, reflects the notion that people have a right to proper treatment as dignified human beings, and it is the role of the personnel manager to intervene in the supervisor–subordinate relationship to ensure this occurs. Human resource management, however, places the care of employees more directly in the hands of all line managers, rather

than a separate specialist. The employee's welfare and commitment is a 'resource' to manage as part of the whole resources picture (time, materials, money and so forth). HRM focuses particularly on seeking direct employee communication and involvement.
Guest (1987), Torrington and Hall (1998)

humanistic perspective

A view in the behavioural sciences which says that humans are, or at least may be, different in kind from other creatures and objects, and need to be studied in a way which recognizes this. It grew out of the philosophical tradition of humanism which approached humans as free agents, capable of improving their lot through education and enlightenment. This perspective may be contrasted with the logical positivist view of Ayer (1910–1989), and the behaviourist approach of Skinner (1904–1990). In Skinner's work, experiments were done to find what responses can be associated with what stimuli, taking the human being from which the response comes as a 'black box'; the behaviourists do not deny that something interesting is going on in the black box, but they say that it is in principle impossible to study it, because it cannot be seen. If you restrict yourself to what can be seen, you can be more sure that what you are studying is really happening, they argue. The humanist argument has been put by Harré and Secord, among others, when they proposed an anthropomorphic model of man. By this they mean that we should study human beings as we actually know them to be, and not pretend that we know nothing of what goes on in the mind of a human. It is not appropriate to study our **actions** in the same way we study the behaviour of electrons. Humanist social researchers would argue that we should not be restricted in our studies by scientific method as it applies to the natural sciences; instead, we should adapt our methods to the matter being studied. Among the distinctly human qualities that may be worth studying is **meaning**; without considering meaning, and the extent to which it is produced by individual interpretation, much of what we know about organizing would be lost. This book is an example of the humanist perspective.
Harré and Secord (1972), Skinner (1966)

identity

The way a person sees him/herself, what makes him/her different from others and a unique individual. If the fact that I go

wind-surfing is very important to my view of what it means to be me, then we say that it is part of my identity. It is possible, but not easy, for people to change their views of themselves. On the whole, people respond quite differently to criticism when the matter in question is part of their identity. If you mock all wind-surfers, and wind-surfing is one of my hobbies, I may not mind. But if that hobby is part of my identity I may feel personally attacked, and wish to defend myself. Identity is often connected with job position. If you ask people what they do, the answer will reveal something about their identity; they may answer in terms of a profession ('I am a doctor'), an organization ('I work for IBM'), a rank ('I am a lieutenant colonel'), or an activity ('I act as a sounding board for people'). In addition to the work we do, many of the objects we consume become part of our identity. Erikson argued that identity is far from easy to construct. Individuals may go through periods of identity crisis, when they are not sure exactly who or what they are meant to be. Identity crises are most common during life's major transitions, such as adolescence. Hewitt has pointed out some of the confusions surrounding identity. He distinguishes between (a) identity, a person's sense of their place relative to others, (b) social identity, which is the others' cumulative sense of that person's place, (c) situated identity, the sense of who the person is in a particular situation, and (d) situated social identity, which is the others' view of who the person is in that particular situation.
Erikson (1968), Hewitt (1984)
See also **alienation, resistance**

impersonality

A dominant feature of modern **bureaucracies**, in which many transactions and relations are stripped of their human inter-personal content and reduced to their formal dimension. Contrast the impersonal procedure of being selected for a course in higher education on the basis of your application form by people who have never met you, with the complex inter-personal relations with your friends and relatives. Arguably, impersonality confers some advantages to organizations. It limits the time spent on irrelevant chatter, it reduces arbitrariness and inconsistency and it goes some way to ensuring equal treatment. If everyone is treated as a number, everyone will be treated equally. Being treated like a number, however, is not something that most people appreciate. Impersonality is often seen as a major contributing factor to **alienation, meaninglessness** and **anomie**. Within modern organizations, lamented Max Weber, 'the performance of each

individual is mathematically measured, each man becomes a little cog in the machine and, aware of this, his one preoccupation is whether he can become a bigger cog' (in Mayer, 1956: 126–7).
Mayer (1956)

implicit personality theory

In perceiving, and making judgements about, other people we focus on a number of features or cues – their clothes, their voice quality, their size, their posture, any previous knowledge we have of their character, and so forth. What do these perceptions add up to? What kind of behaviour or attitudes can we expect from the people we perceive? It is here that our implicit personality theories come into play; the kinds of actions we *believe* go with particular personal qualities. For example, one study showed that, on voice alone, 'breathiness' in men was believed to suggest a young, artistic person, whereas in a female it was regarded as indicating a pretty and shallow person. An experiment conducted by Kelley back in 1950 illustrates the point. He gave students brief written descriptions of a new guest lecturer shortly before the man performed. The description was the same for all students, except for one item – which portrayed the man as 'rather cold' for half the students, and 'very warm' for the other half. After the lecture the 'warm' group rated the lecturer as significantly more considerate, informed, sociable and popular than the 'cold' group. In other words, these qualities were seen to go with a warm, not a cold, person. We call on our implicit personality theories to make our social judgements and they can affect how we view and treat other people. They may not be accurate in an objective sense, and they may foster **stereotyping**, but they are convenient and economical.
Deaux and Wrightsman (1984), Hinton (1993), Kelley (1950)

impression formation

We form our impressions of other people by using the cues available, such as of dress, voice, gait, accent, setting. We then fit them together with our 'assumptive framework': what we *expect* people to be who dress like..., talk like..., are in places like..., to be and do. Our **implicit personality theories** are important in this process, as are our **prejudices** and **stereotypes**. Generally, these all serve to help make complex judgements manageable, regardless of their accuracy. The signs and **symbols** which facilitate impression formation are amenable to manipulation, to the extent that 'impression management' has become an academic field of interest in its own right. Like professional actors we learn what 'mask' to wear for what occasion, our aim being to create the socially desired impression. So we 'need' to look jolly at parties, and 'should' look authoritative at meetings. Impression management is exploited for commercial purposes – such as in the training of sales staff, waiters, receptionists and flight attendants to appear neat, bright and positive. Some executives, like professional politicians, are coached on how to look and sound right in front of an audience or camera. Also job applicants can receive detailed instruction on how to sharpen their self-presentation skills in order to impress an interviewer.

Giacalone and Rosenfeld (1991)

See also **interview**

informal networks

Informal networks refer to the personal connections and **communications** instigated by people within and between organizations, and maintained to serve their interests. Informal networks reflect the need for **action** or influence that formal channels impede or inhibit. They are based on personal friendships, family associations, or ties from shared professional, club, sect or religious interests. Informal networks often involve reciprocal favours, shared secrets and jokes, as well as a common mistrust or dislike of third parties. Studies of informal networks reveal that they can be a major, often invisible, force influencing how resources are allocated in an organization, how staff appointments are made, and how certain jobs get done. The informal network can act well as an antidote to inflexible **bureaucracy**; on the other hand, it can reinforce power elites and **oligarchies**.

Davis and Powell (1992), Tichy and Fombrun (1979)

See also **groups, politics**

informal organization

See also **groups, informal networks**

information

Spoken words, telephone calls, e-mails, computer printouts, compact discs and videodiscs are all *sources* of information. Strictly speaking, we cannot speak meaningfully about them as information until they have *informed* someone, until they are selected and interpreted by the receiver. For this reason they are better viewed more neutrally as data, stimuli generated in some form of **communication**. They become information when they reinforce or change one's thoughts, feelings, **attitudes** or beliefs. Because data are now often presented in so many different ways, in enormous quantity and speed, we often encounter problems of selection and interpretation. Which data produce valuable information and which are redundant? We speak of information overload when we try to assimilate and use more data than we can handle.

See also **groups, informal networks**

information technology

This phrase is often used to refer to recent electronic advances in handling information, but may also be seen more widely. Computers are an important part of information technology. So too are electronic diaries, manual card indexes, typewriters, telephones and even paper and pens. In fact, all technologies concerned with storing, processing, retrieving and communicating information can be seen as information technologies, and as such the label might well relate to knowledge management. Yet, the phrase 'IT' has now come to denote exclusively electronic types of information technology. The emphasis on savings and **rationalization** accomplished through the use of IT has tended to obscure some of its effects on styles and quality of **work**. Weick has identified five types of deficiency resulting from working with computerized information systems: action deficiencies, because you get less feedback (sounds, smells, and so on) from an information system than you do from, say, the factory that it is informing you about; comparison deficiencies, because you cannot walk round and look at it from the other side, as you would with a physical object; affiliation deficiencies, because you are less likely to form your opinions by talking through the output from an information system with others; deliberation deficiencies, as you struggle to see the wood for the trees (a particularly appropriate metaphor when thinking about the piles of printout that can come from a computer); and consolidation deficiencies, as you may assume that the hard work of thinking through the conclusions has already been done (because it all looks so final when it comes from the computer). However, these deficiencies do not prevent us all from relying more and more on such technology, and often from finding this an interesting and enjoyable experience.
Weick (1985)

institution

A set of practices, a **system** of relations or an **organization** which is infused with **value** and recognized as part of the way of doing things. The monarchy in Britain, a regular television soap opera, the Superbowl, Harvard University, Rolls-Royce and marriage are all institutions. Institutions sometimes acquire venerability with time as they become invested with special **meaning** and as they prove their staying power by becoming traditions. In *Leadership and Administration*, Philip Selznik argued that the task of a **leader** is to infuse organizations with meaning, thus turning inert **bureaucracies** into institutions. Institutions have a sense of permanence, consistency, clear **rules**, and are objectified. Selznik's argument has resurfaced in the recent literature of **corporate culture**, in which a primary function of leaders is the **management** of an organization's values and meanings. In industrial relations, collective bargaining is seen as an institution, that is, not just as a set of practices and procedures, but as the right, sensible and decent way of dealing with **conflicts** of interest between employers and employees. It is for this reason that collective bargaining is said to have institutionalized industrial conflict, by preventing it from assuming violent uncontrolled proportions, with outcomes unlikely to please all parties.

Hyman (1989), Peters and Waterman (1982), Selznik (1957)

institutionalization

The process of (a) becoming dependent on an institution (e.g. patients), (b) becoming contained by an institution (e.g. political or industrial **conflict**), and (c) turning into an institution (e.g. turkey at Christmas). The second and third meanings of the term are explained under **institution**, so we restrict our comments here to the first. People who have worked or lived in an organization for a long time may find life outside frightening and confusing. This is a well documented effect for people who have been in 'total institutions' for a long time, like prisons, secure psychiatric hospitals, ships or military organizations. Such organizations control large areas of the lives of their members or inmates, eliminating choices about what time to get up in the morning, what to wear, where to go and so on. Life outside gradually becomes difficult to imagine and the person becomes unable to function independently. Similar processes occur among long-serving employees of some **organizations**, for whom working for another company becomes unimaginable. Such employees may find the transition to retirement especially taxing.

Goffman (1961)

instrumental orientation

See **extrinsic rewards**

intelligence

Intelligence is a controversial concept with definitions varying from 'whatever an intelligence test measures', to a 'profile of a range of mental abilities'. The latter includes deductive reasoning, memory, number facility and verbal comprehension. Measured intelligence is often expressed as a numerical score, an 'intelligence quotient' (IQ) in relation to the population group to which the person belongs: such as men, women, adults, children, adolescents. Some psychologists argue that intelligence is so important that if we measure it early enough in a child's school career, his or her educational achievement can be predicted and planned. Others see intelligence as susceptible to many of life's influences and hard to measure fairly, given differences in people's culture and socio-economic background. In response, so-called 'culture fair' paper-and-pencil tests have been devised which rely less, or not at all, on conventional language facility. These, however, often fail to account for people who have a strong practical intelligence – they show their ability through doing things. An argument has raged for years as to what proportion of measured intelligence is due to social environmental (nurture) factors, and what proportion we are born with (nature). On balance, one can conclude that both play a part, but often a stimulating learning environment will significantly boost intelligence scores.
Anastasi (1990), Vernon (1979)

interpersonal attraction

The topics of sexual attraction and love have probably been treated as effectively and convincingly in novels and plays as in formal research studies. The mechanical view of attraction found in some cheap romantic fiction ('Darling – this thing is bigger than both of us – we have to give in to it. . .') is unconvincing to most of us, whereas the more complicated accounts of attraction produced by great novelists and dramatists have been tested out by readers over time, and are thus probably more thoroughly tested than even the best scientific theories. Going more widely into attraction, Kleinke has reviewed the studies of who attracts whom. Landfield has shown that pairs with similar **cognitive** styles (as measured by their **repertory grids**) are

more likely to work well together, but are less likely to produce creative ideas. It may be that attraction and repulsion are related, and that the opposite of both is indifference. People often find themselves moving from attraction to repulsion or vice versa in their feelings towards another, but indifference seems to be more stable.
Duck (1992), Kleinke (1986), Landfield (1971)

interpersonal skills

The particular **competencies** we have in relating to one another, face to face. Just as someone might be skilled at painting, lathe-turning, bricklaying or word processing, so we may be skilled in the way we socially interact. Typical interpersonal skills include listening, communicating, diagnosing, negotiating, talking and assertiveness. We can become more proficient in these **skills** with training and practice. Consequently, there are training programmes available (within and outside companies) where interpersonal skills can be learned. In some occupations, such as medicine, lecturing, dentistry, social work and hairdressing, interpersonal skills are intrinsic to effective performance. Ironically, though, many of these occupations do not offer interpersonal skills **training** for new recruits.
Bigelow (1991), Chung and Megginson (1981)

interview

Interviews have become virtually taken for granted by employers and job candidates. They are seen to be an important way of evaluating a person's character and **competence**. Nevertheless, studies such as those of Dulewicz frequently show interviews to be questionable in their reliability and validity. In other words, the judgements made are often inconsistent and are poor predictors of later performance on the job. In addition, interviews are often conducted by specialist recruiters who may have little idea of the detail of the job for which they are interviewing, but may be concerned above all not to make an embarrassing recruitment decision. The 'halo' effect is a common problem, where one quality or trait of the candidate swamps the interviewer's judgement – such as attractiveness, the type of school attended, **race, ethnicity** or age. As Mainiero points out, this may need to be overcome deliberately. Research indicates that many decisions are made within the first few minutes of an interview, and the interviewer often spends the remaining period seeking evidence to support that judgement. Well prepared and skilled interviewers are able to reduce some of these

difficulties. This involves a careful study of the job in question and its personal requirements, and a thorough familiarization with pre-interview material – application forms, references, **psychological tests**. The use of co-interviewers may help, so long as the structure of the interview, the roles to be played, and how it stands in relation to any other selection methods being used have all been agreed in advance.
Dulewicz (1991), Lewis (1985), Mainiero (1994)
See also **impression formation**

intrinsic orientation

See **extrinsic rewards**

job satisfaction

Early theories of **management** and administration focused on ways of enhancing worker productivity, and assumed the major incentive to work was money. This assumption was challenged by a series of studies from the 1930s onwards which indicated that many people will seek job satisfaction by meeting social and emotional needs at work, as well as financial ones. Influential **motivational** theorists, such as Abraham Maslow, Douglas McGregor, Frederick Herzberg and David McClelland, supported this line of thought, which coalesced in the 1950s and 1960s into a **Human Relations** perspective in organizational behaviour. This explored various ways in which job satisfaction can be achieved, and how opportunities for achievement, self-actualization (realizing one's potential) and control can be designed into a job. In the 1970s job satisfaction ideas were expanded in a wider Quality of Working Life movement which placed a strong accent on the importance of worker **participation** in the decisions which affect their lives. Elements of this thinking have become standard practice in 1990s **human resources** management.
Hellriegel et al. (1992), Steers and Porter (1975)
See also **group, informal networks, motivation**

Jokes

Like **myths**, stories and **rituals**, these are ingredients of organizational **culture**, which offer insights into the feelings and **desires** of organizational members. Freud argued that jokes offer a partial amnesty, allowing repressed desire to surface and taboo ideas to be expressed. More recently, it has been argued that jokes provide a symbolic route of escape out of the iron cage of **bureaucracy**, enabling the individual to poke fun at a system which is **impersonal** and inhuman.

Davies (1988), Freud (1905), Gabriel (1991)

knowing

A word with a considerable range of connected meanings, from the completely relational ('Adam knew Eve his wife') to the completely propositional ('I know the periodic table'). In between are innumerable shades of knowing, with different degrees of relationship between the knower and the known. School science training tends to emphasize the separation of the knower and the known, in the interests of **objectivity**. This means that what is known about, the object, is treated as separate from the subject, the one who knows. This is commonly regarded as a worthy goal in the interests of finding the unbiased 'truth' of the matter. However, at higher levels in the physical sciences, scientists' accounts suggest much more involvement between themselves and the objects of their knowledge. In studying people and organizations there is always likely to be some kind of relationship between the knower and the known. Indeed many writers argue that such a relationship is desirable. It enables us to use our insight into other people, something that we are all practised at doing. To pretend that in the interest of objectivity we can look at our fellow human beings or our organizations as if they were electrons, without forming a relationship with them, may lead us to throw away the best-quality knowledge available to us.

Reason (1988)

See also **cognition**

labour

The ability of human beings to use their creative capacities in moulding nature to their needs. Marx argued that labour is what makes humans distinctly human, and that through labour intellectual, spiritual and technical capacities develop. Capitalist production impoverishes labour, **alienating** men and women from their products, from their creative activities, and from their fellow humans. Instead of marking the proud and joyful deployment of people's creative powers, labour comes to be equated with oppression, exploitation and dehumanization. In such labour, man becomes like an animal, and only in leisure can he obtain a taste of freedom and fulfilment. Marx's uncompromising equation of labour with what makes man distinctly human has been criticized, or at least complemented, by other uniquely human qualities, notably **symbolic** communication and **desire**. Nevertheless, Marx's contention that the organization of labour in a society has profound repercussions on the society's cultural, religious, legal and family **institutions** has found substantial support in the work of anthropologists. In the last 20 years, many sociologists have been moving away from work towards leisure and consumption activities as the area of life where **identities** are shaped.

See also **work, work ethic**

language

'The limits of my language are the limits of my world.' Managers spend most of their time on **talk** and **discourse**, much of it in **metaphor**. As their activity is mediated by language, they need to be good at it. For visionary or charismatic leaders, language is crucial in conveying images. The images of an 'Iron Curtain' or a 'Cold War' were central in post-Second World War politics. Studying the language people use in organizations can help us understand many of its processes. Types of address (first names, surnames, titles), jargon and so on can tell much about an organization's **culture** and **hierarchy**. Different types of word convey different kinds of **information**. For example, if you want to look at the style in which things are done, look at the adverbs used to talk about it: 'quickly', 'impatiently', 'sensitively', and so on. Language is of special significance in international **communication**. Important nuances may be lost in translation, or even between different versions of the same language. People whose second language is English often find it easier to understand each other, even when speaking English, than to understand Americans or British people. The study of language has assumed extraordinary importance in the human sciences in the 20th century. It is now widely accepted that language is not merely a means of expression but a central faculty of the human mind, directly affecting the ways we think and feel.

Beattie (1983), Tannen (1995)

leadership

Leadership theorizing has been prolific in organizational behaviour writings. Many different approaches have been taken. The most commonsense one has been to seek the personal ingredients for leader success – the **personality** characteristics which mark out leaders from followers, or successful leaders from unsuccessful ones. Despite a multitude of studies, this line of inquiry has been fairly sterile. What we do learn, though, is that 'it all depends'. In some situations some people can be effective leaders, in other situations they are not. But we need to be clear about what we mean by effective. For example, high output may be achieved, but at the cost of much stress and depressed morale. Consequently, work has gone into creating **'contingency theories'**, mapping out the kinds of personal qualities and behaviours which link with particular characteristics of situations to produce different leadership effects. The style of leader behaviour ('people' or 'task' orientation), his or her power, the structure of the task, and the particular needs of the followers, are some of the ingredients that have been put into the contingency equation. Contingency theories can be complex and difficult to translate into practice. Recent attention has moved towards a more subtle understanding of the way that followers and leaders interact, and the role of the leader's face-to-face **interpersonal skills** in moulding and directing that interaction. This can involve the leader using various **symbols** – **language**, strong images, **metaphors**, physical settings – to influence the way people see their worlds; the leader 'manages their **meanings**'. Sometimes this activity is aimed at **empowering** people to direct their energy and enthusiasm to organizational **goals**; at other times it may amount to little less than emotional manipulation and devious influence.

Bryman (1986), Chemmers and Aman (1993), Srivastva (1986), Warr (1987), Wright and Taylor (1984)

See also **management, management of meaning**

learning

There are various perspectives on learning and it has attracted a huge amount of attention amongst psychologists. How do we know something is learned, retained and understood? What are the conditions or experiences that facilitate learning? Kolb suggests that people leave school with passive models of learning, as symbolized by a classroom or a textbook, where 'jugs' full of knowledge are poured into the 'mugs' who are listening to them. This may not be the best way of equipping people to undertake the continuous learning required throughout life. Kolb proposes that learning in organizations happens as a four-stage cycle: concrete experience (something happens), leading to reflection and observation (thinking about it), leading to abstract conceptualization (coming up with an idea), leading to active experimentation (trying that idea out), leading once more to concrete experience. Other views of learning draw from an area of psychology called 'learning theory'. Learning theory focuses on the precise way that observable behaviour can change – under what circumstances and to what degree. 'Classical conditioning' is one feature of learning theory, deriving from the early work of Russian physiologist Pavlov (1849–1936). It refers to unconscious changes in our behaviour, when we automatically associate one thing with something else. A 'stimulus' elicits a 'response'. Pavlov 'conditioned' dogs to salivate at the sound of a bell (associated with seeing and eating food). The closest we get to classical conditioning in organizational life is in the shaping of consumer preferences – such as advertisements which aim to make us (condition us to) choose a particular product because of its association with a sexy image. 'Operant' conditioning, emanating from the work of B.F. Skinner, looks at our conscious learning from doing. It refers to the rewards, or punishments, that we receive when our specific actions lead to specific outcomes. It describes how such associations are strengthened, or 'reinforced', to bring about learnings. Complex schedules of reinforcement (breaks, different types of rewards, different timing of rewards) may be required to master, and sustain effort on, specific tasks. These principles have been applied to the design of systems of pay, **motivation** and **training** in industry. Learning theory has also been extended to 'social learning' where people are seen to learn by modelling their behaviour on what they see others do. They watch others, develop a mental picture of the behaviour and its results, and imitate. If it works for them (they achieve positive results), learning occurs. The organizational applications of learning theory are not without controversy. By its very nature, learning theory does not take heed of 'inner' psychological processes, such as people's feelings, desires and personality. Only changes in outward behaviour matter. More crucially, some aspects can be criticized as being manipulative – effectively bribing, or forcing, people to do things, where the conditions and controls are in someone else's (usually the managers') hands.

Bandura (1977), Kelly (1972), Kolb et al. (1979), Luthans (1992)
See also **experiential learning**

learning organization

This is a term much in vogue at the present; many organizations characterize themselves as 'learning organizations', and many

consultants offer to help your organization to become a 'learning organization', but not always with complete clarity about how they might know when this has been achieved. The term is best applied to organizations which are able regularly to monitor and reflect on the assumptions by which they operate, so that they can learn quickly about themselves and their working environment, and change as a matter of course – rather than traumatically, in a crisis. Typically, most enterprises are not learning organizations. They become defensively locked into beliefs and working patterns that they have operated with for a long time, and are unable to re-constitute them without a major upheaval. There is good reason for this, in that it can be expensive to maintain continual awareness of what is going on around the organization, and learning and change are incompatible with maximizing efficiency. The organization that attempts to be as lean and efficient in the short term as possible cannot be a learning organization.

Argyris et al. (1985), Easterby-Smith et al. (1998), Kanter (1989), Torbert (1987)

management

Both a set of functions and activities as well as the people carrying them out. Management functions are present whenever several people work together. Yet, management as a distinct **group**, separate from the owners of businesses, requiring specialized knowledge and **training**, is a late 19th- and 20th-century phenomenon. Classical theory of management derives from the work of Henri Fayol (1841–1825) and Frederick Taylor (1856–1915), and approaches management essentially as 'running a business'. This involves functions like (1) co-ordination, (2) **communication**, (3) **control**, and (4) planning, aimed initially at profit making. By contrast, the term *administration* was used for the civil service and state organizations, and while it involved similar functions, its **goals** were not market driven. Since the 1920s and the work of the **Human Relations** school the human side of management has been highlighted; its preferred definition would be 'getting things done through people' and its main emphasis has been on employee **motivation**. In the 1980s, the **symbolic** function of management has acquired prominence in the literature, with management being seen as 'the ability to define reality for others'. Instead of looking at managers as individuals who can run **organizations** smoothly, the emphasis now is on managers as agents of **change** and renewal. This brings the concept of management very close to that of **leadership**, and a substantial debate is going on as to whether managers and leaders are the same. Henry Mintzberg has criticized many of these approaches for focusing on what managers *should* be doing rather than on what they actually do. Based on intensive observation of actual managers, he found that much of their work involves **talking** or **communicating** and that it is conducted in short bursts of activity. Handling crises and emergencies takes a substantial part of their time; they have little time for systematic thought or planning and make most **decisions** on the basis of ad hoc information.

Mintzberg (1973)

management of meaning

The notion that **meaning** can be managed presupposes that the social world comprises individuals who strive to make sense, or meaning, out of their interactions and tasks. To some extent our meanings will reflect our own backgrounds and personal desires, so they are partly self-managed. However, they can also be influenced by the actions of those around us, so we can talk about leaders and managers as people who manage other people's meanings. This involves the manipulation of **symbols** which convey a particular message. For example, furniture is arranged informally; the boss's door is left open; staff are trusted to manage their own budgets; secretaries do not intercept telephone calls; maternity and paternity allowances are generous, and so forth. In this way, the leader is signalling how he or she would like people to think of the organization (and its leader) – as open, liberal and caring. The way meaning is managed can be political in that it can be manipulated to achieve personal ends – such as power, to control others, to capture scarce resources (budgets, equipment) or to gain status.

Deal and Kennedy (1982), Morgan (1986)

See also **culture, leadership, meaning**

masculinity

A term used to describe equally the major components of male **sexuality** and the **role** attributes of the male **gender**. The study of masculinity has lagged behind that of **femininity**, the **assumptions** being (a) that everyone knows what 'real men' are like, and (b) there is no problem about men being 'real men'. Many **stereotypes** of masculine behaviour are currently being questioned, leading to an increased interest in masculinity, notably in the United States. Books like Robert Bly's *Iron John: A Book about Men* and Sam Keen's *Fire in the Belly: On Being a Man* have argued that the attainment of real manhood is problematic for men as are stereotypes of macho masculinity. Such books have sought to promote a new vision of masculinity as at once caring and heroic, founded not on hate or contempt for women but on strong male bonding and a reappraisal of the relation between fathers and sons. Masculinity has generally been seen as unproblematic in **organizations**; those stereotypical traits associated with the male gender, such as **rationality**, assertiveness and **compolitiveness**, have been seen as serving organizations very well. The new debate on masculinity, however, with its emphasis on a different set of male **values, desires** and needs, threatens to undermine the earlier cosy coexistence. Organizations, it is now argued, place almost as formidable constraints on masculinity as they do on femininity.

Bly (1990), Keen (1992)

matrix structure

Traditional organizations have divisional or functional **structures**, typically shaped like a pyramid. They have a command structure which is narrow at the top, where the chief sits, and wide at the base where the lower management and workers can be found. There is unity of command, as in a military unit. A matrix organization breaks down the single command structure, and is shaped more like a flat rectangle with operating 'cells' of expertise (managers and workers) which come together in different ways at different times. The matrix organization has a dual **authority** system, and is suited to organizations that change projects or products fast, in several functional areas at once – such as in manufacturing, marketing, engineering and finance. Each of the specialist functions serves a separate project or product, which has its own manager and team. The project/product units share the specialized functional resources with other units, so preventing duplication of these resources. Matrix structures can be extremely flexible, unlike the traditional hierarchy. But they have their drawbacks. Without unity of command everyone has two bosses, a functional manager and a project manager, so there is potential for conflict, confusion in loyalties.

Hellriegel et al. (1992), Mintzberg (1983)

meaning

Human beings can be seen as 'meaning-seeking' animals; words have meanings, as do stories and myths. Meaning is what one seeks to convey through the use of **language** or other forms of **communication**, like gestures and expressions. In this sense, meaning is the ultimate object of human communication. However, humans seek to discover meaning even in phenomena where no other human being is explicitly trying to communicate anything; since time immemorial, people have looked for the meaning of dreams, of solar eclipses, of the death of their loved ones, of the position of the stars and planets at the time of their birth, or even, as Aristotle remarked, in the accidental collapse of a statue. In some of these instances, people are looking for a meaning which they think a super-human being is trying to convey to them. Meaning is linked to **symbolism**, since meaning is what the symbol stands for. Discovering the meaning of anything, like a joke, a poem or an action, requires a process of *interpretation*. Sociologists, especially those known as symbolic interactionists, argue that meaning is the product of human interaction, with people trading interpretations and inferring contrasting meanings. Depth psychologists on the other hand, emphasize that the meanings of mental phenomena, like dreams, accidents, obsessive acts, slips of the tongue or pen (the famous 'Freudian slips'), are linked to repressed **desires**. Existential psychologists argue that men and women strive to create meaning through decisive acts of will, because without them life is unbearable. These views are not incompatible but illustrate some of the diversity of **discourses** surrounding the concept. As far as work is concerned, all three approaches have a significant contribution to make. Sociologists have argued that the meaning of work differs across different cultures, each of which has a distinct **work ethic**. Depth psychology emphasizes that many incidents of organizational life are invested with meanings which derive from unconscious desires and wishes. Existential psychology stresses that meaningless work is unbearable work, and engages in a critique of production techniques, like Taylorism, which deny work its meaning and purpose.

Becker (1962), Blauner (1964), Schwartz (1987)

meaninglessness

Meaninglessness is often seen as a malaise or a disease of our civilization. Trapped in Weber's 'iron cage of **bureaucracy**' and reduced to a cog by **deskilling technologies**, the individual experiences feelings of emptiness, hollowness and purposelessness. Work, instead of adding meaning to most people's lives, becomes an endurance course (see **survival**), adding little to their sense of **identity** and self. Blauner argued that meaninglessness is one of the four dimensions of **alienation**, brought about by mass-production techniques, which contrasts with the pride and self-esteem experienced by craft workers, whose work is a source of meaning in their lives. Other social trends which have been linked to meaninglessness are the decline of religion, the growing cynicism about politics and politicians and the rampant growth of consumerism. This last links **meaning** to the ownership of commodities, such as cars and clothes, but ultimately enhances meaninglessness. As soon as the **desired** item has been purchased its magic and its mystique disappear, and the desire for a new commodity has taken its place.

Blauner (1964), Gabriel and Lang (1995)

mentor

New members of organizations are often now formally given a senior member to act as their mentor; and even when no such scheme is in place, they may find themselves 'adopted' by existing members who become their mentors. The role of the mentor is generally to give counselling, help, protection and to assist with career development. The relationship between mentors and their protégés has a **political** dimension, as an alliance. It may also have a psychological dimension, the mentor adopting a fatherly or motherly role and expecting in return total loyalty and devotion. Kanter has noted that one of the barriers to women's careers is their difficulty in establishing mentor relationships with men without fuelling sexual innuendo and gossip. Sometimes the mentoring may be implicit, as when one person takes another as a **role** model.

Kanter (1977), Morgan (1986), Ragins (1997)

metaphors

People talk in metaphors, and we also do some of our thinking in metaphors. These metaphors can affect the actions that are taken. If people use military metaphors ('we won the battle but we still have to win the war') in their organizational conversation, this can signify the **meaning** of organizational life to them and indicate how they approach conflict – such as permitting 'no surrender', and taking 'no prisoners'. When we employ metaphors we are mapping one area of life on to another as a way of capturing our feelings and the images of our experiences; and we can get carried away by the metaphors we use. If we say that 'organizations are machines', the metaphor allows us and others to consider the organization *as if* it were a machine. We may then see 'levers' for change, 'components' for repair, as well as the impersonality and functionality of the organization. Metaphors necessarily obscure as well as illuminate. If we replace the machine metaphor with 'organizations are rivers', as employed in this book, we can then see movement, flow, competing interests and storms – as well as calm.

Morgan (1986)

mid-career crisis

The sense of shifting aspirations and unfulfilled expectations that many people report in the middle years of their career. Some writers argue that the crisis is part of a wider life shift where increasing age and family commitments combine with existential questions of the sort: 'Where am I *really* going; what should I do next with my life?' The response from those who experience a mid-career crisis varies. Some will embark on a dramatic change of direction 'before it's too late' – such as a new job, a complete switch in career, or a return to full-time education. Others will try to re-model what they already have – at home and/or at work – so that the coming years offer new stimulation. Still others will consider themselves too entrenched in the organization to risk a move. The security benefits of some career posts can act as a strong disincentive to change (see **institutionalization**) – when change would probably ultimately benefit both the organization and the individual.

Cooper and Torrington (1981), Howard and Bray (1988), Levinson (1979)

See also **burnout, career**

motivation

Motivation refers to forces acting on or within an individual which initiate and direct behaviour. Motivational theories attempt to explain the source, strength and form of those forces. There are different types of theory. For example, need-deficiency theories examine the effects of unmet 'needs'. Just as hunger will direct our behaviour towards seeking food, so will our psychological hungers require satisfying, such as for self-esteem, security and achievement. An influential, and controversial, theory by Maslow (1943) suggests that our needs are arranged in a hierarchy, starting with basic physical ones, progressing through safety and social needs, ego needs, to peak with the need to fulfil oneself – 'self-actualization'. He argues that one need-level has to be relatively satisfied before we are able to move on to the next. Other need theorists, such as McClelland, have focused on specific needs which seem particularly relevant to business activity, such as achievement, affiliation and power. Another form of theory is represented by the work of Herzberg (1959). He examined the content of jobs that motivate people. His research suggests that people will receive positive *satisfaction* from certain factors intrinsic to the job, such as its scope for achievement, recognition and responsibility. Extrinsic factors, though, such as pay and working conditions, simply staved off *dissatisfaction*. Some motivational theories attempt systematically to model, and measure, the specific attractiveness or otherwise of a particular **action**, and predict the motivational effort that will ensue. These have been termed *expectancy theories*. They are a close relation to *equity theories*, which examine the importance for motivation of how fairly people feel they are being treated and rewarded, compared with others. Finally, there are motivational theories which look deeply into inner psychological processes. These *psychodynamic* approaches, many rooted in the work of Freud (1856–1939), show how our particular **desires**, conflicts, anxieties and aspirations result from our relationship with family members, and our adjustment to stages of development from childhood to adult. The sources of our motivation will often be unconscious, but will still significantly influence our work conduct and preferences.

Herzberg et al. (1959), Katzell and Thompson (1990), Luthans (1992), Maslow (1943), McClelland (1961), Steers and Porter (1987)

myth

Commonly used predominantly to signify 'popular untruths', as in 'Ten myths about slimming'. As an ingredient of organizational **culture**, myths are usually based on embellished accounts of events in an organization's history, such as the overcoming of obstacles, major crises or disasters and embarrassing or amusing incidents. Myths have **meanings**; if different people all read the same meaning in a particular myth, it can have a galvanizing effect on morale and strengthen **group** cohesion. Often, however, people may read very different meanings into the same stories. While myths are not necessarily accurate narratives of events, their grip on individuals stems from the powerful **needs** which they fulfil. For this reason, the preferred types of myths within an organization reveal some of the underlying emotional factors. In some cases, myths degenerate into self-deceptions by clouding judgement and thought, leading to delusions of invulnerability and grandeur (see **group**). Some organizations have failed because of the inability of their members to detach themselves from such myths. Schwartz, for example, has argued that some major failures, such as the disaster of the American space shuttle *Challenger* (1986), occur when mythologies and **fantasies** get in the way of technical and scientific calculations.

Gabriel (1991), Schwartz (1988)

needs

See **desire**

non-verbal communication

This book is a mainly verbal **communication**. We have a little control over its layout, and none over the circumstances in which you read it or the picture that you have of us, but we do have control over the words that we use. However, the judgement you make of the book will have been affected by non-verbal factors too – do you find the presentation attractive, for example? Many communications are like this: the communicator concentrates on the verbal aspects, but the person receiving the communication will be heavily influenced by non-verbal factors. In conversation the communication is usually multi-channelled: verbal and non-verbal communication are taking place simultaneously. There is strong evidence that the non-verbal is very influential. When people first meet, they focus on the non-verbal almost to the exclusion of the verbal. Non-verbal communication includes body language, but also includes intonation, clothes, the way you arrange your office and so on. If the non-verbal communication does not seem to fit with the verbal, then this is at least disconcerting. Some people smile when they give you bad news. This is probably embarrassment, but it can lead to distrust, because the non-verbal smile and the verbal news do not seem to fit together. It is often said that it is impossible not to communicate. Sitting silently can often be a powerful non-verbal communication. Various attempts have been made to codify non-verbal communications, but in most Western

cultures there is considerable individual variety in the meaning of particular gestures, and the enterprise becomes unreliable.
Argyle (1975), Kharbanda and Stallworthy (1991)

norm

Norms are standards of behaviour which result from the close inter-action of people over time. They are social inventions which help the **group** to control and regulate its activities, and to express its identity and values. In work **organizations** norms arise as complementary, and/or in opposition, to the company **rules** and regulations. Some norms may be divulged openly to new group members: 'Now you've joined us what you need to do is... '. Others will be inferred from the characteristic behaviour of established members. In practice, norms can determine dress code, where people sit and eat, time-keeping, productivity levels (maybe different from management expectations), appropriate **language**, and the sanctions for those who deviate. In short, norms often influence and control our behaviour in subtle ways by becoming part of us – by being internalized.
Champoux (1996) Forsyth (1990)
See also **culture, group, informal network, socialization**

objectivity

Viewing objects or events without bias, dispassionately or, in a more literal meaning, viewing something as an object – as a thing, distinct from yourself. It is possible to come closer to objectivity when consid-ering people and events about which we do not care and in which we have no interest. But even under these circumstances, objectivity is elu-sive. What people may mean when they say that they have been 'objective' is that they have tried to be rigorous and critical in making their subjective judgement; they did not take their first impressions as conclusive. It is possible to take steps to check on the quality of our subjective judgements. For example, if you think a particular manager is good, you can check your judgement by discussing it with other people, looking at the financial performance of her department, ask-ing her about what she is doing and so on. But the judgement remains essentially subjective – a well tested subjective judgement. When a number of people come to a similar judgement, this is sometimes referred to as 'intersubjectivity'. To be objective, one would need to be able to stand outside the situation being considered, neither affecting it nor being affected by it. This is possible in talking about measurable characteristics ('she is 1.75 metres tall'; 'he has hepatitis'), because these qualities are not affected by the person making the judgement. My presence, absence or consciousness has no impact on her height or his hepatitis. Such 'standing outside the situation' is not possible when talking about personal **meanings** and social judgements.

oligarchy

Oligarchy is the rule of the few over the many. Based on a study of the German Social Democratic Party in the early part of the century, Robert Michels (1876–1936), argued that all organizations are subject to an 'Iron Law of Oligarchy'. Arguing against his mentor, Max Weber, Michels claimed that **organizations** are not **rational** instruments for the accomplishment of administrative **goals**; instead, he saw political systems through which small elites control the masses. Organizational survival takes precedence over the achievement of any goals, since without it the **power** and privileges of the **leaders** disappear. To this end, goals become displaced, **values** and doctrines are constantly compromised and organization becomes an end in itself. Michels argued that leaders have formidable mechanisms for overcoming any internal threats. They **control** information and appointments, they can reward those loyal to them and marginalize those against them. They can divide the opposition or accuse it of 'rocking the boat'. Finally, and most importantly, they build their strength on the *apathy* of the organizational members, who have not the time, the expertise or the inclination to challenge the leaders' **decisions**. Michels's view approaches organizations as natural **systems** or biological organisms, preoccupied with survival, rather than as rational systems or tools, after the Weberian tradition. He draws attention to the organizational **environment** which was left outside Weber's ideal type **bureaucracy**. His view of bureaucracy has more in common with the common pejorative sense of self-perpetuating and unaccountable officialdom, than does Max Weber's view. In spite of its power, Michels's rather cynical view has attracted criticism. Gouldner has argued that there is an Iron Law of Democracy opposing the oligarchic tendencies identified by Michels and uses as examples the numerous cases of tyrants who were eventually overthrown through popular mobilization.
Gouldner (1961), Michels (1949)

organization

Most formal definitions are unclear as to which human associations should be thought of as organizations (large corporations, armies, universities, trade unions) and which should not (football crowds, theatre audiences, nuclear families, tribes, gangs). We propose a set of criteria which define the general space occupied by organizations, though not all organizations need fulfil all of these criteria:

1 Organizations are associations of several people, who are aware of being members, and who are generally willing to co-operate.
2 Organizations are mainly long term, and survive changes of personnel.
3 Organizations profess some objectives or **goals** which they pursue in a methodical, no-nonsense manner. These goals will be more or less shared by the members.
4 Organizations involve a certain division of labour, with different people assigned to different tasks. This may amount to a **hierarchy**, a **matrix**, or some other **structure**.
5 Organizations involve a certain degree of formality and **impersonality**.

Strictly, it makes little sense to say that organizations have goals, that they **act**, that they **control** individuals' behaviour. It is people, not organizations, that have goals, act and control. Nevertheless, these are convenient ways of describing behaviours and actions of large numbers of people associated with each other. Furthermore, people talk and behave *as if* organizations act. Organizations can be thought of as the aggregates of the actions of numerous individuals. These actions are not arbitrary; the way people behave in a particular organization can be distinctive because of the **culture** and **norms** of that organization. An organization can be thought of as more than just the sum total of the individual efforts and inclinations of its members.

participation

A general principle in politics that people should participate in the making of political **decisions** which will affect them, either by openly expressing their views or by electing representatives to the bodies which make the decisions. Yet participation in organizations sometimes tends to degenerate into an empty slogan behind which **oligarchy** reigns. Within organizational literature, participation is discussed in connection with **leadership** (seen as a feature of democratic or participatory styles) and decision making. It is often argued that successful implementation of organizational **change** requires the participation of those affected by it in the decision-making process. Various techniques of participation have been tried, ranging from consultation to suggestion boxes and quality circles (regular meetings by groups of employees in company time to discuss improvements in working practices and to resolve organizational problems), some of which have attracted criticism as attempts to manipulate workers. In Britain workers have been reluctant to participate in decisions which can be seen as compromising them or incorporating them in the process of **management**. In Germany, however, since 1952 workers' representatives have participated on the boards of directors in companies above a certain size. Socialists have frequently scoffed at participation, seeing it as an extension of **management control**, and have advocated instead 'workers' control': the management of the organization by the workers themselves. Different forms of workers' control have been devised, including elected managers, works councils and workers' co-operatives, the latter emerging in the 19th century, inspired by the ideas of Robert Owen in Britain and Charles Fourier in France. Workers co-operatives can boast a number of successes, but with some notable exceptions (like the Mondragon co-operatives in Spain) they have not been able to challenge capitalist firms, nor have they matched the success of consumers' or farmers' co-operatives.

perception

Perception refers to the processes by which we create subjective **meaning** from the stimuli received by our senses. Our perceptions are our personal interpretations of the world: the shaping of experiences and events into some coherent whole. Some philosophers and psychologists argue that it is only through perception that we can know anything, so we can never know of an **objective** world beyond our perceptions. The notion of perception in organizational behaviour leads us to anticipate that people's perceived worlds may differ and that difference can explain, at least in part, what they think and do. There are factors which influence the shape and content of perceptions. We often 'see' what we want to see: our needs, **motivations** and **emotions** will, unconsciously, start the perceptual-shaping process. For example we will more readily perceive negative characteristics in people with whom we are in conflict. Conversely, love is blind to faults. Ideological stance, **stereotypes** and **prejudices** will also play their part. It is often in the interests of trade union members to perceive managers as exploitative of labour; while, in turn, managers may 'want' to perceive their workers as preoccupied with minimizing their efforts and maximizing their pay.

Hellriegel et al. (1992), Luthans (1992)

See also **construct, meaning**

performance

An ambiguous word in the literature on organizing. Performance can be used to refer to a fairly mechanistic notion of how well someone is doing, rather like talking about the performance of a car. So in some of the literature on appraisal you will hear references to gauging a person's performance, and in some companies managers will take on performance targets. Performance is also used in the sense of 'putting on a performance', or acting. There is a 'dramaturgical' way of looking at organizations, which sees them as being stages for a performance (Mangham). This can be traced back through Shakespeare ('all the world's a stage') and beyond. Snyder has suggested that performance includes 'self-monitoring', which is the extent to which people are able to take the stance of an audience watching their own performance. High self-monitors are continuously aware of the performance they are putting on and of the impact it is having on others. Low self-monitors are not aware of performing, tend to come over as more centred and 'all of a piece', and may see high self-monitors as slippery. High self-monitors meanwhile wonder why low self-monitors are not putting more energy into their performance, and may see this as a lack of commitment.

Mangham (1986), Snyder (1987)

performance appraisal

Many organizations use systems of performance appraisal to evaluate their employees' work progress. Performance appraisals are used to make decisions on salary, promotions, retention or termination. They can also provide an opportunity for feedback to an employee to identify strengths, weaknesses and training needs. The format of appraisal can vary from the highly structured, using pencil-and-paper rating scales, to an open-ended counselling session. The effectiveness of performance appraisal depends on how well prepared both parties are, how serious they are about the event (is it 'for real' or an empty ritual?), the skills of the appraiser, the reliability and validity of the rating scales, its regularity, and the extent to which decisions or agreements from the appraisal are honoured. Chung and Megginson (1981), Cummings and Schwab (1973), Wigdor and Greene (1991)

See also **performance**

persona

A persona is the appearance or character an individual presents to an audience. We may adopt a range of personae, according to the different situations we are in. At work we may adopt a 'hard-working, harassed' persona; at parties we change to appear 'jolly and sociable', while at home with our children we are the 'attentive, good parent'. This view leaves us with difficult questions about whether there can be a real self which is more than simply one persona among many.

Argyle (1975), Goffman (1959)

See also **impression formation, personality**

personality

Personality is a concept which refers to the totality of a person's individuality. Personality theories, of which there are many, attempt to explain how our individuality forms, develops, changes and is structured. 'Developmental' theories look at the influence of genetically inherited characteristics compared with those which are shaped or created by key learning, especially in our infancy and childhood. 'Structural' theories aim to locate ways of dividing up our personality into key ingredients. For example, some believe we are best described as a bundle of traits – such as friendly, warm, cold, secure, insecure, gloomy, bright, and so forth. Others argue that we can reduce the almost endless list of possible traits to a small number of major factors with which any person can be described and distinguished. These may be 'types' such as extrovert or introvert; neurotic or stable. Sigmund Freud is credited with one of the most influential, and controversial, personality theories which examines the effects of early psychosexual periods of development on individuality, and how unconscious, primitive 'id' forces will seek expression through the control of 'ego' and 'superego' layers of personality. Tests of personality are used in personnel selection and appraisal to help match people to jobs, or to spot potential. They form a major element of vocational guidance. They can be easily misinterpreted or misused, so their availability is usually restricted to psychologists or other specially trained users.

Deaux and Wrightsman (1984), Furnham (1992), Hilgard et al. (1980)

See also **implicit personality theory, intelligence, persona**

politics

In organizations, power and influence are traded in a complex, exciting and sometimes very serious and painful **game** known as organizational politics. The members of an organization form alliances, do deals with each other, plot the downfall or the promotion of colleagues, or mobilize coalitions continually. The military and combative words used in the last two sentences may suggest that this is an undesirable and destructive activity, but it is also true to say that it is a universal activity, and most people engage in organizational politics for what they see as the good of the organization. Organizations with strong **ethical** systems, such as hospitals and churches, are notorious for the robustness of their organizational politics. Bailey says that the more people believe that what they are doing is for the good of others, the dirtier the tricks they are prepared to resort to, to get their way. To label something as 'politics' in your organization is in itself a political action, because what you see as politics may be seen by the person doing it as just what needed to be done.

Bailey (1977), Hickson (1990)

See also **oligarchy, power**

post-modernism

A movement in many fields of intellectual and artistic endeavour, including the study of organizations. Post-modern philosophies describe social order as temporary, fragmented and unmanageable, unlike the regularities of modernism that have imbued rational thinking, organizational design and management practice. The post-modern world is also highly relativistic; there are no absolute standards and there are no fundamental reasons to privilege one type of understanding or 'fact' over another. Post-modernism in the arts has often implied a colourful, playful approach which incorporates several different styles at once, without demanding consistency or coherence. In organizing, a post-modern approach would be one that acknowledges several different ways of understanding things without trying to establish one of those as superior to the others, and without expecting to be able to make firm logical links between them. Boje et al. (1996), Cooper and Burrell (1988)

power

'Power is the medium through which conflicts of interest are ultimately resolved. Power influences who gets what, when and how' (Morgan, 1986: 158). Early work on organizations took a *unitary* view, which implied that it is possible to discover common organizational **goals** towards which all members of an organization work. Anything which stood in the way of unity should be dealt with, so that harmony and organizational health could prevail once again. Within this view, power does not figure very significantly. For many recent thinkers about organizations, however, power is a key concept. Some adopt a *pluralist* perspective, according to which individuals and **groups** in an organization can have diverging or even conflicting interests and goals, which they seek to promote through **politics**, drawing on a variety of sources of power to do so. This generates **conflict**, in which power is exercised and contested through confrontation and negotiation. Politics involves the forming and breaking of deals, alliances and truces, the use of force or the threat to use force. Within a pluralist view of organizations, power is vital. French and Raven identified five types of power depending on their source: *reward* (being able to reward behaviour that you like with promotions, money, praise and so on); *coercive* (being able to punish behaviour that you do not like with reprimands, dismissal, sarcasm or threats); *legitimate* (being seen as having the right to a particular kind of power); *referent* (being liked, and therefore influential); and *expert* (being seen as knowing best). Other thinkers on organizations have adopted a *radical* view. Like the pluralists, radical theorists see power in almost everything that goes on in organizations. Almost everything involves a power dimension: the trading, sharing or using of power. Radical theorists view organizations as composed of different groups and individuals with different interests, like the pluralists, but without a level playing field. Power is very unequally distributed. Some groups and individuals are seen as highly disadvantaged or disenfranchised on the basis of their class, **race** or **gender**. Denied legitimate sources of power, such groups may seek to undermine or disrupt organizational life through acts of resistance or rebellion. Lukes proposed a three-dimensional model of power, associated with the three perspectives. In the first dimension, you have power over someone else if you can force them to do something which they would not otherwise do. In the second dimension, you have power over someone if you can manage the situation so that there is no open discussion of anything that can damage you. For example, in a telephone call with your parents, you may be able to keep the conversation to safe topics! In the third dimension, you have power over someone if you can affect their view of what is in their own interests. Social and organizational factors generate power inequalities, leaving some individuals and groups with little or no power (see **powerlessness**). Such individuals or groups may still work hard for the organizations which dominate them; they may have no other source of income or they may be victims of **rhetoric**, **propaganda** or manipulation. People in organizations often assume that power lies elsewhere, usually at a more senior level. Some senior managers are surprised, however, to find how constrained their **actions** seem to be. Burrell and Morgan (1979), French and Raven (1959), Lukes (1975), Morgan (1986), Pfeffer (1981, 1992)

See also **authority, empowerment, leadership, politics**

powerlessness

A condition of lack of **control**. The term is widely used to describe individuals' feelings within **organizations** and, coupled with **meaninglessness**, it is generally seen as a dimension of **alienation**. Some of the same factors which account for meaninglessness, such as Tayloristic working practices, **deskilling, bureaucracy**, and the vast scale of some organizations, also produce powerlessness. Many low-placed members of the organization see themselves as unable to control what they do, how fast they work, what they produce or a whole range of decisions which affect their lives. These decisions are made in distant boardrooms, by people they have never met and who may have little regard for their happiness or well-being. Powerlessness may lead to fatalism and resignation which may in turn translate into absenteeism from work or poor **performance**; it may, on the other hand, lead to alternative forms of organization, such as trade unionism, and resistance. When the collective voicing of discontent is continuously blocked, powerlessness may lead to devious attempts at revenge through **sabotage, fiddles**, rumours and character assassination.

prejudice

A form of **attitude**, literally a pre-judgement that a person is prepared to make of another. Allport has noted that pre-judgement is a normal human response; human **groups** tend to separate from each other, and to look for characteristics of the other group that can be used to justify that separation. Sherif's classic studies showed that dividing a group of boys arbitrarily into two groups, and giving each group a name, was enough to generate prejudice between them. Studies of neighbours have shown that most prejudice occurs when there is proximity without contact. If people of different **ethnic** backgrounds or colour live in adjoining flats, and the doors to the flats point in opposite directions so that those people do not meet, they are likely to form negative prejudices about each other. **Gender**, sexual preference, **race**, age and social class are common areas of prejudice in organizations.

Allport (1958), Dovidio and Gaertner (1986), Sherif (1966)

See also **authoritarianism, ethnic groups, race, sexism, stereotyping**

problems

'What most people spend most of their time talking about in most organizations.' They occur when something is not as someone would like it to be, and the person is not sure what to do about it. They have the twin characteristics of something needing to be done or thought, and a degree of anxiety about whether the person can in fact deal with the problem. Puzzles are related to problems, but they tend to be tidier and with the potential for a more clearly defined solution. To set up a spreadsheet in unfamiliar software may be a puzzle, because it may take some time and thought to get it working. However, there is little doubt that it will work, and the person trying to do it will know when they have got it working. Problems are usually muckier than this. Much time in organizations is spent trying to persuade other people to see problems the same way that you do; 'The real problem is...' is one way of introducing such an attempt at influence. The definition of problems in organizations is one of the main topics dealt with in the process of organizational **politics**.

Bryant (1989), Eden et al. (1983)

professions

Professions were traditionally those occupations which, like medicine and law, fulfil a number of criteria, like the following: (1) a systematic body of knowledge and monopoly powers over its applications; (2) a self-regulating code of ethics, emphasizing **values** such as respect for the confidentiality of the client; (3) the sanction of the community at large; (4) **control** over the profession's own qualification and entry procedures; and (5) an altruistic orientation, stressing the value of the profession's service to the community over strictly monetary rewards for the professionals. Professionals enjoy a unique source of **power** within **organizations**, which is rooted in their technical expertise. Nevertheless, doubts about the altruism and lofty motives of professionals have persisted, summed up in Bernard Shaw's mischievous definition of a profession as 'a conspiracy at the expense of laity'. This cynical view sees professions as labour cartels, which control entry into an occupation through the erection of a variety of barriers, such as over-lengthy traineeships and examinations or the use of incomprehensible jargon to mystify and confuse the non-professionals.

propaganda

Propaganda is an important mechanism for influencing others through the careful manipulation and presentation of **information**. This can involve a selective presentation of facts (being 'economical' with the truth), presenting facts out of context so as deliberately to create a false impression, using emotive **language** (like 'fatherland' or 'treason'), powerful **symbols** (like flags or anthems) or **metaphors** (like 'iron curtain'). The Nazis officially recognized propaganda as a function of the state meriting a ministry to itself, headed by the notorious Dr Josef Goebbels. Successful propaganda shares many ingredients with successful **leadership**, notably an ability psychologically to 'read' the needs of those who will receive the message, to time and fine-tune the message exactly for the occasion and to build cumulatively on the effect of each message. The line between devious and callous manipulation, on the one hand, and good leadership, through legitimate influence, **motivation** and information is often a thin one; sometimes it is only a matter of different perspectives. Within **organizations**, propaganda is usually referred to in polite terms like public relations and advertising.
See also **rhetoric**

psychological contract

The unwritten set of expectations that exist between people in an organization, this is closely related to the concepts of **norm** and **role**. A psychological contract usually goes well beyond a legal contract of employment; it is psychological because it refers to mutual

perceptions and informal understandings. Psychological contracts are in the eye of the beholder. They imply that co-workers meet certain mutual expectations and obligations arising from the fact that they share the same organizational space and activities. These may include basic courtesies, respecting each other's dignity and worth, working to the spirit rather than letter of the formal work contract, constructive feedback, providing work which is not demeaning, understanding career expectations as well as responding to non-work, personal, crises. The nature of the psychological contract sets the spirit and tone of an enterprise and its development can be crucial to the organization's success and to individuals' well-being.
Rousseau and Parks (1993), Schein (1980)

psychological testing

Psychological testing has become a common feature of employee selection and appraisal processes, and vocational guidance. It is based on the assumption that key features of our personality – abilities, skills, motives, attitudes, values – can be inferred from our performance on specially devised exercises or questionnaires. The best researched have been carefully structured, tried out on a lot of people in advance, and have extensive 'norms' – population scores against which to compare individual scores. They provide relative measurement, and are restricted in availability to qualified users. Psychologists will judge a test by its published reliability and validity; that is, how consistent it is and how well it predicts behaviour or performance. Tests used in industry may be behavioural simulations – such as measuring performance on a set of 'real' decision-making tasks, under time pressure. Also used are standardized pencil-and-paper questionnaires which tap areas such as interests, specific aptitudes and abilities, and personality qualities.
Anastasi (1982), Hilgard et al. (1980), Toplis et al. (1991)
See also **intelligence, personality**

race

A difficult and politically sensitive concept to define. Unlike **ethnic groups**, races are usually thought of as involving some inherited physical characteristics, most notably colour. Yet physical differences between human groups tend to be far less significant in terms of biology than in terms of the political and symbolic **meanings** attached to them. The Nazis tried to develop biological 'theories' of race, mainly as a justification of racist and genocidal practices. Some psychologists have tried to link **intelligence** to race, arguing that this accounts, at least in part, for educational and social inequalities between races. Such arguments approach both race and intelligence as objective, scientific concepts, obscuring the extent to which they are socially defined **constructs**, as well as usually constructing correlations that ignore other factors such as the **culture**-based nature of the **psychological tests** used and indeed of the variables for which they are trying to test. Race acts as a common basis for negative **stereotyping**, as well as for **prejudice** and **discrimination**. Many organizations seek to overcome these injustices through an equal opportunities policy, explicitly excluding colour, gender and so on as factors in hiring or promoting staff. In the United States, Canada and South Africa, affirmative action or 'positive discrimination' programmes go considerably further by seeking actively to encourage the hiring and promotion of members of disadvantaged groups. This is sometimes achieved through the setting of quotas or the relaxation of qualifications and standards for entry into the organization. Such programmes are at times criticized as undermining the 'best man [sic] for the job' principle. Yet, without active encouragement, past inequalities tend to reproduce themselves. Disadvantaged groups find it difficult to break out of a vicious circle of powerlessness, prejudice and discrimination. Disadvantages in housing reinforce disadvantages in education which, in turn, reinforce disadvantages in employment opportunities.

Skellington (1996)

rationality

Rationality is generally thought of as the unique property of human beings to make **decisions** on the basis of careful assessment of **information**. Economists incorporate **assumptions** of rationality in their theories of economic behaviour, employing a model sometimes referred to as '*rational economic man*'; consumers, for example, will try to get the best value for money when faced with a purchasing decision. Max Weber distinguished between two kinds of rationality. Rationality of means implies that, given a certain set of goals, one adopts the optimum means for its achievement, on the basis of careful search, calculation and evaluation of the alternatives. The system of **rules** underpinning **bureaucracy** is rational inasmuch as it is carefully devised to enhance the achievement of organizational **goals**. This type of rationality is based on expert **knowledge** of the alternative courses of **action** available. It is the foundation of technical efficiency, even though it may be applied to entirely evil, insane or arbitrary goals. For example, one can go about very rationally burning down one's own house. The rationality of the ends or rationality of values is the second type of rationality identified by Weber, though his view is that science is of little help here. Modern economists have argued that the classical criteria for rational action are too strict; if the consumer was intent on buying carrots at the lowest price, he/she would end up spending his/her entire life comparing the prices in different shops. The same goes for organizations. Instead of decisions based on absolute rationality, Simon has suggested that they are based on 'bounded rationality': one makes a decision as soon as one has found a solution which is 'good enough', or 'satisfying'. Rational models of human behaviour, like those favoured by economists and Taylorist management, tend to disregard or underestimate people's impulsive, **emotional, desiring** and irrational qualities. These are of central importance to certain schools of thought in social psychology (like the **Human Relations** school) and depth psychology.

March and Simon (1958), Simon (1947), Weber (1948)

rationalization

A term used to signify three different things: (1) increasing the efficiency of an organization by eliminating redundant or non-profitable elements (including departments, operations and people); (2) the provision of credible or plausible motives for one's **actions** which conceal the real motives; this includes the finding of convenient excuses; and (3) the tendency of organizations and societies to shed their traditional, emotional, supernatural, aesthetic and moral qualities in favour of ever-increasing concern with economic efficiency.

See also **rationality**

reality

In philosophy and in different branches of social science, reality is a problematic concept. Is reality something absolute, constant and existing to be discovered 'out there' through ever more sophisticated methods of scientific inquiry? This is *positivism*. But how can we ever know reality other than through our own senses and perception? *Phenomenology* explores this, a view that focuses on human consciousness. Phenomenologists contend that our world consists of many different phenomena which we come to know in many different ways, other than through formal scientific inquiry – such as via our feelings, superstitions, prejudices, religions and beliefs. They constitute 'common sense' that we take for granted, as well as our unique sense of reality. *Hermeneutic* theorists develop this further, arguing that reality consists of a process of striving to make experiences meaningful. Hermeneutics is an ancient discipline, originally concerned with the interpretations of religious texts. Modern hermeneutics says that all **meaning** and understanding is strongly influenced by our culture and our place in it, and this 'ontological fact' is the starting point for the study of reality. Whatever we are, or now feel, is always situated in a cultural and historical context, which shapes how we come to know what is meaningful. But we also live in a world that has many social realities, which are formed and re-formed through interactions between people by different **cultural** and social **norms**. Reality here is a **social construction**, subject to the kind of regularities and disparities that are a feature of any social gathering. These distinctions are important for practice. In organizations, what kinds of realities are we operating with? Whose reality is being imposed on whom? Is the corporate strategic vision fixed on a single, objective view of its working environment, or is it one that sees a shifting, negotiated setting? Are individuals' existential realities honoured – what they are feeling and experiencing in their work?

Berger and Luckmann (1967), Gadamer (1975), Stablein (1996)

See also **objectivity**

repertory grid

A device introduced by George Kelly (1905–66) to identify personal **constructs**. In the original repertory grid, a person was presented with three elements – for example three different people – and asked in what way any two of them were similar and different from the third. 'Two of them are...whereas the other one is...'. The answers to these questions are the two opposite poles of one of that person's constructs. Some have argued that Kelly's genius was as a mathematician, in producing something as neat and effective as the repertory grid which could give us a clear but subtle measurement of personal constructs. Kelly, however, told one of his younger colleagues that he wished he had never invented the repertory grid. Apparently this was because of the extent to which repertory grid research had proceeded as an easily mechanized and possibly misleading form of **psychological testing**, rather than as a means for discovering personal constructs. The extent to which repertory grids appear objective has been abused by some researchers and consultants. Instead of discovering the richness of a personal construct system, they have used the repertory grid as just another way of collecting manageable but not necessarily meaningful data.

Adams-Webber (1978), Bannister and Fransella (1971), Kelly (1955)

resistance

A wide range of activities through which members in organizations seek to oppose official or unofficial forms of **control**. Resistance may be organized or disorganized, individual or collective, conscious or unconscious, active or passive, continuous or one-off. It can take a great diversity of forms, including strikes, **sabotage**, restriction of output, go-slow, insubordination, ritualistic compliance, jokes, sarcasm, bloody-mindedness, whistle blowing and cynicism. Resistance is part of organizational **politics**, yet it can take highly **symbolic** forms. Even small gestures, such as keeping a button undone or inscribing company property with graffiti, can be acts of resistance. Resistance can be an important part of an individual's **identity**.

rhetoric

Rhetoric is the art of persuasion, and is inherent in our use of **language** – conversational and written. The skilled rhetorician learns to shape phrases and select words and **metaphors** in ways which enhance their attractiveness, or accentuate a given message or **meaning**. Politicians are often marked apart by how well they form their rhetoric. Rhetoric is often seen in pejorative terms as dealing with surface appearances and lies. While such interpretations have validity, some academics – who study rhetoric as a discipline – argue that, to a greater or lesser extent, all **reality** is shaped by rhetoric; it is a fundamental part of human communication.

Billig (1987), Simons (1989)

See also **influence, management of meaning, propaganda**

rite of passage

Rites of passage, as first documented by anthropologists, describe the way people ritualize and celebrate key social transitions in their communities – such as birth, coming of age, marriage and death. We see, for example, the importance of the bar mitzvah in the Jewish

tradition when the 13 year old boy becomes a man after reading a specifically prepared piece of the Old Testament within a carefully orchestrated **ritual** in the synagogue. Rites of passage in organizations also mark a change of personal status. They can be informal and/or formal occasions. For example, a craft apprentice can earn full craftsman status by passing formal tests and exams. However, colleagues can also create their own tests – such as of abuse or humiliation. This latter type of rite of passage can be meted out to new recruits in the military, or to new prisoners by their cellmates. In each case the initiate is having to earn his or her new or changed place in the organization by 'passing' or **surviving** the tests. More gently, there is the rite of passage out of the organization after a successful career. The leaver is expected to receive gifts and praise at a ceremony, give thanks, celebrate – and leave.
Kuper (1977), Trice and Beyer (1984)

ritual

A formal **action**, normally repeated in a standardized way. While people often associate the idea of rituals with religions, organizations too generate rituals. Some of the rituals, like the singing of the company anthem in Japanese corporations, are formal, while others, like the purchasing of a new Rolls-Royce by each incoming chairman of ICI, are informal. In both cases, the essence of ritual is its **meaning** and **symbolism**. Knowing how to perform the important rituals in an organization is a crucial part of being seen as a fully fledged, competent insider, even if they are only to do with the normal way of greeting someone or parting from them; people are surprisingly strongly offended by not being greeted in what they regard as a proper way, or by having to wait while someone else goes through what they regard as an over-elaborate ritual. Rituals are generally thought of as having a strong bonding effect, though their compulsive repetitive quality gives them a similarity to certain neurotic traits, like the compulsive washing of hands (itself a form of ritual in several religions). Trice and Beyer have identified six different types of ritual in organizations, including **rites of passage**, rites of degradation and rites of renewal.
Trice and Beyer (1984)

role

A central unit of analysis in sociology and social psychology. It refers to the duties, obligations and expectations which accompany a particular position. We can visualize ourselves as a member of a 'role set', a number of significant people who influence how we should behave – they are our 'role senders'. A married man could have his wife, children, best friend, boss, mother and clergyman all setting different role expectations for him which may conflict with, or complement, each other – or some mix of the two. At work we may experience role conflict – such as expectations on us to increase productivity without sacrificing quality – two seemingly incompatible demands. Or there is ambiguity of role – unclear or confusing messages about what is expected of us. Reconciling various role demands can be a significant source of **stress**. Students, for example, often report the enormous pressures they feel in trying to satisfy the academic demands of their different lecturers, while also meeting social obligations that are regarded as an essential part of being a student.

Brown (1986), Champoux (1996), Kahn et al. (1964)

rules

Most organizations have formal rules governing working hours, safety practices and so on. These rules often go unchallenged (and quite possibly unread), although on occasions an organizational rule will be challenged as being in conflict with social or national laws; for example, rules about retirement age in some organizations have been challenged as they have come into conflict with laws banning **discrimination**. There are also informal rules. Few large companies lay down what their managers should wear, but without being told, the managers do not turn up on Monday morning in the jeans and jumpers they have been wearing over the weekend. Such informal rules operate like **norms**, and those who infringe them are likely to be ridiculed or ignored rather than openly punished. There are also the rules of the **game** of organizational life; in some organizations you are allowed to advertise your individual **success**, in some you are allowed to boast of having tricked a competitor, whereas in other organizations the same behaviour would not be legitimate.

Berne (1964), Hood (1986)
See also **bureaucracy, rationality**

sabotage

Although infrequently discussed in textbooks, sabotage is reported in numerous empirical studies. Sabotage is the deliberate destruction of employers' property (including machinery) or more generally the hindering of the work process. In its simplest form, sabotage can be an individual act of defiance, the throwing of the proverbial spanner in the works. However, sabotage is frequently an organized activity aimed at slowing the pace of work or even at re-asserting some **control** over the productive process, especially as a last resort for the **powerless** and disenfranchised.

Beynon (1973), Hyman (1989)

scapegoating

In biblical times, the sins of the Jewish people would be collectively reassigned to a goat, which would then be allowed to wander off into the wild, **symbolically** taking their sins away. From this procedure has come the term 'scapegoating', which usually means blaming one member of a group, or one group within an organization, for everything that goes wrong. It is often used as a means of not confronting what is going wrong. It can be particularly potent and toxic when combined with **stereotyping** and **prejudice**, as some person or group finds itself blamed for everything simply because it is of a type or race that is currently an object of blame.

Hirschhorn (1988)

Scientific Management

This school of **management** is associated with Frederick Taylor (1856–1915), an American mechanical engineer. Taylor, struck by what he regarded as the inefficiency of many production systems, argued that there was one best way to perform any particular task, and that way could be discovered 'scientifically'. Human–machine operations should, therefore, be precisely tracked and measured using time-and-motion studies, standardized tools, individual financial incentives and close supervision. His *cause célèbre* was a detailed study of the handling of pig iron which, once exposed to the rigours of his analysis, was redesigned to considerably increase output and decrease waste. The vestiges of Scientific Management can be seen in many of today's mass production and service operations – from cars to hamburgers. Taylor's work partly mirrored the times – high unemployment and cheap, poorly organized labour – and Taylor himself, who was an engineer. But he spectacularly failed to recognize the importance of social needs at work, non-financial incentives, informal work practices and non-directive supervision.

Rose (1988)

See also **control, deskilling**

self-presentation

We present ourselves differently to different audiences, partly because of the various **roles** we play in life. In other words, we assume the face, mannerism, dress, language and posture that is expected of us. This might mean disguising how we feel or how we want to be. Like the stage actor, we take on the characteristics required of the role. A 'dramaturgical' view of organizational behaviour suggests that much of social life can be regarded as us working, consciously and unconsciously, at our self-presentations, and making them acceptable for the various situations and audiences in which we find ourselves. **Problems** occur if (a) we do not know what image is required, (b) we are insufficiently skilled to present the desired image, and/or (c) the required image is uncomfortably different from how we feel.

Giacalone and Rosenfeld (1991), Goffman (1959)

See also **impression formation, persona**

sex

If it is not identified with sexual intercourse, or used to distinguish between males and females (see **gender**), sex is a rather difficult concept to define. Sex is a quality of whatever arouses **desire**, especially physical desire. It can be sparked by a poster, an image, a person, an item of clothing, a sound, a smell, a word (consider words with instant sexual connotations). Different **cultures** have very different ideas as to which things are meant to generate sexual feelings and which not as well as different ideals of physical attractiveness (see **interpersonal attraction**). What is certain is that we can learn to respond sexually to a diverse range of stimuli, something which has not escaped the attention of advertisers and marketers. For this reason Germaine Greer has described it as the 'lubricant of consumer society', adding that 'in order to fulfil that function the very character of human **sexuality** itself must undergo special conditioning' (1984: 198). The range of consumer items whose appeal is linked to sex is bewildering – from cars to clothes, and from airlines to computer software. The sexualization of everyday objects underlines two important features of sexuality. Firstly, activities, objects and states of being that appear to have little sexual content may be symbolic expressions of sexual **desires** and attempts to fulfil these desires in **fantasy**; for example, the desire to appear masculine and virile is expressed in driving a fast car. The car has come to stand for virility: it has become its **symbol**. Secondly, in Western cultures, fantasy, rather than passion, love or obsession, has emerged as the chief representation of sexuality. It is as a shared complex of fantasies rather than as anything else that sex stakes its public terrain.

Freud (1905/1977), Greer (1984), Packard (1957), Tavris (1992)

sexism

A negative **attitude** or **prejudice** about a person on the basis of their sex. This has been considered mostly in the prejudice that men have about women, where many jobs have been kept as a male preserve. While this may not be as flagrant as it was in the past, there is still plenty of evidence of sexism at work; in many professions, women face a 'glass ceiling' – an invisible barrier to how high they can go in their jobs. They are excluded from the informal friendship and **mentoring** which is crucial in organizational **politics** and they are often assumed to be less concerned about their work than men, and to be willing to subordinate their **careers** to the career of a male partner. Underlying this may be the male ego – the enormous need of many men for approval and admiration, and their fear of women who are independent enough not to choose to give them such approval and admiration. Sexism is also found in the prejudice against **homosexuals**. (For equal opportunities and affirmative action programmes, see **race**.)

Alvesson and Billing (1992), Gutek et al. (1996), Marshall (1984)

sexual harassment

A concept dating from the early 1970s describing the experience of unwanted attention – physical, or verbal, direct or by innuendo – of a sexual nature. Harassment can range from offensive **language** and **sexist jokes**, the use of exaggerated compliments and negative **stereotypes**, to the use of moral blackmail to extort sexual favours. The victim of sexual harassment is likely to feel anxious and oppressed by what is happening. Most, although not all, reported cases are of men harassing women, and here the issue interacts with the **power** structure of organizations and society – which tends to favour men. A number of studies suggest that harassment is more commonly directed towards those women who are perceived by men as threats. This supports feminist arguments that sexual harassment is not exceptional, nor just an individual's problem, but a wider symptom of power relations between the **genders**. Sexual harassment is difficult to manage institutionally because of its sensitive and personal nature, fear on behalf of the woman that her complaint will not be taken seriously, even ridiculed, and the possibility of the accusation being contested by the harasser. **Perceptions** may well differ about what was 'only a bit of fun', and there are cultural and sub-cultural differences on what is regarded as acceptable sexual attention in the workplace.

DiTomaso (1989), Gutek (1985), Tinsley and Stockdale (1993)

sexuality

Sexuality is the complex of physical **desires** and their expressions. The expressions of sexuality may be physical, emotional, verbal, or even artistic, but, in a direct or indirect way these desires aim at *pleasure*. While the sexuality of most individuals may seem consistent and stable (most desires, for example, are directed towards pleasure through heterosexual intercourse), social and psychological research indicates that sexuality is highly complex and variable. In contrast to animal sexuality which is mechanically linked to instinctual behaviour, human sexuality is mediated by desires, a large part of which are either learned or **symbolically** constituted. Sociologists and anthropologists have observed wide variations of sexual behaviour across different cultures and societies. Malinowski, for example, studied the highly promiscuous sexual behaviour of the Trobrianders, which contrasted sharply with the rigidly controlled behaviour of some of their neighbours. Western **cultures**, it is argued, spotlight one feature of sexuality, **fantasy**, as it is uniquely suitable to the demands of both consumer society and modern organization (see **sex** and **gender**); they also create an obsessive preoccupation with penetrative sex and orgasm as the aim of all sexual activity, at the expense of other forms of pleasurable behaviour. Psychologists have made two important observations regarding human sexuality: (a) It is dynamic, that is it develops through early childhood, going through a number of important stages, where different complications may arise. Freud (1856–1939), in particular, observed four stages of development: (1) the oral, in which most desires focus around the area of the mouth; (2) the anal, when most desires revolve around the control of the bowel movement; (3) the phallic, when the penis and the clitoris come into the centre of sexual feeling; and (4) the genital, which represents the usual terminus of adult sexual development, but which incorporates features of the earlier stages. (b) It is complex, involving numerous desires, many of which may conflict, and most of which are unconscious. No line between 'normal' and 'perverse' behaviour can be drawn, since the sexuality of 'normal' people invariably contains repressed desires that could be classified as perverse.

Freud (1905/1977), Mitchell (1975)

skill

Skill describes a competent or even virtuosic performance in virtually any kind of activity. Carpentry, playing the violin, telling jokes, speaking a language – all involve skills. Skills are generally acquired **competencies**; they require learning, practice and application. Yet there can be no doubt that people differ widely in their ability to develop different skills. Organizational life requires a great diversity of skills, yet there is no general agreement on the precise skills involved in organizing. Some skills required by organizations are social and interpersonal, such as communication, team-building or problem-solving skills. Other skills are of a more technical nature, for example computer programming or engineering. One of the ironies is that many people with highly developed skills (for instance at playing a musical instrument or doing mathematical computations) are incapable of talking about them. Perhaps this is not surprising; high levels of skill operate at a subconscious level. Those who have greater difficulty with acquiring a particular skill may have to think about it more, and thus be better able to talk about it. Improving your skill in the short term may involve some **deskilling**. This is because instead of focusing on the task at hand, the novice tends to focus on the way the task is carried out. Improvement in performance comes when the new skill has become natural, i.e. subconscious. High levels of skill in sport, martial arts, and probably in organizations, may depend on being able to practise and develop the skill in **fantasy**. While some individuals in organizations display highly skilled performances, under the influence of **Scientific Management** many employees throughout the 20th century were engaged to carry out highly deskilled tasks. Deskilling brought down the costs of labour and bolstered management **control** over the productive processes. It also made the quality of output independent of the skills of individual employees. However, the strategy of deskilling is one that no longer seems to work in an increasing number of industries, where employee commitment, flexibility and learning are of paramount importance.

Braverman (1974), Legge (1995), Strati (1985)

social construction

Social constructionism is a philosophy in its own right, and one which puts interacting individuals at the centre of their own universe as architects, more or less, of their own world views and **meaning systems**. According to social constructionists, when people act they do so on the basis of intersubjective understandings of a particular situation; they *define* the situation in interaction, or negotiation, with others. How people know what to do, how to behave, in a particular social situation comes about from an exchange of many communications and performances – exchanges of voice, eye contact, body posture, facial expression, gestures, testing out old understandings, experimenting with new ones. From these social **reality** is constructed. People weigh up their interpretations of the signs and signals, make judgements about others' intentions and, where necessary, seek shared understandings for the formation of rules of conduct. Such rules are not fixed, immutable; they are always being shaped and re-negotiated as new understandings, as well as misunderstandings, emerge. The socially constructed world is always dynamic, but some shared meanings are more resistant to change than others – because they are familiar and seem to work well most of the time. So we are not always seeking to re-define, within our culture, the courtesies of greeting a stranger, conduct in a smart restaurant, or how to behave in the presence of our boss. These **norms** do shift, but slowly over time. Nor, in the socially constructed world, are we completely free to redefine situations. In the hierarchies of **power** and **status** in organizations – themselves social constructions – we invest some people with more influence than others, so they can impress their definition of situations on us. Less formally, many social interactions in organizations involve give-and-take, where we sacrifice some of our own interpretations in the interest of co-operation and collaboration.

Berger and Luckmann (1967), Harré (1992), Nash (1985)

socialization

Socialization is the process by which people become part of a social unit. It is the taking on of the beliefs, **values** and mores of the society or organization to which they belong. Key agents of socialization are parents, teachers, peers, and possibly religious officials. Competing hard with these traditional sources are the mass media and entertainment – magazines, television, film, pop stars. From these various sources we learn our national cultural ways, including what is appropriate behaviour for our sex, social class and educational background. Organizational socialization is a microcosm of these processes. Companies seek to mould employees to their way of thinking and doing things. They do this by stressing their values and expectations at the recruitment stage. These are then reinforced by the joining **rituals, rites of passage, training**, promotional criteria, and various forms of organizational literature. Some companies are known for their heavy-handedness in such efforts, reflecting the desire to create a 'strong' organizational **culture** (IBM, McDonald's, Xerox). Others achieve their aims more subtly; a less visible, 'hands off' socialization.

Brown (1986), Schein (1978)

See also **institutionalization**

stakeholder

A group or individual seen as having some special interest, or *stake,* in the outcome of an organization's activities. Most organizations have core stakeholders, such as its owners and shareholders, employees, suppliers and government. Other possible stakeholders are customers, local communities, financial institutions, environmental protection groups and political parties. Stakeholders in organizations may be drawn more or less widely, and the decision about who a company regards as its stakeholders often reflects the organization's partialities and **values**. For example, a radical environmental pressure group may see itself as one of an oil company's stakeholders, but the company refuses to acknowledge such a relationship. A stakeholder perspective for management means that no organization can be considered an island. Managers need to map their key stakeholders, consider their expectations and demands, their interrelationships and their power to influence the organization's outcomes and reputation.

Mason and Mitroff (1981), Wood (1994)

status

Like **role**, status signifies a social position. Yet status goes beyond role, as it embodies an evaluation of merit, prestige or honour. Age, gender, birth, education, acquaintances and lifestyles are all important sources of status, though how they affect an individual's status may differ across different **cultures**. A person's job or occupation is an extremely important source of status in our cultures, frequently referred to as 'socio-economic status'. Within organizations, **professionals** and clerical workers usually enjoy superior status to manual workers; they are also more concerned about the social status of their job than manual workers. Status **symbols** are visible signs establishing an individual's or a group's status. A BMW as well as a Volkswagen Beetle can be status symbols, as are the size of an executive's office, a fashionable pair of trainers, a title such as Sir or Dr, an address in a fashionable part of town, or a badge on a piece of clothing.

stereotyping

This term was introduced in 1922 by the journalist Walter Lippman, who described stereotypes as 'pictures in our heads'. Stereotypes have been described by Wilson and Rosenfeld as 'clusters of preconceived notions'. Stereotyping means assuming that all the objects in some category will be similar in ways other than the one used to categorize them. Thus all students do have something in common – they are all studying. Stereotyping would go on from there to assume that all students will have other features in common too, such as all being prone to get up late, drink too much and not do much work. Stereotypes can be positive too; for example, the expectation that all doctors will be intelligent and caring is a positive stereotype. Stereotyping is one of the ways in which **prejudice** operates. People may fall victim to their own stereotypes: managers who are men may start to behave in peculiarly unaware, macho ways because they have absorbed a stereotype that this is how a 'real manager' should behave.
Wilson and Rosenfeld (1990)
See also **attitude, prejudice, scapegoating**

strategy

Strategies are major courses of **action** that an organization plans to take in order to meet objectives. At its simplest, and in its military origin, it means looking several steps ahead and considering what to do over the longer term, rather than looking only to the immediate term ('tactics'). Most often, strategies are formulated by the top management team – as an expression of their interests, inclinations and views about the purpose of the business. The process of strategic planning has become central to the operation of many organizations. It involves decisions on the organization's mission in the light of opportunities and threats, and on the long-term outlook for the business. Strategic planning will also include the allocation of resources – money, personnel, plant, land and equipment. Within the overall strategic plan, tactical planning will take place – short-term decisions, such as how a particular department will spend its own budget and achieve its production targets. Much recent research in organizations has been devoted to the process of strategy making, and to the types of strategies which seem to pay off. The word 'strategy' has become debased in recent years, as the fashion has grown for describing oneself as 'thinking strategically' or working at a 'strategic level' without the label having any particular meaning beyond that the speaker thinks they are important. Those new to reading about organizations should be warned that a number of old ideas have been repackaged, had the label 'strategy' stuck on them, and are now being offered as if they were new. The counter-argument to enthusiasts for strategy has been to say that what is important is timely, opportunistic action. It may be that strategy making helps people to think through a situation, and prepares them to be effective in operating opportunistically; in effect, strategy making may be best if you do not then feel you have to follow your strategy.

Joyce and Woods (1996), Pearce and Robinson (1991), Pennings (1985)

stress

Stress normally refers to unpleasant feelings and/or physical responses that people experience when they are working beyond their capacities and levels of tolerance. The signs and symptoms of stress include anxiety, irritability, fear, skin ailments, high blood pressure, gastric complaints and heart disease. Certain work situations are likely to be potentially more stressful than others, such as where there are high levels of noise, poorly designed equipment, conflicting **role** demands, a very high workload, poor support and supervision, and unpredictable changes. One approach to stress management, therefore, lies in improving the design and supervision of work. But the mechanisms of stress are also very individual. It depends on a person's **perception** of how threatening a particular **problem** or situation is, and his or her capacities to cope. Long periods of unresolved stress can lead to **burnout**, even death. In recent years it has become more acceptable to talk openly about stress problems. Some companies run stress management training programmes and offer counselling support. Yet a difficulty arises when stress becomes the only permissible way of talking critically about one's job or employer or a catch-all term for all the afflictions caused by modern organizations.

Cooper and Marshall (1978), Luthans (1992), Matteson and Ivancevich (1987), Smith (1991)

structure

A concept which derives from engineering, where it is used to describe bridges, buildings, towers or other constructions made up of different interconnected components. Structure has come to signify the patterned relations of components which make up any **system**. You can think of the structure as a framework on which different interconnected components are attached; it is not generally easy to alter one component without affecting the others. Organizations have different types of structure: in formal terms some are structured in geographical or product divisions, others in functional areas (such as marketing, finance, personnel and so on) and yet others form **matrix** structures. In more substantial terms, some have rigid mechanical structures dominated by formal **roles, rules** and regulations, while others have more informal and flexible structures in which people collaborate and communicate in a less highly **controlled** manner. Some organizations operating in particularly turbulent and uncertain **environments** tend to adopt an extremely fluid task-oriented structure known as adhocracy.

See also **bureaucracy, contingency theories, hierarchy, matrix structure**

sub-culture

The concept of **culture** originated with societies, as in 'European culture' or 'Amazonian culture'. It was then applied to organizations, where 'organizational culture' meant those distinctive features of an organization which make life in it so different from other organizations. Within organizations you may find quite different sub-cultures. For example, staff in a computer department often follow a different, more relaxed dress code than staff in other departments. The sub-culture of different groups of students within a university, such as engineers and business students, may also be very different, with different **norms** of dress and behaviour. As with all forms of culture, the inhabitants are usually largely unaware of the nature of their own culture. People often become aware of different sub-cultures only when two different sub-cultures meet. For example, they are in the company sports club with a friend from a different department, and meet a colleague from their own department. They may then find themselves aware for the first time of the norms of each sub-culture, and unsure as to which sub-cultural norms to adopt.

success

An integral part of the Protestant **work ethic**, success in the form of material prosperity, fame and honour was regarded as a sign of God's favour and a reward for hard work. Protestantism, according to Max Weber (1860–1920), encouraged a methodical and calcu-lating attitude in the pursuit of wealth, which provided capitalism with the work ethic required for its early growth in the 16th century. Nowadays, success has lost its religious and moral underpinning; it is no longer seen by everybody as the product of hard work, nor is it seen as generating a set of responsibilities and duties towards the community. Instead, some people would regard success as the result of careful planning, clever deals or good luck. Maccoby has argued that the successful businessman of today is essentially one who is good at **games**. Instead of hard **work** or ruthless ambition, cunning and risk-taking are seen as the requirements for success. Although different people may see success differently, it remains a powerful feature of middle-class cultures in the West as well as in the East, as part of a system of **values** which includes self-reliance, individualism and material well-being but also entrepreneurship and risk. Some individuals may gauge success in terms of visible signs and **symbols** while others tend to assess it through personal indicators, such as contentment, happiness or love.
Furnham (1990), Maccoby (1976)

survival

In many organizations, people's psychological well-being cannot be taken for granted. Constantly bombarded with **information**, over-whelmed by different demands and requests, worried about the future, surrounded by people whom they hardly know or like, work-ing in large organizations can be experienced as surviving an assault course. Other more subtle pressures threaten people's identity, integrity or self-respect. In order to survive within an organization, people employ a variety of coping mechanisms. **Jokes, gossip** and griping are safety valves for frustration. Practical jokes and **games** break the monotony of work. Some people distance themselves from the organization, adopting a cynical attitude and seeking to protect their 'patch' or wallowing in nostalgia for a golden past. Others try to survive by identifying fully with the organization, its **goals** and **values**. These people occasionally become very disillusioned and experience profound feelings of disappointment or **burnout**.

Hochschild (1983), Schwartz (1987)

See also **stress**

symbolism

A symbol is something that 'stands for', or signifies something beyond the literal properties of the symbol itself. So a national flag can symbolise (stand for) a nation, its freedom and independence. A small lapel badge can symbolise membership of an exclusive club or sect. Consumer products are often designed to be attractive for what they stand for as much as, if not more than, for what they actually do. To own a car of a particular make, colour and shape can give others a recognizable sign that you are the sort of person who has 'made it'. Similarly, wearing specific clothes can symbolise one's wealth, youth, **status**, occupation, or identification with a **sub-culture**. The words, deeds and products of organizational managers can influence those whom they manage as much through the symbolism used as through any more direct content. The symbols may be very obvious ones, such as the frequency of managers' presence and availability; the size, shape and furnishing of their rooms; the style of their memos and announcements; the way they conduct meetings; their **language** and **rhetoric**; the kinds of cars they drive; and the salaries they take and award. All these can be taken as symbols of their own **values**, style, and degree of concern for others. Less obvious symbols relate to areas such as trust and reliability – subtle features of the psychological contract. Do managers deliver what they promise? Are confidences respected? Is promotion seen to be fair? Are all staff listened to? Inconsistency in managerial symbols can soon undermine people's confidence and enthusiasm. Such as, for example, when bank staff are told they need to live up to the company's public slogan of 'the listening, caring bank', yet these same staff receive little attention or care from their own managers.

Czarniawska-Joerges (1992), Gagliardi (1990), Turner (1990)

See also **meaning, status**

system

Organizations are often studied as systems. Systems are separated from their **environment** by a boundary which is crossed by inputs and outputs. An organization's inputs from the environment may include raw materials, expertise, and money, while its outputs may include products, services and waste. Systems themselves are seen as being made up of components in orderly relationship, each component having specific functions of benefit to the system as a whole. These relations make up the system's **structure**. Biological systems, like animals or plants, are seen as having sub-systems, such as respiratory or nervous. Generally systems are seen as responding to changes in their environment, either by adapting or by seeking to change and control their environment. While the concept of a system has been used extensively to describe phenomena as diverse as the solar system, the transport and educational systems of a country, the global ecosystem or an information system, it has been criticized for obscuring **conflict** and disorder, and presenting too tidy and rational an image of the world. This textbook has highlighted organizations as terrains in which people make **decisions**, create **meanings**, face choices and experience **emotions**; these are all features which are generally underplayed by systems theory, which in the last resort tends to look at organizations using the **metaphors** either of machines or of biological organisms.
Keys (1991)

talk

A major part of most people's lives and, in particular, the main part of what managers do. Studies of managerial life by Mintzberg and Stewart show that the greater part of managerial activity is conducted through talk. Managers talk for their living as much as teachers, actors or chat show hosts do, a topic that has received lively and informative coverage by Tannen. Relatively little time is spent, or **action** taken, by managers on their own. Talk has been studied as a form of behaviour (Beattie), in a process called 'conversational analysis'. In a less behaviourist fashion, recent research has focused on **language, rhetoric** (Billig) and **discourse** (Potter and Wetherell). Talk is not always serious. People talk and **gossip** for pleasure as well as profit; such conversations may be conducted in the spirit of idle chatter, but can still have a considerable impact on later events, when the **information** that was passed on reaches someone who wishes to make use of it. It may be left deliberately unclear as to whether such talk is idle chatter or should be taken more seriously, as a way of testing out others' reactions before being too firm oneself. The role of talk and gossip has been grossly understated in most management theorizing, which has seen it as a transparent medium by which messages are conveyed from one person to another, rather than as a substantive activity in itself. The richness and joy of talk, the influence that can be wielded by an effective talker, the activities of the virtuoso talker (who will deliberately offer a brilliant display for the joy of showing that it can be done), the significance of telling stories well, and the role of gossip in keeping informed about what is happening in your organization, are all under-emphasized if talk is viewed as simply a functional way of conveying intended meaning.

Beattie (1983), Billig (1987), Mintzberg (1973), Potter and Wetherell (1987), Stewart (1967), Tannen (1995)

See also **gossip, language**

Taylorism

See **Scientific Management**

team-work

Organizations are full of teams, and many managers and theorists have argued for the importance of good team-work for the achievement of complex tasks. Teams are better than individuals on complex tasks which require either more work than one person can give, or more knowledge or **information** than one person will have. They are also important where a task calls for different **roles** or **skills** to be brought into play. But teams can also be arenas for **conflict**, and this conflict can come to hold more interest to the members than their task. Since the 1970s, there has been extensive team development work in many organizations, usually with the intention of producing more closely knit teams, and enabling team members to be more open with each other. However, well-developed teams also manifest some difficulties. They are prone to 'risky shift' – taking more risky decisions than the members would individually. They are also at risk of 'groupthink' (Janis), of going along with the opinions of their team-mates, particularly if they trust and respect them, whatever their personal doubts. Some practitioners have argued that too much work is done in teams, stifling individualism; they have then offered team destruction as an alternative package to team building.

Goold and Campbell (1998), Janis (1972), Lembke and Wilson (1998), Schein (1980)

See also **group**

technology

Technology can be thought of as ways of automating or mechanizing complex processes to enable them to be done in a more certain and economical way. A list of things you must remember to do would come within this definition of technology, as would a diary, or an **information system**. Technology may relieve you of the **stress** and potential overload of trying to do a task unaided. For a typical example of the double-edged character of technology, a person may be more relaxed when they have off-loaded the things they are trying to remember to their action list. At the same time, they are relinquishing some **control** over their life. There would be no point in their having an action list if they did not sometimes look at it and let it have some influence over what they did. Word processors limit where you may sit, and affect your view of the document you are working on. Technology also carries with it a risk of system failure; action lists get lost, central locking on cars fails to function, and computers become infected with viruses. The more technology seems able to help its users, the more likely they are to let it control them, and the more they feel lost when systems fail.

Rose (1988)

See also **alienation, contingency theories, deskilling, information technology**

teleworking

Teleworking is a term applied to people who work at a distance from their customer, client, colleagues or headquarters, but the physical distance is bridged by telecommunications technology. Traditionally, the telephone with a computer modem attached to a PC in the worker's home or local telecottage has provided the necessary link, but this has now been supplemented with sophisticated additions such as portable telephones, fax lines, electronic mail and video conferencing. Teleworking offers flexibility over one's place of work, which can range from the corner of a kitchen to the car. Using computer links, people can rapidly transmit documents over huge distances, so reducing the need for face-to-face meetings – and much travel and commuting (hence the phrase 'telecommuter'). The advantages of teleworking can be considerable to those who live in isolated communities, or who wish to avoid congested towns or cities. Large companies can save on expensive office space by encouraging teleworking. On the other hand some teleworkers, while initially liking the opportunity to work at home, feel too tied to the technology, lonely working without colleagues, cramped or stressed in their home workspace, and less secure about their work status. Teleworking is particularly suited to some jobs – such as computer software services, journalism, publishing, sales, and some types of consultancy. It is also well suited to some of the lowest paid and most repetitive jobs in society, such as data entry.

Jackson and van der Wielen (1998), Kinsman (1987), Townsend et al. (1998)

See also **information technology**

trade unions

Trade unions are **organizations** formed by employees to promote their common interests. They emerged in the early part of the 19th century out of the **powerlessness** of the individual worker when confronted by the **power** of the employer. They grew out of the realization that by forming an association, workers could offer mutual protection and improve their conditions of work. Most early unions were craft associations, seeking to limit the supply of labour in skilled trades, thus raising the market value of these **skills**. Gradually, however, industrial unionism shifted the emphasis towards uniform conditions of work and rates of pay through industrial action, like strikes, and collective bargaining with the employers. In this way, unions have sought to limit the powers of employers to hire and fire at will, unilaterally to impose conditions of work on a 'take it or leave it' basis, and to guarantee only minimal standards of protection and welfare as part of the terms of employment. In most industrial countries, following periods of acute conflict and confrontation, employers accepted unions as legitimate expressions of their employees' collective interests and recognized the legitimacy of collective bargaining as an **institution** for settling **conflicts** of interest. In recent years, however, unions have been on the defensive in

Britain and the United States, as a result of (1) new **technologies** which have wiped out traditional strongholds of unions in the skilled trades, (2) new **management** philosophies which have placed heavy emphasis on the individual employee as a bargaining agent or as a member of a corporate **culture**, (3) the emergence of new sectors in the economy, notably in services, where unionization is difficult, and (4) globalization of production which allows companies to shift productive operations relatively easily to countries where costs are low.

Hyman (1989)

See also **alienation, contingency theories, deskilling, information technology**

training

Bringing people to higher levels of **skill** or new **competencies**. The concepts of training and education are sometimes used interchangeably, but they have important differences. Training is bringing about or deepening specific pieces of learning, with the expectation that the person who has learned will be able to make use of this at work more or less straight away. Education implies more personal development: a change in the understanding that the person has of the world. Training is what brings you to competence in a specific technique; you should be able to go out and do something immediately with the results of your training. Education would enable you to respond more actively, to evaluate new techniques in which you are offered training, and to be able to decide when to apply the techniques you have been trained in. The example of sports training is helpful here. Training may make you fitter and able to perform at a higher level than you could before the training. Education might enable you to ask more critical questions, such as whether it is worth becoming better at the skill in which you are training, what you think about the **ethics** of competition, or whether there is some quite different way of going about your sport which might be more effective.

unemployment

The study of unemployment can reveal much about the role of employment, especially the social and psychological features of work that people take for granted. Paid employment has become a major feature of all industrialized societies, and provides a major source of **meaning** for those who work – even in jobs which are dreary and

alienating. The unemployed often report a loss of time-structure to the day, difficulties with their status and personal identity, a lack of 'place' at home, and more generally a sense of purposelessness and **meaninglessness** in their lives. **Stress** and illness are often greater amongst the unemployed. Poverty, or being less creditworthy, adds considerably to these difficulties; paid work is one of the few (legal) ways of acquiring money to purchase the various commodities which have become essential to survival in modern consumerist societies. Often the loss of work can be traumatic, particularly to people who are unable easily to re-enter the workforce because of their age, out-of-date skills or infirmity. In high unemployment communities we find school leavers expecting not to work, and pools of long-term unemployed men and women. For some, unemployment can become a way of life, so widely shared in their community that it does not feel a stigma. However, the unemployed can rarely participate in the wealth, opportunity and consumption enjoyed by those who do work, therefore high levels of unemployment can be socially divisive – and have been linked to social unrest and crime.

Fineman (1983, 1987), Winefield et al. (1993)

See also **meaning, work ethic**

values

In the end, what do you care about? What do you think is ultimately important? These are your values. If you ask yourself why you are doing something, take your answer, and keep asking the same question, you end up with a value. Why are you reading this book? To pass the exam. Why do you want to pass the exam? To get a better job. Why do you want a better job? To get more money. Why do you want more money? To feel secure. Why do you want to feel secure? I don't know, I just do. In this case, feeling secure is probably a value. Much of the research on values stems from Rokeach, who said that a value is 'an enduring belief that a specific mode of conduct or end state of existence is personally and socially preferable to alternative modes of conduct or end states of existence' (1973: 159). Some recent debate has questioned whether the noun 'value' can ever be more than a trivial simplification of the activity of human beings caring about what they are doing. The concept of individual values has also been questioned; what people care about is both formed and sustained in a community.

Rokeach (1973)

See also **attitude, culture, meaning, norm**

work

Unlike **labour**, which is a concept drawn from political economy, work is in the main a sociological and a psychological concept. It incorporates a wide range of cultural assumptions regarding what constitutes work, what is the purpose and **meaning** of work, and what its values and rewards are. 'What work do you do?', for example, is a question which cannot be answered without understanding the meaning which a **culture** attributes to work, the expectation of receiving payment or the **status** and prestige of different kinds of work. Different cultures have assigned widely diverging meanings to work and its corollary, leisure. Some have approached it as a primeval curse afflicting humanity, some as the true road to holiness and **success**, and some, like the Ancient Greeks, as a lower form of occupation unworthy of free individuals. Clusters of meanings around work, especially those regarding the relations between work and the good life, are often said to constitute **work ethics**.

work ethic

The notion of 'work ethic' implies a moral driving force in individuals to work; it suggests that people ought personally to labour, producing goods or services. There is debate about the strength and direction of the work ethic in different populations, especially whether it has declined amongst young people. The 'ought' implied in the work ethic is associated with the 17th-century rise in Protestantism in Europe where working was regarded as a religious imperative: a major route to spiritual salvation. The link between Protestantism and business activity was explored extensively by Max Weber (1864–1920) in his influential book *The Protestant Ethic and the Spirit of Capitalism*. The religious roots of the work ethic are today diffused by the broader influences of national and community cultures. We can see significant competing 'ethics' in people's lives, such as leisure and various forms of self-development. Those who lament the apparent decline in the work ethic point to a 'welfare ethic' – people who are now keen to live off the social provisions of the state. Inevitably, however, discussions about the work ethic become intermingled with the availability of jobs, and the extent to which non-workers are personally blamed for their predicament.

Furnham (1990), Weber (1958)

See also **success**

Bibliography

Abramis, D.J. (1992). 'Humor in healthy organizations', *HRMagazine*, August, 37 (8): 72–4.

Adams-Webber, J. (1978). *Personal Construct Theory: Concepts and Applications*. New York: Wiley.

Adorno, T.W., Frenkel-Brunswick, E., Levinson, D. and Sandford, N. (1950). *The Authoritarian Personality*. New York: Harper.

Ajzen, I. and Fishbein, M. (1980). *Understanding Attitudes and Predicting Behavior*. Englewood Cliffs, NJ: Prentice-Hall.

Aktouf, Omar (1996). *Traditional Management and Beyond*. Montreal: Morin.

Alderfer, C.P., Alderfer, C.J., Tucker, L. and Tucker, R. (1980). 'Diagnosing race relations in management', *Journal of Applied Psychology*, 16: 135–66.

Allison, G.T. (1971). *Essence of Decision: Explaining the Cuban Missile Crisis*. Waltham, MA: Little, Brown.

Allport, G.W. (1958). *The Nature of Prejudice*. Garden City, NY: Doubleday Anchor.

Alvesson, M. and Billing, Y.D. (1992). 'Gender and organization: towards a differentiated understanding', *Organization Studies*, 13: 73–103.

Anastasi, A. (1982). *Psychological Testing*. London: Macmillan.

Anastasi, A. (1990). *Psychological Testing*, 6th edn. New York: Macmillan.

Anthias, F. (1982). 'Connecting "race" and ethnic phenomena', *Sociology*, 26(3): 421–38.

Argyle, M. (1975). *Bodily Communication*. London: Methuen.

Argyris, C. and Schön, D.A. (1974). *Theory in Practice: Increasing Professional Effectiveness*. San Francisco, CA: Jossey-Bass.

Argyris, C., Putnam, R. and Smith, D. (1985). *Action Science*. San Francisco, CA: Jossey-Bass.

Arthur, M. (1994). 'The boundaryless career: a new perspective for organizational inquiry', *Journal of Organizational Behavior*, 15: 295–306.

Arvey, R.D. and Campion, J. (1982). 'The employment interview: a summary and review of recent literature', *Personnel Psychology*, 35: 281–322.

Asch, S. (1951). 'Effects of group pressure upon the modification and distortion of judgement', in M.H. Guetzkow ed., *Groups, Leadership and Men*. Pittsburgh, PA: Carnegie Institute of Technology Press. pp. 117–90.

Ashforth, B.E. and Humphrey, R.H. (1995). 'Emotion in the workplace – a reappraisal', *Human Relations*, 48 (2): 97–125.

Austrin, Terry, (1994). 'Positioning resistance and resisting position: human resource management and the politics of appraisal and grievance hearings', in J. Jermier, W. Nord and D. Knights eds, *Resistance and Power in Organizations*. London: Routledge. pp. 25–68.

Bailey, F.G. (1977). *Stratagems and Spoils*. Oxford: Blackwell.

Bandura, A. (1977). *Social Learning Theory*. Englewood Cliffs, NJ: Prentice-Hall.

Bannister, D. and Fransella, F. (1971). *Inquiring Man*. Harmondsworth: Penguin.

Bansal, P. and Howard, P. (1997). *Business and the Natural Environment*. Oxford: Butterworth-Heinemann.

Barnard, C.I. (1938). *The Functions of the Executive*. Cambridge, MA: Harvard University Press.

Bate, P. (1994). *Strategies for Cultural Change*. Oxford: Butterworth-Heinemann.
Baudrillard, J. (1988). *Selected Writings*, ed. M. Poster. Cambridge: Polity Press.
Bauman, Z. (1988). *Freedom*. Milton Keynes: Open University Press.
Bauman, Z. (1992). *Intimations of Postmodernity*. London: Routledge.
Beattie, G. (1983). *Talk*. Milton Keynes: Open University Press.
Becker, E. (1962). *The Birth and Death of Meaning*. Harmondsworth: Penguin.
Belbin, M. (1981). *Management Teams: Why They Succeed or Fail*. London: Heinemann.
Bennis, W. (1989). *Why Leaders Can't Lead. The Unconscious Conspiracy Continues*. San Francisco, CA: Jossey-Bass.
Bennis, W. and Nanus, B. (1985). *Leaders: Strategies for Taking Charge*. New York: Harper and Row.
Bentham, J. (1897). *An Introduction to the Principles of Morals and Legislation*. Oxford: Clarendon Press.
Berger, P.L. and Luckmann, T. (1967). *The Social Construction of Reality*. Harmondsworth: Penguin.
Berne, E. (1964). *Games People Play*. New York: Grove Press.
Beynon, H. (1973). *Working for Ford*. London: Allen Lane.
Bigelow, J.D. (1991). *Managerial Skills: Explorations in Practical Knowledge*. Newbury Park, CA: Sage.
Billig, M. (1987). *Arguing and Thinking: A Rhetorical Approach to Social Psychology*. Cambridge: Cambridge University Press.
Bion, W.R. (1961). *Experiences in Groups*. London: Tavistock.
Blackburn, R.M. and Mann, M. (1979). *The Working Class in the Labour Market*. London: Macmillan.
Blauner, R. (1964). *Alienation and Freedom*. Chicago, IL: University of Chicago Press.
Bloomfield, B.P. (1989). 'On speaking about computing', *Sociology*, 23 (3): 409–26.
Bly, R. (1990). *Iron John: A Book about Men*. Reading, MA: Addison-Wesley.
Boje, D.M. and Dennehy, R.F. (1993). *Managing in the Postmodern World: America's Revolution Against Exploitation*. Dubuque, IO: Kendall-Hunt.
Boje, D.M., Gephart, R.P. and Thatchenkery, T.J. (1996). *Postmodern Management and Organization Theory*. Thousand Oaks, CA: Sage.
Bowen, D.E., Ledford, G.E. and Nathan, B.R. (1991). 'Hiring for the organization, not the job', *Academy of Management Review*, 5 (4): 35–50.
Brady, F.N. (1990). *Ethical Managing*. New York: Macmillan.
Brandt, J. (1996). 'In praise of fools', *Industry Week*, 1 April 245 (7): 6.
Brant, C. and Too, L. (1994). *Rethinking Sexual Harassment*. London: Pluto Press.
Braverman, H. (1974). *Labor and Monopoly Capital*. New York: Monthly Review Press.
Brown, A. (1995). *Organisational Culture*. London: Pitman.
Brown, D. and Brooks, L. eds (1990). *Career Choice and Development*. San Francisco, CA: Jossey-Bass.
Brown, R. (1986). *Social Psychology*. New York: Free Press.
Bruner, J. (1990). *Acts of Meaning*. Cambridge, MA: Harvard University Press.
Bryant, J. (1989). *Problem Management: A Guide for Producers and Players*. Chichester: Wiley.
Bryman, A. (1986). *Leadership and Organizations*. London: Routledge and Kegan Paul.
Bryman, A. (1992). *Charisma and Leadership in Organizations*. London: Sage.
Bryman, A. (1996). 'Leadership', in S. Clegg, C. Hardy and W. Nord, *Handbook of Organizational Studies*. London: Sage.
Buchanan, D. and Huczynski, A. (1997). *Organizational Behaviour*, 3rd edn. Hemel Hempstead: Prentice-Hall.
Burns, J.M. (1978). *Leadership*. New York: Harper and Row.
Burns, T. and Stalker, G.M. (1961). *The Management of Innovation*. London: Tavistock.
Burrell, G. and Morgan, G. (1979). *Sociological Paradigms and Organizational Analysis*. London: Heinemann.
Cannon, T. (1994). *Corporate Responsibility*. London: Pitman.

Carlzon, J. (1989). *Moments of Truth*. New York: Harper and Row.

Champoux, J.E. (1996). *Organizational Behavior*. Minneapolis/St Paul: New York.

Chemmers, M. and Aman, R. eds (1993). *Leadership: Theory, Practice, Perspective and Direction*. New York: Academic Press.

Child, J. (1977). *Organizations: A Guide to Problems and Practice*. London: Harper and Row.

Chodorow, N. (1978). *The Reproduction of Mothering: Psychoanalysis and the Sociology of Gender*. Berkeley: University of California Press.

Chung, K.H. and Megginson, L.C. (1981). *Organizational Behavior: Developing Managerial Skills*. New York: Harper and Row.

Clampitt, P.G. (1991). *Communicating for Managerial Effectiveness*. Newbury Park, CA: Sage.

Cockburn, C. (1991). *In the Way of Women*. Basingstoke: Macmillan.

Collins, E. and Blodgett, T.B. (1981). 'Sexual harassment: some see it, some won't', *Harvard Business Review*, March-April.

Collinson, D.L. (1994). 'Strategies of resistance: power, knowledge and subjectivity in the workplace', in J. Jermier, W. Nord, and D. Knights eds, *Resistance and Power in Organizations*. London: Routledge.

Conrad, C. and Witte, K. (1994). 'Is emotional expression repression or oppression? Myths of organizational affective regulation', in S.A. Deetz ed., *Communication Yearbook 17*. Thousand Oaks, CA: Sage. pp. 417–28.

Cook, S.L. (1982). *The Writings of Steve Cook*, eds K. Bowen, A. Cook and M. Luck. Birmingham: Operational Research Society.

Cook, S. and Yanow, D. (1993). 'Culture and organizational learning', *Journal of Management Inquiry*, 2 (4): 373–90.

Cooper, C.L. and Marshall, J. (1978). *Understanding Executive Stress*. London: Macmillan.

Cooper, C.L. and Torrington, D.P. eds (1981). *After Forty*. Chichester: Wiley.

Cooper, R. and Burrell, G. (1988). 'Modernism, postmodernism and organizational analysis: an introduction', *Organization Studies*, 9 (1): 91–112.

Crompton, R. and Jones, B. (1984). *White Collar Proletariat*. London: Macmillan.

Cummings, L.L. and Schwab, D.P. (1973). *Performance in Organizations*. Glenview, IL: Scott Foresman.

Cummins, T.G. and Worley, C.G. (1993). *Organization Development and Change*, 5th edn. St Paul, MN: West.

Czarniawska-Joerges, B. (1992). *Exploring Complex Organizations*. Newbury Park, CA: Sage.

D'Zurilla, T.J. and Goldfried, M.R. (1971). 'Problem solving and behaviour modification', *Journal of Abnormal Psychology*, 78: 107–26.

Dalton, P. and Dunnett, G. (1992). *A Psychology for Living: Personal Construct Theory for Professionals and Clients*. Chichester: Wiley.

Davidson, M.J. and Cooper, C.L. (1992). *Shattering the Glass Ceiling: The Woman Manager*. London: Paul Chapman.

Davis, G.F. and Powell, W.W. (1992). 'Organization-environment relations', in M.D. Dunnett and L.M. Houg eds, *Handbook of Industrial and Organizational Psychology*, 2nd edn. Palo Alto, CA: Consulting Psychologists Press. pp. 316–75.

Davies, C. (1988). 'Stupidity and rationality: jokes from the iron cage', in C. Powell and G.E.C. Paton eds, *Humour in Society*. London: Macmillan. pp. 1–32.

Deal, T.E. and Kennedy, A.A. (1982). *Corporate Cultures*. Reading, MA: Addison-Wesley.

Deaux, K. and Wrightsman, L.S. (1984). *Social Psychology in the 80s*. Monterey, CA: Brooks/Cole.

Difonzo, N., Bordia, P. and Rosnow, R.L. (1994). 'Reining in rumors', *Organizational Dynamics*, Summer: 47–62.

DiTomaso, N. (1989). 'Sexuality in the workplace: discrimination and harassment', in J. Hearn et al. eds, *The Sexuality of Organization*. London: Sage.

Doray, B. (1988). *From Taylorism to Fordism: A Rational Madness*. London: Free Association Books.

Douglas, T. (1983). *Groups*. London: Tavistock.

Dovidio, J.F. and Gaertner, S.L. (1986). *Prejudice, Discrimination and Racism*. Orlando, FL: Academic Press.

Drucker, P.F. (1989). *The Practice of Management*. Oxford: Heinemann.

Du Gay, P. (1996). *Consumption and Identity at Work*. London: Sage.

Duck, S.W. ed. (1982). *Personal Relationships 4: Dissolving Personal Relationships*. New York: Academic Press.

Duck, S.W. (1992). *Human Relationships*, 2nd edn. London: Sage.

Dulewicz, V. (1991). 'Improving assessment centres', *Personnel Management*, June: 50–5.

Duncan, W.J. and Feisal, J.P. (1989). 'No laughing matter: patterns of humor in the workplace', *Organizational Dynamics*, Spring, 17 (4): 18–30.

Durkheim, E. (1951). *Suicide*. New York: Free Press.

Dutton, J. (1997). 'Strategic agenda building in organizations', in Z. Shapira ed. *Organizational Decision Making*. New York: Cambridge University Press.

Easterby-Smith, M., Burgoyne, J. and Araujo, L. eds (1998). *Organizational Learning and the Learning Organization: Developments in Theory and Practice*. London: Sage.

Edelwich, J. and Brodsky, A. (1980). *Burn-Out*. New York: Human Sciences Press.

Eden, C. and Ackermann, F. (1988). *Making Strategy: The Journey of Strategic Management*. London: Sage.

Eden, C. and Radford, J. eds (1990). *Tackling Strategic Problems: The Role of Group Decision Support*. London: Sage.

Eden, C., Jones, S. and Sims, D. (1983). *Messing about in Problems: An Informal Structured Approach to their Identification and Management*. Oxford: Pergamon.

Eden, S. (1996). *Environmental Issues and Business*. Chichester: Wiley.

Edwards, R. (1979). *Contested Terrain: The Transformation of the Workplace in the Twentieth Century*. London: Heinemann.

Egan, G. (1990). *The Skilled Helper: A Systematic Approach to Effective Helping*, 4th edn. Pacific Grove, CA: Brooks/Cole.

Erikson, E. (1968). *Identity, Youth and Crisis*. New York: Norton.

Festinger, L. (1957). *A Theory of Cognitive Dissonance*. Evanston, IL: Row Peterson.

Festinger, L. and Carlsmith, J. (1959). 'Cognitive consequences of forced compliance', *Journal of Abnormal and Social Psychology*, 58: 203–10.

Fiedler, F. (1967). *A Theory of Leadership Effectiveness*. New York: McGraw-Hill.

Fineman, S. (1983). *White Collar Unemployment*. Chichester: Wiley.

Fineman, S. (1985). *Social Work Stress and Intervention*. Aldershot: Gower.

Fineman, S. ed. (1987). *Unemployment: Personal and Social Consequences*. London: Tavistock.

Fineman, S. ed. (1993). *Emotion in Organizations*. London: Sage.

Fineman, S. (1996a). 'Emotion and organizing', in S. Clegg, C. Hardy and W. Nord eds, *Handbook of Organization Studies*. London: Sage.

Fineman, S. (1996b). 'Emotional subtexts in corporate greening', *Organization Studies*, 17 (3): 479–500.

Fineman, S. (1997). 'Constructing the green manager', *British Journal of Management*, 8: 31–8.

Fineman, S. and Clarke, K. (1996). 'Green stakeholders: industry interpretations and response', *Journal of Management Studies*, 33 (6): 715–30.

Fineman, S. and Mangham, I.L. (1978). 'Leadership: contingencies and training', in P. B. Warr ed. *Psychology at Work*. pp. 243–70. Harmondsworth: Penguin.

Fineman, S. and Sturdy, A. (1999). 'The emotions of control: a qualitative study of environmental regulation', *Human Relations*, 52 (5): 631–63.

Fisher, A. (1996). 'What's so funny, jokeboy?' *Fortune*, 9 December 134 (11): 220.

Fiske, J. (1989). *Understanding Popular Culture*. London: Unwin Hyman.

Fletcher, C. and Williams, R. (1992). *Performance Appraisal and Career Development.* Leckhampton: Thornes.

Fontana, A. (1980). 'The mask and beyond: the enigmatic sociology of Erving Goffman', in J. Douglas, *The Sociologies of Everyday Life.* Boston, MA: Allyn and Bacon.

Ford, H. (1923). *My Life and Work.* London: Heinemann.

Forsyth, D.R. (1990). *Group Dynamics.* Pacific Grove, CA: Brooks/Cole.

Foucault, M. (1965). *Madness and Civilization.* New York: Random House.

Foucault, M. (1971). *The Birth of the Clinic.* London: Tavistock.

Foucault, M. (1977). *Discipline and Punish.* London: Allen and Unwin.

Foucault, M. (1979). *The History of Sexuality.* New York: Vintage Books.

French, J.R.P. Jr and Raven, B.H. (1959). 'The bases of social power', in D. Cartwright ed., *Studies in Social Power.* Ann Arbor: University of Michigan Press.

Freud, S. (1905). *Jokes and their Relation to the Unconscious.* London: Hogarth Press.

Freud, S. (1905/1977). 'Three essays on the theory of sexuality', in *Freud on Sexuality.* Harmondsworth: Penguin. pp. 33–169.

Friedman, M. (1970). 'The social responsibility of business is to increase profits', *New York Times Magazine*, 13 September: 122–6.

Frost, P.J., Moore, L.F., Louis, M.R., Lundberg, C.C. and Martin, J. eds (1991). *Reframing Organizational Culture.* London: Sage.

Fryer, D. and Ullah, P. (1987). *Unemployed People: Social and Psychological Consequences.* London: Tavistock.

Furnham, A. (1990). *The Protestant Work Ethic: The Psychology of Work-Related Beliefs and Behaviours.* London: Routledge.

Furnham, A. (1992). *Personality at Work.* London: Routledge.

Gabriel, Y. (1988). *Working Lives in Catering.* London: Routledge.

Gabriel, Y. (1991). 'On organizational stories and myths: why it is easier to slay a dragon than to kill a myth', *International Sociology*, 6 (4): 427–42.

Gabriel, Y. (1992). 'Heroes, villains, fools and magic wands: computers in organizational folklore', *International Journal of Information Resource Management*, 3 (1): 3–12.

Gabriel, Y. (1995). 'The unmanaged organization: stories, fantasies, subjectivity', *Organization Studies*, 16 (3): 477–501.

Gabriel, Y. (1998). 'Same old story or changing stories: folkloric, modern and postmodern mutations', in D. Grant, T. Keenoy and C. Oswick eds, *Discourse and Organization.* London: Sage. pp. 84–103.

Gabriel, Y. and Lang, T. (1995). *The Unmanageable Consumer: Contemporary Consumption and its Fragmentation.* London: Sage.

Gadamer, H.G. (1975). *Truth and Method.* New York: Seabury Press.

Gagliardi, P. ed. (1990). *Symbols and Artifacts: Views of the Corporate Landscape.* Berlin: De Gruyter.

Gardner, C.B. (1995). *Passing By: Gender and Public Harassment.* Berkeley: University of California Press.

Giacalone, R.A. and Rosenfeld, P. (1991). *Applied Impression Management.* Newbury Park, CA: Sage.

Giddens, A. (1991). *Modernity and Self-Identity: Self and Society in the Late Modern Age.* Stanford, CA: Stanford University Press.

Goffman, E. (1959). *The Presentation of Self in Everyday Life.* Garden City, New Jersey: Anchor.

Goffman, E. (1961). *Asylums.* Garden City, NJ: Anchor.

Goldthorpe J.H., Lockwood, D., Beckhofer, F. and Pratt, J. (1968). *The Affluent Worker: Industrial Attitudes and Behaviour.* Cambridge: Cambridge University Press.

Goleman, D. (1996). *Emotional Intelligence.* London: Bloomsbury.

Goodman, P.S. (1982). *Change in Organizations.* San Francisco, CA: Jossey-Bass.

Goold, M. and Campbell, A. (1998). 'Desperately seeking synergy', *Harvard Business Review*, 76 (5): 131–44.

Gordon, D.M., Edwards, R. and Reich, M. (1982). *Segmented Work, Divided Workers: The Historical Transformation of Labor in the United States.* Cambridge: Cambridge University Press.

Gouldner, A.W. (1954). *Patterns of Industrial Bureaucracy.* Glencoe, IL: Free Press.

Gouldner, A.W. (1961). 'Metaphysical pathos and the theory of bureaucracy', in S.M. Lipset and N.J. Smelser eds, *Sociology: The Progress of a Decade.* Englewood Cliffs, NJ: Prentice-Hall. pp. 469–505.

Greenspan, S.I (1997). *The Growth of the Mind.* Reading, MA: Addison-Wesley.

Greer, G. (1970). *The Female Eunuch.* London: Granada.

Greer, G. (1984). *Sex and Destiny: The Politics of Human Fertility.* London: Secker and Warburg.

Grey, C. (1994). 'Career as a project of the self and labour process discipline', *Sociology,* 28 (2): 479–97.

Guest, D. (1987). 'Human resource management and industrial relations', *Journal of Management Studies,* 24 (5): 503–21.

Gunz, H. (1989) *Careers and Corporate Cultures.* Oxford: Blackwell.

Gutek, B.A. (1985). *Sex and the Workplace: Impact of Sexual Behavior and Harassment on Women, Men and Organizations.* San Francisco, CA: Jossey-Bass.

Gutek, B.A., Cohen, A.G. and Tsui, A. (1996). 'Reactions to perceived sex discrimination', *Human Relations,* 49: 791–813.

Hall, D.T. (1986). *Career Development in Organizations.* San Francisco, CA: Jossey-Bass.

Hall, D.T. (1996). *The Career is Dead: Long Live the Career!* San Francisco, CA: Jossey-Bass.

Hall, D.T., Bowen, D.D., Lewicki, R.J. and Hall, F.S. (1978). *Experiences in Management and Organizational Behavior.* Chicago, IL: St Clair Press.

Handy, C.B. (1976). *Understanding Organizations.* Harmondsworth: Penguin.

Hannigan, J.A. (1995). *Environmental Sociology.* London: Routledge.

Harré, R. (1992). 'What is real in psychology?', *Theory and Psychology,* 2 (2): 153–8.

Harré, R. and Secord, P.F. (1972). *The Explanation of Social Behaviour.* Oxford: Blackwell.

Harri-Augstein, S. and Thomas, L. (1991). *Learning Conversations.* London: Routledge.

Harries, R. (1998). 'Outmocking the mockers', *Times Higher Education Supplement,* 24 April: 29.

Harrison, E.F. (1981). *The Managerial Decision-Making Process,* 2nd edn. Boston, MA: Houghton Mifflin.

Harrison, R. (1972). 'How to describe your organization', *Harvard Business Review,* September-October.

Harvey-Jones, J. (1988). *Making it Happen.* Glasgow: Fontana.

Hatch, M.J. and Ehrlich, S.B. (1993). 'Spontaneous humour as an indicator of paradox and ambiguity in organizations', *Organization Studies,* 14: 505–26.

Hearn, J. and Parkin, W. (1987). *'Sex' at 'Work': The Power and Paradox of Organization Sexuality.* Brighton: Wheatsheaf.

Hearn, J., Sheppard, D.L., Tancred-Sheriff, P. and Burrell, G. eds (1989). *The Sexuality of Organization.* London: Sage.

Hellriegel, D., Slocum, J.W. and Woodman, R.W. (1992). *Organizational Behavior,* St Paul, MN: West.

Herriot, P. and Pemberton, C. (1995). *New Deals: The Revolution in Managerial Careers.* Chichester: Wiley.

Herzberg, F., Mausner, B. and Snyderman, B. (1959). *The Motivation to Work.* New York: Wiley.

Hewitt, J. (1984). *Self and Society: A Symbolic Interactionist Social Psychology,* 3rd edn. Boston, MA: Allyn and Bacon.

Hickson, D.J. (1990). 'Politics permeate', in D.C. Wilson and R.H. Rosenfeld eds, *Managing Organizations*. London: McGraw-Hill. pp. 175–81.

Hilgard, E.R., Atkinson, R.C. and Atkinson, R.L. (1980). *Introduction to Psychology*. New York: Harcourt Brace Jovanovich.

Hinton, P.R. (1993). *The Psychology of Interpersonal Perception*. London: Routledge.

Hirschhorn, L. (1988). *The Workplace Within*. Cambridge, MA: MIT Press.

Hochschild, A. (1983). *The Managed Heart*. Berkeley: University of California Press.

Hochschild, A. (1989). *The Second Shift*. New York: Viking.

Hofstede, G. (1991). *Cultures and Organizations: Software of the Mind*. New York: McGraw-Hill.

Hood, C. (1986). *Administrative Analysis: An Introduction to Rules, Enforcement and Organization*. Brighton: Wheatsheaf.

Hopfl, H. (1991). 'Nice jumper Jim! dissonance and emotional labour in a management development programme', paper presented at 5th European Congress – The Psychology of Work and Organizations, Rouen, 24–27 March.

Hovland, C., Janis, I. and Kelley, H.H. (1953). *Communication and Persuasion*. New Haven, CT: Yale University Press.

Howard, A. and Bray, D.W. (1988). *Managerial Lives in Transition: Advancing Age and Changing Times*. New York: Guilford Press.

Howe, I. (1986). 'The spirit of the times: greed, nostalgia, ideology and war', *Dissent*, 33 (4): 413–25.

Huczynski, A.A. (1996). *Management Gurus*. London: Thompson.

Huczynski, A.A. and Buchanan, D. (1991). *Organizational Behaviour*, 2nd edn. London: Prentice-Hall.

Huse, E.F. and Cummings, T.G. (1985). *Organization Development and Change*. St Paul, MN: West.

Hyman R. (1989). *Strikes*. Basingstoke: Macmillan.

Iaccoca, L. (1984). *Iaccoca*. London: Bantam Books.

Jackall, R. (1988). *Moral Mazes*. New York: Oxford University Press.

Jackson, M.C. and Keys, P. (1986). *New Directions in Management Science*. Aldershot: Gower.

Jackson, P.J. and van der Wielen, J.M. eds (1998). *Teleworking: International Perspectives*. London: Routledge.

Jahoda, M. (1982). *Employment and Unemployment*. Cambridge: Cambridge University Press.

Janis, I.L. (1972). *Victims of Groupthink*. New York: Houghton Mifflin.

Jaques, E. (1976). *A General Theory of Bureaucracy*. Oxford: Heinemann.

Jermier, J.M., Knights, D. and Nord, W.R. eds (1994). *Resistance and Power in Organizations*. London: Routledge.

Jones, E.E. (1990). *Interpersonal Perception*. New York: Freeman.

Joyce, P. and Woods, A. (1996). *Essential Strategic Management: From Modernism to Pragmatism*. Oxford: Butterworth-Heinemann.

Kahn, R.L., Wolfe, D.M., Quinn, R.P., Snoek, J.D. and Rosenthal, R.A. (1964). *Organizational Stress: Studies in Role Conflict and Ambiguity*. New York: Wiley.

Kamata, S. (1984). *Japan in the Passing Lane*. London: Allen and Unwin.

Kanter, R.M. (1977). *Men and Women of the Corporation*. New York: Basic Books.

Kanter, R.M. (1983). *The Change Masters*. New York: Simon and Schuster.

Kanter, R.M. (1984). *The Change Masters*. London: Unwin Hyman.

Kanter, R.M. (1989). *When Giants Learn to Dance*. London: Simon and Schuster.

Katz, D. and Kahn, R.L. (1978). *The Social Psychology of Organizations*, 2nd edn. New York: Wiley.

Katzell, R.A. and Thompson, D.E. (1990). 'Work motivation: theory and practice', *American Psychologist*, 45: 144–53.

Keen, S. (1992). *Fire in the Belly: On Being a Man*. London: Piatkus.

Keisler, C.A. and Keisler, S.B. (1969). *Conformity*. Reading, MA: Addison-Wesley.

Kelley, H.H. (1950). 'The warm–cold variable in first impressions of persons', *Journal of Personality*, 18: 431–9.

Kelley, H.H. (1972). 'Attribution in social interaction', in E.E. Jones, D.E. Kanouse, H.H. Kelley, R.E. Nisbett, S. Valins and B. Weiner eds, *Attribution: Perceiving the Causes of Behaviour*. Morristown, NJ: General Learning Press. pp. 1–26.

Kelly, G.A. (1955). *The Psychology of Personal Constructs*, Vol. 1: *A Theory of Personality*. New York: Norton.

Kelly, G.A. (1972). *A Theory of Personality*. New York: Norton.

Kets de Vries, M.F.R. (1990). 'The organizational fool: balancing a leader's hubris', *Human Relations*, 43 (8): 751–70.

Kets de Vries, M.F.R. and Miller, D. (1984). *The Neurotic Organization*. San Francisco, CA: Jossey-Bass.

Keys, P. (1991). *Operational Research and Systems: The Systemic Nature of Operational Research*. New York: Plenum.

Kharbanda, O.P. and Stallworthy, E.A. (1991). 'Verbal and non-verbal communication', *Journal of Managerial Psychology*, 6 (4): 10–13.

Kinsman, F. (1987). *The Telecommuters*. Chichester: Wiley.

Kleinke, C.L. (1986). *Meeting and Understanding People: How to Develop Competence in Social Situations and Expand Social Skills*. New York: Freeman.

Knights, D. and Morgan, G. (1993). 'Organization theory and consumption in a post-Modern era', *Organization Studies*, 14 (2): 211–34.

Knights, D. and Willmott, H. eds (1990). *Labour Process Theory*. Basingstoke: Macmillan.

Kolb, D.M. and Putnam, L. (1992a). 'The multiple faces of conflict in organizations', *Journal of Organizational Behavior*, 13: 311–24.

Kolb, D.M. and Putnam, L. (1992b). 'The dialectics of disputing', in D.M. Kolb and J.M. Bartunek eds, *Hidden Conflict in Organizations: Uncovering Behind the Scenes Disputes*. Newbury Park, CA: Sage. pp. 1–31.

Kolb, D.A., Rubin, I.M. and McIntyre, J.M. (1979). *Organizational Psychology: An Experiential Approach*, 3rd edn. Englewood Cliffs, NJ: Prentice-Hall.

Kotter, J.P. (1979). *Power in Management*. New York: Amacon.

Kotter, J.P. (1982). *The General Managers*. New York: McGraw-Hill.

Kuper, A. (1977). *Anthropology and Anthropologists*. London: Routledge and Kegan Paul.

Landfield, A.W. (1971). *Personal Construct Systems in Psychotherapy*. Chicago, Il.: Rand McNally.

Lasch, C. (1980). *The Culture of Narcissism*. London: Abacus.

Lasch, C. (1984). *The Minimal Self: Psychic Survival in Troubled Times*. London: Pan Books.

Lawler, J.L. and Elliot, R. (1996). 'Artificial intelligence in HRM: an experimental study of an expert system', *Journal of Management*, 22 (1): 85–112.

Leavitt, H.J. (1951). 'Some effects of certain communication patterns on group performance', *Journal of Abnormal and Social Psychology*, 46: 38–50.

Legge, K. (1995). *Human Resource Management: Rhetoric and Realities*. Basingstoke: Macmillan.

Lembke, S. and Wilson, M.G. (1998). 'Putting the "team" into teamwork: alternative theoretical contributions for contemporary management practice', *Human Relations*, 51 (7): 927–44.

Levinson, D. (1979). *The Seasons of Man's Life*. New York: Ballantine.

Levitt, B. and March, J. (1988). 'Organizational Learning', *Annual Review of Sociology*, 14: 319–40.

Lewis, C. (1985). *Employee Selection*. London: Hutchinson.

Lewis, S. and Cooper, C. (1989). *Career Couples*. London: Unwin.

Locke, R. (1996). *The Collapse of the American Management Mystique*. Oxford: Oxford University Press.

Lukes, S. (1975). *Power: A Radical View*. London: Macmillan.

Luthans, F. (1992). *Organizational Behavior*. New York: McGraw-Hill.

Maccoby, M. (1976). *The Gamesman: New Corporate Leaders*. New York: Simon and Schuster.

Machlowitz, M. (1980). *Workaholics*. New York: Mentor.

MacIntyre, A. (1981). *After Virtue*. London: Duckworth.

Maier, N.R.F. (1970). 'What makes a problem difficult?', in N.R.F. Maier ed., *Problem Solving and Creativity in Individuals and Groups*. Belmont, CA: Brooks/Cole. pp. 179–88.

Mainiero, L.A. (1994). 'Getting anointed for advancement: the case of executive women', *Academy of Management Executive*, May: 53–67.

Mangham, I.L. (1986). *Power and Performance in Organizations: An Exploration of Executive Process*. Oxford: Blackwell.

Mangham, I.L. and Pye, A.J. (1991). *The Doing of Managing*. Oxford: Blackwell.

Manning, P. (1992). *Organizational Communication*. New York: Aldine De Gruyter.

March, J.G. (1997). 'Understanding how decisions happen in organizations', in Z. Shapira ed., *Organizational Decision Making*. New York: Cambridge University Press. pp. 9–32.

March J.G. and Simon, H.A. (1958). *Organizations*. New York: John Wiley.

Mars, G. (1982). *Cheats at Work: An Anthropology of Workplace Crime*. London: Allen and Unwin.

Mars, G. and Nicod, M. (1984). *The World of Waiters*. London: Allen and Unwin.

Marshall, J. (1984). *Women Managers: Travellers in a Male World*. Chichester: Wiley.

Marshall, J. (1995). *Women Managers Moving On: Exploring Careers and Life Choices*. London: Routledge.

Martin, J. (1992). *Cultures in Organizations: Three Perspectives*. New York: Oxford University Press.

Marx, K. (1975). *Early Writings*. Harmondsworth: Penguin.

Marx, K. and Engles, F. (1848/1972). 'The Communist Manifesto', in Robert C. Tucker ed., *The Marx-Engles Reader*. New York: Norton.

Maslow, A.H. (1943). 'A theory of human motivation', *Psychological Review*, 50: 654–61.

Mason, R.O. and Mitroff, I.I. (1981). *Challenging Strategic Planning Assumptions*. New York: Wiley.

Matteson, M.T. and Ivancevich, J.M. (1987). *Controlling Work Stress*. San Francisco, CA: Jossey-Bass.

Mayer, J.P. (1956). *Max Weber and German Politics*. London: Faber and Faber.

McCall, M.W. and Kaplan, R.E. (1990). *Whatever It Takes: The Realities of Managerial Decision Making*, 2nd edn. Englewood Cliffs, NJ: Prentice-Hall.

McClelland, D. (1961). *The Achieving Society*. New York: Free Press.

McClelland, D. (1971). *Assessing Human Motivations*. Morristown, NJ: General Learning Press.

McDonagh, P. and Prothero, A. eds (1997). *Green Management: A Reader*. Dryden.

McGuire, W.J. (1985). 'Attitudes and attitude change', in G. Lindzey and E. Aronson eds, *Handbook of Social Psychology*, Vol. 2, 3rd edition. New York: Random House.

McLean, A., Sims, D., Mangham, I. and Tuffield, D. (1982). *Organization Development in Transition: Evidence of an Evolving Profession*. Chichester: Wiley.

Michels, R. (1949). *Political Parties*. New York: Free Press.

Milgram, S. (1974). *Obedience to Authority*. New York: Harper and Row.

Miller, G.A., Galanter, E. and Pribram, K.H. (1960). *Plans and the Structure of Behavior*. New York: Holt, Rinehart and Winston.

Mintzberg, H. (1973). *The Nature of Managerial Work*. New York: Harper and Row.

Mintzberg, H. (1983). *Structure in Fives: Designing Effective Organizations*. Englewood Cliffs, NJ: Prentice-Hall.

Mitchell, J. (1975). *Feminism and Psychoanalysis*. Harmondsworth: Penguin.

Moingeon, B. and Edmondson, A. eds (1996). *Organizational Learning and Competitive Advantage*. London: Sage.

Morgan, G. (1986). *Images of Organization*. London: Sage.

Morita, A. (1987). *Made in Japan*. London: Collins.

Mouzelis, N. (1975). *Organisation and Bureaucracy*. London: Routledge.

Mumford, L. (1934). *Technics and Civilization*. New York: Harcourt, Brace and World.

Myers, D.G. (1994). *Exploring Social Psychology*. New York: McGraw Hill.

Nash, J. (1985). *Society and Self*. St Paul, MN: West.

Nichols, T. and Beynon, H. (1977). *Living with Capitalism: Class Relations and the Modern Factory*. London: Routledge.

Nkomo, S.M. (1992). 'The emperor has no clothes: rewriting "race in organizations"', Acadamy of Management Review, 17 (3): 487–513.

Oakley, A. (1972). *Sex, Gender and Society*. London: Temple Smith.

Oates, W. (1971). *Confessions of a Workaholic: The Facts about Work Addiction*. New York: World Publishing.

Omi, M. and Winant, H. (1987). *Racial Formation in the United States*. London: Routledge.

Ouchi, W.A. (1981). *Theory Z: How American Business Can Meet the Japanese Challenge*. Reading, MA: Addison-Wesley.

Packard, V. (1957). *The Hidden Persuaders*. Harmondsworth: Penguin.

Parker, M. (1998). *Ethics and Organizations*. London: Sage.

Pascale, R. and Athos, A. (1981). *The Art of Japanese Management*. Harmondsworth: Penguin.

Pearce, J.A. and Robinson, R.B. (1991). *Strategic Management*. Homewood, IL: Irwin.

Pedler, M., Burgoyne, J. and Boydell, T. (1997). *The Learning Company: A Strategy for Sustainable Development*, 2nd edn. Maidenhead: McGraw-Hill.

Pennings, J.M. (1985). *Organizational Strategy and Change*. San Francisco, CA: Jossey-Bass.

Peters, T.S. and Waterman, R.H. (1982). *In Search of Excellence*. New York: Harper and Row.

Pfeffer, J. (1981). *Power in Organizations*. Marshfield, MA: Pitman.

Pfeffer, J. (1992). *Managing with Power*. Boston, MA: Harvard Business School Press.

Phillips, N. and Brown, J.L. (1993). 'Analyzing communication in and around organizations: a critical hermeneutic approach', Academy of Management Journal, 36: 1547–77.

Pines, A. and Aronson, E. (1989). *Career Burnout*. New York: Free Press.

Polanyi, M. (1964). *Personal Knowledge*. New York: Harper and Row.

Pollert, A. (1981). *Girls, Wives, Factory Lives*. Oxford: Macmillan.

Pondy, L.R. (1967). 'Organizational conflict: concepts and models', Administrative Science Quarterly, 12: 296–320.

Porter, M.E. (1985). *Competitive Advantage*. New York: Free Press.

Potter, J. and Wetherell, M. (1987). *Discourse and Social Psychology: Beyond Attitudes and Behaviour*. London: Sage.

Powell, G. (1993). *Women in Management*. Newbury Park, CA: Sage.

Probst, G. and Buchel, B. (1997). *Organizational Learning: The Competitive Advantage of the Future*. London: Prentice-Hall.

Radford, K.J. (1986). *Strategic and Tactical Decisions*. Toronto: Holt McTavish.

Rafaeli, A. and Sutton, R.I. (1987). 'Expression of emotion as part of the work role', Academy of Management Review, 12 (1): 23–37.

Rafaeli, A. and Sutton, R.I. (1989). 'The expression of emotion in organizational life', Research in Organizational Behavior, 11: 1–42.

Ragins, B.R. (1997). 'Diversified mentoring relationships in organizations: a power perspective', Academy of Management Review, 22: 482–521.

Ray, J.J. (1990). 'The old fashioned personality', Human Relations, 43: 997–1013.

Reason, P. (1988). *Human Inquiry in Action: Developments in New Paradigm Research*. London: Sage.

Reason, P. and Hawkins, P. (1988). 'Storytelling as inquiry', in P. Reason, ed. *Human Inquiry in Action: Developments in New Paradigm Research*. London: Sage.

Roddick, A. (1991). *Body and Soul*. London: Ebury Press.

Rodrigues, S.B. and Collinson, D.L. (1995). '"Having fun?" Humor as resistance in Brazil', *Organization Studies*, 16: 739–68.

Rokeach, M. (1973). *The Nature of Human Values*. New York: Free Press.

Rose, M. (1988). *Industrial Behaviour*. Harmondsworth: Penguin.

Rosener, J.B. (1990). 'Ways women lead', *Harvard Business Review*, 68 (6): 119–25.

Rosnow, R.L. (1980). 'Psychology in rumor reconsidered', *Psychological Bulletin*, May: 578–91.

Rousseau, D.M. and Parks, J.M. (1993). 'The contracts of individuals and organizations', in L.L. Cummins and B.M. Staw eds, *Research in Organizational Behavior*, Vol. 15. Greenwhich, CT: JAI Press. pp. 1–43.

Russell, B. (1946). *The Philosophy of Bertrand Russell*, ed. P.A. Schilpp. Evanston, IL: Library of Living Philosophers.

Salaman, G. (1981). *Class and Corporation*. London: Fontana.

Schaufeli, W.B., Maslach, C. and Marek, T. eds (1993). *Professional Burnout: Recent Developments in Theory and Research*. New York: Hemisphere.

Schein, E.H. (1978). *Career Dynamics*. Reading, MA: Addison-Wesley.

Schein, E.H. (1980). *Organizational Psychology*, 3rd edn. Englewood Cliffs, NJ: Prentice-Hall.

Schein, E.H. (1985). *Organizational Culture and Leadership*. San Francisco, CA: Jossey-Bass.

Schein, E.H. (1988). 'Organizational socialization and the profession of management', *Sloan Management Review*, Fall: 53–65. (Original work published in 1968.)

Schein, E.H. (1995). *Career Survival: Strategic Job/Role Planning*. San Diego, CA: Pfeiffer.

Schön, D.A. (1971). *Beyond the Stable State: Public and Private Learning in a Changing Society*. London: Maurice Temple Smith.

Schwartz, H.S. (1987). 'Anti-social actions of committed organizational participants: an existential psychoanalytic perspective', *Organization Studies*, 8 (4): 327–40.

Schwartz, H.S. (1988). 'The symbol of the space shuttle and the degeneration of the American dream', *Journal of Organizational Change Management*, 1 (2): 5–20.

Schwartz, H.S. (1990). *Narcissistic Process and Corporate Decay*. New York: New York University Press.

Selznik, P. (1957). *Leadership and Administration*. New York: Harper and Row.

Senge, P. (1990). *The Fifth Discipline*. London: Random House.

Sharpe, E. (1984). *Double Identity: The Lives of Working Mothers*. Harmondsworth: Penguin.

Sherif, M. (1936). *The Psychology of Social Norms*. New York: Harper.

Sherif, M. (1966). *In Common Predicament: Social Psychology of Intergroup Conflict and Cooperation*. Boston, MA: Houghton Mifflin.

Simon, H.A. (1947). *Administrative Behavior*. New York: Macmillan.

Simons, H.W. (1989). *Rhetoric in the Human Sciences*. London: Sage.

Sims, D. (1979). 'A framework for understanding the definition and formulation of problems in teams', *Human Relations*, 32 (11): 909–21.

Sims, D. (1985). 'Fantasies and the location of skill', in A. Strati ed., *The Symbolics of Skill*. Trento: University of Trento. pp. 12–17.

Sims, D. (1986). 'Mental simulation: an effective vehicle for adult learning', *International Journal of Innovative Higher Education*, 3: 33–5.

Sims, D. (1992). 'Information systems and constructing problems', *Management Decision*, 30 (5): 21–7.

Sims, H.P. and Lorenzi, P. (1992). *The New Leadership Paradigm: Social Learning and Cognition in Organizations*. Newbury Park, CA: Sage.

Skellington, R. (1996). *'Race' in Britain Today*, 2nd edn. London: Sage.

Skinner, B.F. (1966). 'An operant analysis of problem solving', in B. Kleinmuntz ed., *Problem Solving: Research, Method and Theory*. New York: Wiley. pp. 225–58.

Smith, A. (1997). *Integrated Pollution Control*. Aldershot: Ashgate.

Smith, D. (1993). *Business and the Environment*. London: Paul Chapman.

Smith, M. ed. (1991). *Analysing Organizational Behaviour*. London: Macmillan.

Snyder, M. (1987). *Public Appearances, Private Realities: The Psychology of Self-monitoring*. New York: Freeman.

Sorrell, T. and Hendry, J. (1994). *Business Ethics*. Oxford: Butterworth-Heinemann.

Spencer, A. and Podmore, D. (1987). *In a Man's World*. London: Tavistock.

Srivastva, S. (1986). *Executive Power*. San Francisco, CA: Jossey-Bass.

Stablein, R. (1996). 'Data in organization studies', in S. Clegg, C. Hardy and W. Nord eds, *Handbook of Organization Studies*. London: Sage.

Stacey, R. (1995). 'The science of complexity: an alternative perspective for strategic change', *Strategic Management Journal*, 16: 477–95.

Stacey, R. (1996). *Complexity and Creativity in Organizations*. San Francisco, CA: Berrett-Koehler.

Statt, D.A. (1994). *Psychology and the World of Work*. Basingstoke: Macmillan.

Stauber, J. and Rampton, S. (1995). *Toxic Sludge is Good for You*. Monroe, ME: Common Courage Press.

Steers, R.M. and Porter, L.W. eds (1975). *Motivation and Work Behavior*. New York: McGraw-Hill.

Steers, R.M. and Porter, L.W. eds (1987). *Motivation and Work Behavior*, 4th edn. New York: McGraw-Hill.

Stewart, R. (1967). *Managers and Their Jobs*. London: Macmillan.

Strati, A. (1985). *The Symbolics of Skill*. Trento: University of Trento Press.

Sturdy, A. (1998). 'Customer care in a consumer society: smiling and sometimes meaning it?', *Organization*, 5 (1): 27–53.

Tajfel, H. (1981). *Human Groups and Social Categories*. Cambridge: Cambridge University Press.

Tancred-Sheriff, P. (1989). 'Gender, sexuality and the labour process', in J. Hearn, D.L. Sheppard, P. Tancred-Sheriff and G. Burrell eds, *The Sexuality of Organization*. London: Sage.

Tannen, D. (1995). *Talking from 9 to 5*. New York: Morrow.

Tavris, C. (1992). *The Mismeasure of Woman*. New York: Simon and Schuster.

Taylor, F.W. (1911). *Principals of Scientific Management*. New York: Harper.

Thomas, D.A. (1993). 'Mentoring and Irationality: The Role of Racial Taboos', in L. Hirshhorn and C.K. Barnett eds, *The Psychodynamics of Organizations*. Philadelphia, PA: Temple University Press.

Thomas, K.W. (1977). 'Towards multidimensional values in teaching: the example of conflict behaviors', *Academy of Management Review*, 12: 484–90.

Thomas, W.I. and Thomas, D.S. (1928). *The Child in America: Behavior Problems and Programs*. New York: Knopf.

Thompson, P. (1990). 'Crawling from the wreckage: the labour process and the politics of production', in D. Knights and H. Willmott eds, *Labour Process Theory*. London: Macmillan. pp. 95–124.

Tichy, N.M. and Fombrun, C. (1979). 'Network analysis in organizational settings', *Human Relations*, 32: 923–65.

Tinsley, H.E.A. and Stockdale, M. (1993). Special issue on sexual harassment. *Journal of Vocational Behavior*, 42 (1).

Toplis, J., Dulewicz, V. and Fletcher, C. (1991). *Psychological Testing: A Manager's Guide*. London: Institute of Personnel Management.

Torbert, W. (1987). *Managing the Corporate Dream*. Homewood, IL: Dow Jones-Irwin.

Torrington, D. and Hall, L. (1998). *Human Resource Management*. London: Prentice-Hall.

Townsend, A.M., DeMarie, S.M. and Hendrickson, A.R. (1998). 'Virtual teams: technology and the workplace of the future', *The Academy of Management Executive*, 12 (3): 17–29.

Trice H.M. and Beyer, J.M. (1984). 'Studying organizational cultures through rites and ceremonials', *American Management Review*, 9: 653–69.

Turner, B. (1990). *Organizational Symbolism*. Berlin: De Gruyter.

Van Maanen, J. and Kunda, G. (1989). '"Real feelings": emotional expression and organizational culture', *Research in Organizational Behavior*, 11: 43–103.

Vernon, P.E. (1979). *Intelligence: Heredity and Environment*. San Francisco, CA: Freeman.

Waldron, V.R. (1994). 'Once more with feeling: reconsidering the role of emotion in work', in S.A. Deetz ed., *Communication Yearbook 17*. Thousand Oaks, CA: Sage. pp. 338–416.

Walton, C.W. (1988). *The Moral Manager*. New York: Harper.

Warr, P.B. (1987). *Psychology at Work*. Harmondsworth: Penguin.

Waterhouse, K. (1975). *Billy Liar on the Moon*. London: Joseph.

Weber M. (1948). *From Max Weber: Essays in Sociology*, eds H.H. Gerth and C. Wright Mills. London: Routledge.

Weber, M. (1958). *The Protestant Ethic and the Spirit of Capitalism*. New York: Scribner.

Weick, K.E. (1985). 'Cosmos vs chaos: sense and nonsense in electronic contexts', *Organizational Dynamics*, Autumn: 50–64.

Weick, K. (1995). *Sensemaking in Organizations*. Thousand Oaks, CA: Sage.

Weizenbaum, J. (1976). *Computer Power and Human Reason: From Judgement to Calculation*. New York: Freeman.

Welford, R. (1995). *Environmental Strategy and Sustainable Development*. London: Routledge.

Welford, R. (1997). *Hijacking Environmentalism*. London: Earthscan.

Wigdor, A.K. and Greene, B.F. (1991). *Performance Assessment and the Workforce*. Washington, DC: National Academy Press.

Wilkinson, B. (1996). 'Culture, institutions and business in East Asia', *Organization Studies*, 17 (3): 422–47.

Wilkinson, B., Morris, J. and Mundy, M. (1995). 'The iron fist in the velvet hand', *Journal of Management Studies*, 32 (6): 819–30.

Willis, P. (1990). *Common Culture: Symbolic Work at Play in the Everyday Cultures of the Young*. Milton Keynes: Open University Press.

Wilson, F.M. (1995). *Organizational Behaviour and Gender*. London: McGraw-Hill.

Wilson, D.C. and Rosenfeld, R.H. (1990). *Managing Organizations: Texts, Readings and Cases*. London: McGraw-Hill.

Winefield, A.H., Tiggermann, M., Winefield, H.R. and Goldney, R.D. (1993). *Growing up with Unemployment: A Longitudinal Study of its Psychological Impact*. London: Routledge.

Wolf, N. (1990). *The Beauty Myth*. London: Chatto and Windus.

Womack, J.P., Jones, D.T. and Roos, D. (1990). *The Machine that Changed the World*. London: Macmillan.

Wood, D.J. (1994). *Business and Society*. New York: Harper Collins.

Woodward, J. (1965). *Industrial Organization: Theory and Practice*. Oxford: Oxford University Press.

Wright, P.L. and Taylor, D.S. (1984). *Improving Leadership Performance*. London: Prentice-Hall.

Yarwood, D.L. (1995). 'Humor and administration: a serious inquiry into unofficial organizational communication', *Public Administration Review*, 55: 81–90.

Zaleznik, A. (1977). 'Managers and leaders: are they different?', *Harvard Business Review*, May–June: 47–60.

Zuboff, S. (1988). *In the Age of the Smart Machine*. Oxford: Heinemann.

Index

Entries in **bold** type refer to the Thesaurus